Diversity of Sacrifice

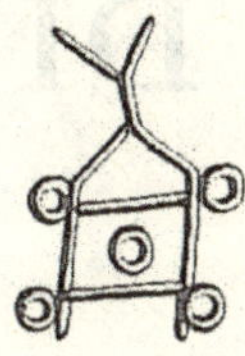

DIVERSITY OF SACRIFICE

Form and Function of Sacrificial Practices in the Ancient World and Beyond

IEMA Proceedings,
Volume 5

EDITED BY
Carrie Ann Murray

STATE UNIVERSITY OF
NEW YORK PRESS

Logo and cover/interior art: A vessel with wagon motifs from Bronocice, Poland, 3400 B.C. Courtesy of Sarunas Milisauskas and Janusz Kruk, 1982, Die Wagendarstellung auf einem Trichterbecher au Bronocice, Polen, *Archäologisches Korrespondenzblatt* 12: 141–144

Published by
State University of New York Press, Albany

For information, contact
State University of New York Press, Albany, NY
www.sunypress.edu

Production, Eileen Nizer
Marketing, Michael Campochiaro

Library of Congress Cataloging-in-Publication Data

Diversity of sacrifice : form and function of sacrificial practices in the ancient world and beyond / edited by Carrie Ann Murray.
     pages cm. — (SUNY series, The Institute for European and Mediterranean Archaeology distinguished monograph series)
     Includes bibliographical references and index.
     ISBN 978-1-4384-5995-0 (hc : alk paper)
     ISBN 978-1-4384-5994-3 (pb : alk. paper)
     ISBN 978-1-4384-5996-7 (e-book)   1. Sacrifice—Europe—History—To 1500—Congresses.   2. Sacrifice—Meditarranean Region—History—To 1500—Congresses.   3. Social archaeology—Europe—Congresses. 4. Social archaeology—Meditarranean Region—Congresses. 5. Archaeology and religion—Europe—Congresses.   6. Archaeology and religion—Meditarranean Region—Congresses.   7. Material culture—Europe—History—To 1500—Congresses.   8. Material culture—Meditarranean Region—History—To 1500—Congresses.   9. Social interaction—Europe—History—To 1500—Congresses.   10. Social interaction—Meditarranean Region—History—To 1500—Congresses. I. Murray, Carrie Ann, 1976–   II. University of Buffalo. Institute for European and Mediterranean Archaeology.

     BL570.D58 2016
     203'.40936—dc23   2015013508

10 9 8 7 6 5 4 3 2 1

For my grandfather, Detective Louis Linton Miller,
who died while protecting the people of New York City

Contents

Part III
Exploring Exceptional Cases of Sacrifice

Part IV
Formularizing and Regularizing Sacrifice

Illustrations

The Value and Power of Sacrifice

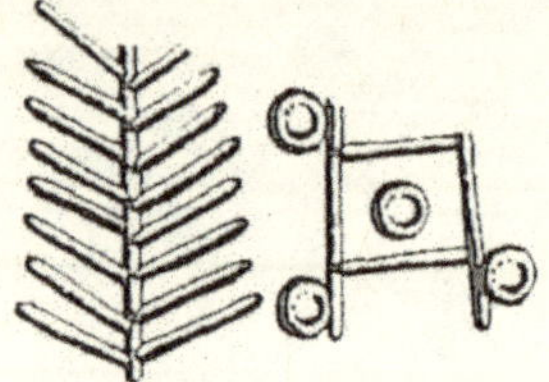

Carrie Ann Murray

ISSUES OF SACRIFICE IN SCHOLARSHIP

An experience that affects all of the senses—the impetuses and consequences of sacrificial practices relate to more than purely religious considerations. The continuous presence of sacrifice, in widely varying forms, from ancient to contemporary contexts is testament to its perceived long-term significance. Its relevance applies to the community, family, and individual. Evidence from archaeology, epigraphy, ethnography, history, and literature provides a wealth of insights into a multitude of sacrificial practices from across a wide spectrum of contexts. There is an abundance of scholarship informing our understanding of sacrifice in its different guises. Publications often explore the significance of sacrifice within the confines of separate contexts: ancient, contemporary, pagan, Christian, and others. The isolated perspectives often reach little consensus regarding what seems so neatly packaged as a single term, "sacrifice," in our parlance, but what is a complex and varied transhistorical and transcultural phenomenon.

To begin, let us consider how "sacrifice" can be defined. Sacrifice in the ancient world has been defined as a "central act of Greek and Roman religious ritual, an offering to the gods, heroes, or the dead" (Stafford 2006:775). Here, as elsewhere, the emphasis is placed on a means of gift giving from humans to the supernatural and the otherworldly. The recipients of sacrifice—deities and the deceased—are very different in nature, but are combined in definitions of sacrifice to distinguish these practices from purely mundane and secular actions. Discussions of other aspects of sacrifice, such as scale, types of offerings, and procedures are subsumed within these descriptions. These variables can diverge wildly without affecting what is seen as the essence of sacrifice, allowing us to categorize different types of sacrifice, for instance: blood, bloodless, animal, human, civic, private, etc. Typologies of sacrifice, as with most attempts to rationalize and compartmentalize social action, come with benefits and limitations. Identifying different contexts and purposes has been fundamental. Yet, such fine-grained distinctions between sacrificial rites of different contexts can also obscure aspects of sacrifice that present continuities rather than oppositions.

With so much discussion at present, this will be a (re)formative period for the study of sacrifice in its many guises. For instance, in Knust and Vrhelyi's edited volume (2011), central themes include questioning the centrality of animal sacrifice over bloodless in the ancient world, the meaning of "sacrifice," and our categorization of it. In addition, in Faraone and Naiden's edited volume (2012) some contributors also question the centrality of animal sacrifice in the ancient world. Perhaps in direct contrast, Naiden in his own monograph (2013) explores an innovative perspective emphasizing the role of the gods for Greek sacrificial practices and the repercussions that potential divine rejection of prayers and offerings had on the development of regulations and priestly roles, as well as confronting contexts of consumption of nonsacrifical meat. Clearly, rather than reaching a consensus, these studies enable us to question our investigative frameworks and create new avenues to explore.

THEMES IN SCHOLARSHIP

Several themes recurrent in sacrifice-related scholarship have formed the structure of many key texts on the subject. Two of the core issues have been the role of violence and the role of meat in sacrifice.

THE ROLE OF VIOLENCE

The question of violence has formed a long-standing debate, where sacrifice can be described as a transformed form of hunting (Burkert 1972:16–22, 1985:58; Detienne 1989:5; Meuli 1975:999) and a ritualized type of killing (for animal sacrifice see Girard 1977, 1986, 1987; Hubert, Mauss 1964:67–70; Smith 1987:197; for human sacrifice see Green 2001 esp. 163–176; Burkert 1985:63), or as an act not necessarily related to hunting or perceived of as violent in specific contexts (see Bremmer 2010:141; Vernant 1989:85–86).

Many studies of sacrifice attempt to explain how sacrifice serves society in functional terms. Bremmer agrees that sacrifice is ritual slaughter, does constitute a community, and is killing for eating, as advanced by Meuli, Burkert, and Vernant respectively, but argues that these represent "secular" reductionist explanations that lack insight into the aims of the participants, in this case ancient Greeks (Bremmer 2010:144). Reason and meaning can vary as to the individual even when a social practice is organized at a community level. Scholarship sometimes struggles to evaluate social action within sacrifice by questioning the appropriateness of emic and etic perspectives of analysis and interpreting potentially culturally specific views.

THE ROLE OF MEAT IN ANIMAL SACRIFICE

Categorizing Greek and Roman sacrificial practices is not a simple matter. Greek sacrificial practices are often described as the normative core, and Roman sacrificial practices taken as largely replicating these Greek practices. Our comparison of these cultures' customs requires care. The modern lens used to compare and contrast these cultures must tread a careful path. Does emphasizing similarity or difference between aspects of Greek and Roman sacrificial practices privilege or undermine the importance of separate belief systems or interaction between cultures? These issues are not easily resolved, but must be confronted.

For instance, comparing the role of meat in animal sacrifice of Greek and Roman practices illustrates how limiting it can be to draw conclusions within a narrow dichotomy to describe the two cultures. Animal sacrifice in ancient Greek contexts in particular, has received attention as a primary source for meat in the diet (Bloch 1992:24–45; Detienne 1989:esp. 3; Detienne, Vernant 1989). The consumption of the meat through animal sacrifice enables collective participation within precise social structures. Apart from dietary benefits, animal sacrifice is also connected to all levels of politics within a Greek city, ranging from the collective meals of prisoners to the founding of a colony (Detienne 1989:3–4). Even the Pythagoreans' abstinence from particular types of meat invites a political-religious interpretation, according to Detienne (1989:5ff). The distribution of types and portions of meat and other substances from animal sacrifice also creates a hierarchy among the participants and those excluded (for instance Sælid Gilhus 2006:116).

A growing dialogue acknowledging the consumption of animal meat outside of sanctuary space, even apart from hunting contexts (especially Ekroth 2007; Parker 2010), has improved our means of understanding the complicated relationships between sacred and secular acts in Greek and Roman societies. For a time, there was a notion that the quintessential difference between Greek and Roman animal sacrifice was the inviolability of meat consumption outside of a sacred setting for the Greeks and the potential to sell meat in the marketplace in Roman society (for the view of meat in the Greek world having sacrificial origins see Lietzmann 1949; for the sale of meat and Roman markets see Holleran 2012:160–180; an interesting instance is debated in McDonough 2004:74–75; Scheid 2003:90–91).

The particular contexts of meat consumption in both cultures are more complex. Given the numerous lararia and altars from domestic settings preserved in Campania (Boyce 1937; Gioccobella 2008), and information concerning sacred rituals performed in conjunction with the consumption of meat in Roman domestic settings, a more nuanced analysis is required to understand the relationship between public and private Roman religion and how animal sacrifice and the consumption of meat related to each other in the Roman world.

The Greek world too, however, has produced literary and epigraphic evidence that refutes the notion that sacrifice was compulsory for the consumption of meat of any sort. Examples of meat being consumed outside of sanctuary settings indicate that commercial and practical concerns were involved at least sometimes (Naiden 2013:232–275; Parker 2010:140–144). Literary evidence affords evidence of meat of some description being sold in the marketplace via Theophrastus's Shameless Man (*Characters* 9.4). Other accounts indicate the sale of sacrificial meat in the market, including a description of Aesop purchasing the tongues of sacrificed pigs in the market (G and W *Vita Aesopi*; see Isenberg 1975:272–273), and ravenous kites on Elis refraining from eating the flesh of sacred victims, but getting scraps of the meat as it is carried through the market (Aristotle *De mirabilibus auscultationibus* 123, 842a34–842b2). A description of historical unrest during the rule of Dionysius I at Syracuse indicates that animals appropriate for sacrifice were not always dealt with in such a way when the citizens slaughtered and sold their herd animals in protest to imposed taxes, and when the tyrant imposed a limit to the number of animals that could be slaughtered daily, the citizens began to sacrifice the animals (Aristotle *Oeconomica* 1349b 11–14). A piece of epigraphic evidence suggests that meat from a sacrifice related to the Lesser Panathenaia was distributed in two settings, some immediately on the Acropolis and some later to each deme elsewhere, possibly in the Kerameikos (IG II 334.10–16, see Ekroth 2008:277; Rhodes and Osborne 2003, no.81). Some of these instances of meat consumption outside of sanctuaries mention the inclusion of nonsacrificial meat, which can include animal species not appropriate for sacrifice and animals that died of natural causes (Naiden 2013:232–275; Parker 2010:140–144). One vivid example is the case Naiden makes for the consumption of pork in the messes of Sparta (2013:250–258). The Greek world, just as the Roman world, requires further thought as to the role of sacrificial meat across public and private settings.

The addition of Christianity to these contexts adds another interesting level of concern over the source of meat for sale in markets. For example, we may explore the complexity of the relationship between sacrificial practices in the Greek and Roman worlds through Paul's First Epistle to the Corinthians (1 Corinthians 10:25–29; see also Isenberg 1975:271). This text reveals interpretations of sacrificial practices varying according to time and location. In this case, Corinth, as a Greek city that, in the Roman period, particularly in the mid-first century C.E., was rife with cultural interactions, including a number of Christian residents who found themselves navigating their way through a complex set of circumstances concerning religious belief and diet. Paul gives advice whether or not to purchase meat from the market or partake in a meal if in either case the Christian does not know if the meat was sacrificed in honor of a pagan god. This indicates that meat at a market or at a home in Corinth then could have been from (pagan) animal sacrifice or from a nonsacrificial slaughter.

Opening the discussion to consider unexpected dynamics of sacrificial practices both within and beyond the Greek and Roman worlds allows for new insights. The conference allowed scholars working in different periods and locations across the Mediterranean and Europe to voice their own understandings of central issues related to different forms of sacrificial practices.

FRAMEWORK OF THE CONFERENCE

The occasion of the conference was held as the annual symposium for the Institute for European and Mediterranean Archaeology (IEMA) at the University at Buffalo, SUNY. It was organized as an opportunity to explore the rite of sacrifice from multiple perspectives across an array of contexts. The scholars involved represent a broad gamut of disciplines that tackle the concept and practice of sacrifice, including: anthropology, archaeology, epigraphy, literature, and theology. In the end, the participants' work spans ancient to contemporary contexts across the Mediterranean and much of Europe, exploring case studies from a variety of contexts: prehistoric, protohistoric, Egyptian, Near Eastern, Greek, Punic, Iberian, Etruscan, Roman, Christian, and post-domestic. There was general recognition that the seeming ubiquitous existence of offering-based practices that might be described as sacrifice was an exciting common ground for discussing disparate contexts and different issues. There was no searching for universal truths, but rather a collaborative exploration of the rich variety of sacrificial practices and experiences.

As editor I suggested various areas for the participants to explore as they saw fit. The overt functions of sacrifice set in a specifically religious sphere often involve many other levels; sacrifice joins sacred and secular elements in part to serve social needs. As described below, these areas included such questions as the importance of actors, substances, time, space, and regulations.

Sacrifice is a powerful means of transformation; individual actors can gain specialized social roles, and objects, places, and actions can take on additional meanings. This rite offers a means of communication with a deity, which could have profound effects on the lives of the participants. The substances involved in sacrifice act as physical links between the mundane and the holy. Blood and wine, smoke and incense can travel into the earth or to the heavens carrying with them the sacrificers' vows and requests. The presence of these substances led to the confinement of many sacrificial practices within special physical places, protected from impure actions and persons. The necessity of purification for people, animals, objects, and spaces involved in sacrifice helps restrict and heighten the process. Part of the powerful meanings involved in sacrifice involves the concept of tradition through time and space. Repetition and the sense of inheritance of a practice begun before one's lifetime give importance, continuance, and respect to a social and religious practice at the individual and social scales. Also, because sacrifice is present in public and private contexts, this helps demonstrate how the functions of sacrifice can be meaningful on levels from the personal to the communal, for an individual's health, a family's well-being, an army's victory, or a city's protection. In particular, it is interesting to consider how sacrifice offers an effective means of communicating with a deity. The importance placed on sacrifice is also seen in the detail. Many cultures take great care in following formulae and procedures during a sacrifice. In many contexts incorrect utterances or actions can nullify the entire process. There is a strict means of communicating with deities in order to successfully have a request fulfilled or an offering of thanks accepted.

THEMES EXPLORED IN THE VOLUME

The essays here are not divided into strict disciplinary or chronological groupings. Regions, types of offerings, and other criteria are intermingled to highlight less obvious connections among the scholars. During the IEMA conference, three other presentations were made, but are not included in this volume; Philip Kiernan discussed the use of sacrificial knives in Roman western provinces; Tom Palaima discussed the potential political significance of sacrifice in Mycenaean culture, with particular analysis of Linear B tablets from Pylos; Andrew Reynolds questioned the meaning of non-funerary weapon deposition in Anglo-Saxon Britain.

Part I: Defining and Redefining the Boundaries of Sacrifice

The essays in this section include views on the theory of sacrifice, questions of universality, and explorations of the significance of sacrifice in the landscape from different disciplinary backgrounds, while trying to understand the sacrificial practices from the perspectives of the participants.

Phillips Stevens Jr. offers a broad and thorough discussion of anthropological scholarship on the topic of sacrifice. The importance of ethnographic fieldwork is suggested to be a vibrant pool from which classicists and other scholars can share in the building of understandings of humanity through the variegated, but universal presence of sacrificial practices around the world. He stresses the importance of considering multiple perspectives for the functions and reasons behind sacrifice and to appreciate its different elements and forms.

Turning to archaeology, Åsa Berggren questions the appropriateness of viewing sacrifice as a universal concept. She is primarily concerned with problematizing the journey from theoretical perspectives to archaeological interpretation, and the categorization of "sacred" and "sacrificial" in these two arenas. Berggren's case study is set in the fens of southern Sweden with long-term development from the Late Mesolithic to the Early Bronze Age and is used as a means of testing practice theory. She questions if the wetland deposition of varied materials should be viewed as ritualization of practice, whose meaning can be investigated by understanding what relationships were created through the practice at Hindbygården fen. The role of memory, as seen through long-term, physical action in the landscape plays a key role.

Understanding the functions of material deposits is also central for Christoph Huth's essay. Here he discusses deliberate depositions of metalwork during the Bronze and Iron Ages in several locations across Europe. Huth argues for the importance of conceptualizing mythic functions of precious weapons and vessels. Contemporary iconography of weapons and vessels are employed to demonstrate the importance of these items within nonutilitarian and divine spheres, and so are gifts from the gods that are offered back to them via permanent deposition.

In a very different arena, Samantha Hurn explores through extensive ethnographic fieldwork the recent circumstances of foxhunting in the United Kingdom as a form of sacrifice. In particular, the concept of a population divided over different relationships with animals, landscapes, and agriculture is seen at the core of divergent perceptions of this practice. Many "post-domestic" non-agriculturalists view foxhunting as a violent and unnecessary sport, while many others involved in foxhunting, particularly farmers, express different views, including the need to protect flocks of sheep. Hurn argues that seeing the hunt as a form of sacrifice in a secularized society with industrialized food production produces a new understanding of the relationship between humans and animals, as well as violence and food consumption.

Part II: Sacrifice across the Mediterranean World

The essays of the second section span a cross-section of classical contexts (Egyptian, Carthaginian, Greek, and Etruscan) by focusing on myth and iconography held within material culture and human remains involved in sacrifice.

Mary-Ann Pouls Wegner investigates the importance reflected in the material culture of sacrifice for all levels of society in extramural ritual landscapes of ancient Egypt. She particularly highlights contexts of sacrifices to the god Osiris in Abydos. Pouls Wegner demonstrates how the presence of the weskhet-dishes supports the textual and iconographic evidence indicating that the ritual processions and donations act to reaffirm social hierarchies.

The flames of the ongoing debate concerning child sacrifice at Carthage are stoked here with Jeffrey H. Schwartz's detailed examination of the osteological evidence. Schwartz argues that interpretations based on noncontemporary written sources, as well as enigmatic inscriptions and iconography, neglect the physical evidence of neonatal and perinatal remains. Several recently contentious issues are addressed, including: potential tooth crown shrinkage, visibility of neonatal-lines, the sex of the individuals, and the type of wood fuel in the cremations.

Tyler Jo Smith addresses the consummate form of evidence for Greek sacrifice, Attic vases. Here, Smith uses Folkert van Straten's influential work as a foundation on which to build. She examines the visual language of sacrifice in specific painted vases in relation to contexts of production, use, and deposition. The concepts of performance and gaze inform the social actions within the choices made by the vase painters and the viewers' engagement with the vessels.

The Etruscans are brought to the fore with Nancy T. de Grummond's investigation into human sacrifice by elucidating the intriguing archaeological evidence of long-term ritual action from the Pian di Civita, Tarquinia. De Grummond details the ten depositions of human remains from the site and argues for different sacred practices at work, including: an honorable burial of an epileptic child who may have been deemed as having oracular powers, donative offerings of infants, and sacrifice or ritual killing of a potential prisoner of war. She stresses the importance of the myth of Tages, and iconography of human sacrifice in Etruscan art for better understanding the role of children in Etruscan religious belief.

Part III: Exploring Exceptional Cases of Sacrifice

The essays in this section question the notions of violence and resolution in sacrifice through discoveries from the archaeological record, focusing on human and animal remains.

Andrea Zeeb-Lanz and her colleagues present the fascinating results from Herxheim, a Neolithic site in Germany. Belonging to the Linear Bandkeramik Culture, Herxheim is unique not only because of the remains of human sacrifice of more than 500 individuals, but also because of the evidence of cannibalism. The physical remains of the sacrifice are sewn into the fabric of the landscape by their deposition in a ditch system surrounding the settlement. Zeeb-Lanz et al. question how the definitions of "sacrifice" can be used within archaeological interpretation. They also propose a need for a better understanding of the relationships between levels of violence and human sacrifice in a society.

Enriqueta Pons and her two colleagues present their findings from a site dating from the fifth to second century B.C.E., Mas Castellar de Pontós, Spain. The site holds an interesting key to examining animal sacrifice, in this case dog sacrifice, within a context where the animal is seen to perform sacred and secular roles by the varying forms of deposition. The canine remains at Mas Castellar are found in the use and reuse of pits for votive deposits and the collection of food waste, as well as in the remains of structures that combine domestic and ritual activities. Considering the different methods of treatment, their disposal, and their association with other animal remains presents new questions regarding the varying relationships between humans and dogs.

Guinevere Granite explores the enigmatic array of evidence of bog bodies in northwestern Europe. She presents the early stages of her research on bog bodies by considering the multiple theories currently used to interpret them. Granite argues that while some of the individuals might have been sacrificed as part of religious rituals, there are alternate plausible circumstances for others. The individual bog bodies must be examined individually and contextually, rather than supporting one general explanation for all.

PART IV: FORMULARIZING AND REGULARIZING SACRIFICE

In this section, the essays explore issues of meaning and transformation of sacrifice through language and symbols. Roger D. Woodard explores the power of words and signs in religious ritual in the forms of speech, writing, and sacred offering as recorded in a unique passage in the Hebrew Bible, concerning the Sotah. At the core of this ritual, a wife suspected of adultery undergoes a rite, whereby a prayer to Yahweh and an offering to Him via the woman's body are used to discern the truth, which will be made manifest through the woman's potential reproductive morbidity. The offering consists of water, tabernacle dust, and the dissolved alphabetic signs of the priest's request. Woodard demonstrates that the alphabetic signs themselves, written and dissolved into the potion to be drunk, are a powerful sacrificial offering, that is, something that is ultimately a gift from God that is returned to Him.

The importance of language continues with Michael Gagarin's investigation of the Greek laws on public sacrifice. He uses a number of public inscriptions concerning sacrifices in association with sacred spaces. Chief among this type of inscription concerning sacrifice is the sacred calendar, usually delineating the date or frequency, the divine recipient of the sacrifice, and the type of animal offering. Gagarin argues that these inscriptions of Greek laws function on both legal and religious levels. The cost of the events needed to be mandated to ensure that both civic duty was fulfilled and the gods were honored.

S. Mark Heim discusses one of the most influential areas of study in Western scholarship for understanding sacrifice, the death of Christ. Here, he questions the concept and terminology of describing the death of Christ as a "sacrifice." By contrasting early Christian texts and iconography, Heim highlights how the circumstances surrounding the death of Christ, before and after, make for what could be seen as an unlikely example of the quintessential sacrifice for Christians. Heim explores the development of the cross as a central Christian icon, not adopted before the fifth century C.E., which initially related more to execution in a secular sense, rather than sacrifice within a sacred sphere. In particular, Heim counters René Girard's anti-sacrificial reading of the death of Christ in terms of the scapegoat effect.

Considerations Raised through Discussion

Estimating Value

Strict categorizations were avoided here; the aspects of compartmentalization are largely artificial for practical reasons of organizing text into a traditional format. In reality, various issues are woven throughout many of the essays regardless of context or disciplinary framework. The shared common ground and unexpected divergences testify to the relevance of investigating sacrificial practices as a theme in an interdisciplinary forum to foster new ideas and question old ones. Unanticipated areas that came into focus for this volume, as the editor sees it, concern the estimation of the value of sacrificial offerings, the effects of social power for participants of sacrificial practices, and the importance of setting.

Discerning the relative "value" of sacrificial offerings necessitates appreciating the context-specific circumstances in each case. Our assumptions based on modern, Western perspectives, for instance, of the value of human life versus (nonhuman) animal life and inanimate objects, must be examined. The offering of human life is often presumed to be the highest, most costly, powerful, or meaningful type of offering to lose through sacrifice. If the life in question, however, is from outside of the community, as discussed by Andrea Zeeb-Lanz et al. and Nancy de Grummond (potentially, in one instance), or is part of a ritual execution of a criminal as discussed by Guinevere Granite or even S. Mark Heim's essay, then how does that affect the value of the offering as perceived by the sacrificer(s) and the rest of the participants? For communities that lose members to the human sacrifices held elsewhere, the sense of loss and gain brought about through this ritual is felt even more widely, which could be considered abstractly in such cases as described by Andrea Zeeb-Lanz et al. or very clearly in the case of Christians as described by S. Mark Heim. If the infant remains at Carthage represent funerary—rather than sacrificial—ritual, as Jeffrey Schwartz suggests, then human life at this early stage could have garnered value in a very different sense in the Carthaginian culture from other contemporary, ancient cultures, which lack high concentrations of infant burials.

The Effects of Social Power

"Power," too, must be examined within its particular contexts to consider the individuals involved in social dynamics surrounding a sacrifice, and the consequences both at and beyond the altar. Social power is at stake in issues of inclusion in and exclusion from sacrificial practices. A unique type of sacrificial rite can even include a powerful threat of curse over an individual's life as described by Roger D. Woodard, which potentially affected the behavior of others in the community. As Christoph Huth describes, the deposits of exemplary weapons and vessels could have been used to lay socially powerful claims of connections between mortal and divine through the bearing and returning of gifts from the gods.

The social power and relevancy of sacrifice also relates to the functions it provides, as explained by Phillips Stevens Jr. Sacrifice need not relate purely to sacred functions. If, in ancient Greece, animal sacrifice served as a primary source of meat in the diet, then secular and practical aspects of sacrifice must be acknowledged elsewhere. The sacrifice in Enriqueta Pons et al.'s piece demonstrated that some of the dogs were butchered, presumably for consumption. Samantha Hurn described how foxhunting provided a sense of community in several ways, always including a communal meal, but of lamb, rather than fox meat. Equally, Michael Gagarin demonstrated how the Greek inscriptions describing sacrificial practices involved practical concerns to ensure the correct execution of the rites.

IMPORTANCE OF SETTING

The scale and breadth of social power for the participants of sacrifice can also be dependent upon the physical settings of public or private locations and the political contexts of either conformity or subversion. A community's long-term development of a defined landscape through sacrificial practices is revealed in Åsa Berggren's discussion. Similarly, political power seems to be expressed publicly through the human depositions in direct association with monumental architecture in the case described by Nancy T. de Grummond, and the vast amounts of human remains used to encircle an entire village in Andrea Zeeb-Lanz et al.'s essay. Pouls-Wegner asserts the importance of the perceived marginal, extramural ritual deposits to Osiris as important contexts for negotiating a wide range of social statuses. The clandestine circumstances of locations and participation lay at the heart of Samantha Hurn's essay to subvert the larger, dominant community in order to maintain a smaller community. The choices made in the depiction of space and participation in Greek vase sacrificial imagery can also illuminate a deeper understanding of these ritual practices, as Tyler Jo Smith argues.

FINAL THOUGHTS

This volume explores how sacrifice plays a key role in the overlapping sacred and secular spheres for a number of societies in the past and present. Members of several disciplines have contributed their perspectives on disparate examples that share issues and themes that are beneficially considered in combination. The unique strengths of this project involve the incorporation of theory, material culture, and textual evidence at a number of case studies spanning a wide variety of contexts across the Mediterranean region and Europe.

The importance of sacrifice as a phenomenon with widespread social implications cannot be overstated. Insight into the sacrificial practices can illuminate the immediate context-specific circumstances, as well as the often long-term traditions surrounding their origins and transformations in a given society. Eschewing universal and reductive explanations, this collection instead considers new and divergent data from past and present case studies that can help broaden our field of vision while raising new questions and drawing new conclusions.

There is still more room to investigate cross-cultural and interdisciplinary similarities and dissimilarities of sacrificial practices for insights into the social contexts of sacrifice. Such potential approaches include complicating the presumed dichotomies between public and private worship, and practical and spiritual functions of worship. In so many cases, one can see that sacrificial practices are not just isolated acts within a temple precinct, but actions that relate to other areas of social life. A simple explanation will not help explore an area so vast and changing. How religious beliefs and practices can be integral parts of life on individual and community levels is of fundamental importance to understanding the past and present.

ACKNOWLEDGMENTS

I would like to thank the members of the Institute for European and Mediterranean Archaeology, and Peter Biehl in particular, for supporting this project during my fellowship. Many thanks to all of the contributors to this volume; it has been an honor working with all of you. I would like to express my thanks to the reviewers for their valuable feedback on my introduction and the whole volume. Thank you also to John Dugan and Rebecca Krawiec for their generous help. Any mistakes that remain are, of course, my own.

REFERENCES CITED

Beazley, J. D. 1956 *Attic Black-Figure Vase-Painters.* Clarendon, Oxford.

Bloch, M. 1992 *Prey into Hunter. The politics of Religious Experience.* Cambridge University Press, Cambridge.

Boardman, J. 1974 *Athenian Black Figure Vases.* Thames and Hudson, London.

Bothmer, D. von 1944 The Painters of "Tyrrhenian Vases." *American Journal of Archaeology* 48:161–170.

Boyce, G. K. 1937 *Corpus of the Lararia of Pompeii.* Memoirs of the American Academy in Rome, Vol. 14. American Academy in Rome Rome.

Bremmer, J. N. 2010 Greek Normative Animal Sacrifice. In *A Companion to Greek Religion*, edited by D. Ogden, pp. 132–144. Wiley-Blackwell, Oxford.

Burkert, W. 1972 *Homo Necans. The Anthropology of Ancient Greek Sacrificial Ritual and Myth.* University of California, Berkeley.

Burkert, W. 1985 *Greek Religion. Archaic and Classical.* Blackwell, Oxford.

Detienne, M. 1989 Culinary Practices and the Spirit of Sacrifice. In *The Cuisine of Sacrifice among the Greeks*, edited by M. Detienne and J.-P. Vernant, pp. 1–20. University of Chicago, Chicago.

Detienne, M., and J.-P. Vernant (editors) 1989 *The Cuisine of Sacrifice among the Greeks.* University of Chicago, Chicago.

Ekroth, G. 2007 Meat in Ancient Greece: Sacrificial, Sacred, or Secular? *Food and History* 5.1: 249–272.

Ekroth, G. 2008 Meat, Man, and God. On the Division of the Animal Victim at Greek sacrifices. In *Mikros Hieronmnemon: Studies in Memory of Michael H. Jameson*, edited by A. Matthaiou and I. Polinskaya, pp. 259–290. Greek Epigraphic Society, Athens.

Faraone, C. A., and F. S. Naiden 2012 *Greek and Roman Animal Sacrifice. Ancient Victims, Modern Observers.* Cambridge University Press, Cambridge.

Gilhus, I. S. 2006 *Animals, Gods, and Humans. Changing Attitudes to Animals in Greek, Roman and Early Christian Ideas.* Routledge, London.

Giacobello, F. 2008 *Larari pompeiani: Iconografia e culto dei Lari in ambito domestic*. Il Filarete, University of Milan, Milan.

Girard, R. 1977 *Violence and the Sacred*. Johns Hopkins University Press, Baltimore.

Girard, R. 1986 *The Scapegoat*. Johns Hopkins University Press, Baltimore.

Girard, R. 1987 Generative Scapegoating. In *Violent Origins. Walter Burkert, René Girard, Jonathan Z. Smith on Ritual Killing and Cultural Formation*, edited by R. G. Hamerton-Kelly, pp. 73–105. Stanford University Press, Stanford.

Green, M. A. 2001 *Dying for the Gods. Human Sacrifice in Iron Age and Roman Europe*. Tempus, Stroud.

Hamerton-Kelly, R. G. (editor) 1987 *Violent Origins. Walter Burkert, René Girard, Jonathan Z. Smith on Ritual Killing and Cultural Formation*. Stanford University Press, Stanford.

Holleran, C. 2012 *Shopping in Ancient Rome. Retail Trade in the Late Republic and the Principate*. Oxford University Press, Oxford.

Hubert, H., and M. Mauss 1964 *Sacrifice, Its Nature and Functions*. University of Chicago Press, Midway Reprint, Chicago.

Isenberg, M. 1975 The Sale of Sacrificial Meat. *Classical Philology* 70: 271–273.

Knust, J. W., and Z. Várhelyi (editors) 2011 *Ancient Mediterranean Sacrifice*. Oxford University Press, Oxford.

Konrad, C. F. 2004 *Augusto augurio. Rerun humanarum et divinarum commentationes in honorem Jerzy Linderski*. Steiner, Stuttgart.

Lietzmann, H. 1949 *An die Korinther I–II*. Mohr, Tübingen.

McDonough, C. M. 2004 The Pricing of Sacrificial Meat: *Eidolothuton*, the Ara Maxima, and Useful Misinformation from Servius. In *Augusto augurio. Rerun humanarum et divinarum commentationes in honorem Jerzy Linderski*, edited by C. F. Konrad, pp. 70–76. Steiner, Stuttgart.

Meuli, K. 1975 *Gesammelte Schriften*. Schwabe, Basel.

Naiden, F. S. 2013 *Smoke Signals for the Gods. Ancient Greek Sacrifice from the Archaic through Roman Periods*. Oxford University Press, Oxford.

Ogden, D. (editor) 2010 *A Companion to Greek Religion*. Wiley-Blackwell, Oxford.

Parker, R. 2010 Eating Unsacrificed Meat. In *Paysage et religion en Grèce antique, mélanges offerts à Madeleine Jost*, edited by P. Carlier and C. Lerouge-Cohen, pp. 137–145. de Boccard, Paris.

Rhodes, P. J., and R. Osborne 2003 *Greek Historical Inscriptions 404–323 BC*. Oxford University Press, Oxford.

Scheid, J. 2003 *An Introduction to Roman Religion*. Indiana University Press, Bloomington.

Shipley, G., J. Vanderspoel, D. Mattingly, and L. Foxhall (editors) 2006 *The Cambridge Dictionary of Classical Civilization*. Cambridge University Press, Cambridge.

Smith, J. Z. 1987 The Domestication of Sacrifice. In *Violent Origins. Walter Burkert, René Girard, Jonathan Z. Smith on Ritual Killing and Cultural Formation*, edited by R. G. Hamerton-Kelly, pp. 191–235. Stanford University Press, Stanford.

Stafford, E. 2006 Sacrifice. In *The Cambridge Dictionary of Classical Civilization*, edited by G. Shipley, J. Vanderspoel, D. Mattingly, and L. Foxhall, pp. 775–776. Cambridge University Press, Cambridge.

Vernant, J.-P. 1989 At Man's Table: Hesiod's Foundation Myth of Sacrifice. In *The Cuisine of Sacrifice among the Greeks*, edited by M. Detienne and J.-P. Vernant, pp. 21–86. University of Chicago Press, Chicago.

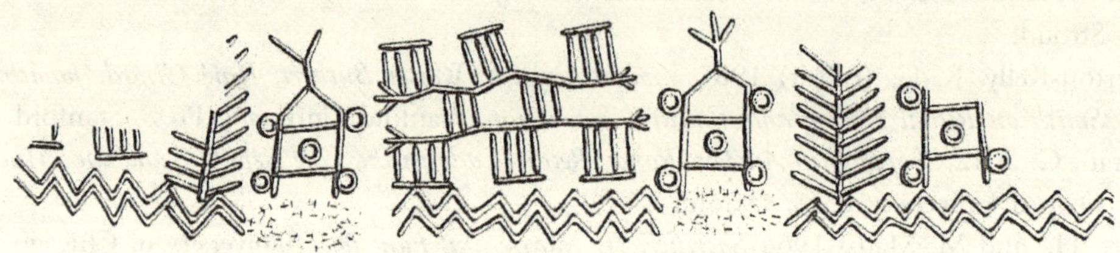

PART I

Defining and Redefining
the Boundaries of Sacrifice

CHAPTER ONE

Anthropology and Sacrifice

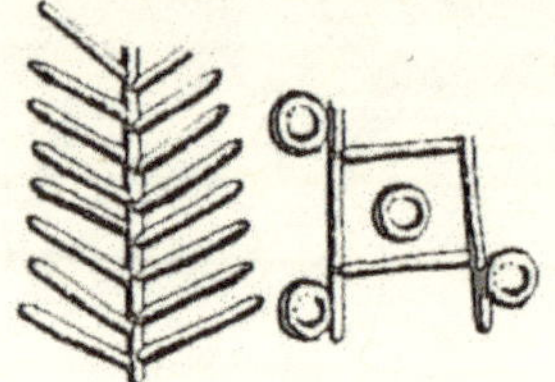

Phillips Stevens Jr.

Abstract   *As "sacrifice" was the theme of the 2011 IEMA conference, this was an ideal occasion for a summary overview of what the field of cultural anthropology has had to say about the subject. In the late nineteenth and early twentieth centuries, sacrifice was a popular topic, but in the later twentieth century, interest in the subject was sporadic, and in the twenty-first century, many discussions of the anthropology of religion omit it entirely. This paper reviews the meaning of "anthropology" and of "sacrifice," considers the history of interests in sacrifice, and reviews and assesses the works of noted early and classical scholars on the topic. Modern fieldwork-based anthropology offers new and better perspectives on this important and complex institution; as H. sapiens is fundamentally cognitively similar everywhere and throughout the history of the species, the insights of modern anthropology should be applied by classicists.*

As "sacrifice" was the theme of the 2011 IEMA conference, this was an ideal occasion for a summary overview of what the field of cultural anthropology has had to say about the subject. And it is a fortuitous occasion for both IEMA and the field of anthropology, because some of the earliest studies with lasting influence were by classicists. In the late nineteenth and early twentieth centuries, sacrifice was a popular topic, but in the later twentieth century interest in the subject was sporadic, and in the twenty-first century discussions of the anthropology of religion in many general textbooks omit it entirely. A critical survey of anthropological views on the subject reveals it as a rich source of insight into human culture and can help to correct many misconceptions about it. A great many misconceptions of modern times, as we will see, have come down to us from early European assumptions about the rest of the world.

I have changed the title somewhat. My IEMA conference paper was entitled "The Anthropology of Sacrifice." The field of anthropology today allows for so many perspectives on a given issue that to call a study *the* anthropology of something sounds presumptuous; moreover, many of the early influential studies of the subject were by European classicists and philologists. Some of these were influenced by scholars formally trained as anthropologists, but "anthropology" has had different meanings in Europe, the British Isles, and America. It could be said that for many early-twentieth-century scholars it was considered a theoretical and methodological approach as well as an academic discipline. Looking at the literature on sacrifice, we might discern two separate "anthropological" approaches: what we could generously call "philological anthropology" (though not all scholars under this heading were strictly philologists; this avoids the derisive label "armchair anthropology") and, perhaps, "field anthropology." The former draws from others' writings to speculate on a culture that is quite distant geographically or temporally from the writer, who might interpret other customs, beliefs, and morals through the tenets of his/her own; the other assumes that any statements about a culture must be dependent upon direct observation of, and testimony by, those within that specific culture. (From the latter twentieth century we might argue for a third approach, an "ethnological anthropology" that assumes certain regularities in the behavior of *H. sapiens,* so that some level of generalization is justified; we'll elaborate on this below). So, our application of the label must not be dogmatic, and must allow for inclusion of different observations on the human condition.

I mean "sacrifice" in its broadest sense, to indicate giving up something valuable, and this discussion will include all offerings from people to supernatural agencies. The practice of sacrifice is surely universal to religious ritual, and is an expression of the classic sociological theory of religious concepts being projections of social ones, the theory given the most eloquent expression by Emile Durkheim (1915).

Scholars often preface their explanations with some form of classification. A widely applicable classification of sacrifice is based in the situation in which sacrifice seems called for: *calendrical,* usually corresponding to seasonal change, especially horticultural cycles, but which also includes the so-called "first fruits" rituals found in all societies, including those of hunters and gatherers; and *critical*: sacrifice in response to some unforeseen crisis. Sacrifice at passages through stages in the life cycle has been classified as "critical," insofar as such life cycle events are regarded as "life crises"; in fact, such ceremonies may be markedly calendrical. Individual scholars have proposed other bases for classifying sacrifice, such as according to its apparent purpose. Valerio Valeri (1985:81–82) proposed a scheme based on a deity's chief function and the corresponding type of sacrifice selected: "nomocentric" sacrifices are for supernatural agencies who protect social groups; "ergocentric" sacrifices are for agencies who govern economic, specifically tool-making, activities; and "genocentric" sacrifices render specific species available for human consumption (e.g., "first fruits" offerings). Any method may be useful, depending on what we are looking for.

EARLY THEORIES

Perhaps the oldest interpretation of sacrifice is as economic exchange, modeled directly on that institution in human society; just as human social relationships are both established and maintained by the satisfaction of expectations and obligations by economic means, so too are human-supernatural relationships governed. It has been recognized for a long time—indeed, millennia before Marcel Mauss's *The Gift* (1923)—that gifts are indemnifying; Plato in his *Dialogues* (fourth century B.C.E.) asserted that the gods could not be bribed (*Euthryphro* 14, *Laws* 716–17; Malefijt 1968:209). E. B. Tylor (1871) explained sacrifice in terms of economic motives: indemnification, homage, and abnegation. But from classical times to the present, the economic cost of sacrifice has been an issue; it would seem that the wealthy have an edge on supernatural favor. Hesiod had stated that "one must sacrifice according to one's means" (Burkert 1987:143), and this issue leads to discussions of principles of sacred morality, and the tolerance of the gods for substitutes, and their appreciation of intention over substance (e.g., the "widow's mite" in Christian offering advice; Luke 21:1–4). In one of his later works, Walter Burkert (1996) summarizes Western discussions of this issue; we will return to it.

Robertson Smith (1889) set the sociological frame; being so bold—some said heretical—to apply objective science to the Bible, he emphasized the nature and social functions of the communal meal that so often followed the sacrificial ritual, and his theory was strongly influential on James George Frazer, Henri Hubert and Marcel Mauss, Mircea Eliade, and Emile Durkheim, and some lesser-known scholars, as we'll see below. Frazer's fanciful theory of the dying god/divine king (1890), which he saw reflected in agricultural societies in the classical world, and which some scholars as heretical as Smith saw in the Jesus cycle, was influential in Victorian thinking, but not strongly respected in later anthropology. Science in the latter nineteenth century, impacted strongly by Charles Darwin's theory of evolution, was obsessed with ascertaining the stages that marked the progressive evolution of cultural phenomena. Frazer focused mainly on the material being offered, and his evolutionary scheme of sacrifice—like most others of his era, and many later—posited that the earliest sacrifices were human beings, specifically priests, because they were closest to the gods; then animals replaced people, and as agriculture spread, plant products became the dominant sacrificial material. And he noted that in agricultural societies, plant materials— corn, grains, rice, and fruit—were offered in the same manner as animals had been in hunting societies; he stated that a principal aim of agrarian sacrifice was the fertility of the fields. These observations were topics of discussion among several of the twentieth-century European scholars whom we will look at shortly.

Henri Hubert and Marcel Mauss (1964; orig. 1898) wrote the first major treatise on sacrifice, which became the obligatory starting point for all later discussions. They stated that the primary function of sacrifice was as communication, and in so doing, they established the structural/functionalist theoretical framework for subsequent explanations for the next six decades or more. They expressed indebtedness to Tylor, Smith, and Frazer; and they correctly criticized Smith and Frazer for framing their theories in totemism, the geographic distribution of which is quite limited, and other unjustified assumptions. They seem ahead of their time in their criticism of Smith for classifying his materials according to his own system of logic, "a characteristic common to English anthropologists" (1964:7). They set their theories on Biblical and early Hindu Sanskrit texts, "doctrines that belong to a definite era . . . drawn up by the participants themselves in their own language, in the very spirit in which they enacted the rites" (1964:7). But in their reliance on early Indo-Iranian oral traditions, the Vedic cosmogonic myths of *soma* and the *purusha,* and their search for parallels in other religions to establish a prototypic symbol of divine sacrifice in the manner of Frazer, they also are on fragile theoretical ground. In his foreword to the 1964 translation, E. E. Evans-Pritchard said, "I find its conclusions . . . rather lame, but as a study of the structure, or one might almost say the grammar, of the sacrificial rite, the Essay is superb" (1964:viii). Hubert and Mauss found it important to distinguish between the one who performs the actual sacrificial ritual, the "sacrificer," and the person or party on whose behalf the sacrifice is performed, the "sacrifier," and these terms have been used in English discussion ever since.

An evolutionary concern persisted, but the "functionalist" and "structuralist" approaches dominated European conversation for the next several decades. Most influential were Emile Durkheim's classic work on the sociology of religion (1915), and Claude Lévi-Strauss's structuralism (See, e.g., 1953, 1966). Three monographs by European scholars: Walter Burkert (1983; orig 1972), Luc de Heusch (1985), and Valerio Valeri (1985), deserve special and more detailed discussion.

Burkert's Homo Necans

Walter Burkert, whose many works followed a "history of religions" approach, is a recognized authority on classical, especially Greek, religion. The title of his major work could be translated "Killing Man," or "Man the Killer"; and the subtitle is "The Anthropology of Ancient Greek Sacrificial Ritual and Myth." Following the search for origins or earliest forms set by the nineteenth-century evolutionists, he elaborated on a thesis proposed by various others, that sacrifice arose out of the culture of early hunters, and served the critical social functions of channeling man's innate aggression, and of fostering social unity. He credits Karl Meuli (1946) for the recognition of the hunter's basic dilemma: he needs to kill to feed his people; but in killing, he destroys a vital link in the natural cycle, and he depletes his own source of sustenance. In a combination of remorse and concern for his future welfare, the hunter makes an offering of apology and a plea to the gods for replenishment of nature. Meuli, however, and other students of Greek sacrificial ritual noted that, in the ubiquitous communal meal, people got the choice cuts of meat, and the gods got only "the bones, the fat, and the gall bladders." And, sardonically, Burkert asks, "Is the god 'to whom' the sacrifice is made any more than a transparent excuse for festive feasting?" (Burkert 1983:7), echoing a sentiment of various early discussants of Greek culture. Here is a sentiment of the "armchair anthropologist" that justifies Europeans' claim of naivety and childishness among "primitive" peoples—and completely misses a very basic aspect of sacrifice: that it is not the material but the spiritual, the life force, the core *essence* of the animal or object that is transmitted to the supernatural. This is similar to the attitude held by modern missionaries, which assumes that the primitive sacrificer's belief is that the idol or whatever object is addressed in the ritual is the god itself; and conversion is assisted by destruction of idols and religious paraphernalia. The error might be rectified in understanding the ritual use of blood, to which we will return later.

Burkert, like Meuli, Frazer, and others before him, assumes that human sacrifice was the earliest ideal, and that animals came to substitute for people, and anthropomorphism and personification are involved as the hunter's

> quarry becomes a quasi-human adversary, experienced as human and treated accordingly. Hunting concentrated on the great mammals, which conspicuously resembled men in their body structure and movements, their eyes and their "faces." Their breath and voices, in fleeing and in fear, in attacking and in rage . . . [o]ne could, perhaps, most clearly grasp the animal's resemblance to man when it died. Thus, the quarry turned into a sacrificial victim. Many observers have told of the almost brotherly bond that hunters felt for their game, and the exchangeability of man and animal in sacrifice recurs as a mythological theme in many cultures. (1983:20)

Sacrifice is ritual, and through its repetitiveness and "theatrical exaggeration," (Burkert 1983:23) "ritual creates and affirms social interaction." Ritual's repetition is rhythmic, "and auditory signals accompanying the gestures give rise to music and dance. These, too, are primordial forms of human solidarity." He cites both Durkheim and ethologists such as Lorenz and Eibl-Eibesfeldt in support of his theory of biosocial development. Ultimately, his is a functional theory, in which sacrifice is postulated as the basis of not only society itself, but many features of society as well. "The ritual power to kill" is the most powerful binding force of society at all levels; "serious" ritual killing in "a community bound by oaths" provides a more powerful bond than friendly compassion and cooperation (1983:35), and "the closer the bond, the more gruesome the ritual" (1983:36; which may explain why so many conspiracy theories postulate secret societies that perform bloody human sacrifice followed by a cannibalistic communal meal). The physical structures of society are solidified by sacrifice (1983:39); indeed, "any new creation requires ritual killing." Initiation into exclusive organizations often involves symbolic death and rebirth. For "civilization" (meaning here the nineteenth-century evolutionists' ultimate stage in human social development), "the death penalty became the strongest expression of governmental power" and execution the ultimate sacrificial act (1983:46).

An important, oft-quoted statement of Burkert's comes early in his book: "Sacrificial killing is the basic experience of the 'sacred.' *Homo religiosus* acts and attains self-awareness as *Homo necans*" (1983:3). Through sacrifice, the sacred (Rudolf Otto's "numen," "numinous," "*mysterium tremendum*," 1923) is directly experienced. Burkert thus recognizes a central property of sacrifice—the realization of the Latin roots of the word, "to make holy"; but he does not dwell on it. This idea is important; I will return to it later.

And, though Burkert explicitly dismisses Freudian theory as passé, some of his reasoning echoes psychoanalytic themes. One of his summary statements recalls both Freud's and Durkheim's use of Australian totemic data: "In the hunting ritual, aggression between men was redirected toward an animal quarry which was thereby raised to the status of a personality, a blood-relation, even a father" (1983:42). Ultimately, for Burkert, the most "serious" way to direct the aggressive instinct outside is "by integrating large groups of men in a common fighting spirit, i.e., war. . . . War is ritual, a self-portrayal and self-affirmation of male society," which brings us full cycle: "For the ancient world, hunting, sacrifice, and war were symbolically interchangeable" (1983:47), and in this last sentiment,

Burkert foreshadows proponents of psychohistory and the psychoanalytic study of society, as exemplified today by Lloyd de Mause, Richard Koenigsberg, and others.

There are both useful insights and unprovable speculation in Burkert's work, but like the following two scholars, to whose work I will give considerably less space, a hidden benefit of reading it is that it provides insights from lesser-known scholars, some of whose works were not translated into English. We have noted Burkert's debt to Karl Meuli; he also cites Marcel Detienne, French historian and classicist, and Jean-Paul Vernant, historian and anthropologist, who together sought to apply a Lévi-Straussian structuralist anthropology to the culture of classical Greece. For our interest here, we can refer to their interesting study of the myth of the introduction of sacrifice by Prometheus, his prescription of the menu for the communal meal, and the resultant curious relationship Greeks had with meat and grain (Detienne and Vernant 1979; trans). Because of his interest in human violence, Burkert is also attracted to the work of René Girard, literary critic, historian, and "anthropological philosopher," who saw sacrifice as originating in the human social need for a scapegoat (Girard 1972; trans 1977). Some of the writings on ritual killing by Burkert, Girard, and historian of religion Jonathan Z. Smith were brought together in a 1988 collection by Robert Hamerton-Kelly. Burkert also brings in the work of an early German scholar, Wilhelm Mannhardt (1875) whose thoughts on the nature of sacrifice have implications for the magical element, to which we will return later.

Luc de Heusch and Valerio Valeri

Two important monographs in the fieldwork-based anthropology of sacrifice were written by these scholars, and should receive special mention. De Heusch's *Sacrifice in Africa: A Structuralist Approach* (1985) is a product of the Systems of Thought in Black Africa Laboratory discussions of sacrifice in the mid-late 1970s, motivated by the lack of focus on the topic in African studies; earlier *cahiers* on sacrifice had been produced by the Laboratory in 1976, 1978, 1979, and 1981, all in French. De Heusch assembled materials from several field anthropological studies, including his own fieldwork in the Belgian Congo: Germaine Dieterlen's and Marcel Griaule's study of the Dogon and Bambara, and Max Gluckman's work with the Thonga, and from special classes that he held focusing on Swazi, Rwanda, and Zulu; he also consulted the published works of many other scholars.

De Heusch begins with a thorough critique of Hubert and Mauss for their armchair theorizing and the narrow application of their pronouncements, and takes us through many of the same sources that Burkert had credited. He states as his aim the clarification and delineation of the "ideologies that are set up around the immolation of a human or animal victim" (de Heusch 1985:15), which can really be done satisfactorily only through fieldwork. He freely compares African themes and practices with those of classical Greece and Brahmanic India, which had been Hubert and Mauss's starting point, and the subject of an important monograph by Madeleine Biardeau and Charles Malamoud (1976). He discusses Evans-Pritchard's famous Nuer studies (1953, 1956) at length, and criticizes that scholar's theoretical interpretation for its apparent reliance on Judeo-Christian theology. He curiously does not mention Burkert, but he dismisses Girard's scapegoat theory. In what he characterizes as "merely a reconnoitering trip" (1985:213), he illustrates the complexity and heterogeneity of African systems, and in a good expression of the principles of modern anthropology, he notes the vast range of sacrificial practices and their correlations with social and political structures and subsistence practices, and with finer details of hunting, ritual, cooking, stock raising, etc. He argues convincingly for greater and more specific ethnographic examination of African (and any other) systems before allowing any generalizations. He stresses the importance and the complexity of symbolic thought and communication systems that must be examined and understood.

> One must listen patiently to the ideological speeches of a multitude of sacrificers, in the most diverse societies, before reaching a conclusion. One must ask oneself, in each particular case, what is the symbolic coherence of the set of sacrificial rites which often appear incongruous; one must not fail to connect them with neighbouring rites, with the entirety of the symbolic thought in the society under study. (1985:23)

De Heusch was previously known for his insights on African kingship (1972, 1982). In this work, he distinguishes two major sacrificial schemas: one is a set of domestic and culinary practices intended for the ancestors, and the other is a set of royal and cosmogonic sacrifices, in which are included all sacrificial practices associated with sacred kingship or with the mythic sovereignty of a god doomed to die in order to be born again. On the theme of African ritual regicide, he says, "I have resolutely joined Frazer's camp. It cannot be doubted that the sacred king, the formidable master of natural forces, is, after a reign of varying lengths, condemned to die prematurely, to become a sacrificial victim. The ritual killing of the king is part of his fate; it is the ultimate expression of the prohibitions that hedge in his excessive power, his monstrous counter-cultural nature" (1985:98–99).

Valerio Valeri's 1985 work, deriving from his examination of sacrifice in Hawaii, is about twice the length of de Heusch's, and also is valuable beyond its own central focus. Valeri conducted anthropological fieldwork in Micronesia, Indonesia, and Malaysia as well as Hawaii. One work on sacrifice from his intensive work in Huaulu, Moluccan Islands, was published (1994) before his untimely death; at least three monographs were expected to appear posthumously. His great work on Hawaiian kingship and sacrifice was described by Marshall Sahlins in an obituary notice (University of Chicago Chronicle 1998) as "the best book ever written on Polynesian ethnology. It offers an innovative theory of sacrifice, as well as a theory of divinity, that engages with the best Western writings on comparative theology and takes its place among them." In her positive review of Valeri's book, Joyce Linnekin showed ways in which conscientious anthropological fieldwork is supplemented by archival work: it is "based on exhaustive and meticulous ethnohistorical research. . . . He appears to have consulted virtually all the non-Hawaiian accounts of the early society as well as the major Hawaiian-language texts relating to ritual, and he discusses the biases, strengths, and reliability of each source" (Linnekin 1985:788–789). Valeri's work is incredibly rich and far too complex to be fully laid out and explicated here; I will make just two points about it. The first, drawing from Linnekin's review, summarizes his main points about Hawaiian ritual and what Sahlins has called his "innovative theory of sacrifice." His analysis, following Durkheim and G. W. F. Hegel, shows in detail how all levels of Hawaiian society are replicated through sacrificial ritual. *Luakini* is the temple traditionally consecrated for royal human sacrifice, and its rituals:

> Valeri's premise is that sacrificial rituals "hierarchize" subjects by relating them to different gods. Lower-ranking men sacrifice to inferior deities; the king offers the most valued sacrifice and "creates society" by establishing the rank of all those below him. The Hawaiian gods are anthropomorphic and personify types of social beings. Their function is therefore normative: they symbolize and represent men in the course of the ritual. Valeri likens the *luakini* rites to "programmed learning through activities that involve the apperception of codes, principles, concepts, and their reproduction in practice" (p. 344). In one phase of the *luakini* ritual, a god-image is tamed, passing from a wild, disordered, and individual state to an ordered collectivity. The god thus "reconstitutes" society through its ritual transformation, and the king's role is crucial because he serves as the ideal man in this passage—an exemplar and also a mediator between the human and the divine. (Linnekin 1985:789)

My second point is to say that Valeri's work is an exemplary illustration of de Heusch's advice about what kinds of investigations and considerations are necessary before statements about sacrifice can be deemed legitimate.

Valeri cites and assesses most of the principal writers on sacrifice (including Burkert), and his themes are clearly framed within the structuralist mode. He specifically acknowledges Evans-Pritchard (1956) "and especially . . . Lienhardt (1961)" (1985:346), praising the latter's view of supernatural agencies as "representations" or "images" or "schemes" of experience, having constructed "an explicit empiricist model of the passage from experience to concept." Burkert had stressed "experience"; here is the same emphasis from a field anthropologist.

ANTHROPOLOGICAL TRUTHS AND EXCEPTIONS

Twentieth-century anthropology up to the 1970s was marked by ethnographic study, and important statements about sacrifice by several other fieldworkers, for example, Robert Lowie (1935), Kalervo Oberg (1940), John Middleton (1960), Melville Herskovits (1967), Raymond Firth (1967), and the celebrated structuralist Claude Lévi-Strauss (1953, 1966), include conclusions drawn from their own fieldwork. The latter third of the last century might be labeled the Age of Ethnology, anthropology's powerful cross-cultural comparative method, which aims at comparing specific ethnographic data across and between regions, and correlating cultural data with ecological and other factors, in order to make general statements about humanity. One critical conclusion from ethnology is that *H. sapiens* is cognitively similar around the world and throughout history; people everywhere tend to arrive at very similar solutions to the most fundamental problems of life. The most useful statements that we can make about sacrifice today benefit from both perspectives.

Like most cultural institutions, sacrifice has been explained by meaning and purpose; and its meaning is multilayered and complex. I have mentioned the economic dimension; many supernatural beings are conceptualized as either kin or broadly ancestral to the people, and the most important of all kinship obligations, sharing, may be a primary motive. Perhaps the most common explanation is expiation, atonement for some transgression; this explanation is widely applicable, as many supernatural recipients of offerings are regarded as supervisors and monitors of human social behavior. Anthropologists have recognized for a long time that sacrifice involves communication; a message is transmitted through the language of symbolism (e.g., Hubert and Mauss 1964; Lévi-Strauss 1953; Leach 1976). This element is clear in the ritual of divination, which commonly follows a sacrifice, to ascertain the result of the sacrificial offering. The communicative medium is symbolic; it may carry words spoken directly to it by the sacrificer. The object is often something of which the recipient is known to be particularly fond, and sometimes, through the magical principle of similarity, it is meant to link directly to some aspect of the nature of its recipient—e.g., a black bull for the god of night or the underworld. Thanks to Burkert (1983:44), we learn of the work of the little-known Wilhelm Mannhardt, who wrote several ethnological works in German in the late nineteenth century (see his *Wald- und Feldkulte*, 1875) and who recognized such links (though it is not clear that he recognized them as magical connections). Mannhardt coined the label "*Vegetationsdämon*" to signify the spirit of the agricultural cycle. In his Note 39, Burkert (1983:45) says:

> The fact that it is precisely the "Vegetationsdämon" who is killed time and time again in the ritual has been explained in various ways: the drowning is weather-magic for rain (1875:214, 417), the immolation is a purification (607–608), the burying is intended for sowing and germination (419–21), the whole process stimulates the annual cycle of the death and rebirth of vegetation.

And sacrifice has been performed as a corrective measure, to reestablish balance or alignment among some cosmic elements—the central purpose of the great *Eka Dasa Rudra* festival of Bali, the "Festival of the Eleven Powers," as held and filmed in 1979, to restore the balance to the world, which had been overturned by decades of violent conflict in Southeast Asia (Gartenstein 1980).

The most common explanation, and perhaps scientifically the weakest, is one based in function. Functions change; and an act can be seen to have multiple functions simultaneously. So a functionalist explanation may not be very helpful. The sociologists were correct, of course, in many of their general pronouncements; sacrifice has powerful sociological functions—cohesion, order, purpose, psychological release, confidence, and control. A sociobiological explanation is offered by Scott Atran (2002) who points out that the sacrificer might seek the most economical object; nevertheless, as we have noted earlier, any sacrifice is costly, and the costs of some are extraordinary. Atran suggests an explanation in terms of the evolutionary phenomenon of altruism. And sacrifice illustrates a latent function of all ritual, elevating the profane to the level of the sacred, a main point of Hubert and Mauss (1964 [1899]) and later of Durkheim (1915). Such an act has important implications for the sociology of status. Who performs the act? The practitioner has been sacralized, "purified" perhaps, so as to handle the sacred without harm. Blacksmiths are the sacred executioners at the great sacrifice to the Eleven Powers in Bali; there and elsewhere blacksmiths are already endowed with special power. This function also has implications for the communicative aspects of sacrifice; the sacrificial object or victim also must undergo a process of sacralization (consecration), so that it can act as mediator.

We can elaborate a bit on Smith's focus on the communal meal—around the world, dining is a social event, an event of intimacy, domesticity, and trust, sharing with others the very bases of subsistence; Smith understood this very clearly in the cultures of the Middle East. Mircea Eliade told us in many of his works that an aim of ritual is to identify with the supernatural, and this is clear in the communal meal. It is wrenchingly, disturbingly clear in the cannibalistic ritual of the Eucharist, explainable by Smith as a survival of an earlier totemic religious system, in which the participants sought to absorb something material of the totem with which they so thoroughly identified. As Hubert and Mauss had noted, this falling back on totemism was the weakest part of Smith's theory, a popular theme that ensnared both Durkheim and Freud as well, but it serves to sanctify and smooth over the viscerally abhorrent act of cannibalism.

Elaborating further on an economic explanation for sacrifice, scholars have emphasized the value of the sacrificial object, and sought correlation between its social value and the gravity of the ritual. Through some incomplete correlations, some have pointed out that very valuable items are sacrificed rarely or not at all; that in times of hardship, the supernaturals will accept substitute items of lesser value—as in Evans-Pritchard's celebrated Nuer substitution of a cucumber for a cow (1956). But some stated correlations are wrong, or incomplete. It has been generally accepted, for example, that only domestic animals are sacrificed, not wild ones—but ethnographic accounts are replete with descriptions of hunters' "first-fruits" offerings of a season's first kill of a particular species (and I witnessed this myself, in fieldwork among the Bachama of northeastern Nigeria, 1969–71). Only partially satisfactory is the widely heralded awareness of traditional peoples that they and nature are vitally interconnected, and the death of an occupant of nature leaves both a gap and a function unfulfilled, and some effort to restore that deficiency is obligatory.

Whatever the material, care is taken to ensure that its essence is transmitted to the other dimension. As we have noted, early observers of traditional material sacrifice, already biased about "savages," completely misunderstood the material elements of sacrifice, including the offering itself, and the "target"—the altar or the structure on it, the temporary domicile of the spirit—the material representation of the god, sometimes an idol. They commented disparagingly about the offerings by "primitives" and "savages" of costly utilitarian objects such as tools, weapons, and prepared foodstuffs—similar to the interpretations of grave goods in classical burials. Such views showed a critical misunderstanding, like the classic assumption about idolatry: that the idol is the god and that people believe that the idol consumes the offering. They failed to grasp the core of the sacrificial act; it is the mystical *essence* of the thing, not its material shell, that is transmitted. If they had stayed a few days, as anthropologists did later, and seen the utilization of the sacrificial objects by the sacrificers and their relatives and creditors, they might have realized their error. Because of such early misunderstandings, some important aspects of the sacrificial complex need further examination.

ALTARS

Anthropologists have not been much interested in altars—why not? An anthropological assessment really must give substantial attention to the altar. The altar is sacred space, but more than that, it is highly charged with mystical supernatural power, hence dangerous. The concentration of power at that point, the exact point of sacrifice, is like that experienced by Moses after his personal meeting with God, when "his face shone" and his people were terrified when he came down from the mountain (Exodus 34:29–30), or like the power that killed Uzzah when he touched the Ark (2 Samuel 6:6–7, 1 Chron. 13:9–10). Around the world, people construct shrine objects imbued with power the sole purpose of which is to enhance the power of the altar, to assist in the accomplishment of its purpose. It has been interesting through my career to note that art historians have been far more interested in altars than anthropologists have, mainly because of the fine quality of some of the shrine enhancements.

Around the world, horns have power. In Hebrew scriptures, God instructs the people how to build altars for different purposes, for incense or burnt offerings or for sin offerings; in Exodus (27 and 29) he gives specific instructions for adding horns to the four corners of the altar, and "its horns shall be of one piece with it" (Exodus 27:2). Several horned altars, built of stone blocks, have been excavated in Israel; just a few years ago, a solid horned altar was discovered in the hills of Judea (Elitzur and Nir-Zevi 2004). Burkert had famously said that sacrifice "is the basic experience of the sacred." And it happens on an altar.

Libations and Burnt Offerings

Liquid offerings are common throughout the world, and the properties of the liquid accord exactly with the economic attributes of other sacrificial objects that we have discussed. Liquids are almost always representative of life, or subsistence, or of pleasure, such as fermented or distilled liquids. And of course, the fermentation or distillation concentrates the power of the liquid, just as incineration of the sacrificial material in a burnt offering removes the dross and concentrates the essence in smoke, the odor of which, as the Bible says, "is pleasing to God" (Genesis 8:21; Exodus 29;18; Leviticus 1:9; elsewhere).

Blood

No matter what it is, the fullest meaning of the liquid is symbolic; and there is nothing more deeply symbolic than blood. Indeed, blood is at once real *and* symbolic. We cannot overstate the universal power and ritual significance of blood. It is the essence of life; it *is* life. A full appreciation of the cross-cultural meaning of blood is essential for the fullest understanding of sacrifice (see, e.g., Buckley and Gottlieb 1988).

Blood is most often the true sacrificial element in live sacrifice; indeed, blood is often regarded as the property of the divine; flesh, mundane and profane, is shared among the supplicants (remember the errors of our early classicists and missionaries). But by its source, blood (human *and* animal) can differ greatly: in ancient Hebrew culture, menstrual blood and blood of childbirth and blood of circumcision are very different, each having very different power, which determines instructions for pollution and purification, and for sacrifice (in Exodus, Leviticus, and Deuteronomy; see especially Eilberg-Schwartz 1990). The process of rendering meat *kasrut* (kosher)—or *halal*, in Islam—involves the ritual separation of blood from the slaughtered carcass, and a symbolic offering of that blood to its divine source.

Blood is the all-purpose sacrificial liquid, satisfying to all supernatural agencies in all imaginable occasions. It is readily available to individuals in crisis situations; Robert Lowie (1935) describes the Crow Indian vision-seeker's act of severing a finger and offering it and the freely flowing blood to the potential guardian spirit, in a solemn contract. And my colleague Bob Dentan (2008:69ff.) describes how Semai slash themselves and throw their blood to Nkuu, the terrible god of the thunderstorm who can destroy whole villages with his breath.

HUMAN SACRIFICE

This is a good place to confront the gorilla in the room, what jumps to most minds when the word *sacrifice* is heard. The sacrifice of a human being represents the ultimate offering to the supernatural, and the idea of it is very probably universal. It dominated early scholarship. It was assumed that human sacrifice was rare among kin-based noncentralized peoples, such as foragers, herders, and simple horticulturalists; but that it was fairly common among centralized, stratified, heterogeneous peoples; and in such instances the victims were somehow marginal to the dominant group: slaves or captives. Frazer's elaborate account of the dying god-king, and Eliade's (1964) assumption that we are dealing with a ritual reenactment of a primordial reality, fostered the assumptions of a wide distribution of human sacrifice in the early world.

Ethnological research, however, has revealed that, like cannibalism, human sacrifice existed mostly as allegation; in actual fact, it was far less common than assumed (see, e.g., Obeyesekere 2005). Much has been made of the Aztec case, with famous explanations. The records of the act seem accurate, and many are supported by indigenous sources including ancient glyphic art, but careful research suggests that the incidence of human sacrifice was greatly exaggerated, especially by the Spanish who themselves came from a tradition that assumed widespread human sacrifice—and cannibalism—in the traditional world. Descriptive models of Aztec ritual included the communal meal—and assumed routine cannibalism; and serious explanations have been offered based on the idea that the cannibalistic communal meal satisfied a protein deficiency in the population. We are wiser now, with a great debt of thanks to Bill Arens (1979), and we know that the twin allegations of cannibalism and human sacrifice are widespread epithets, commonly made by one group about some other, in the traditional world.

The story of Abraham and Isaac (Genesis 22) has many layers of meaning; we should realize that on one level it is a type of myth, which we could entitle "The End of Human Sacrifice" (see Thompson 1955).[1] God said, "I appreciate your gesture, but don't do it, your numbers will diminish." It is likely that variants of the myth exist cross-culturally, and it explains why human sacrifice seems rare among egalitarian homogeneous peoples, and why complex stratified peoples select victims from outside the dominant group. The suggestion that the notion of human sacrifice resides deep in the human psyche is attested to by its dominance in worldwide folklore about witches and evil Others, in the form of "ritual murder," especially of children. The narrative of evil exists today, in belief in murderous Satanists in Christian areas of the world in the 1980s and 1990s, and witches in developing areas. Many scholars gave serious treatment to the notion of the "fetal Eucharist," a legendary element of the "Black Mass" that has existed in Christian lore for centuries.

What Else Can We Say?

Perhaps the most important contribution of ethnology is its reinforcement of Tylor's old definition of culture as a "complex whole," and its insistence that a cultural context be established for just about everything that we want to explain. Anthropological questions, therefore, include: "What else is going on?" Jan Bremmer, in his introduction to his *The Strange World of Human Sacrifice* (2007), asks anthropological questions.

Sacrifice, especially of live beings, is spectacular, and the sight of flowing blood generates universal reaction in all primates. The fact of sacrifice has been used by itself as diagnostic of many things—especially as part of an earlier European understanding of "savagery" among "primitive" peoples—but really, it is meaningful only within its broader ritual context. It is always part of something much larger, and mustn't be separated from that whole. Sacrifice is ritual, and the great literature on ritual should be perused.

My final observation is that Western studies of traditional religion, based on their authors' own experience, have assumed a much greater distance between human beings and the supernaturals than actually exists in local cultural conception. From my several decades as a professional anthropologist, including several years of fieldwork in Africa and parts of the Caribbean, it is clear to me that traditional peoples consider the supernatural close and quite easily accessible; indeed, as many anthropologists have pointed out, the "super" is misleading—there is just one realm. In that realm, human beings and supernatural beings and things in nature are all interconnected in a never-ending cycle of day-night, seasonal change, and life, death, and rebirth. A very real but neglected aspect of ritual is that it represents the human effort to keep the natural cycle going. Ritual generates energy that can stimulate both supernaturals and the mystical forces of the cosmos. Sacrifice, especially live-animal sacrifice, sends a rush of life energy into the cosmos. Imagine simultaneous multiple blood sacrifices, such as happens once a century in the great Ceremony of the Eleven Powers, the *Eka Dasa Rudra* of Bali, when the blood of hundreds of individuals of all known local species is released at once to restore the balance between the cosmic forces of good and the forces of evil (Gartenstein 1980).

Whatever else it is, sacrifice is always a return of life to its source and the resultant regeneration of that source.

Acknowledgments

I gratefully acknowledge the invaluable comments offered by Jan Bremmer on the conference draft of this article, editor Carrie Murray, and the help of Cindi Tysick, anthropology librarian at the University at Buffalo.

NOTE

1.   Thompson's magnificent motif index is 55+ years old and there is now a lot of material to update it. This motif might fit after his A1545.2, "animal substitute for human sacrifice."

REFERENCES CITED

Arens, W. 1979 *The Man-Eating Myth: Anthropology and Anthropophagy*. Oxford University Press, Oxford.

Atran, S. 2002 *In Gods We Trust: The Evolutionary Landscape of Religion*. Oxford University Press, Oxford.

Biardeau, M., and C. Malamoud 1976 *Le sacrifice dans l'Inde ancienne*. Presses Universitaires de France, Paris.

Bremmer, J. N. (editor) 2007 *The Strange World of Human Sacrifice*. Peeters, Leuven, Belgium.

Buckley, T. C. T., and A. Gottlieb 1988 *Blood Magic: The Anthropology of Menstruation*. University of California Press, Berkeley.

Burkert, W. 1996 *Creation of the Sacred: Tracks of Biology in Early Religions*. Harvard University Press, Cambridge.

Burkert W. 1983 *Homo Necans: The Anthropology of Ancient Greek Sacrificial Ritual and Myth*. Translated by P. Bing. University of California Press, Berkeley.

de Heusch, L. 1982 *Rois nés d'un cœur de vache. Mythes et rites bantous II*. Gallimard, Paris.

de Heusch, L. 1982 *The Drunken King, or, The Origin of the State*, Translated by R. Willis. Indiana University Press, Bloomington.

de Heusch, L. 1985 *Sacrifice in Africa*. Indiana University Press, Bloomington.

de Heusch, L. 1985 *Sacrifice in Africa: A Structuralist Approach*. Manchester University Press, Manchester.

Dentan, R. K. 2008 *Overwhelming Terror: Love, Fear, Peace and Violence among Semai of Malaysia*. Rowman & Littlefield, Lanham, Maryland.

Detienne, M., and J. P. Vernant 1989 *The Cuisine of Sacrifice among the Greeks*. Translated by P. Wissing. University of Chicago Press, Chicago.

Durkheim, E. 1915 *The Elementary Forms of the Religious Life*. Translated by J. Ward Swain. George Allen & Unwin, New York.

Eilberg-Schwartz, H. 1990 *The Savage in Judaism: An Anthropology of Israelite Religion and Ancient Judaism*. Indiana University Press, Bloomington.

Eliade, M. 1964 *Myth and Reality*. Translated by R. Willard. Allen & Unwin, London.

Elitzur, Y., and D. Nir-Zevi 2004 Four-horned Altar Discovered in Judean Hills. *Biblical Archaeology Review* (May-June): 35–39.

Evans-Pritchard, E. E. 1964 Foreword. In *Sacrifice: Its Nature and Function,* by Henri Hubert and Marcel Mauss pp. vii–viii. Translated by W. D. Halls. University of Chicago Press, Chicago.

Evans-Pritchard, E. E. 1956 *Nuer Religion*. Clarendon, Oxford.

Evans-Pritchard, E. E. 1953 The Sacrificial Role of Cattle among the Nuer. *Africa* XXIII(3):181–197.

Frazer, J. G. 1890 *The Golden Bough*. Macmillan, London.

Firth, R. 1967 *Tikopia Ritual and Belief*. Beacon Press, Boston.

Gartenstein, L. (producer) 1980 Film, *The Eleven Powers*. Orson Welles, Narrator; Frank Heimans, Director.

Girard, R. 1977 *Violence and the Sacred*. Translated by P. Gregory. Johns Hopkins University Press, Baltimore.

Hamerton-Kelly, R. 1987 *Violent Origins: Walter Burkert, René Girard, and Johnathan Z. Smith on Ritual Killing and Cultural Formation*. Stanford University Press, Stanford.

Herskovits, M. 1967 *Dahomey: An Ancient West African Kingdom*. 2 vols. Northwestern University Press, Evanston.

Hubert, H., and M. Mauss 1964 *Sacrifice: Its Nature and Function*. Translated by W. D. Halls. University of Chicago Press, Chicago.

Leach, E. R. 1976 *Culture and Communication*. Cambridge University Press, Cambridge.

Lévi-Strauss, C. 1966 *The Savage Mind*. University of Chicago Press, Chicago.

Lévi-Strauss, C. 1953 Social Structure. In *Anthropology Today*, edited by A. L. Kroeber pp. 524–553. University of Chicago Press, Chicago.

Lienhardt, G. 1961 *Divinity and Experience: The Religion of the Dinka*. Clarendon, Oxford.

Linnekin, J. 1985 Review of Valeri, *Kingship and Sacrifice*. *American Ethnologist* 12(4):788–790.

Lowie, R. 1935 *The Crow Indians*. Farrar & Rinehart, New York.

Malefijt, A. de Waal 1968 *Religion and Culture: An Introduction to Anthropology of Religion*. Macmillan, New York.

Mannhardt, W. 1875 *Wald- und Feldkulte I: der Baumkultus der Germanen unter ihrer Nachbarstämme: Mythologische Untersuchen*. Berlin.

Meuli, K. 1975 *Gesammelte Schriften*, vol. 2. Reprinted. Schwabe, Stuttgart. Originally published 1946 "*Griechische Opfergebräuche*," in *Phyllobolia*, Festschrift for Peter von der Mühll, 185–288.

Middleton, J. 1960 *Lugbara Religion. Ritual and Authority among an East African People*. Oxford University Press, Oxford.

Oberg, K. 1940 The Kingdon of Ankole in Uganda. In *African Political Systems*, edited by M. Fortes and E. E. Evans-Pritchard, pp. 121–162. Oxford University Press, London.

Obeyesekere, G. 2005 *Cannibal Talk: The Man-Eating Myth and Human Sacrifice in the South Seas*. University of California Press, Berkeley.

Otto, R. 1923 *The Idea of the Holy: An Inquiry into the Non-rational Factor in the Idea of the Divine and Its Relation to the Rational*. Translated by J. W. Harvey. Oxford University Press, Oxford.

Smith, W. R. 1889 Sacrifice. Lecture VII, in *Lectures on the Religion of the Semites*. Appleton, New York.

Thompson, S. 1955 *Motif-index of Folk Literature*. 6 vols. Indiana University Press, Bloomington.

Tylor, E. B. 1871 *Primitive Culture*. 2 vols. Murray, London.

University of Chicago 1998 Obituary: Valerio Valeri. *Chronicle* 17, 15, April 30.

Valeri, V. 1994 Wild Victims: Hunting as Sacrifice and Sacrifice as Hunting in Huaulu. *History of Religions* 34(2):101–131.

Valeri, V. 1985 *Kingship and Sacrifice: Ritual and Society in Ancient Hawaii*. Translated by P. Wissing. University of Chicago Press, Chicago.

CHAPTER TWO

A View from a Fen

On the Concept of Sacrifice and the Possibility of Understanding Neolithic Wetland Depositions

Åsa Berggren

Abstract   *How do we approach a concept such as sacrifice when we are studying archaeological material from a prehistoric period? In a review of the use of the sacrificial concept in Scandinavian archaeology, several problematic assumptions are discovered. For example, sacrifice is often regarded as universal and is thus taken for granted. Also, the concept of sacrifice is sometimes used as a covering term, which may homogenize our understanding of what seem to be rather varying practices. The term is also burdened with baggage that is not always addressed in archaeological studies. This paper deals with questions concerning theoretical perspectives and archaeological interpretation. Practice theory and the concepts of ritualization, embodiment, and objectification are used as a starting point, leading to alternative results that may complement or replace the sacrificial category. The theoretical discussion presented here is illustrated by prehistoric wetland depositions, especially a case study of a fen at Hindbygården in Malmö in the south of Sweden. The material is dated from the Late Mesolithic to the Early Bronze Age. Relations were created by people at the fen through their sensuous experiences of the acts that were carried out there. The relations were part of both ritualization strategies and social strategies in their societies.*

THE HINDBYGÅRDEN FEN

This paper is based on my thesis, which mainly deals with questions concerning theoretical perspectives and archaeological interpretation (Berggren 2010). The starting point is the use of the concept of sacrifice in Scandinavian archaeology, specifically concerning wetland depositions, and the conclusion is an attempt to interpret wetland deposited material with an alternative theoretical perspective, practice theory.

The archaeological material of my case study consists of artifacts deposited in a fen in the south of Sweden during a period spanning 3,400 years, including most of the Neolithic. As per many wetland depositions, this material was interpreted as being sacrifices or offerings during the archaeological excavation. Even though I did not participate in the excavation, this material was handed to me to write up (Berggren 2007). During my analysis of the material, an implicit concern was becoming increasingly bothersome: Was the sacrificial category really an adequate interpretation for this material? Was this interpretation argued for or was it taken for granted?

There are several questions we could ask ourselves. How do we approach an understanding of a phenomenon like sacrifice when the material we are studying is many thousands of years old? When there are no written documents and no iconography? When all we have are fragments of the material world that once was the reality of the people whom we are trying to understand, which at best give us a sketchy picture of their world?

One issue that comes to mind is whether or not we may assume that sacrifice took place at all times during human history. Have all people, in all cultures, used what we define as sacrifice? I believe that this interpretation should be argued, rather than assumed.

How should we argue about the interpretations of sacrifice within archaeology? I will get back to this question after a brief presentation of the material. The archaeological material from the fen, situated at Hindbygården in southwest Scania in southern Sweden, is dated to a main period from the Late Mesolithic to the Early Bronze Age. The material is both extensive and varied. It consists of hundreds of artifacts, including flint tools such as axes, scrapers, sickles, and daggers, as well as cores and flakes, ground stone tools such as axes, hammer- and grinding stones, and other worked stones, bone and horn tools, and one bronze axe. There were also 5.6 kilograms of pottery, 136 kilograms of animal bones (interpreted as remains of meals and slaughter), and 13 tons of unworked stones. A small amount of human bone—of at least three individuals: two adults and a child—was also found in the peat. Some wooden structures in the fen include a plank of oak, arranged as a footbridge over the deepest part of the fen, and some pointed poles driven down into the peat. Around the fen there were many pits, some filled with stones, and there were layers that indicate activities including burning. Two urn burials were also dug into the ground near the fen. An archaeobotanical study has shown how the vegetation in and around the fen has changed over the millennia, which in its turn has indicated the changes of the water table in the fen. This has allowed inferences of the spatial structures in the fen created by the water and the vegetation as well as how these structures changed over time.

How can we understand material like this? It is very varied and deposited over a very long period of time. Should it all be categorized as sacrifices? In my analysis of this material, I wanted to go back to the question, "What is this?" rather than assuming the material was sacrificial.

Sacrifice in Archaeology—Some Underlying Problems

How has the interpretation of sacrificial practices been argued in archaeology? In a review of the use of the sacrificial concept in Scandinavian archaeology during the past 140 years, I have studied the arguments that are used to favor an interpretation of wetland deposited artifacts as sacrifices, as well as the various meanings that the concept of sacrifice is considered to have. Underlying both the arguments and meanings, there are several assumptions, both explicit and implicit, that may be problematic when the sacrificial concept is applied to prehistoric society.

First of all, sacrifice is assumed to be a universal category. It is taken for granted that all people in all cultures have practiced what we define as sacrifice. This assumption may lead to questionable ways of reasoning, for example, in connection to how we divide archaeological material into categories. In Scandinavian archaeology, there are three categories, proclaimed as the major categories for understanding prehistoric (preferably Neolithic) material: finds from settlements, burials, and offering sites (Andersson 2004:147; Lekberg 2002:172; Rydbeck 1918:3f). These categories have a long history in Scandinavian archaeology and have had a strong influence on our thinking. They are not problematic in themselves, but their use may be. It is problematic when these categories are implicitly assumed to be all-encompassing. This assumption leads to interpretations by way of ruling out other alternatives. If an object cannot be explained as belonging to a settlement or a burial, the sacrificial interpretation is used, as it is the only alternative left. To reach an interpretation through this kind of reasoning, we have to assume that the categories are all-encompassing, representing all aspects of a prehistoric society. This is very problematic and most would agree that we cannot assume a total understanding of any prehistoric period through our categories.

Secondly, a separation between ritual and nonritual phenomena is often assumed when depositions are interpreted. The term *hoard* may be used, and the significance of a hoard is often considered to be a choice between ritual and nonritual explanations. The nonritual alternatives are often ruled out one by one, for instance, by evaluating whether the deposited objects were possible to retrieve or not, and in the end, a ritual explanation may be arrived at, explained as an offering or sacrifice. This division between interpretations in terms of ritual and nonritual types leads us to a third problematic assumption, as it often also means a division between sacred and profane deposits, which in turn assumes a division between a sacred and a profane sphere in prehistoric society. This is due to the connection often made between ritual and religion. Profane rituals or other formalized activities are seldom discussed as alternative interpretations, and the modern constructions of sacred and profane categories are often not questioned in terms of their appropriateness for prehistoric societies.

At the base of these problematic issues connected to the use of the concept of sacrifice lies the assumption that sacrifice is universal; as if it is just a matter of figuring out where in the archaeological material it may be visible. With this approach to the material, the variation is at risk of getting lost. In fact, the sacrificial category is in many cases used as a covering term, which may homogenize our understanding of what seem to be rather varying formalized practices. The concept of sacrifice has perhaps turned into what may be called a black box, or to use the words of Christopher Tilley, a frozen metaphor (Tilley 1999:82ff).

The significance given to the concept of sacrifice in Scandinavian archaeology during the past 140 years echoes contemporary works in anthropology and other academic fields. Early archaeological studies were influenced by scholars such as Tylor (1871), Robertson Smith (1997, originally 1889), and Frazer (1922), but also Durkheim (1915) and Mauss and Hubert (1898). One can also say that they influence our use of the term *sacrifice* today. The concept brings with it layers of meaning formed during the past centuries. The significance of the sacrificial concept is taken for granted in archaeology today. In some archaeological studies, older works are referenced in which the term is defined, but in many, there is no mention of the significance of the term at all. After 140 years of archaeological sacrificial interpretations, it may seem unnecessary. But the term is not unproblematic, and some issues have been addressed in anthropology and other fields. One important line of criticism concerns the implicit Judeo-Christian values embedded in the concept, which stem from the older sacrificial theories formulated in the late eighteenth and early nineteenth centuries. These were colored by how society and religion were regarded at this time. The evolutionistic content and other problematic issues of these theories have been discussed in recent years. For example, the way that other religions are judged according to Judeo-Christian values and how other religions are considered less evolved has been criticized (Bloch 1992; de Heusch 1985; Strenski 2003; Vernant 1989). The term *sacrifice* is thus burdened with baggage that is not always addressed in archaeological studies. This way, we risk this baggage of evolutionism and implicit values becoming a hidden part of our archaeological interpretations.

There have been calls for more ambiguous concepts in archaeological interpretation in order to allow for the ambiguous nature of social reality. There are several ways for archaeologists to reduce uncertainty in the process of interpretation, for example, "washing" the data from ambiguity and making interpretations more homogenous (Gero 2007). I believe that this is what concepts such as sacrifice, as well as megalith (Tilley 1999) and ritual (Bradley 2003a), have become, that is to say, homogenizing terms that hide the variation of the material. So, how can we approach the material, allowing social ambiguity into our interpretations? I have chosen a theoretical approach that focuses on human practice and the term "ritualization" as a starting point, but I do not want to assume that the deposited artifacts in the fen were the results of ritualized acts. Instead, with this perspective, it is possible to argue whether or not the acts were ritualized.

To conclude, the term *ritual deposition* could be a more relevant, general category when interpreting wetland depositions. But the concept of ritual is not without problems. It too has been regarded as universal. Many definitions of ritual are instrumental. They consist of a number of criteria that an action has to meet to be defined as a ritual act. These criteria may include repetition, formalism, and durability. Catherine Bell (1992) has pointed to issues that make these definitions problematic; actions considered ritual by the participants might fall outside of the definition. The concept of ritualization describes a more context-dependent phenomenon, which demands a greater understanding of the social context by the archaeologist.

Practice Theory

As mentioned, I have chosen to apply the perspective of practice theory to the depositions made in the fen at Hindbygården. In practice theory, meaning is viewed as generated in the performance of an act. Actions are thus not regarded as representing anything outside themselves, such as ideas or thoughts. The meaning that is generated through practice consists of relationships between phenomena (Bourdieu 1977:120), a statement that I have made the main point of my study.

Ritual in Practice Theory

In order to understand whether the depositions in the fen were the results of ritual acts or not, I use the concept of ritualization, as presented in an influential study by Catherine Bell (1992), where ritual, as seen through a practice-theory perspective, is termed ritualization. Using the ideas of Bell, I have broken this term down into five overlapping points to underline the consequences that its implementation has for a corpus of archaeological material.

- Human practice may be regarded as acts in a continuum of formalism, from everyday routines to formal ceremonies. Rituals tend to be placed at the outermost end among the more formalized acts, but they may be found anywhere on this continuum. As a result, we cannot separate rituals from other acts solely by examining the degree of formalism of the performance.

- Ritualization is a differentiation of acts, and all acts may be ritualized. The strategies of differentiation may be visible in the archaeological record, as they often have a material component.

- Ritualization is dependent on context. Every culture produces its own strategies of differentiation to ritualize certain acts. Any attempt to instrumentally define ritual in a general or universal fashion is thus fruitless.

- Ritualized acts do not communicate, but create, meaning. Explicit meaning may vary between contexts and between individuals, but there has to be compliance with a social consensus or a minimal consent, or else the act is not ritualized. Interpretations of material remains of ritualized acts may be aimed at understanding this social structure rather than the explicit meaning that varies between individuals.

- The meaning created by ritualization is relational. It establishes relationships between persons, things, places, and anything else that plays a part in the act, some aspects of which may be a part of the archaeological record.

EMBODIED PRACTICE AND OBJECTIFICATION

Practice theory enables me to focus on the relationships that are created in human practice, the structuring effect of practice, and the role of human action according to a long-term perspective. Thus, the question I ask is: What relationships were created by the practices carried out at the Hindbygården fen? This question is separated into two parts: What structures were embodied and what structures were objectified at the fen? An analysis of those structures enables researchers to have a discussion of differentiation strategies and whether or not they were parts of ritualization processes or other social-differentiation processes.

The concepts of embodiment and objectification are central as theoretical tools within this perspective and have been increasingly used in archaeology (e.g., Hamilakis, Pluciennik, and Tarlow 2002; Kus 1992; Miller 2005; Nilsson Stutz 2003; Tilley et al. 2006). As practice theory focuses on physically performed acts, the body is of great importance. The relationships, and thus the structures that are created by practice, are embodied by the participants. Individuals experience the world, and thus structures, through their bodies and through their senses, something that is stressed in what may be named "an archaeology of the senses" (Brüch 2005; Hamilakis 2002; Houston and Taube 2000). What individuals experience through seeing, hearing, smelling, tasting, and feeling is a part of the creation of various structures. I want to stress that sensual experiences are not to be regarded as universal. There is a biological foundation that we all share, but the experiences are culturally specific.

Through sensuous experiences, structures were embodied by the participants as they were created. I use this as one of the starting points for the analysis of the structures created by the depositions made in the fen. If I can grasp the sensuous experiences of the participants in the activities at the fen, I can understand the structures created there.

Embodiment and objectification are two sides of the same process. The structures that are embodied by the participants are also objectified in the things used in the acts and in the spatial structures where the acts take place. Thus, the materiality of things and places is of central importance for understanding the creation of structures in practice. Material culture may be regarded as an active social agent, rather than a passive reflection of culture. Objectification is a part of the process that is described in practice theory, as it is a method of studying the relationships between things, or the order of things. An order of things is given a homology, a counterpart, in other orders in society. In this way, a social order, for example, is given a material base (Bourdieu 1977:143; Miller 2005:6f; Tilley 2006:65). Material culture puts persons into context. As Daniel Miller puts it: "We cannot know who we are, or become what we are, except by looking in a material mirror, which is the historical world created by those who lived before us. This world confronts us as material culture and continues to evolve through us" (Miller 2005:8). This circular process is the process of objectification.

TIME AND THE SIGNIFICANCE OF THE PAST

In archaeology, there has been increased interest in the conception of time during recent decades. In ritual theory, however, not much attention has been paid to how rituals are maintained and changed over long periods. Nevertheless, in practice theory, and especially in the theories of materiality, there are several accounts of how references to the past and memories are created in interaction with things and places.

In practice theory, material things are crucial for creating memories of the past. In fact, to Nadia Seremetakis (1994), things are material memories. Places may play similar roles. To have "a sense of place" means to experience it as its past events (Van Dyke and Alcock 2003). In the construction of history, it is not just what is remembered, but also what is forgotten, that is important (Küchler 1993). In the processes of creating the past, things and places play important roles both in the collective memory and in forgetfulness.

Memories are created and stored in material things, and as objectification and embodiment are two sides of the same process, bodily practices also create memories. Rituals are specifically mentioned in connection with bodily memories (e.g., De Boeck 1995). Incorporated social practice may be implicit and may not be reflected, and thus remain unquestioned. There is a certain inertia built into bodily practices that may explain how a practice may stay unchanged for long periods of time.

Some say that a memory of an actual event may survive for anything from two generations up to 200 years. After this, a tradition may start to resemble a myth (Bradley 2002:8, 2003b; Meskell 2003). History may be divided into two categories—genealogical history and mythical history. The first consists of known individuals or events connected in a continuous sequence from now into the past. The second is perceived as events that took place in a distant past, without continuity with the present time. Both kinds of history may coexist in a society and neither may be more authentic than the other (Gosden and Lock 1998).

Relationships and Structures Created at the Hindbygården Fen

The processes of objectification and embodiment that took place during the performance of practices at the fen created relationships that varied during the long period of use. They may at times have contributed to differentiation in ritualization strategies as well as social differentiation. It is not possible to give an in-depth description of the relationships and structures in this chronological account due to the limited space of this text, but an overview gives an idea of the results of the analysis.

The Late Mesolithic

The earliest dated depositions in the fen took place during the Late Mesolithic, about 4500–4000 B.C.E. At that time, a dense forest surrounded the fen, with a few open wetlands in the area. The fen had sparse vegetation, including bushes and trees and areas of open water. The sensuous experiences of the place set the fen apart from its surroundings. Through processes of embodiment and objectification, the fen was related to its surroundings through sensations of contrast. To anyone approaching the fen, it was experienced as a light and open glade in contrast to a dark, dense environment, but there was also contrast between what was wet and dry as well as what was seen and hidden from view. Even if the fen was not unique, as there were other wetlands nearby, it may have appeared isolated; it was not possible to see it from a distance and it was not possible to see the surroundings from the fen. In this respect, it was a well-defined and delimited place.

The depositions left during this period consist of core axes deposited on the border of peat-growth at the deepest part of the fen, and stones deposited in the water in the center of the deepest area. These depositions made the persons performing them a part of the spatial order, as they became a part of the encircling or the encircled structure in the fen through processes of objectification.

The way the fen was experienced as separate from the surroundings suggests that acts performed there created a differentiation and a ritualization of the acts. The acts also created relationships, or differences, between those who were inside and outside of the borders of the fen, those who became wet and those who remained dry on the outside, those who became encircled and those who enacted encircling by depositions, etc. Several phenomena in the fen suggest that a variety of relationships and social positions were created there, such as the varying degrees of access to the water at the center of the fen, the objectified presence of the participants in the stones thrown into the fen, the positions of the participants as either hidden or visible, and so on.

The social organization created by the practices performed at the fen was rather complex. It gave the participants various social positions and identities in relation to each other. It was probably not just a leader who created his or her position vis-à-vis the rest; it seems that other positions were created as well. This social organization was not necessarily a strict hierarchical structure, and the relationships may have been temporary. However, there must have been inertia in the structure that caused the social patterns to be repeated.

Someone conducted the first deposition in the fen sometime during the Late Mesolithic. But this should not be regarded as an inauguration of the fen as place for the creation of social relations. Instead, the first deposition referred to the spatial structures that were recognized at the fen, known from collective memory. The depositions of objects such as axes in the fen during this time were few in number. Other depositions took place in other wetlands, which made it a known practice. The deposition in the fen created a special social position for the person performing the deposition. Stone depositions were performed in the fen somewhat more frequently. Some may have had personal memories of earlier depositions at this place, but most knew about the correct way to perform a deposition through general knowledge about the practice and collective memories.

THE EARLY NEOLITHIC

During the Early Neolithic, about 4000–3300 B.C.E., both the surroundings and the fen changed. During the earliest part of the Early Neolithic, the fen may still have been experienced as an open and relatively well-demarcated place in the dense forest. During the latter part of the Early Neolithic, however, the vegetation in and around the fen changed, as did the relationship between the fen and its surroundings. The vegetation in the fen grew denser and, in the surroundings, there were small, cultivated areas and small pastures within the forest. From a distance, the fen may at this time have been experienced as a grove among small open areas in the forest. This means that the fen was perceived as a delimited place separated from the surroundings during both the early and the late part of the Early Neolithic.

During the Early Neolithic, the fen became drier, the open water covered a smaller area, and certain plants spread around the drier edges like a frame around the center. This frame of vegetation may have been experienced as a boundary and a threshold, which may have added to the experience of separation of the fen from the surroundings. During the summer, the plants in the frame were tall and perhaps difficult to see through or over.

At this time, funnel beakers were placed in the edge vegetation, perhaps objectifying the boundary around the fen, pronouncing the difference between the fen and the surroundings. Other objects were deposited in the shrinking water pool, some by persons standing on the edges as well as on a footbridge placed across the deepest area, some by persons walking into the water, digging the artifacts down into the peat.

The spatial structures and differences were embodied by the participants. This may have been a differentiation strategy to ritualize certain activities that took place at the fen. For example, the sensuous experience of walking though the edge vegetation (Figure 2.1) embodied the boundary around the fen and the separation of the place. During the early part of the period, the differentiation strategy seems to have concerned the place on a general level, as the fen was differentiated from the surroundings. Later in the Early Neolithic, however, as the number of depositions increased, the differentiation strategies became more varied. On one level, differentiation may have ritualized certain acts, but on other levels it functioned as social differentiation. Differences between groups were created by the difference embodied and objectified between structure as inside and outside, visible and hidden, dry and wet. Both the social structures and the ritualization strategies became increasingly complex and varied during the course of the Early Neolithic. Perhaps more individuals, or more groups of individuals, were involved in the activities at the fen.

It may have been the local populations that used the fen. During the early part of the Early Neolithic, the landscape was collectively organized and most persons could have had access to the fen. Yet only a few performed depositions there. Some of those who did, did so openly and created their social positions officially, while others were hidden and their positions were perhaps unofficial. The change of structures in the fen during the Early Neolithic may be connected to a change of movement patterns in the landscape. More and larger settlements led to changed routes through the landscape, and more persons seem to have had access to the fen.

The knowledge of the spatial structures in the fen was passed from generation to generation. Embodied memories and stories kept the tradition alive. In the kin-based society, perhaps a few persons in every generation partly created their position within the kin group by performing depositions at the fen. Earlier generations may have been important, and the fen a place to reconnect with them, as a complement to burials and a genealogical history. The stories at the fen may have been genealogical, but the mythical

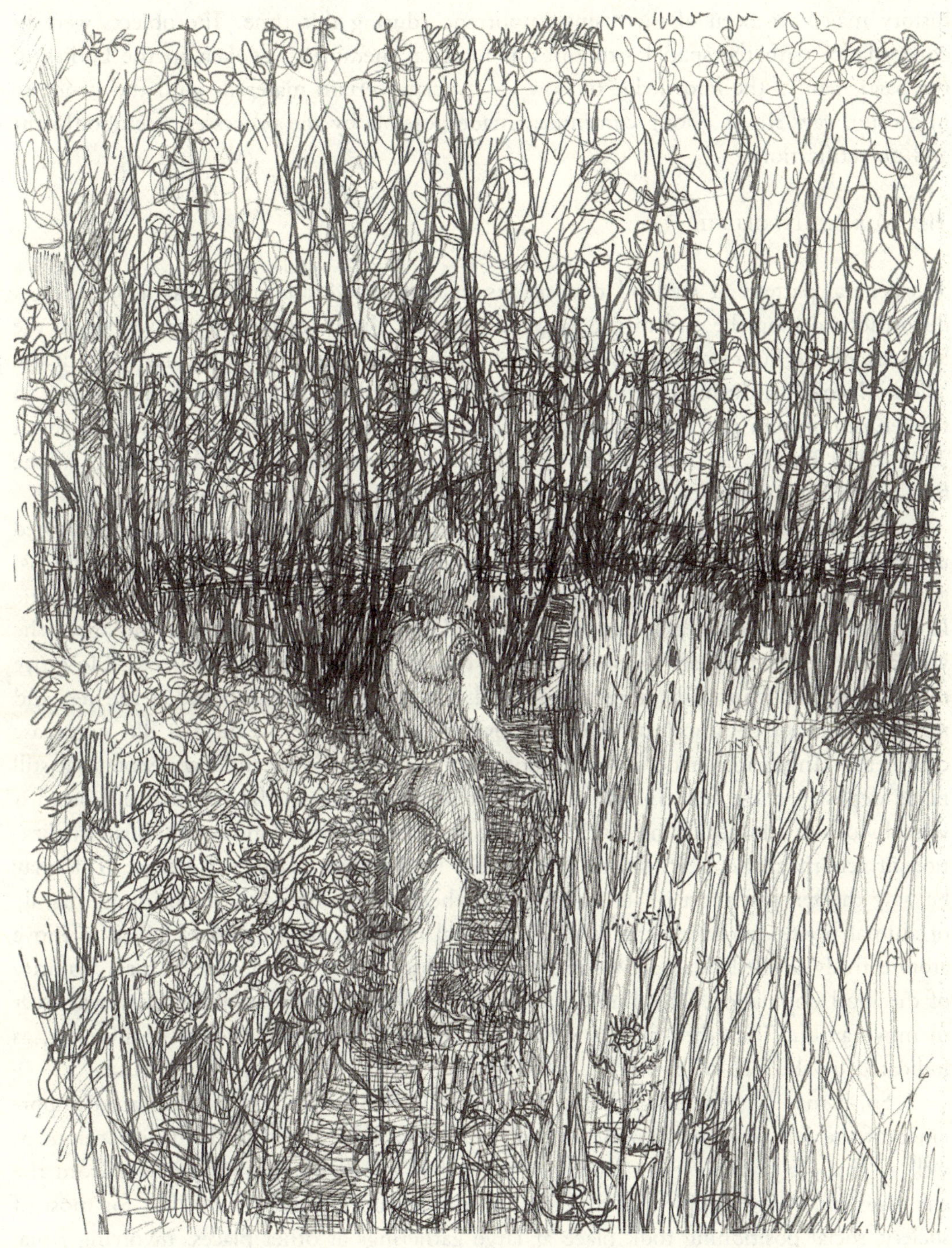

Figure 2.1 A person is walking through the vegetation edge of the fen during the Early Neolithic. Illustration: Hans Ekerow.

history may have been of increasing importance during this time. The objects were in concordance with the spatial structures as material memories, awoken in the bodies of the participants. The knowledge of how to associate certain materials with the structure in certain ways shows a long continuity, made possible by the processes of embodiment and objectification.

The Middle Neolithic

The general pattern of wetland depositions in Southern Scandinavia was a decrease of depositions during the end of the early part of the Middle Neolithic, equivalent to the last part of the Funnel Beaker culture, and an increase again during the last part of the Middle Neolithic, during the time of the Battle Axe culture. The depositional pattern in the fen did only in part follow this general pattern. The Middle Neolithic period, about 3300–2300 B.C.E., is characterized by a decrease in the number of depositions in the fen. It lost its importance as a place for the creation of social relations.

During the first part of the period, the environment around the fen remained unchanged. There were still open areas for cultivation and grazing nearby. From the last part of Middle Neolithic A and through the Middle Neolithic B to the Late Neolithic I, however, the open areas were overgrown. Many people may have left the area. The vegetation in the fen itself became denser. The fen thus changed from a visible grove to an integrated part of a more closed landscape. The difference between the fen and the surroundings became less obvious. However, the activities at the fen did not cease completely. The spatial structures were not clearly experienced by the few people that still made deposits in the fen. The difference that separated the fen from the area around it was obvious at the beginning of the period, but later differentiation and thus ritualization of acts may have been difficult to achieve in the same manner as before. This may be why the fen lost most of its importance. There were only a few depositions, mainly of animal bones, perhaps remains of communal meals or feasting. The ability to move around freely in the landscape was more limited during this period, at least for a majority of the local population. This limited access to the fen. The elite of the society was freer to move around, but they do not seem to have used the fen for social positioning, as indicated by the lack of prestigious objects.

So, it may be concluded that during the Middle Neolithic A the decreased importance of the fen was partly connected to the general decrease in wetland depositions as well as changes in the vegetation, making the fen less delimited and separate from the environment. A few people still deposited in the fen during this period, but for most of society, social positioning took place at large gatherings at other places, involving ritual meals and feasting. Perhaps a few opposed this new order by sticking to the old tradition and the old myths. The past was of special significance for them. The opposition and the old way may have been embodied in the acts at the fen.

During the Middle Neolithic B, wetland depositions were once again of increasing importance in society, but the fen was still not used to any great extent. Only a few people performed depositions there. The fen was still not a delimited place, which made it less suitable for ritualization. Perhaps the few depositions that did take place were only ritual-like acts (Bell 1997:138f), to commemorate the mythical past of the place.

The Late Neolithic and the Early Bronze Age

The majority of the depositions in the fen were made during the Late Neolithic and the early part of the Bronze Age, around 2300–1300 B.C.E. At the beginning of the Late Neolithic, the vegetation in the fen was still rather dense and the fen was perceived as a part of a closed landscape, not a well-defined and delimited place. During the middle of the Late Neolithic, human influence on the environment changed and became strong once again. The landscape was opened up through cultivation and grazing. The fen constituted a dense grove in the open landscape, a well-defined and delimited place, separate from the surroundings. It was separated so that differentiation and ritualization were again easily achieved. The spatial structure objectified the difference and was embodied in the people who came to the fen. Activities that took place there were acted out in the open, visible from a distance. The vegetation right next to the fen was worn down through frequent usage or large gatherings, evidenced by sand that eroded down into the peat. There is also evidence of fires near the fen, perhaps in connection with cooking and consumption of food (Figure 2.2) The fires were visible from a distance, especially if used at night. This period of strong human impact on the landscape lasted until the end of the analyzed sequence of peat in the fen, that is, until around 1300 B.C.E. or the end of Bronze Age period II.

The fen itself became drier as the water level decreased and the vegetation became more dense and homogenous. The impression of a frame around the center became weaker. The fen may have been perceived more as a whole entity during this time, without internal spatial structures. This means there was no experience of a boundary or threshold, and the fen may have been experienced as easier to access. Perhaps it was open to more people? At least it was used more intensely. The majority of the material found in the fen was deposited during this time. Most of the deposited artifact types were spread over the whole surface, with only a slight concentration at the deepest part in the north. Several tons of the unworked stones were deposited at this time and a large part of the deposited material consisted of well-used artifacts, taken from the daily lives of the local population. The objects objectified their users on a general level, but the highly varied material indicates a complex and varied social organization.

Depositions of artifacts such as axes or daggers were performed by a small number of individuals, while the more numerous depositions of stone or bone perhaps recurred every year, as a part of everyday life. The knowledge of the structures in the fen was a part of an embodied memory, perhaps unspoken by the majority of participants. Through continuous practice, the structures were recreated, even as the vegetation and environment in the fen slowly changed. It is possible that many individuals had personal memories of earlier events at the fen, especially if they occurred annually, but at times of less frequent depositions, collective memories played a more important role.

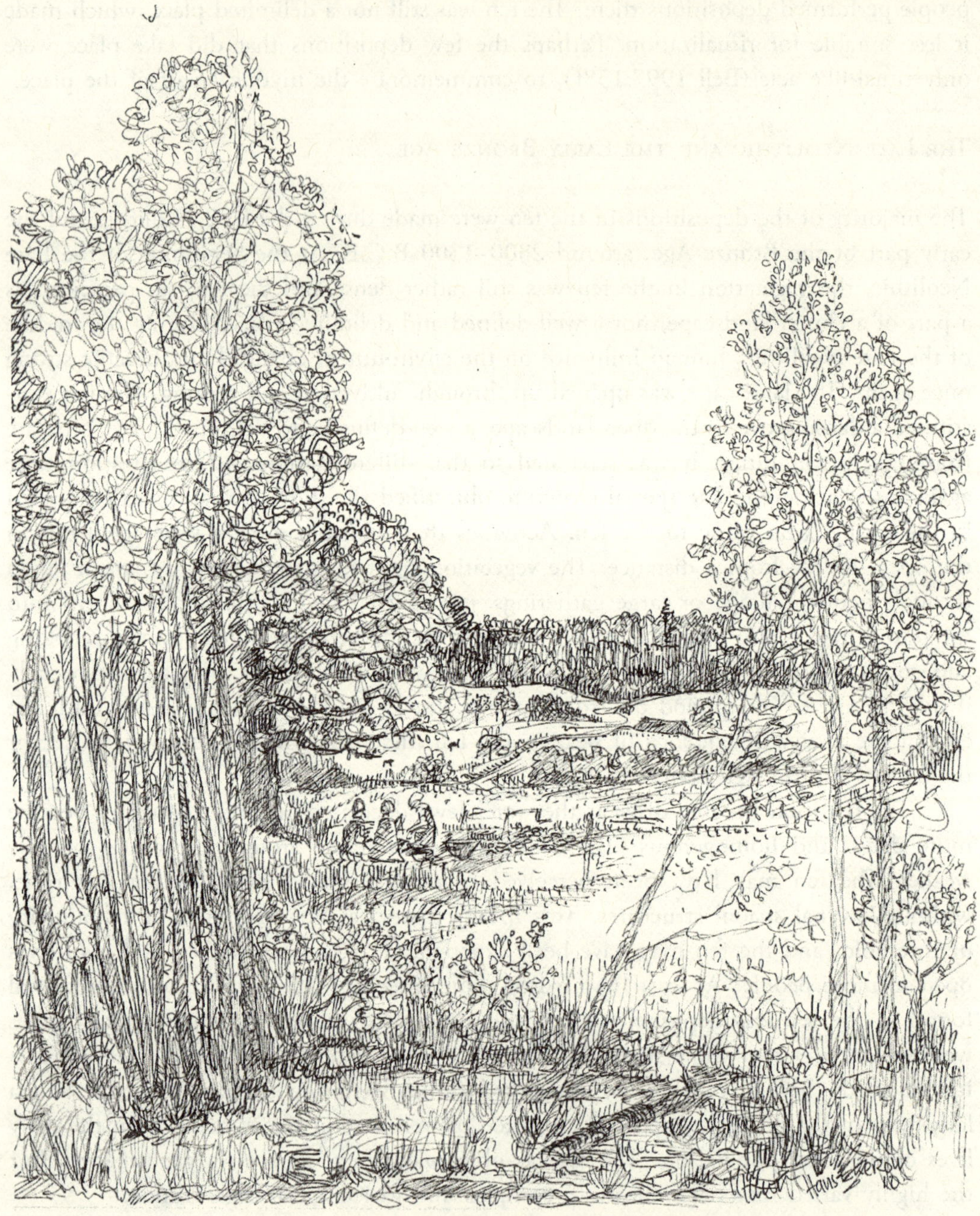

FIGURE 2.2 A group of people are cooking and eating a meal near the fen during the Late Neolithic or Early Bronze Age. Illustration: Hans Ekerow.

As indicated by commonplace objects, the rather large group of persons who used the fen was a part of the local population closely connected to the cultivation of land in the vicinity. They were not a part of the elite who positioned themselves socially with exotic objects, contact with distant peoples, and big herds of livestock. The material in the fen indicates that the materially less privileged population was not an unstratified mass of people, but had a rather complex social organization. The past played an important role for them, as the activities at the fen seem to have been retrospective, with the place itself as the most evident indication.

A View from a Fen

As archaeological material meets theory, we create the prerequisites to discuss the lives of the prehistoric people whom we are studying. At the same time, we may evaluate both the empirical material and the theories. The following is an evaluation of the theoretical concepts used and a discussion of the interpretations that constitute the archaeological results.

On a general note, the combination of the archaeological material, the questions, and the theoretical tools used in this study has enabled a more nuanced image of the activities at the fen, as compared to an interpretation of the fen as a sacrificial place.

The processes of embodiment and objectification create the same structures, but the two concepts constitute different starting points. As they are applied to the material, they result in different, complementary images of relations and structures. The bodily process is often indirectly represented in the material while the objects constitute the material. Regarding the bodily processes, I have concentrated on the sensuous experiences, which has enabled me to focus on the people that once used the fen and its physical activities.

I have discussed objectification processes in both spatial structures and artifacts. The physical environment and the character of the vegetation and its changes are of great importance for the interpretation of social differentiation and ritualization strategies. Detailed knowledge of the vegetation is a prerequisite for a more nuanced interpretation of the fen. Patterns of movement and sequences of acts are also important, placing the objects in a context, instead of a one-sided focus on the artifacts. The great variation of artifact types is characteristic of the material. It makes it difficult to grasp as a whole but is large enough to indicate general tendencies. The processes of objectification seem to point in a variety of erratic directions, but the superior order seems to be connected to the place itself, and its historical significance. All artifacts have something in common: a recontextualization as the objects were deposited in the fen. The act of depositing something in the fen may have been more important than the specific object. However, it was not insignificant what was deposited, as indicated by the patterns of deposition.

The practices that were carried out in the fen generated relationships and thus structures that were a part of the social organization of society. The structures that are discernable in the fen are very detailed and somewhat basic. As such, they are close to the persons who performed the acts, close to their bodies and sensuous experiences. However, it is not unproblematic to place these detailed structures in a wider societal context. There is a discrepancy between the detailed structures visible in the fen and the general social structures that are normally discussed. Many studies are focused on the higher end of the social hierarchy of society, but the persons who used the fen were not a part of that social stratum. They were also organized in a web of social relations and positions, but we lack the terminology to describe them. The social groupings that are normally discussed, for example, divisions by age and gender, are not apparent in the fen.

The difference between the fen and its surroundings is a major theme in the history of the fen. This was used by the people as a general and very long-lived strategy of ritualization. At a more detailed level, many of the acts performed at the fen were structured and formalized. They were repeated and unchanged for long periods. This does not automatically mean that we should view them as ritualized, even though they had a structuring effect on the participants. There were several levels of differentiation strategies in effect at the fen. Some may have been ritualization strategies, but others were social differentiation strategies, and it is not evident which are which. Perhaps it is not always possible to draw a distinct line between different categories of acts, and perhaps it is not always necessary, if the aim is to interpret the social interplay of the past.

The choice of ritualization strategy is always dependent on the cultural context. In the case of the fen, the cultural context underwent many changes during the time that it was used. The ritualization strategy probably stayed largely unchanged. This illustrates how the interaction between the participants and the physical environment created and recreated the context, as they made it their own, a part of their culture. The cultural context may have changed rather quickly, but the environment changed slowly, and as it too became a part of the cultural context through the people's practice; the ritualization strategy based on the environment could stay unchanged.

The meaning that was created as the acts were performed was instantaneous and varied between individuals. Its implicit and ambiguous character enabled every individual to adapt the ritual to his or her understanding of the whole. At the same time, explicit meanings may have existed, varying over time, but were not decisive for the long continuity of the strategy. Yet the significance of the past may have been of importance for most of the period, and the explicit meanings may have told both a genealogical and a mythical history.

Is practice theory a relevant alternative to the concept of sacrifice when interpreting wetland deposits? The result of this study is an image of rather complex social relations and structures created by the activities at the fen. The concept of sacrifice would have had a homogenizing effect on this image, and the complexity of the interpretation may have been lost. The result also illuminates the still unsolved problem of the categorization of acts. It is not always possible to say whether an act has been ritualized or not. But this may not be a problem after all. It is still possible to interpret the social strategies of the societies.

By implementing a practice theory perspective, I have shifted focus from the motives behind the acts to the structuring effect of the acts. Instead of making inferences about beliefs and religion, the results concern the relationships of the people and the social structures of its members. Thus, this is a question of what kind of results we want to achieve and find acceptable. I am not suggesting that inquiries into beliefs and religion are uninteresting, but a practice theory approach to this material may lead to another—and perhaps new—knowledge of the people and their relationships and social structures.

REFERENCES CITED

Andersson, M. 2004 Domestication and the First Neolithic Concept, 4800–3000 BC. In *Stone Age Scania. Significant Places Dug and Read by Contract Archaeology*, edited by M. Andersson, P. Karsten, B. Knarrström, and M. Svensson, Skrifter No 52:143–190, Riksantikvarieämbetet, Stockholm, Sweden.

Bell, C. 1992 *Ritual Theory, Ritual Practice*. Oxford University Press, New York.

Bell, C. 1997 *Ritual. Perspectives and Dimensions*. Oxford University Press, New York.

Berggren, Å. 2007 *Till och från ett kärr. Den arkeologiska undersökningen av Hindbygården*. Malmöfynd 17. Malmö Kulturmiljö, Malmö.

Berggren, Å. 2010 *Med kärret som källa. Om begreppen offer och ritual inom arkeologin*. Vägar till Midgård 13. Nordic Academic Press, Lund.

Bloch, M. 1992 *Prey into Hunter. The Politics of Religious Experience*. Cambridge University Press, Cambridge.

Bradley, R. 2002 *The Past in Prehistoric Societies*. Routledge, London and New York.

Bradley, R. 2003a A Life Less Ordinary: the Ritualization of the Domestic Sphere in Later Prehistoric Europe. *Cambridge Archaeological Journal* 13(1):5–23.

Bradley, R. 2003b The Translation of Time. In *Archaeologies of Memory*, edited by R. Van Dyke and S. Alcock, pp. 221–227. Blackwell, Malden, Massachusetts.

Brück, J. 2005 Experiencing the Past? The Development of a Phenomenological Archaeology in British Prehistory. *Archaeological Dialogues* 12(1):45–72.

de Boeck, F. 1995 Bodies of Remembrance: Knowledge, Experience, and the Growing of Memory in Luunda Ritual Performance. In *Rites et ritualization*, edited by G. Thinès and L. de Heusch, pp. 113–138. Librairie Philosophique J. Vrin och Institut Interdisciplinaire d'Etudes Epistémologiques, Paris and Lyon.

Durkheim, E. 1965 [1915]. *The Elementary Forms of Religious Life*. Translated by J.W. Swain. Collier, New York.

Frazer, J. 1994 [1922]. *Den gyllene grenen. Studier i magi och religion*. Translated by E. Klein. Natur och kultur, Stockholm.

Gero, J. 2007 Honoring Ambiguity/Problematizing Certitude. *Journal of Archaeological Method and Theory* 14(3):11–327.

Gosden, C., and G. Lock 1998 Prehistoric Histories. *World Archaeology. The Past in the Past: The Reuse of Ancient Monuments* 30(1):2–12.

Hamilakis Y. 2002 The Past as Oral History: Towards an Archaeology of the Senses. In *Thinking through the Body: Archaeologies of Corporeality*, edited by Y. Hamilakis, M. Pluciennik, and S. Tarlow, pp. 121–136. Kluwer Academic/Plenum, New York.

Hamilakis, Y., M. Pluciennik, and S. Tarlow (editors) 2002 *Thinking through the Body. Archaeologies of Corporeality*. Kluwer Academic/Plenum, New York.

Houston, S., and K. Taube 2000. An Archaeology of the Senses: Perception and Cultural Expression in Ancient Mesoamerica. *Cambridge Archaeological Journal* 10(2):261–294.

Hubert, H., and M. Mauss 1964[1898] *Sacrifice, its Nature and Function*, translated by W. D. Halls. University of Chicago Press, Chicago.

de Heusch, L. 1985 *Sacrifice in Africa, a Structuralist Approach*. Translated by L. O'Brien, and A. Morton. University of Manchester Press, Manchester.

Küchler, S. 1993 Landscape as Memory: The Mapping Process and its Representation in a Melanesian Society. In *Landscape. Politics, and Perspectives*, edited by B. Bender, pp. 85–106. Berg, Providence/Oxford.

Kus, S. 1992 Toward an Archaeology of Body and Soul. In *Representations in Archaeology*, edited by J-C. Gardin and C. Peebles, pp. 168–177. Indiana University Press, Bloomington and Indianapolis.

Lekberg, P. 2002 *Yxors liv, människors landskap. En studie av kulturlandskap och samhälle I Mellansveriges senneolitikum*. Kust till kust 5. Uppsala universitet, Uppsala, Sweden.

Meskell, L. 2003 Memory's Materiality: Ancestral Presence, Commemorative Practice, and Disjunctive Locales. In *Archaeologies of Memory*, edited by R. Van Dyke and S. Alcock, pp. 34–55. Blackwell, Malden, Massachusetts.

Miller, D. 2005 Materiality: An Introduction. In *Materiality*, edited by D. Miller, pp. 1–50. Duke University Press, Durham.

Nilsson Stutz, L. 2003 *Embodied Rituals and Ritualized Bodies. Tracing Ritual Practices in Late Mesolithic Burials*. Acta Archaeologica Lundensia No 46. Almqvist & Wiksell, Stockholm.

Robertson Smith, W. 1997 (original 1889) *Lectures on the Religion of the Semites: The Fundamental Institutions*. Routledge, New York.

Rydbeck, O. 1918 Slutna mark- och mossfynd från stenåldern i Lunds universitets historiska museum, deras tidsställning och samband med religiösa föreställningar. *Från Lunds universitets historiska museum*, 1918:1–66.

Seremetakis, N. (editor) 1994 *The Senses Still. Perception and Memory as Material Culture in Modernity*. The University of Chicago Press, Chicago.

Strenski, I. 2003 *Theology and the First Theory of Sacrifice*. Brill, Leiden.

Tilley, C. 1999. *Metaphore and Material Culture*. Blackwell, Oxford.

Tilley, C. 2006 Objectification. In *Handbook of Material Culture*, edited by C. Tilley, W. Keane, S. Küchler, M. Rowlands, and P. Spyer, pp. 60–73. Sage, London.

Tilley, C., W. Keane, S. Küchler, M. Rowlands, and P. Spyer (editors) 2006. *Handbook of Material Culture*. Sage, London.

Tylor, E. 1871 *Primitive Culture: Researches in the Development of Mythology, Philosophy, Religion, Language, Arts, and Custom*. John Murray, London.

Van Dyke, R. and S. Alcock. 2003 Archaeologies of Memory: An Introduction. In *Archaeologies of Memory*, edited by R. Van Dyke and S. Alcock, pp. 1–13. Blackwell, Malden, Massachusetts.

Vernant, J-P. 1989 [1979]. At Man's Table: Hesiod's Foundation Myth of Sacrifice. In *The Cuisine of Sacrifice among the Greeks*, edited by M. Detienne and J-P. Vernant, pp. 21–86. University of Chicago Press, Chicago.

CHAPTER THREE

Gifts from the Gods

A New Look at Some Weapons and Vessels from the Metal Ages

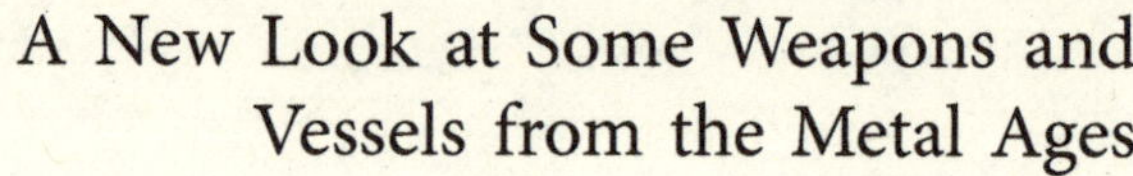

Christoph Huth

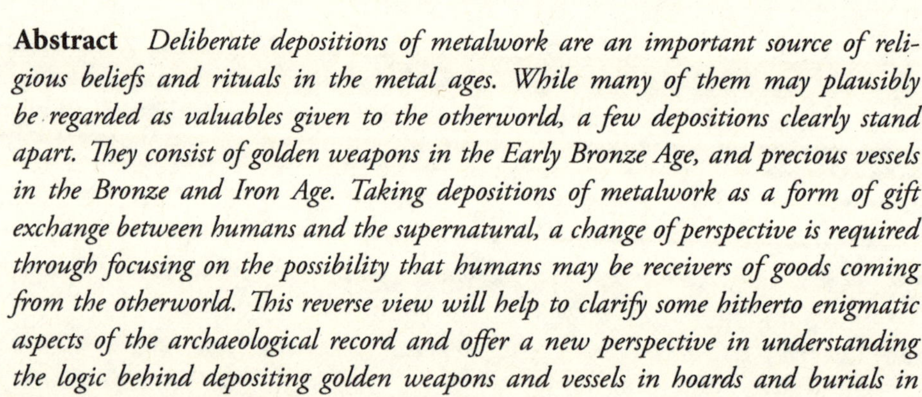

Abstract   *Deliberate depositions of metalwork are an important source of religious beliefs and rituals in the metal ages. While many of them may plausibly be regarded as valuables given to the otherworld, a few depositions clearly stand apart. They consist of golden weapons in the Early Bronze Age, and precious vessels in the Bronze and Iron Age. Taking depositions of metalwork as a form of gift exchange between humans and the supernatural, a change of perspective is required through focusing on the possibility that humans may be receivers of goods coming from the otherworld. This reverse view will help to clarify some hitherto enigmatic aspects of the archaeological record and offer a new perspective in understanding the logic behind depositing golden weapons and vessels in hoards and burials in the Bronze and Iron Age.*

Sacrifice is a form of gift exchange between humans and the supernatural, characterized by giving and receiving. Although this is an oversimplification of a rather complicated relationship, it is useful as a starting point in considering a long-neglected aspect of this matter (i.e., humans as receivers of gifts from the gods).

Much research has been devoted to the human part of this particular relationship, on the actors involved, the gifts presented to the gods, or the sites where sacrifices occurred (Biehl 2001; Burkert 1983; Gladigow 1984; Müller 2002). However, little attention has been paid to the possible gifts received from the gods, apart from general aspects such as health, wealth, and well-being. This may be so because the otherworldly part of this exchange system is entirely fictional to us. So could we reasonably expect to find real objects in the archaeological record that were believed to be gifts coming from the gods?

Obviously for the believers, the otherworld, the ancestors, and gods were no fiction. Thus, it is no surprise that mythological narratives now and then refer to objects that ultimately came from the supernatural world, either received as a gift from the gods or sometimes simply stolen by humans (Burkert 1967). And indeed, there are objects in the archaeological record that are best explained as things that were believed to have come from the gods, mainly weapons and vessels, frequently made of precious metals.

Deliberate Depositions of Metalwork

Why are metal objects so important with regard to Bronze and Iron Age religion? Sacrificial offerings of animals and foodstuff were omnipresent in prehistory; however, they are notoriously difficult to detect in the archaeological record. One reason is because they rapidly decay. The other reason is of an entirely different nature; religious activities in prehistory were entirely ephemeral (Müller 2002). There were no temples, and there were no particular sites where people regularly gathered over a significant stretch of time in order to carry out their sacrificial rituals. Perhaps Neolithic earthworks such as Herxheim belonged to this category (see Zeeb-Lanz this volume), but otherwise there were no such places before the Iron Age at least. For the moment, suffice it to say that depositions of metalwork (copper, bronze, iron, rarely gold) rank among the most significant relics of religious activities, if only for technical reasons such as the durability of the material in use.

Depositions of metalwork are a rather heterogeneous group in the archaeological record. They comprise single items as well as groups of objects, masterpieces of craftsmanship as well as scrap, metalwork buried in dry ground as well as objects deposited in wet places like rivers and swamps, which rendered attempts of recovery impossible for all times (Bradley 1990; Geißlinger 1984). Deposition of metalwork starts in the Copper Age. There is a peak in the Early and the Late Bronze Age to such an extent that depositions of metalwork are commonly regarded as the most typical aspect of the Bronze Age. They vanish in the Early Iron Age, only to reappear in the La Tène period. Altogether, there are thousands of hoards and single deposits that have been discovered.

There has been, unsurprisingly, a lengthy and fierce debate over the proper interpretation of these depositions for 150 years and the debate is ongoing. However, in recent years a theory has become popular that interprets these depositions as gifts to the gods, no matter what their contents (Hänsel and Hänsel 1997). The basic idea is that they may have been valuables presented to the gods according to the principle of *do ut des*. All sorts of valuables were deposited, in fact, for even scrap metal could be seen as something fit for giving away. While this seems very intriguing at first glance, it is too simplistic and reductionist in reality. This theory cannot account for the enormous variety of the archaeological record. Moreover, a theory that explains everything will explain nothing in the end.

On top of that, this theory does not differentiate among the gifts presented to the gods; not among the objects, nor their condition or quality, and neither among the ends to which they were presented to the gods, not to speak of the gods addressed, which are of course entirely unknown in prehistory. Needless to say, these differences are important indeed. As a consequence, many attempts have been made to categorize these gifts and the intentions behind their presentation, as well as the attendant rituals (Colpe 1970; Stjernquist 1963). To these belong sacrifices, offerings, trophies and *ex-votos*. *Ex-votos* stand apart as they are basically not a gift, but rather a message or sign denoting something closely linked with the giving person. *Ex-votos* refer to a promise or vow made among people or equally so between people and god, but at any rate in the name of god, and may take various forms. There are written texts as well as iconic items such as pictures, and, finally, objects symbolizing the promise at the basis of the *ex-voto*. In this case *ex-votos* are also gifts, very much like offerings. Whatever people give to the gods, it must be something the gods want to possess. There is rich literary and ethnographic evidence for this, and without exception (Godelier 1999). We may therefore infer that the situation was not different in prehistoric times.

We are left with a major problem when we turn back to the depositions of metalwork. About 95 percent of the hoards of the Copper and Bronze Age consist of scrap metal or ingots of various forms (Geißlinger 1984; Huth 2008a). While ingots may be regarded to some extent as valuables, though possibly not for the gods, scrap definitely does not look as though it would be very appealing to the gods.

However, there are a small number of hoards that clearly stand apart. They commonly consist either of weapons, ornaments, or vessels, sometimes in large numbers, but typically containing just one type of object, and rarely an admixture of other things. Quite often these objects are masterpieces of craftsmanship, and their condition at the time of deposition was very good. Some were deposited in wet ground, such as swamps or wells or rivers. To these conditions, we may add all those single finds from watery locations, again basically weapons, ornaments, and vessels (Müller 2002; Torbrügge 1996).

We are in the presence of very special depositions here, presumably offerings or *ex-votos* and occasionally trophies or prestige goods buried for a particular reason. Unlike scrap metal and ingots, these objects do belong to a symbolic, if not religious, sphere. Once again, there has been a lengthy discussion as to the nature of these finds. This brings us to those finds that were presumably seen as coming from the otherworld.

DEPOSITIONS OF GOLDEN WEAPONS

The hoard of Perşinari in Romania is certainly the best known of all depositions of weapons made of gold and silver (Primas 1991:184 no. 2; Vulpe 1995). It was unearthed on several occasions between 1954 and 1976, which means there are some doubts as to the completeness of the find. Nevertheless, what has been recovered is impressive enough. The hoard contained a golden rapier, twelve dagger blades made of gold and finally four silver axes (Figure 3.1). The gold weighs about 4.8 kilograms, the silver slightly more than a half-kilogram. Traditionally the find has been dated to the early second millennium, but there are good reasons to place it as early as the mid-third millennium B.C.E. (Hansen 2002:165). Now, there are three aspects which are most remarkable. First of all, the objects are made of gold or silver, which renders any practical purpose impossible. Secondly, the

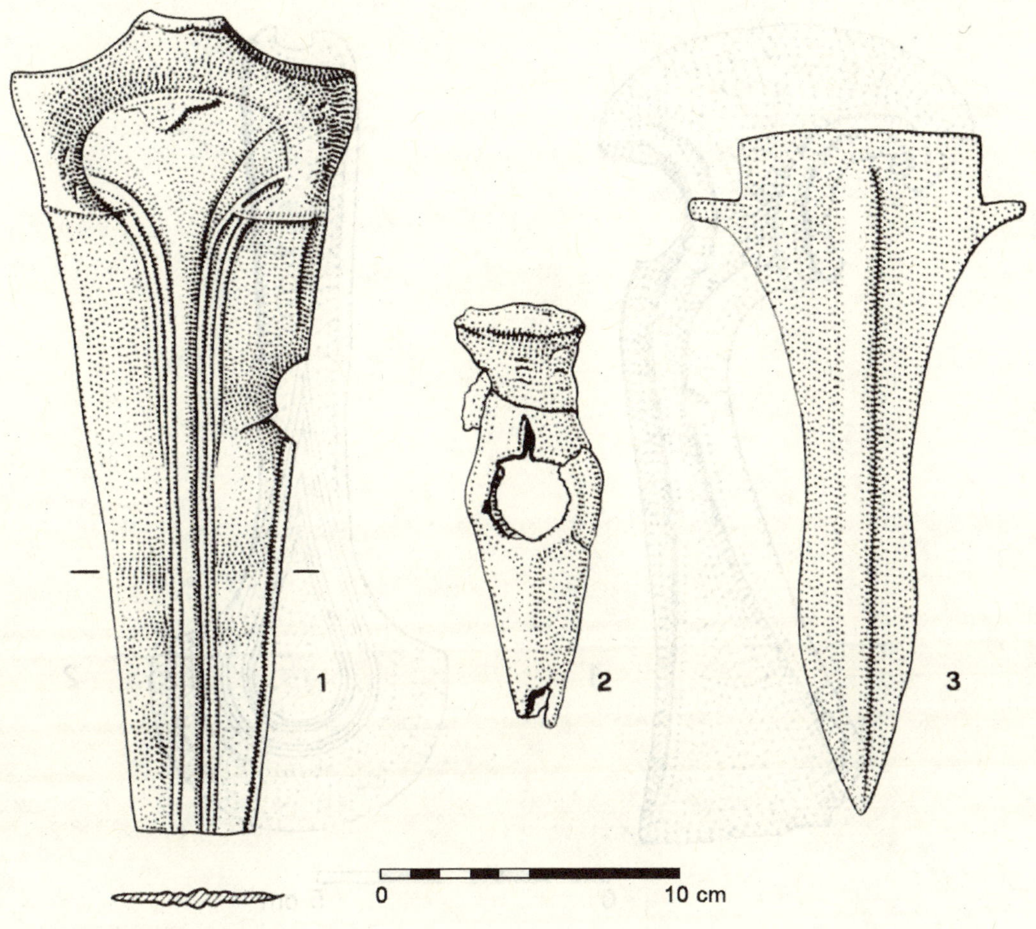

FIGURE 3.1 Rapier, axe and dagger blade made of gold, from Perşinari (ROM, after Primas 1991: 177 fig. 8).

daggers are in an as-cast condition. The edges are blunt and the casting seams have not been removed. Thirdly, there is a whole series of objects in the case of the daggers and the axes. At first sight at least, it does not look like the belongings of a single person.

To this hoard may be added another one from Tufalău, again in Romania, this time definitely belonging to the Early Bronze Age (Primas 1991:185 no. 4). Discovered in 1840, it originally contained four golden axes, one of which survives (Figure 3.2). Another Romanian find from Măcin, again badly documented, consisted of two golden halberd blades and perhaps two golden bracelets as well (Primas 1991:184–185 no. 3). A golden axe was unearthed in Dieskau in East Germany together with a silver neckring and two golden bracelets (Primas 1991:185 no. IX; Schmidt and Nitzschke 1980). A golden dagger blade from Inowrocław in Poland was found in an earthen vessel (Gedl 1980: 41 no. 74). Măcin, Dieskau, and Inowrocław could be burials instead of hoards, but due to the lack of documentary evidence this must remain speculative.

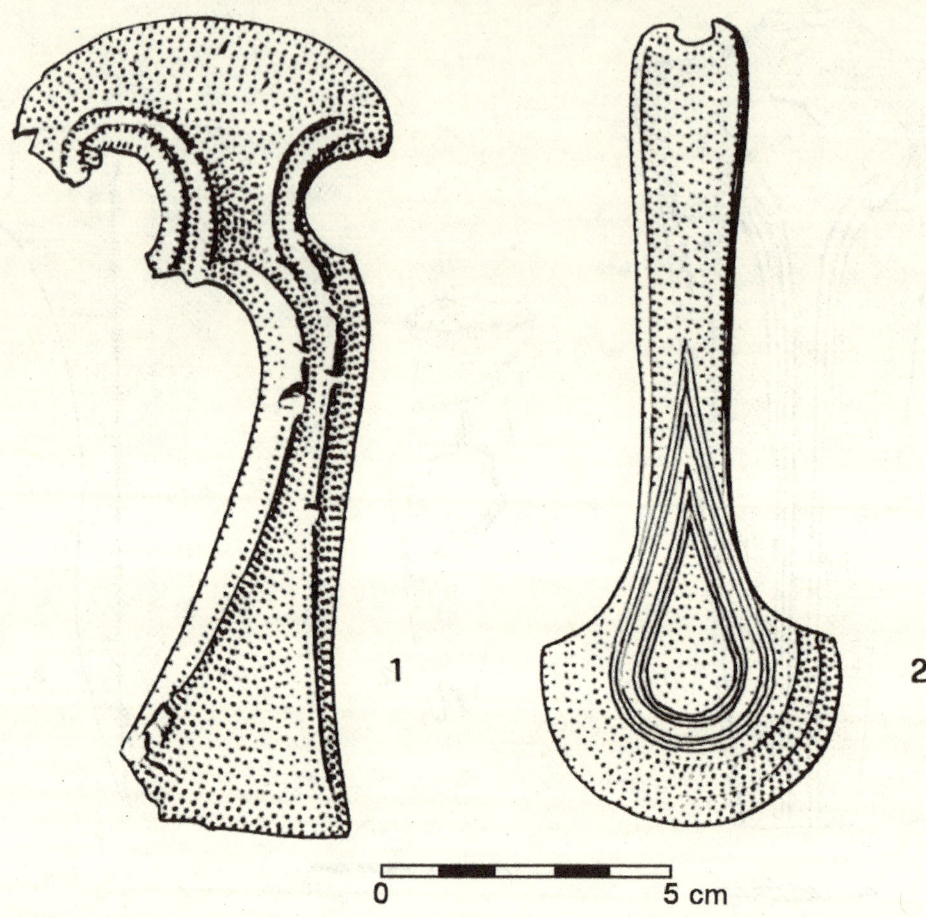

Figure 3.2 Golden axes from Țufalău (ROM) and Dieskau (GER, after Primas 1991: 178 fig. 9).

However, weapons made of precious metal do occur in burials, indeed, as well as in hoards. Twenty years ago, Margarita Primas brought these weapons together in an article covering a wide variety of evidence from the Near East to Central Europe and from the fourth to the second millennium (Primas 1991). Quite obviously, these finds do not represent a homogeneous group nor do they reflect a common cultural or historic background. The depositions in the temple area of Byblos are of particular interest. There, several depositions contain axes and daggers made of gold and silver (Primas 1991:182–183 no. 1–3). At least one golden dagger seems to be an image of a dagger rather than a real weapon. The temple area is dedicated to Reshef, who appears in the form of figurines carrying axes, daggers, and sometimes a spear. It looks as if the weapons deposited in the temple area were regarded as belonging to Reshef. On the other hand, sickle-shaped swords, which are the king's foremost symbol of power, were discovered in three royal burials, but not in the depositions of the temple area (Müller 1987:120–123).

If we go back to Europe, we find similar weapons in rich burials of the Early Bronze Age, particularly in Wessex and in Brittany (Briard 1984; Clarke et al. 1985:107–140, 274–286; Hansen 2002). Although they are not entirely made of precious metals, gold is used to turn them into extraordinary pieces of craftsmanship. Sometimes thousands of tiny gold pins were laid out in a meticulous pattern to adorn the handle of these daggers (Figure 3.3). This devotion to utmost precision is typical of virtually all objects

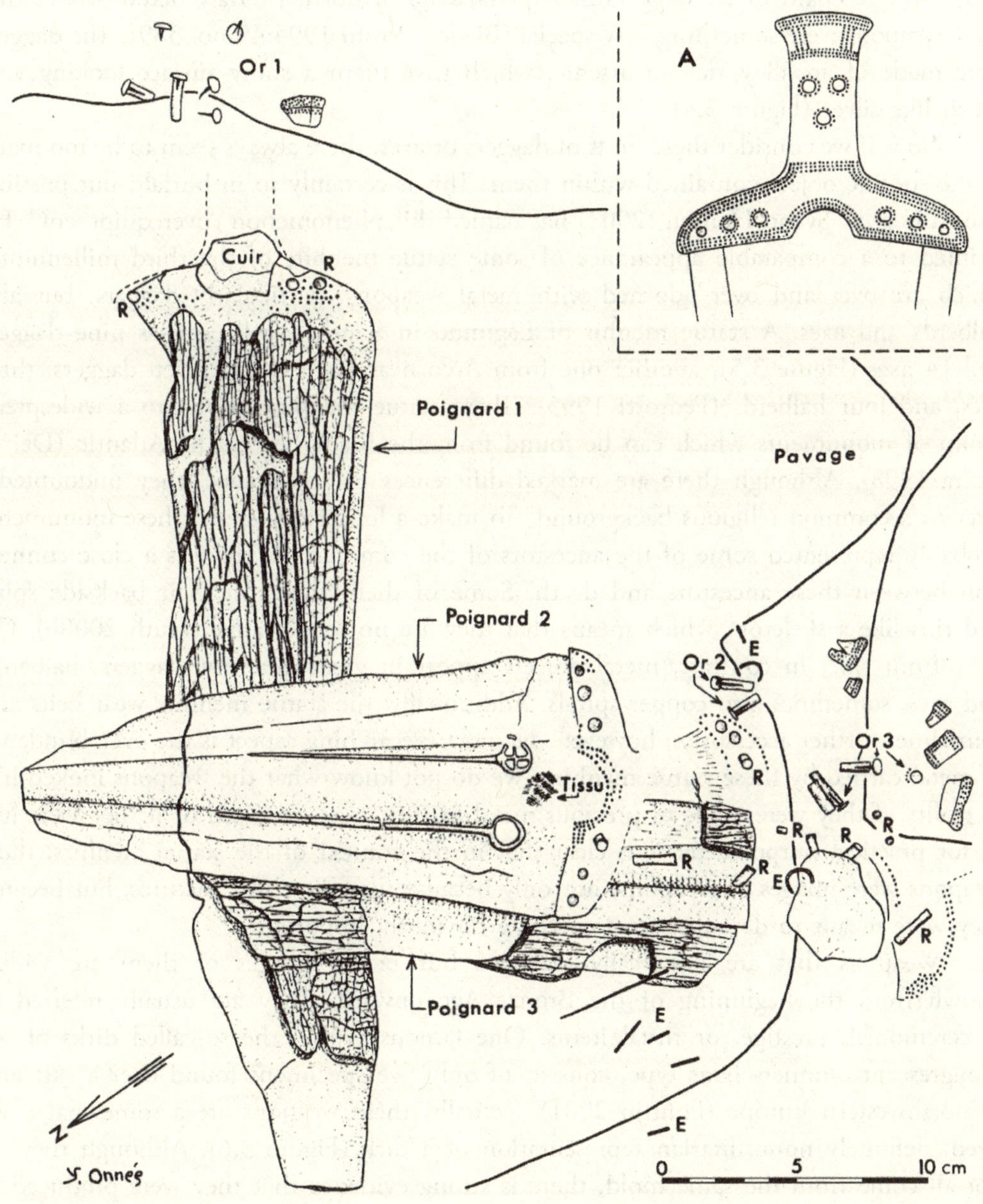

FIGURE 3.3 Daggers adorned with tiny gold pins from Plouvorn (FRA, after Briard 1984: 91 fig. 56).

of a religious meaning in prehistory. With regard to hoards such as Perşinari and Tufalău, one is struck by the fact that these burials do not contain single weapons, but a whole series of weapons, especially daggers. Some graves produced up to twelve daggers, much more than one would expect to be the possession of a single person.

This leads us to a group of hoards consisting of weapons of a single type, yet in great quantities. These, too, can be dated to the Early Bronze Age. We are mainly dealing with daggers and halberds of outstanding quality (Hansen 2002). The hoard from Groß-Schwechten in eastern Germany contained 10 halberds (Wüstemann 1995:81 no. 139–140). A hoard of 25 daggers in Ripatransone in northern Italy demonstrates that these weapons were something very special (Bianco Peroni 1994:49 no. 389). The daggers were made of an alloy rich in arsenic, which gave them a shiny surface looking very much like silver (Figure 3.4).

Now, if we consider these finds of daggers or axes, there always seem to be too many of the specific object contained within them. This is certainly so in burials, but possibly also in hoards. Svend Hansen (2002) has named this phenomenon "overequipment." He pointed to a comparable appearance of some statue menhirs of the third millennium, which are over and over adorned with metal weapons, particularly daggers, but also halberds and axes. A statue menhir of Lagundo in South Tyrolia carries nine daggers and 14 axes (Figure 3.5), another one from Arco near Lake Garda seven daggers, three axes, and four halberds (Pedrotti 1995). These statue menhirs belong to a widespread group of monuments which can be found from the Black Sea to the Atlantic (Dei di pietra 1998). Although there are marked differences in appearance, they undoubtedly refer to a common religious background. To make a long story short, these monuments probably represented some of the ancestors of the community. There is a close connection between these ancestors and death. Some of them show on their backside spine and ribs like a skeleton, which means that they are no longer alive (Huth 2008b). On their front side, in contrast, metal objects appear in great quantity, daggers, halberds, and axes, sometimes also copper spirals. Additionally, the statue menhirs wear belts and sometimes further accessories; however, the most eyecatching aspect is the overabundance of metal carried by these statue menhirs. We do not know what the weapons looked like in reality, if they were made of precious metal, if they were oversized or if they were just fit for practical purpose. Yet it is clear that in the context of the statue menhirs, these weapons were images of weapons, not only because they were just pictures, but because they were meant to demonstrate something obviously important.

Weapons that are not really weapons but rather images of them are widely known from the beginning of the Bronze Age onward. They are usually referred to as ceremonial, prestige, or ritual items. One famous group, the so-called dirks of the Plougrescant-Ommerschans type, consists of only five specimens found over a vast area in northwestern Europe (Fontijn 2001). Actually, these weapons are a somewhat oversized, definitely nonutilitarian representation of a dirk (Figure 3.6). Although they do not all come from the same mold, there is strong evidence that they were produced in the same workshop. Their quality is extraordinary. According to David Fontijn, "They are objects that were deliberately made to look like dirks, but this is not what they were. Rather, they are abstractions evoking the idea of the dirk," in other words, some form

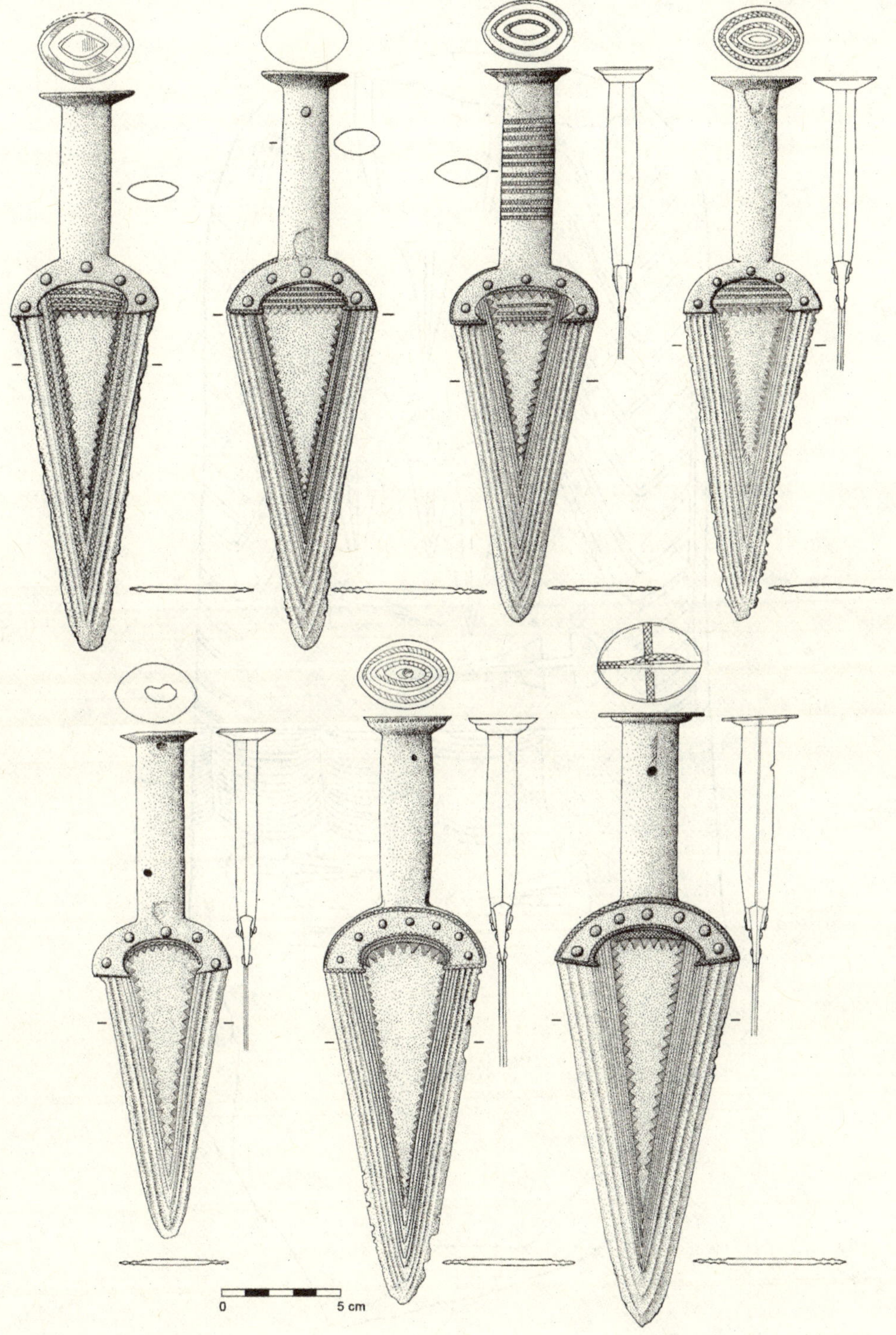

FIGURE 3.4 Daggers from the hoard of Ripatransone (ITA, after Bianco Peroni 1994: pl. 25).

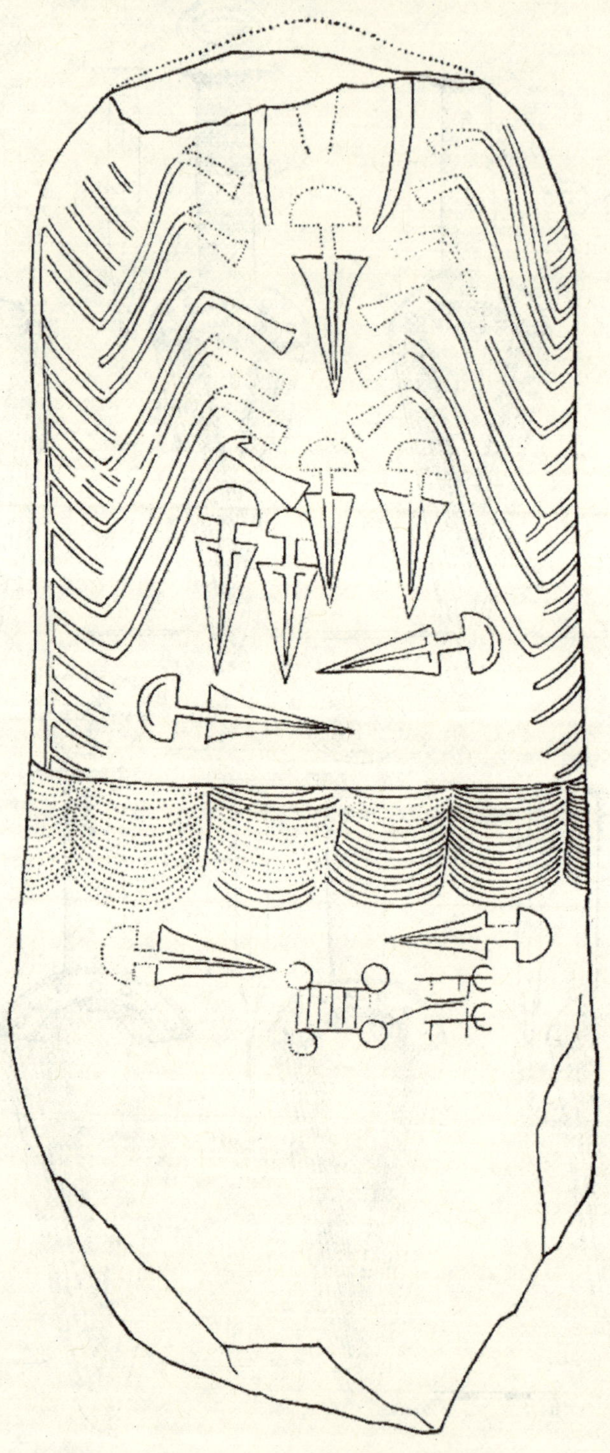

FIGURE 3.5 Statue menhir of Lagundo (ITA), Height = 267 cm (after Dondio 1995: 209 fig. F96).

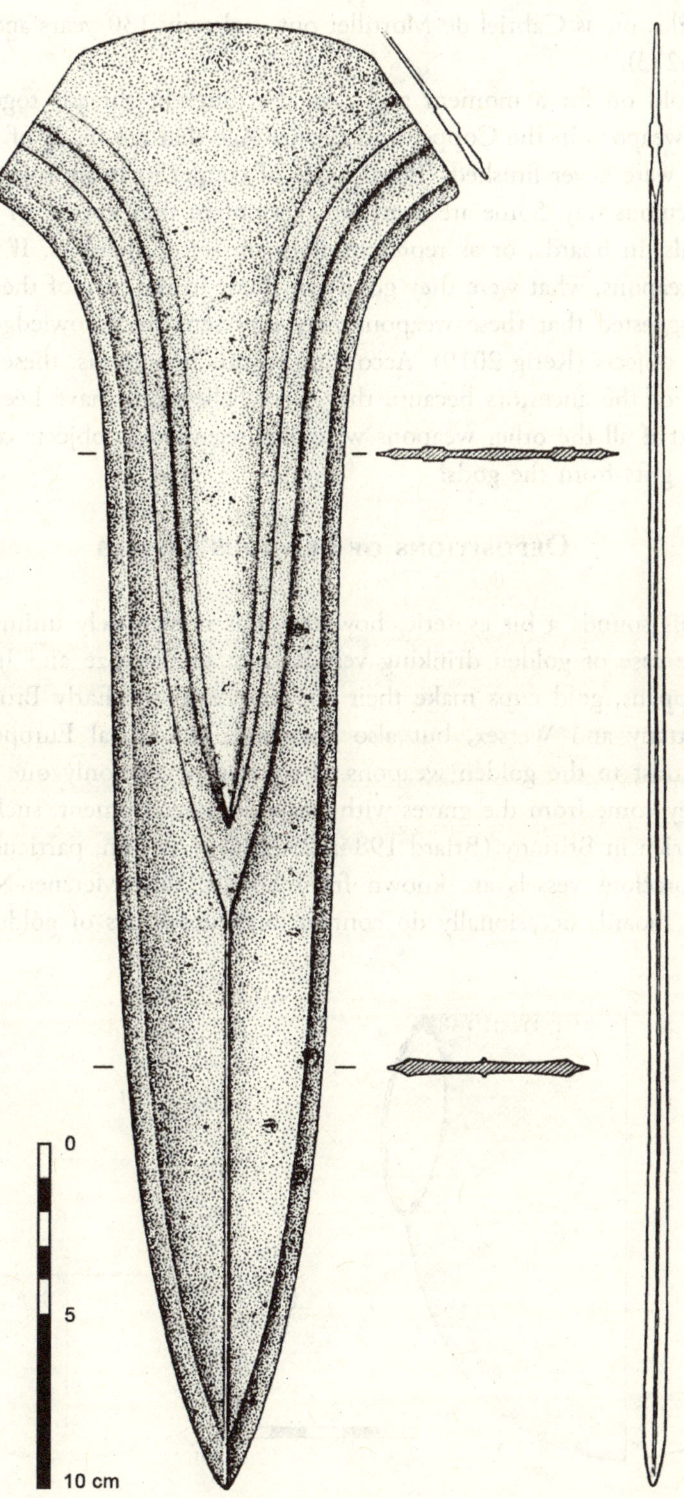

FIGURE 3.6 Bronze dirk from Jutphaas (NED, after Butler, Sarfatij 1972: fig. 3).

of idealized dirks, or, as Gabriel de Mortillet put it already 130 years ago, a simulacrum (Fontijn 2001:273).

Let us hold on for a moment and take the different threads together. There are nonutilitarian weapons in the Copper and Bronze Age that are made of precious metals. Some of them were never finished. Those made of copper or bronze were manufactured in a very meticulous way. Some are oversized. Very often they appear in great quantities, either in burials, in hoards, or as representations on statue menhirs. If we accept them as images of weapons, what were they good for, then? In the case of the statue menhirs, it has been suggested that these weapons may represent the knowledge and power to produce metal objects (Kerig 2010). According to this hypothesis, these objects were in the possession of the ancestors because they were believed to have been received from the gods. What if all the other weapons were also regarded as objects coming from the otherworld, as gifts from the gods?

DEPOSITIONS OF PRECIOUS VESSELS

Admittedly, this sounds a bit esoteric; however, it is not entirely unimaginable, as can be seen in the case of golden drinking vessels from the Bronze and Iron Age (Figure 3.7). As it happens, gold cups make their appearance in the Early Bronze Age in rich burials in Brittany and Wessex, but also elsewhere in Central Europe (Clarke et al. 1985). In contrast to the golden weapons, there is generally only one cup in a grave. Sometimes they come from the graves with weapon overequipment, such as a silver cup from Saint-Adrien in Brittany (Briard 1984:225–226). Later on, particularly in the Late Bronze Age, precious vessels are known from hoards, too (Metzner-Nebelsick 2003). Unlike burials, hoards occasionally do contain large quantities of golden vessels. From

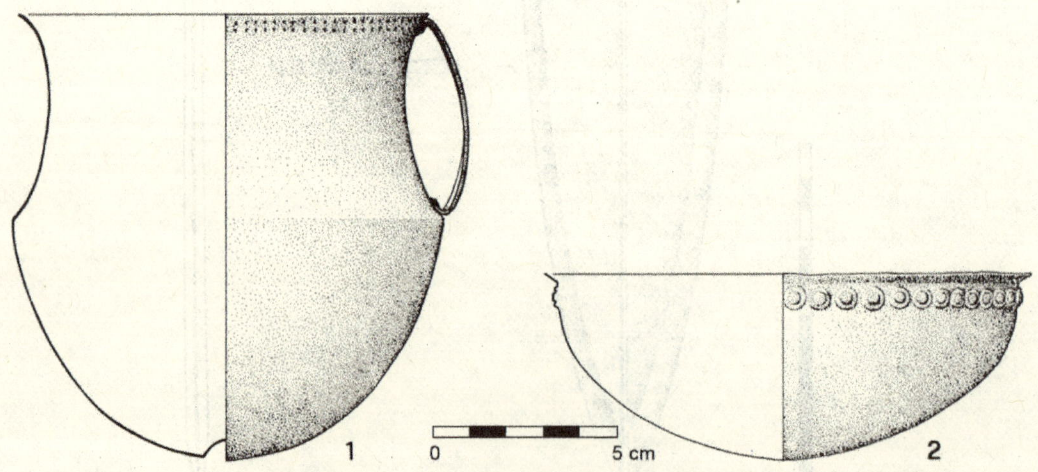

FIGURE 3.7 Gold cups from (1) Fritzdorf and (2) Hochdorf (both GER, after Jacob 1995: pl. 77 no. 406, pl. 79 no. 418).

the Late Bronze Age onward apart from the drinking cups, cauldrons and buckets appear in the archaeological record, sometimes as depositions in watery locations, sometimes in burials (Kimmig 1991). Some of the vessels are mounted on four wheels (Guggisberg 1996). When they belong to burials, there is always a set of drinking vessels along with them. Cauldrons and precious drinking vessels evidently belong together.

The cauldrons mounted on wheels are clearly meant as images of vessels and were not for practical usage. Consequently, they are referred to as ceremonial or ritual cauldrons. These cauldrons have a long tradition lasting into the Iron Age. With the appearance of pictorial representation in the Early Iron Age, it becomes clear what they were good for. On the famous cart of Strettweg in Styria (Figure 3.8), we can see that the

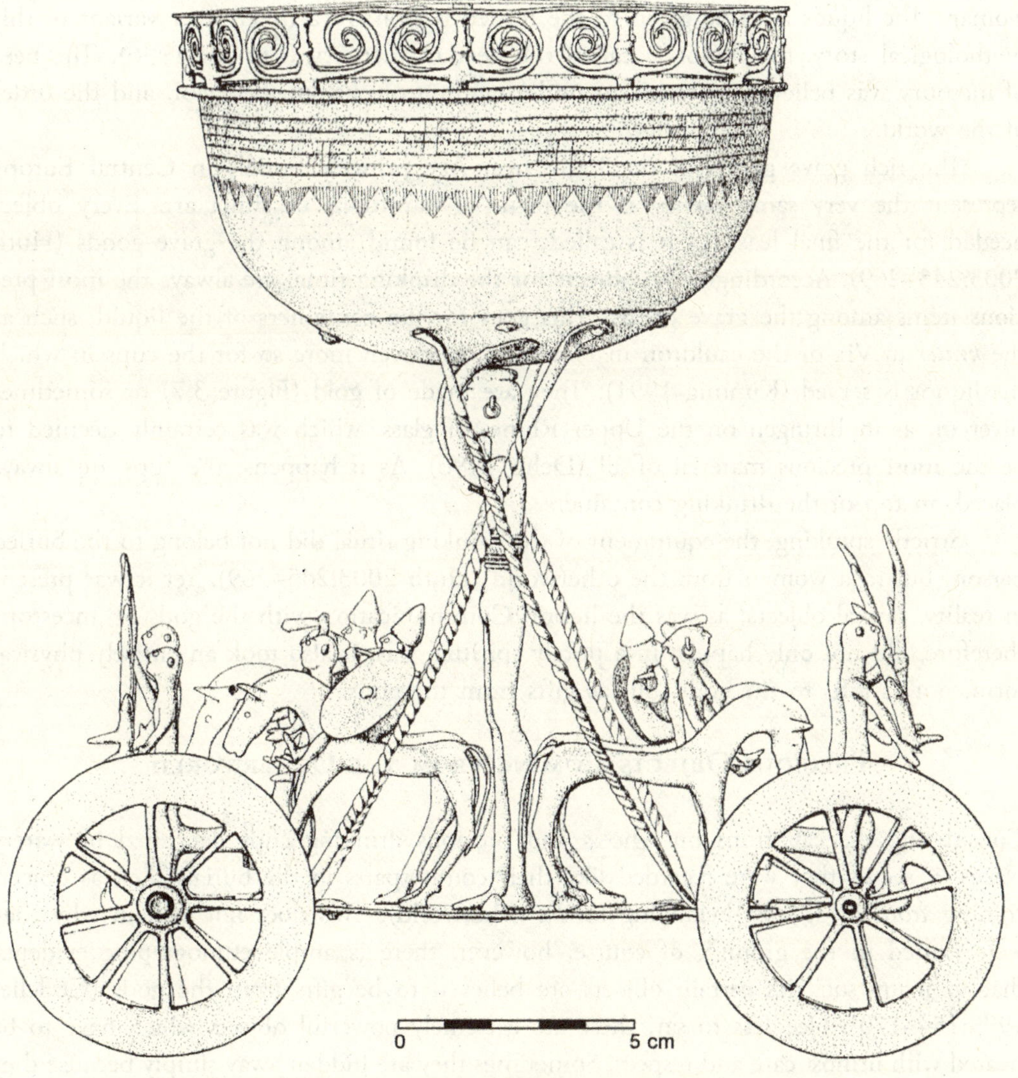

FIGURE 3.8 Ceremonial cart from Strettweg (AUT, after Egg 1996: 27 fig. 17).

cauldron belongs to a richly adorned woman who is carrying it over her head (Egg 1996). Further evidence comes from situla art, the first coherent pictorial narration in European prehistory. Situla art shows how cauldrons and buckets were used in complex religious rituals, be it for sacrifices including beverages and incense, as a prize for ritual combats and musical competitions, and finally as the most important equipment of a ritual leading to the apotheosis of a ruler (Huth 2003). In this ritual, a woman serves a drink to a man sitting on a throne. The drinking ritual is followed by a wedding ritual, a *hieros gamos,* to be exact. Evidently, the woman does not belong to the world of the living.

The motif of the woman with the cup, the hydrophore, has widespread distribution during the first millennium B.C.E. from the eastern Mediterranean to Central Europe (Egg 1996:36–43). She appears in situla art, as well as on the cart of Strettweg. The Strettweg cart plainly demonstrates that the container and its content belong to this woman. The liquor is to be given to the buried person. In a much later variant of this mythological story, the liquor is called the beer of memory (Enright 1996). The beer of memory was believed to entail an understanding of custom, behavior, and the order of the world.

The rich grave goods of the Early Iron Age princely burials in Central Europe represent the very same events as the pictorial narrations of situla art. Every object needed for the final feast, as it is called, can be found among the grave goods (Huth 2003:245–269). Accordingly, the objects for the drinking ritual are always the most precious items among the grave goods. This goes for the containers of the liquid, such as the *krater* in Vix or the cauldron in Hochdorf, but even more so for the cups in which the liquor is served (Kimmig 1991). They are made of gold (Figure 3.7) or sometimes silver or, as in Ihringen on the Upper Rhine, of glass, which was certainly deemed to be the most precious material of all (Dehn 1996). As it happens, the cups are always placed on top of the drinking containers.

Strictly speaking, the equipment of the drinking ritual did not belong to the buried person, but to a woman from the otherworld (Huth 2003:245–269). Yet it was present in reality, as real objects, as was the liquor. Communication with the gods or ancestors, therefore, did not only happen in a purely spiritual way, it also took an entirely physical form, not as gifts to the gods, but as gifts from the gods.

Precious Objects Coming from the Otherworld

Considering the cauldrons on wheels and precious drinking cups deposited in watery places, it seems they were regarded like their counterparts in the burials (i.e., as objects coming from or at least belonging to the otherworld). This does not explain why they were buried in the ground, of course; however, there is ample ethnographic evidence that in many societies certain objects are believed to be gifts from the gods (Godelier 1999:154–170). Needless to say, these are extremely powerful objects which have to be treated with utmost care and respect. Sometimes they are hidden away simply because they are so powerful. As Godelier (1999:169) pointed out, they are inalienable goods which cannot be used in the normal sphere of gift exchange. Going back to the first millennium

B.C.E., the only possibilities to deal with these objects were to store them, hide them in the ground, or use them in burial rituals (a rather similar situation seems to prevail among the huge Neolithic tumuli of Brittany containing jadeite axes (Pétrequin et al. 2010:196). Alternatively, the objects may have been looted, something that happened quite frequently, bearing in mind that most of the princely burials had been robbed in antiquity.

This may sound speculative. But if we take the idea into consideration for a moment, it will certainly help to clarify some hitherto unexplained facts of the archaeological record. At any rate it will help to understand why in the Copper and Bronze Age golden weapons existed at all, why they were meant to be images of weapons, why they were deposited in large quantities in hoards and burials or depicted on statue menhirs believed to represent the ancestors of a community. If we recall the rich burials of the Early Bronze Age in Brittany, it is easy to imagine the logic according to which the relationship between man and the supernatural had been constructed and instrumented. Supplying the dead with objects from the otherworld emphatically demonstrated his close relationship with the ancestors or gods. The deposition of large quantities of identical objects follows a logic according to which the power of a symbol is enhanced by its iteration. One dagger helps a little, many daggers help a lot.

Precious vessels make their appearance when precious weapons gradually vanish in the Early Bronze Age. It is not yet clear if the precious vessels of the Late Bronze and Early Iron Age do follow a tradition established in the Early Bronze Age. In any case, they stand for a very elaborate ideology of descent and power firmly rooted in religious beliefs. Maybe for this reason the iteration of symbolic objects gave way to a complex narrative about the relationship between humans and the supernatural world. Yet gifts from the gods did not lose their importance. Actually, they never did. In Lavinium, the central sanctuary of the Latini and home of *dii penates populi Romani,* the Romans kept objects that had been brought by Aeneas from Troy including precious drinking equipment (Godelier 1999:166–167).

References Cited

Bianco Peroni, V. 1994 *I pugnali nell'Italia continentale.* Steiner, Stuttgart.

Biehl, P. (editor) 2001 *The Archaeology of Cult and Religion.* Archaeolingua Alapítvány, Budapest.

Bradley, R. 1990 *The Passage of Arms.* Cambridge University Press, Cambridge.

Briard, J. 1984 *Les tumulus d'Armorique.* Picard, Paris.

Burkert, W. 1967 Urgeschichte der Technik im Spiegel antiker Religion. *Technikgeschichte* 34:281–299.

Burkert, W. 1983 *Homo Necans. The Anthropology of Ancient Greek Sacrificial Ritual and Myth.* University of California Press, Berkeley.

Butler, J. J., and H. Sarfatij 1972 Another Bronze Ceremonial Sword by the Plougrescant-Ommerschans Smith. *Berichten van de Rijksdienst voor het Oudheidkundig Bodemonderzoek* 20–21, 1970–1971 (1972):301–309.

Clarke, D. V., T. G. Cowie, and A. Foxon 1985 *Symbols of Power at the Time of Stonehenge.* HMSO, Edinburgh.

Colpe, C. 1970 Theoretische Möglichkeiten zur Identifizierung von Heiligtümern und Interpretation von Opfern in ur- und prähistorischen Epochen. In *Vorgeschichtliche Heiligtümer und Opferplätze in Mittel- und Nordeuropa*, edited by H. Jankuhn, pp. 18–39. Vandenhoeck & Ruprecht, Göttingen.

Dehn, R. 1996 Ein Fürstengrab der späten Hallstattzeit von Ihringen (Kreis Breisgau-Hochschwarzwald). In *Trésors Celtes et Gaulois. Le Rhin supérieur entre 800 et 50 avant J.-C.*, edited by S. Plouin, pp. 113–118. Musée d'Unterlinden, Colmar.

Dei di pietra 1998 *Dei di pietra. La grande statuaria antropomorfa nell'Europa del III millennio a.C.* Skira, Milano.

Dondio, W. 1995 *La Regione Atesina nella Preistoria*. Ed. Raetia, Bolzano.

Egg, M. 1996 *Das hallstattzeitliche Fürstengrab von Strettweg bei Judenburg in der Obersteiermark*. Römisch-Germanisches Zentralmuseum Mainz, Mainz.

Enright, M. J. 1996 *Lady with a Mead Cup. Ritual, Prophecy, and Lordship in the European Warband from La Tène to the Viking Age*. Four Courts Press, Blackrock, Co. Dublin.

Fontijn, D. R. 2001 Rethinking Ceremonial Dirks of the Plougrescant-Ommerschans Type—Some Thoughts on the Structure of Metalwork Exchange. In *Patina. Essays Presented to Jay Jordan Butler on the Occasion of his 80th Birthday*, edited by W. H. Metz, B. L. van Beek, and H. Steegstra, pp. 263–280. Amsterdam.

Gedl, M. 1980. *Die Dolche und Stabdolche in Polen*. Beck, München.

Geißlinger, H. 1984 s.v. Depotfund, Hortfund. In *Reallexikon der Germanischen Altertumskunde*, vol. V, pp. 320–338. De Gruyter, Berlin.

Gladigow, B. 1984 Die Teilung des Opfers: Zur Interpretation von Opfern in vor- und frühgeschichtlichen Epochen. *Frühmittelalterliche Studien* 18:19–43.

Godelier, M. 1999 *Das Rätsel der Gabe. Geld, Geschenke, heilige Objekte*. Beck, München (*L'énigme du don*. Librairie Arthème Fayard, Paris 1996).

Guggisberg, M. 1996 Eine Reise von Knossos nach Strettweg. Tiergefäße und Kesselwagen als Ausdruck religiöser Kontakte zwischen der Ägäis und Mitteleuropa im frühen 1. Jahrtausend v. Chr. *Archäologischer Anzeiger* 1996:175–195.

Hänsel, A., and B. Hänsel 1997 *Gaben an die Götter. Schätze der Bronzezeit Europas*. SMPK, Berlin.

Hansen, S. 2002 "Überausstattungen" in Gräbern und Horten der Frühbronzezeit. In *Vom Endneolithikum zur Frühbronzezeit: Muster sozialen Wandels?*, edited by J. Müller, pp. 151–173. Habelt, Bonn.

Huth, C. 2003 *Menschenbilder und Menschenbild. Anthropomorphe Bildwerke der frühen Eisenzeit*. Reimer, Berlin.

Huth, C. 2008a Horte als Geschichtsquelle. In *Vorträge des 26. Niederbayerischen Archäologentages 2008*, edited by K. Schmotz, pp. 131–162. Leidorf, Rahden/Westfalen.

Huth, C. 2008b Darstellungen halb skelettierter Menschen im Neolithikum und Chalkolithikum der Alten Welt. *Archäologisches Korrespondenzblatt* 38:493–504.

Jacob, C. 1995 *Metallgefäße der Bronze- und Hallstattzeit in Nordwest-, West- und Süddeutschland*. Steiner, Stuttgart.

Kerig, T. 2010 Ein Statuenmenhir mit Darstellung einer Axt vom Eschollbrückener Typ? Zu einem enigmatischen Steindenkmal aus Gelnhausen-Meerholz (Main-Kinzig-Kreis). *Praehistorische Zeitschrift* 85:59–78.

Kimmig, W. 1991 Edelmetallschalen der späten Hallstatt- und frühen Latènezeit. *Archäologisches Korrespondenzblatt* 21:241–253.

Metzner-Nebelsick, C. 2003 Ritual und Herrschaft. Zur Struktur von spätbronzezeitlichen Metallgefäßdepots zwischen Nord- und Südosteuropa. In *Rituale in der Vorgeschichte, Antike, und Gegenwart*, edited by C. Metzner-Nebelsick, pp. 99–117. Leidorf, Rahden/Westfalen, Germany.

Müller, F. 2002 *Götter, Gaben, Rituale. Religion in der Frühgeschichte Europas*. Von Zabern, Mainz.

Müller, H. W. 1987 *Die Sichelschwerter*. Verlag der Bayerischen Akademie der Wissenschaften, München.

Pedrotti, A. 1995 Le statue-stele e le stele antropomorfe del Trentino Alto Adige e del Veneto occidentale. Gruppo atesino, gruppo di Brentonico, gruppo della Lessinia. *Notizie Archeologiche Bergomensi* 3:259–280.

Pétrequin, P., S. Cassen, and L. Klassen 2010 Zwischen Atlantik und Schwarzem Meer. Die großen Beile aus alpinem Jadeit im 5. und 4. Jt. V. Chr. In *Jungsteinzeit im Umbruch. Die „Michelsberger Kultur" und Mitteleuropa vor 6000 Jahren*, edited by C. Lichter, pp. 191–197. Badisches Landesmuseum, Karlsruhe.

Primas, M. 1991 Waffen aus Edelmetall. *Jahrbuch des Römisch-Germanischen Zentralmuseums Mainz* 35, 1988 (1991):161–185.

Schmidt, B., and W. Nitzschke 1980 Ein frühbronzezeitlicher Fürstenhügel bei Dieskau im Saalkreis. *Ausgrabungen und Funde* 25:179–183.

Stjernquist, B. 1963 Präliminarien zu einer Untersuchung von Opferfunden. Begriffsbestimmung und Theoriebildung. *Meddelanden från Lunds Universitets Historiska Museum* 1962–1963:5–64.

Torbrügge, W. 1996 Spuren in eine andere Welt. Archäologie der vorzeitlichen Wasserkulte. In *Archäologische Forschungen zum Kultgeschehen in der jüngeren Bronzezeit und frühen Eisenzeit Alteuropas*, edited by M. Almagro-Gorbea et al., pp. 567–581. Regensburg, Universitätsverlag Regenburg, Regensburg.

Vulpe, A. 1995 Der Schatz von Perşinari in Südrumänien. In *Festschrift für H. Müller-Karpe zum 70. Geburtstag*, edited by A. Jockenhövel, pp. 43–62. Habelt, Bonn.

Wüstemann, H. 1995 *Die Dolche und Stabdolche in Ostdeutschland*. Steiner, Stuttgart.

CHAPTER FOUR

Post-Domestic Sacrifice

Exploring the Present and Future of Gifts for the Gods

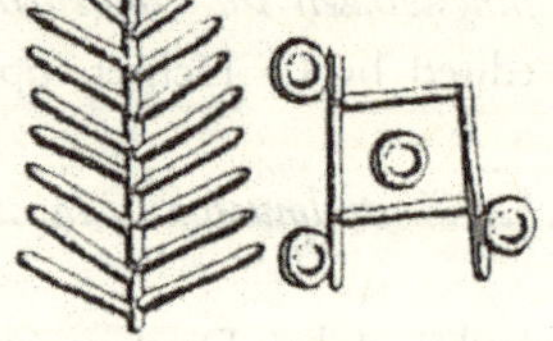

Samantha Hurn

Abstract *This paper considers the contemporary relationships between the human and nonhuman animals involved in foxhunting, an activity traditionally dismissed as "sportive" (and therefore highly immoral) by external commentators. The widespread condemnation of foxhunting is significant in what Richard W. Bulliet terms "post-domesticity," where the vast majority of people are alienated from the "natural" world and processes of agricultural production. This post-domestic separation of consumers from producers and humans from animals has led to an increase in protest against traditional blood sports, culminating in legislation that makes it a criminal offense to pursue a wild mammal with dogs (hounds) in the United Kingdom. In the minds of many, it is, to quote Oscar Wilde, "The unspeakable in pursuit of the uneatable." Yet thousands of animals get killed in the U.K. every day. Ritualization is what makes foxhunting so objectionable, although it might be argued that it is the ritualization that transforms some examples of hunting into sacrifice where sacrifice is viewed as a respectful and reciprocal exchange between two parties. Viewing the hunt as sacrifice facilitates consideration of the complex relationships that occur between the sacred and the profane, and between the human and the nonhuman in the past and present, with important implications for our collective futures.*

"One must observe the proper rites . . ." [said the Fox to the Little Prince]. "What is a rite?" asked the Little Prince. "Those also are *actions too often neglected*," said the Fox. "They are what make one day different from other days, one hour from other hours. There is a rite, for example, among my hunters. Every Thursday they dance with the village girls. So Thursday is a wonderful day for me! I can take a walk as far as the vineyards. But if the hunters danced at just any time, every day would be like every other day, and I should never have any vacation at all." (de Saint-Exupéry 1995:82; emphasis added)

Sacrifice, the act of sacralized violence, is traditionally performed when the perpetrator of that violence seeks either to control circumstances that are otherwise beyond his or her actual ability to control, or to propitiate some higher being following or preceding an act which might, if left unacknowledged, cause offense or imbalance. Sacrifice is a reciprocal exchange between the suppliant and a greater power, whereby the gift of the sacrifice (and the manner in which the offering is made) is given in return for some positive intervention in the real world, or for forgiveness for some transgression. The ritual aspects of sacrifice, including the numerous taboos that must be observed if the rite is to be successful, are part of the gift. Moreover, the adherence to strict taboos can also be regarded as a sacrifice in and of itself, as the suppliant relinquishes certain pleasures (such as sex, alcohol, or luxury foodstuffs) and enters into a period of liminality in a bid to ensure the desired outcome. Typically, the recipient of a sacrificial gift is a deity, ancestor, or other spirit, but in mundane or secular contexts, anthropologists have argued that other tangible beings or profane ideals may take on this role (see for example Miller 1998). However, according to Walter Burkert (1983:3), "Sacrificial killing is the basic experience of the 'sacred'" and so the notion of mundane, profane, or secular sacrifice might appear oxymoronic. Yet in situations where the relationship between humans and the divine is eroded or has disappeared altogether, it stands to reason that other figures important within that particular sociocultural context will supersede a divine recipient. Regardless of who the intended recipient of the sacrifice is, however, the sacrificial victim is typically a surrogate or a substitute for what Burkert (1983:2) terms the "consecrating actor" of the sacrificial violence.

ANIMAL OTHERS

Nonhuman or other-than-human animals (henceforth, "animals") are renowned for being "good to think" (Lévi-Strauss 1963) in that they represent convenient symbolic stand-ins for humans. This notion extends into the realm of sacrifice. Given the fundamental importance of cattle to the Sudanese Nuer, for example, where all social, political, and economic transactions and relationships are (or at least traditionally were) only possible because of the cows an individual had in his possession (Evans-Pritchard 1969), the substitution of cattle for humans in the resolution of blood feuds is understandable. In a Biblical example, the substitution of a ram for the first born son of Abraham is also symbolically redolent. Sheep are metaphors for the human flock, shepherded by a Christian God. In her work on the symbolic importance of sheep in the contemporary U.K., Sarah Franklin has argued that sheep continue to be convenient metaphors for humans (2001, 2007). Sheep and other animals are routinely "sacrificed" in the name of science and agricultural production (Serpell 1999b). Consequently, thinking about these "mundane" processes as forms of sacrificial ritual holds significant value for our understanding of sacrifice more generally.

In the context of the ethnographic fieldwork I have conducted in a rural farming community in west Wales, U.K., I argue that ritualized foxhunting enacted as a form of pest control has become a form of secular sacrifice. As a result of predations on domestic livestock, notably sheep, the red fox (*Vulpes vulpes*) becomes the sacrificial victim, standing in for the human perpetrators of significant acts of violence also enacted against sheep. These ovine domesticates are taken en masse to end their lives at industrial-scale abattoirs which predominate in what Richard W. Bulliet (2005) terms "post-domesticity." Post-domesticity sees the separation of producers from consumers and humans from the "natural" world, with the processes of meat production taking place behind closed doors and shrouded in guilt. In such post-domestic, industrialized agricultural systems there is no opportunity for reverence or propitiation in the process of killing.

In what Bulliet terms domestic or pre-domestic societies, the institutionalized killing and processing of animals into meat and other useful products is traditionally conducted ritualistically, as a form of sacrifice—the animal's life is sacrificed to feed the hunter's family and, in the process, propitiate ancestral gods (e.g., Rappaport 2000). The ritual process allows for the assuaging of guilt through demonstrating a respect for the life of the animal. There are so many instances of this form of "respectful" killing in the ethnographic record that such processes are staple anthropological fodder. And as other contributors to this volume demonstrate, the archaeological record is also littered with examples of the sacrificial killing of other living things not only as gifts with which to bargain with the gods, but also as demonstrations of reverence and respect for the sacrificial victims themselves. Through a consideration of some classic scholarship on the theme of sacrifice, juxtaposed with my own extensive ethnographic fieldwork experience in west Wales, I will argue in this chapter that in the post-domestic world, sacrifice as a fundamental feature of human societies through the ages has not been lost, but rather reinvented in response to the industrialization of food production and secularization of society.

Sacrifice as a Ritual and Rite of Passage

Given that in the process of sacrifice a surrogate victim takes the place of the community or individual making the sacrifice, René Girard suggests that sacrifice presents a means for the community to protect itself from perpetrated violence: "If the community comes too near the sacred it risks being devoured by it; if, on the other hand, the community drifts too far away, out of the range of the sacred's therapeutic threats and warnings, the effects of its fecund presence are lost" (Girard 1992:268).

In most post-domestic contexts, thinking about human social relations via the theoretical concepts of "community" and "sacrifice" might appear, for the most part, unhelpful. The global networks that link contemporary producers and consumers bear little or no resemblance to a community in the traditional anthropological sense of the term (e.g., Davies and Jones 2003). Consumers have drifted too far from the processes of production, and blood sacrifice is no longer an institutionalized or accepted practice. Yet some nodes in the network might still usefully be described as communities. The farming community where I have been conducting fieldwork for more than 12 years is a case in point. Here, farmers raise their flocks and herds on land that has been in their families' possession for generations. They engage with their neighbors face to face, and while their end products, the flesh of the animals in their care, will be exported nationally and internationally for external consumption, while the animals are alive and present, they also constitute extended or peripheral members of the community around whose needs daily activities are organized.

Within this ethnographic context, I suggest that the practice of mounted foxhunting enacted by my farming informants constitutes both a form of sacrifice while also conforming to the classic threefold structure of a rite of passage or ritual activity, as outlined by Victor Turner as follows:

> The first phase of *separation* clearly demarcates sacred space and time from profane or secular space and time. . . . It includes symbolic behavior—especially symbols of reversal or inversion of things, relationships and processes secular—which represents the detachment of the ritual subjects (novices, candidates, neophytes or "initiands") from their previous social statuses. . . . During the intervening phase of *transition* . . . the ritual subjects pass through a period and area of ambiguity, a sort of social limbo which has few . . . of the attributes of either the preceding or subsequent profane social statuses or cultural states. . . . The third phase, called by van Gennep, "reaggregation" or "incorporation" includes symbolic phenomena and actions which represent the return of the subjects to their new, relatively stable, well-defined position in the total society. (Turner 1982:24)

Maurice Bloch, whose work supports Turner's (1982) and van Gennep's (1960) three-stage process, highlights that while both of these theorists recognize the violence inherent in the act of separation, "they completely miss the significance of the much more dramatic violence of the return to the mundane" (Bloch 1991:6). Consequently Maurice Bloch argues for the recognition of two underlying acts of violence: the initial conquest of an inherent weakness within the individual or society (the act of separation), and a "rebounding violence" involving the incorporation of "vitality obtained from *outside* beings, usually animals" (1991:5; original emphasis) typically manifest in blood sacrifice. Both of these acts of violence are integral to an understanding of my farming informants' mounted foxhunting ritual, and will be considered in due course.

ACTS OF VIOLENCE

In the specific context of this rural farming community, it is arguable that the first violent act is that of fox predation and the death of livestock, given as the rationale for the hunt. The initiands are separated from the mundane through the donning of hunting dress (characterized by the red hunting jacket, an item of clothing which is, in reality, only worn by the hunt staff) and their participation in the hunt itself, the sacrificial act. On the sound of the huntsman's horn, followers are plunged into a period of liminality, which continues as they ride over the countryside in pursuit of their quarry. Only when they arrive back at the hosting venue after the fox has been killed are they released from this area of ambiguity and reincorporated back into profane society.

During the hunt itself, the Master and/or Huntsman would take the lead of the mounted field, in pursuit of the hounds in full cry. The riders follow, flanked by hunt staff in red coats, with one of the Field Masters bringing up the rear. The red jackets worn by staff served as boundary markers, perhaps even markers of the field's collective liminality. The hunt staff, after all, were there to do a job of work, and consequently represented the ritual specialists under the "direction" of the "Master." Indeed, as Bloch notes (1991), the transition to the liminal phase involves the symbolic death of the initiands. While the donning of a red hunting jacket certainly means social death in certain circles in the U.K., it might also represent collective transition and symbolic death as the initiands make the transition from the human (mundane) to the natural (sacred) realm, from their "normal" lives as farmers or whatever other profession they were engaged in, via ritual, to their collective life as members of this particular farmers' hunt.

RETURN TO THE MUNDANE

On returning at the end of the day, followers would put the horses away in the lorries or trailers that brought them to the meet, and then the human participants would sit down together to partake in a communal meal (cf. Detienne and Vernant 1989). This meal was (is) always a steaming bowl of lamb *cawl* (a traditional Welsh lamb stew) accompanied by bread and butter and chunks of cheese, and as it is served, consumed, and washed down with a glass of something alcoholic, everyone discusses the day's proceedings, and share their experiences as a group.

This hospitality is integral to the success of the mounted foxhunting ritual in this specific ethnographic context, as not all meets are hosted. Indeed, many (more than half) are held at crossroads, bridges, or other local landmarks, and therefore what is known as the "stirrup cup" is forsaken on these occasions. This clearly demonstrates the functionality of the hunt aside from its social aspects. This particular farmers' hunt is really there to do a job of work. This is in stark contrast to many hunts elsewhere in the U.K., where the literature suggests that mounted meets are always social occasions, with an emphasis on "good riding" (e.g., Bell 1994:182; Marvin 2000). In west Wales, hosted meets allow the farmers who benefit from the pest control service provided by the hunt to reciprocate. They not only allow the hunt staff and followers to ride over their land, but more importantly, provide them with sustenance, and in particular, sustenance comprised of the very animal they are there to save—the sheep. Partaking in this communal meal at the end of a day's hunting therefore further serves to reaffirm the farmers' hunt followers' shared values and interests, in this case, sheep, the animals on which most are dependent for survival.

The communal meal is part of the third stage of the rite of passage, which sees the initiands' reincorporation into profane society by way of "symbolic phenomena and actions" (Turner 1982:24) and especially "symbolic violence" (Girard 1992) or "rebounding violence" (Bloch 1992) and the consumption of the sacrificial animal. In many of my discussions with "antis," the ritual and ceremonial aspects of foxhunting were what marked the activity out as particularly abhorrent (in line with academic condemnations; e.g., Leach 1964; Tuan 1984), and I have been asked repeatedly by friends and colleagues why the fox has to die at the end of the hunt. One made the following point during a rather heated debate:

> I agree it's a sacrificial act, but why the need for death? I don't understand why it would be such a big deal to go drag hunting instead. I mean, lots of "sacrifices" which, in the past, were blood sacrifices, now have a symbolic substitute. I just don't see how the needless death of an animal can be justified in this day and age.

In this part of the world, the statistics for lamb deaths as a result of fox predation are three times higher (61 percent) than anywhere else in the U.K. and, as a result, the kill at the end of the hunt remains an important aspect for hunt staff and followers who are also farmers or at least involved in the agricultural industry. Further and unlike foxhunting in many other parts of the U.K. (notwithstanding other farmers' hunts and foot packs), for the members of this particular hunt, "hunting" is not a sport because the aim is always for the fox to die—it must therefore constitute a *sacrifice*. This may appear as a paradox given that sacrifices are ultimately concerned with *negating* violence, and reconciling hunters and herd animals, not predators. As Tim Ingold notes:

> A hunt that is successfully consummated with a kill is taken as proof of amicable relations between the hunter and the animal that has willingly allowed itself to be taken. Hunters are well-known for their abhorrence of violence in the context of human relations, and the same goes for their relations with animals: the encounter, at the moment of the kill, is—to them—essentially *non*-violent. (Ingold 2000a:69)

Although Ingold is referring to subsistence hunting in pre-domestic societies as practiced by the Skolt Laps or Rock Cree, I would suggest that the willingness of my own post-domestic farming informants to participate in the ritualized act of mounted foxhunting demonstrates their desire to overcome the violence that is inherent in their day to day lives as sheep farmers.

Assuaging Guilt and Animals as Actors

Anthropologically, the collective ritualization inherent in the hunting practices of subsistence hunter-gatherer communities whose members are governed by animistic beliefs serves to alleviate the guilt associated with killing another living thing, as well as to appease the animal spirits. Consequently, examples from elsewhere in the ethnographic record may provide useful comparative material, especially where the "rights" of non-human predator species have been "prioritized" over those of domestic livestock (as is the case in the U.K. following the 2004 Hunting Act) and, by association, the humans who rely on domestic animals for survival. A particularly revealing account is that of pastoralist-wolf conflict described by G. Lindquist (2000). Lindquist discusses the ongoing "battle" between the indigenous Saami, a traditional reindeer herding people from Northern Europe, their reindeer herds, and predatory wolves protected by pan-European legislation.

According to Lindquist, the introduction of laws to protect wild predators, including the wolf, in Sweden in the 1960s left the Saami with no means of protecting their herds, and in recent years the situation has deteriorated as Saami protests have escalated (2000:170, 182). The Saami's main argument in defense of their "right" to hunt wolves is that even though other predators such as bear, lynx, and wolverine are responsible for more reindeer losses than wolves, wolf predation is the most challenging for several reasons (Lindquist 2000:179, see also Kruuk 2002:90; cf. Ingold 1980; Vitebsky 2005). Firstly, wolves live and hunt in packs, with a hierarchical social structure not unlike human society (Kruuk 2002). Consequently, wolves are accorded a greater degree of agency than other predators because of their ability to cooperate, and this is reflected in the fearful (and at times hateful) mythology surrounding wolves in Saami and other pastoralist cultures (for example, Lindquist 2000:180; Vitebsky 2005:270–273).

This disproportionate fear of wolves is also based on their perceived ruthlessness. Wolves, like foxes, are renowned for opportunistically killing more animals than they could possibly eat in one sitting (see Ingold 1980:78 on wolves and Marvin 2000:207 on foxes). Further, they are often cited as cruel because they seldom kill outright, instead inflicting a slow, painful death as the victims of predation are frequently eaten alive. Their natural behavior, combined with the culturally constructed intentionality (and therefore culpability) ascribed to wolves by the Saami makes them particularly problematic predators, whose control requires both skill and ritual preparation.

As Lindquist notes, in Saami folklore:

> The wolf-hunt was looked upon as a dangerous struggle, in which hunters risked their lives; it was often emphasized how important it was to kill the wolf with the first blow. A wounded wolf was believed to always get back at the hunter and take his life. This mysterious, frightening power of the wolf also appears in more recent folklore accounts in which . . . the wolf is said to cast spells on the hunter's bullet so that it misses or on the rifle so that it fails to fire. The wolf was ascribed the ability to read a man's mind; the wolf was said to have the strength of one man and the intelligence of ten. The meat of a reindeer killed by a wolf was considered to be contaminated and inedible. (2000:180)

Wolf predation is a major issue for the Saami reindeer herders because the wolf, like the fox in rural Wales, is regarded as "transgressive" or "subversive." In other words, it appears to consciously undermine human activity and human spheres of influence. Like most pastoralists, the Saami regard themselves as "protectors" of their herds, and the same certainly applies to the Welsh sheep farmers studied here. However, the Saami were traditionally hunter-gatherers and, as Ingold (1980:1) notes, the contemporary process of reindeer herding is in many ways reminiscent of hunting practices, as the reindeer are allowed to roam beyond the control of their human owners.

Further, given the commonly accepted hunter-gatherer ontology, it is not surprising that the wolf is regarded as subversive by reindeer pastoralists. As numerous academic commentaries testify, the "animistic" nature of traditional hunter-gatherer beliefs ensured that the hunted animal was accorded respect, that it was killed humanely as a sacrifice, that the body was treated reverently following the kill, and every part consumed or utilized (for example Ingold 1987, 1994; Lawrence 1993; Morris 2000: 105; Serpell and Paul 1994; cf. Ellen 1986; Krech 2000; Milton 1996; Nadasdy 2005).

This ideology persists in practice among many circumboreal reindeer herding pastoralists and other traditionally animistic peoples. However, such "respectful" interaction with hunted (wild or semi-domesticated) or sacrificed (domestic) animals contrasts starkly against wolf predations, which, as Lindquist notes, are seen as cruel and destructive (Lindquist 2000:179, 182), and therefore in breach of both the "waste not want not" hunter-gatherer premise, and the perceived safety of human protective custody of their livestock;

> "Are the bells so you can find them?"
>
> "*Nye-e-et!*" he answered. "I can always find them. They're to warn wolves that the reindeer are protected—there are humans nearby." (Vitebsky 2005:161)

As the indignant response given by Vitebsky's informant demonstrates, this form of domestication continues to rest on a certain degree of trust between humans and their charges and, more importantly, on the fulfillment of mutual responsibilities between hunter-pastoralists and the animals in their *care*. This point will be returned to in due course. But, for the moment, what of mounted foxhunting in west Wales?

Foxhunting as Sacrifice

It would be difficult to argue that contemporary Welsh farming practices are comparable to the techniques and ideologies of pre-domestic hunter-gatherers or indeed, domestic pastoralists. As Ingold notes, the transition from hunting to domestication in many ways negates the trust that characterizes hunter-gatherer relationships with animals, and replaces it with domination (1999b). For farmers to make their living from animal production they can no longer regard them in animistic terms.

Further, unlike traditional reindeer herding peoples for whom shamanism was integral to their culture for centuries prior to the comparatively recent imposition of Christianity, my informants had been brought up according to the dominance of Christian belief and the widespread subscription to the hierarchy of Cartesian dualisms. Indeed, as in many other quarters of the U.K., human mastery over the natural realm has divine and scientific sanction (for example, Macdonald and Johnson 1996:161; Milton 2005:257; Woods 1998:1222). Therefore, as both Gupta (2006) and Marvin (2000, 2002, 2006:12) note, the fox's predatory tendencies make the chase to the death "justified" in the eyes of those who have lost livestock. Consequently, the foxhunt, like the wolf hunt, can be regarded as an act of negative reciprocity which must be ritually avenged to reestablish social order.

Many hunt followers with whom I have spoken, especially hunt servants and members who are sheep farmers, cite the kill as the most important aspect of the mounted foxhunt for them. For example, as one informant who was given responsibility for laying trails in the early days following the implementation of the Hunting Act stated, "Well if a fox gets in the way, tough luck." It took me a long time to appreciate the significance of this.

Indeed, if, as in an animistic worldview (e.g., de Castro 1998; Kohn 2007; Nadasdy 2007; Willerslev 2007), animals are conscious actors, then they can be held accountable for their actions. But more importantly if animal agency is recognized, the deaths of others in human custody (and therefore human "care") must also be avenged. The recognition of this agency problematizes what, despite the "benefits" of domestication, is nonetheless an exploitative relationship. Indeed, the interactions occurring between humans and animals in this context become even more meaningful when considered in terms of social obligations and reciprocal exchange. As Ingold notes:

> The social identity of the pastoral animal is established through the event of birth; the owner of the mother becomes the owner of the living calf [or lamb] on which his property mark is cut. On the occasion of slaughter, it is converted into an anonymous carcass, whose former identity is no longer verifiable nor relevant. The hunted animal on the other hand acquires social significance through the agency of death. (1980:157)

Consequently just as the "social identity" of animals such as sheep is established through their birth, it can also be established or reinforced through their untimely death. The act of fox predation—what Bloch would refer to as the initial act of violence (1991:6)—causes farmers to reevaluate their relationship with the pastoral animals in their care, not merely because of the economic loss in the unplanned death of lambs, but also because it reminds them of their dependence on these animals, and the lack of "respect" accorded to "livestock" as a direct result of the increasingly industrialized approach to contemporary farming.

According to Alexander, "Ritual defined in the most basic terms is a performance, planned or improvised, that effects a transition from everyday life to an alternative context within which the everyday is transformed" (1997:139). Yet if the farmers who participate in this hunt regularly kill animals, why the need for "a transition from everyday life to an alternative context within which the everyday is transformed"? In other words, why does the act of killing a *fox* in the context of a rural Welsh farming community need to be so heavily ritualized, when the act of killing a *sheep,* or more to the point, thousands of sheep, has no pomp and ceremony associated with it?

Sacrifice and Symbolic Dirt

Garry Marvin asserts that the ritual is important because the fox is anomalous (2000)—or as Mary Douglas would say, "matter out of place" (1966)—and therefore needs to be dealt with under the auspice of ritual activity. So ritual serves to safeguard the community, to protect members from the residual pollution that remains following contact with symbolic "dirt." Ritual also serves to propitiate the sacrificial animals. In my own fieldwork context, I agree with Marvin's belief that the fox is anomalous, killing animals otherwise destined for human consumption, but disagree with his suggestion that the fox is problematic and therefore killed in a ritual manner simply "[a]s a result of the relationships which the fox has with *animals* in its world" (2002:154; emphasis added). I argue instead that it is a result of the relationships *humans* have with animals which determines their relationship with the fox.

As James A. Serpell notes:

> [B]ecause they live together in what is, to some extent, a combined social group, it is not unusual for farmers and herdsmen to establish social bonds with their animals and vice versa. The moral dilemma is, therefore, far more intense for the farmer than the hunter, because killing or harming the animal in this context effectively constitutes a gross betrayal of trust. (Serpell 1999a:42)

Such betrayal therefore necessitates the employment of some form of defense or coping mechanism to deal with the contradiction of caring for animals who are raised as commodities destined for human consumption. The most obvious of these is the use of nomenclature such as "livestock," a well-documented distancing device, and the anonymity of intensive agricultural production. For example, many of my informants had several hundred, and some several thousand, head of sheep in their care at any one time. They explained that while they knew certain key individuals (such as former "pet lambs" or difficult breeders), it was overall extremely difficult to identify personally with such a number, and conversely it was easy to objectify the sheep, or think of them as units rather than individual animals.

What Does It Mean to be Human?

In the specific foxhunting ritual under discussion, the fox assumes the position of the sacrificial victim (Bloch 1991), whose blood must be let to restore the natural balance and divine order, or in this case, the divinely ordained privileges of a people who see themselves as the "guardians of the land" (Page 2004:2–3). This distinction between these farmer-hunters (or hunter-pastoralists) and the other animals upon whose blood loss this particular hunting ritual is contingent (sheep and foxes), rests on the unerring "fact" of farming; that humans are, or at least should be, in control.

Indeed, the hunt's followers enact the mounted foxhunt as a *collective* activity so as to reestablish the social order and hierarchical guardianship (or protective custody) of humans over nonhuman (domestic) animals, which has been blurred by the conscious actions of the fox, a wild animal. Jose Ortega y Gasset suggests that hunting "permits the greatest luxury of all, the ability to enjoy a vacation from the human condition" (1972:139) through the "humbling of man [*sic*] which limits his superiority and lowers him towards the animal" (1972:59). In other words, the act of foxhunting is here viewed as a competition with humans at the mercy of their nonhuman quarry.

Far from being a "vacation from the human condition," I would suggest that mounted foxhunting is a performance of what being human means in this specific cultural context. The ritualized act serves to redress the social imbalance between humans (farmers) who have suffered loss as a result of fox predation, the sheep in the farmers' care, who have lost one or more of their number, and the subversive (Marvin 2000:208) or transgressive (Marvin 2006:17) fox. The mounted foxhunt therefore becomes a retributive act to restore the status quo between humans and animals, and the liminal existence of the domesticated (or post-domestic) realm as a hybrid of nature and culture (Haraway 1989). By encroaching onto human-owned land, and killing and eating animals (sheep) destined for human consumption who should "only be killed by humans" (Marvin 2000:206) the fox also assumes a liminal role via his or her own agency—something that seriously challenges and undermines the human farmer's position.

HUNTERS, PASTORALISTS, AND RANCHERS

Serpell's research, which considers the coping mechanisms adopted by farmers, correlates with my own in that our respective informants placed the blame for the lack of protective care they could afford their livestock (and which in the case of my own fieldwork brought about their untimely deaths) on the increasingly intensive nature of livestock production resulting from consumers' desire for cheap meat (1999b:27). Nonetheless, Serpell points out that the farmers he surveyed saw their livestock as "happy" and " 'better off' than wild animals, in the sense of being safer and more comfortable" (1999b:27). Further, and this was a point I frequently encountered, most domestic livestock breeds "would not exist at all if not for farming. In this way, many farmers tended to cast themselves in the role of 'good shepherd,' i.e. as protective and custodial agents, rather than as purely exploitative ones" (1999:27).

In light of this assertion, a consideration of Ingold's distinction between pastoralists and ranchers becomes particularly pertinent. For Ingold "the symbiotic aspect of pastoralism . . . lies primarily in the *protection* of herds" (1980:27) because "pastoral peoples are those who are dependent chiefly on their herds of domesticated stock for subsistence" (Krader 1959:499 in Ingold 1980:82). Although contemporary Welsh sheep farmers are engaged in the commoditization and exchange of their stock, they are nonetheless "dependent" upon them for "subsistence" because their entire way of life is governed by the farming calendar and the needs of their animals, who, in turn, exist to fulfil the needs of their owners in an almost symbiotic relationship (cf. Theodossopoulos 2005). This is in stark contrast to ranchers.

Indeed, while Strickon (1956:230 in Ingold 1980:236) defines "ranching" as "that pattern of land use which is based upon the grazing of live-stock, chiefly ruminants, for sale in a money market," which most certainly applies to the sheep farming I have witnessed in west Wales, it is Ingold's discussion of the relationship between humans and animals in the context of ranching that makes me uneasy about applying the term to many of my informants. When referring to Brazilian cattle ranching for example, Ingold notes that the relationship between ranchers and their cattle is one of "mutual and violent antagonism" (Ingold 1980:237). However, the relationship between my informants and their sheep was paternalistic, and therefore more closely aligned with pastoralism (such as found amongst the Nuer of Sudan or the Eveny of Siberia) where individuals expend a great deal of time and energy caring for their flocks or herds.

Those farmers in the area who felt the *need* to participate in the mounted foxhunting ritual (and many did not) were those who were more "hands-on" (i.e., who did not use contractors, but undertook the day to day care of their stock themselves), who wanted to defend their livestock, and always sought to kill the hunted fox. Unlike "ranchers," however, not one expressed a desire to "embark on *offensive* campaigns aimed directly at the *extermination* of agents of predation" (Ingold 1980:238; emphasis added).

There is no *ritual* involved in other methods of "pest" management such as the laying of traps, poisoning, gassing, or shooting—this is just killing. Consequently, the farmers who participate in the mounted foxhunting *ritual* as pest control activity do so because, unlike ranchers, these individuals recognize a duty of care toward the animals in their custody which obliges them to act in such a manner. This may seem counterintuitive, but if they really did see other animals as objects, then *all* the farmers in this part of rural west Wales would shoot foxes on their land, and this was certainly not the case. Therefore, I argue that farmers who ride to hounds in this context are in actuality those who exist in a pastoral, or what Bulliet terms "domestic," relationship with their "stock" and therefore experience a certain sense of disquiet about farming's inherently exploitative nature, while those who feel no such need for the sacrifice with its accompanying ritual action to propitiate and avenge the loss of animals in their care, represent ranchers. Nonetheless, both relationships are hierarchical in nature, with the human position accorded priority.

Of Scapegoats and Totems

The ability to make a successful living from farming is contingent on the regular, sometimes daily, violence of nonhuman animal death. These animals live on land (which becomes the "field") that in many cases has been farmed by particular families for generations. Further, as a result of long-term breeding programs developed by the same families to improve their quality, it could be argued that sheep represent the ideal metaphorical substitutes for local farmers and vice versa.

While in much of the pro-hunting literature focused on hunts elsewhere in the U.K., the fox is presented as a totemic figure, I suggest it is sheep rather than foxes who should be regarded as the totems of hunt staff and followers in this particular context because it is the human participants who symbolically represent the sheep in their care, and who are transformed during the mounted foxhunt. Their transformation takes the form of prey into hunter. The fox, on the other hand, becomes a scapegoat and is transformed from the hunter to the prey (see also Blau 1987:270; Turner 1982:13; cf. Descola and Palsson 1996:95–96). Therefore, in the ritual realm, the sheep, who are the actual *victims* of fox predation become actors, represented by their human caretakers (who are also victims—their ownership has been undermined by the fox's agency) with the outcome that the human avengers are able to reassert control and reposition themselves in the social hierarchy above other animals, both wild and domesticated (Marvin 2006:12).

In the act of the mounted foxhunt, the followers who are farmers experience a further role reversal (Turner 1982:24). It is no longer they, as humans, who are responsible for the deaths of livestock in their care (See Serpell 1996, 1999a:44), as the sheep are representatives of their own community, or even their own families. Therefore in the ritual realm, the fox becomes, by way of "projective inversion" (Dundes 1991), a scapegoat for the human actions in the mundane (Arluke 1994; Cohen 1994; Ingold 2000) rather than a totem to be revered (cf. Scruton 1998:2).

In this specific mounted foxhunt therefore, the human participants symbolically die in the wake of livestock losses via the act (in the case of hunt staff) of donning blood-red *woolen* (i.e., part-sheep) hunting jackets. These participants then transcend their human existence, assuming the identity of the sheep, yet behaving in an animalistic manner and emulating the activity of the fox who has wronged them. Indeed, hunt supporters frequently assert that this method of fox control is the most "natural" because it mimics the actions of the fox. As Fiona Bowie notes (2006:62–64), rituals are concerned with negotiating the inevitability of death, while for Girard, rituals serve "to purify violence" (1992:36), and for Bloch sacrifice serves to "bring life and death into harmony, to give death the upsurge of life, life the momentousness and the vertigo of death opening onto the unknown" (1986:92); precisely what this particular mounted foxhunting ritual is all about.

Scruton argues that "hunters" engage in what can be described as "inverse anthropomorphism" (1998:101 n.24). The prey becomes a totemic symbol and dies "on behalf of the species and thereby re-consecrates the sacred identity between species and tribe" (1998:101). Conversely, I would draw attention to the fact that during this specific foxhunt, it is the hounds—for whom the fox is a more likely totem (Pardo and Prato 2005:145)—who pursue and actually kill the fox in the main (an outcome which, under the Hunting Act, is illegal), as opposed to the human protagonists, who are at the mercy of the nonhuman actors (Marvin 2002:140). It is this lack of control which is symbolic in this particular context—control has to be regained during the third and final stage of the ritual—after the killing of the sacrificial animals comes the communal meal.

The Communal Meal

According to Bloch (1991), the final stage of the ritual sees the empowerment of the initiands before their return to the mundane. The initiands experience the symbolic violence of the kill (Girard 1992), which is then followed by the communal meal (Detienne and Vernant 1989). Indeed, Bloch notes that in consuming "the vitality of beings external to himself [*sic*]" (1991:87), the individual initiate is able transcend his or her liminality and be reincorporated back into society as control is once again regained. This act of commensality is important for community identity and solidarity, but more importantly for redefining the classificatory boundaries between humans, the livestock in their care who, as Marvin rightly notes, are intended for human consumption (2000:206), and the transgressive fox who has, via "his" agency, brought wider social relations into question. As Daniel Miller observes,

> The third stage of sacrifice is marked . . . by a turning away from the relationship to the divine and a return to the social relations of profane society and the social consequences of sacrifice . . . the emphasis upon classification in regard to the sacrificial victim is only intended to reaffirm the centrality of sacrifice to another classification, which is the social order of . . . society . . . it is the transference of taxonomic order that most effectively reproduces society as a sanctified formation. It is then in this final action of consumption that the power of the transcendent is used to confirm and reify the social relations of the group. (1998:105–106)

Following a day's mounted foxhunting, the final action of consumption for the hunt's followers was, as noted above, *always* a meal of *cawl*—a stew made not with fox flesh but with *lamb*. The use of lamb in *cawl* is a comparatively recent development, resulting from the shift from dairy to sheep-based agriculture locally, and this is significant. Indeed, Detienne and Vernant (1989) are concerned with "the communal meal which follows the sacrifice and the distribution of the portions of the animal . . . as a means of *objectifying the social relations of the community*" (in Miller 1998:80; emphasis added). If all of the hunt's followers partake of the *cawl* provided at the end of a hosted meet, they are demonstrating their solidarity as a social group, sharing the responsibility for the kills, of both fox *and* sheep.

In light of the above discussion, this particular example of foxhunting represents a life-giving ceremony (Eriksen 2001:222) and "always takes place during the cold season . . . [which] establishes a continuity between the . . . ceremony . . . and . . . death" (Eriksen 2001:222). It is no coincidence that the hunting season, as with other agrarian rituals (Turner 1995:177), runs from October to March. In many ways, this too represents the need for continuity between the essentially "life-giving" ritual of the hunt for participants (in the sense that it is enacted to protect their livestock from predation), and the cold winter, when nothing grows, and farmers must feed their stock additional hay and fodder (but also where lone farmers find themselves socially isolated). The hunt therefore also helps to affirm membership within the wider farming community.

CONCLUSION

As has been demonstrated in this chapter, for members of the farmers' hunt, which has been the focus of my fieldwork, the mounted foxhunt is a means of negotiating the fact that humans are responsible for the nonhuman animals they domesticate, but it is those who are faced with (and troubled by) this daily reality for whom the "hunting" ritual is important, and for whom the hunt becomes a sacrifice.

Indeed, this form of mounted foxhunting can also be interpreted as a "social drama," whereby fox predation constitutes the "breach of regular, norm-governed social relations" (Turner 1974:38) between farmers and the fox. This "breach" must then be maintained during a "crisis" period, when a "problem" fox has taken lambs but has yet to be brought under control. This phase is then followed with "redressive action" (1974:39), whereby the ritual is enacted to either kill (sacrifice) or disperse the transgressive animal, and finally, the "*reintegration* of the disturbed social group or of the social recognition and legitimization of irreparable schism between the contesting parties" (1974:41). This final comment is key to the foxhunting ritual in this specific context. Despite my hunter-pastoralist informants' need to hunt (and sacrifice) the fox to protect their flocks, they nonetheless experience a paradoxical need to coexist with foxes. Indeed, as noted above, farmers locally do not seek to eradicate the fox population (foxes are important for managing rabbit populations, which would otherwise decimate crops), and so in the act of following the hunt, humans and the nonhuman participants resume their symbiotic coexistence. For the human participants, the "recognition of irreparable schism" (Turner

1974:41) remains to justify their participation in future hunts, and further identifies this ritual as a form of sacrifice.

The importance of the fox as both sacrificial scapegoat and metaphor for other encroachments, which the hunt's followers, including those who aren't sheep farmers themselves, have to contend with cannot be overemphasized. Indeed, according to Bruce Kapferer:

> It is possible to regard sacrifice as the core process in most forms that anthropologists study as ritual. This might explain the ubiquity of sacrifice, the reason why such action crops up in numerous areas where human beings *encounter challenges to their existence.* (1997:189; emphasis added)

By actively embracing their "traditional" cultural activities the hunt's followers are able to regain control of a key element of their lives. Indeed, Girard observes that "anything that adversely affects the institution of sacrifice will ultimately pose a threat to the very basis of the community, to the principles on which its social harmony and equilibrium depend" (1979:49). In terms of this specific hunting community, its social harmony rests on the need to "exploit" animals, and sheep in particular, even though members do have a duty of care to their charges. Nonetheless, farmers, by their very nature, must interact with animals in an unequal way as they make their living from raising animals for slaughter. "Hunting" feeds into and arises from this relationship.

Therefore, the challenge to mounted foxhunting in this particular cultural context (i.e., its reclassification as illegal following the 2004 Hunting Act) is also a challenge to the local rural way of life. The research of anthropologists in other comparable ethnographic contexts has led them to conclude that traditional rituals experience a resurgence in the face of foreign opposition, or threats from incomers (Hurn 2009; Mitchell 2001; Moore 1994). The increase in the number of what are colloquially referred to as "white settlers" into this part of rural west Wales, the demise of traditional culture and Welsh language, the withdrawal of agricultural subsidies and the 2004 Hunting Act are all factors that, in combination, have created an acute sense of local disempowerment and frustration.

In his fieldwork with the Merina, Bloch found that "some aspects of the [circumcision] ritual adapted functionally to changing politico-economic circumstances, [while] other aspects remained unchanged through time" (1991:1). This realization led Bloch to look for an "irreducible core of the ritual process," which he felt consisted of "a marked element of violence or . . . *conquest*" (1991:4; emphasis added). In the case of mounted foxhunting, this is the conquest of external encroachment onto a traditional way of life by way of fox predation *and* the erosion of local "culture" by some "white settlers" who become metaphorical foxes (see also Hurn 2009). Viewed in such terms, the interactions between humans and animals involved in the mounted foxhunting sacrificial ritual discussed in this chapter become even more symbolic. As Alberto Bouroncle observes:

> Social violence may have a ritual counterpart, in which the participants not only negotiate and confirm their legitimacy and status, but express their ideology and reflect the balance of power in a *certain historical context in a given society.* (2000:58; emphasis added)

While the hunt in question was established in 1953 to enable participants to "negotiate and confirm their legitimacy and status" as newly established freehold farmers released from the shackles of tenancy, and reflected the socioeconomic changes which local residents were experiencing (e.g., nationalistic political mobilization in pursuit of self-governance; the demise of the gentry estates; the rise in freehold farming; the move from dairy to sheep farming and the concomitant change in the status of the fox), the 2004 Hunting Act also came at a time when the balance of power in this particular community was shifting. These more contemporary changes are also in line with wider societal trends and include social and legal changes to the status of animals more generally, the secularization of society, the cultural devaluation of "farming" and the commoditization and globalization of agricultural production.

In the current context, the mounted foxhunting conducted by this farmers' hunt could be seen as an example of what Arjun Appadurai (1996:197) refers to as both an "implosive" and an "explosive" situation. It is "implosive" in the sense that incomers bring with them many of the problems they have run away from (e.g., crime and a lack of neighborliness), and "explosive" because it is through them and their contacts with the "outside" world, that "local" issues, such as "hunting" have been blown out of proportion, and incorporated into "global" or at least, national, interactions and processes.

So in this chapter, the mounted foxhunting ritual has been considered in terms of a rite of passage and a violent sacrificial act. According to Miller, however, "It is not violence per se that is found in sacrifice but the violence of consumption as expenditure. . . . In some cases this may be through sacrifice itself commencing with a spectacle of violent expenditure" (1998:92).

For Miller then, sacrificial violence in the form of *consumption* "becomes the starting-point or premise behind sacrifice" (1998:92). Moreover,

> If we were to grant that destruction is the very essence of sacrifice then it would represent precisely the liberating transgression that Bataille celebrated. . . . The tight technical constraints upon how exactly sacrifice should take place and the rigorous control of important sacrifices suggest that while it may have to evoke this discourse of transgression, the point of the ritual is to negate it as a possibility and ensure that sacrifice is turned back into an ordered relationship to the divine. (1998:93)

Unlike religious sacrifice, the mounted foxhunt enacted in this ethnographic context actively encourages transgression precisely because of the violence inherent in the livestock industry. Indeed, in this particular "hunt as sacrifice," the "divine" becomes synonymous with divinely ordained human control and the ability to care for animals classified as live*stock*. Further, the sacrifice certainly becomes representative of negotiating consumption, but in this case it is the consumption of the totemic sheep during the communal meal, and the reestablishment of the natural hierarchy of humans over both domestic and transgressive wild animals. In such a model, the fox, whose initial subversive consumption instigates the whole ritual, becomes representative of "consumers" in general—those at whose feet the blame for a more intensive approach to animal husbandry is laid. While, conversely, the hunter-pastoralists whose responsibility it is to feed consumer desire for meat are labeled barbaric for "needing" to participate in the propitiatory sacrifice of the foxhunt.

I started my paper with a conversation between The Little Prince and the fox, and it seems fitting to end with one also, for their conversation demonstrates for me the significance of the mounted foxhunt for farmers in this specific farming community in rural west Wales, U.K.: " 'Men have forgotten this basic truth,' said the fox. 'But you must not forget it. *You become responsible, forever, for what you have tamed* " (de Saint-Exupéry 1995:82; emphasis added). This specific mounted foxhunt is a means of negotiating the fact that humans are indeed responsible for the animals they domesticate, but it is those who are faced with (and troubled by) this daily reality for whom the "hunting" ritual is important (cf. Marvin 2006). This is significant in relation to the future of this sacrificial act, which was criminalized by the U.K. government in 2004, leaving participants with even greater difficulty managing (and coping with) their complex and exploitative multispecies interactions.

ACKNOWLEDGMENTS

I would like to express my deepest thanks to Carrie Murray for inviting me to participate in the IEMA conference, for putting on such a wonderful event, for constructive feedback on earlier drafts of this chapter, and for her patience during the intervening period! Thanks are also due to the other participants at IEMA 2011 for some inspirational papers and comments and for helping to clarify some of the issues under discussion here. Of course, I assume sole responsibility for any inaccuracies that may remain!

REFERENCES CITED

Alexander, B. 1997 Ritual and Current Studies of Ritual: an Overview. In *Anthropology of Religion: a Handbook*, edited by S. D. Glazier, pp. 139–160. Greenwood Press, Westport.

Appadurai, A. 1996 *Modernity at Large: the Cultural Dimensions of Globalization*. University of Minnesota Press, Minneapolis.

Arluke, A. 1994 Managing Emotions in an Animal Shelter. In *Animals and Human Society: Changing Perspectives*, edited by A. Manning and J. Serpell, pp. 145–165. Routledge, London.

Bell, M. 1994 *Childerley: Nature and Morality in a Country Village*. University of Chicago Press, Chicago.

Blau, H. 1987 *The Eye of the Prey. Subversions of the Postmodern*. Indiana University Press, Bloomington.

Bloch, M. 1986 *From Blessing to Violence: History and Ideology in the Circumcision Ritual of the Merina of Madagascar*. Cambridge University Press, Cambridge.

Bloch, M. 1991 *Prey into Hunter. The Politics of Religious Experience*. Cambridge University Press, Cambridge.

Bouroncle, A. 2000 Ritual, Violence and Social Order: An Approach to Spanish Bullfighting. In *Meanings of Violence. A Cross Cultural Perspective*, edited by G. Aijmer and J. Abbink, pp. 55–76. Berg, Oxford.

Bowie, F. 2006 *The Anthropology of Religion.* Wiley Blackwell, Oxford.

Bulliet, R. W. 2005 Hunters, Herders, and Hamburgers: The Past and Future of Human-Animal Relationships. Columbia University Press, New York.

Burkert, W. 1983 *Homo Necans: the Anthropology of Ancient Greek Sacrificial Ritual and Myth.* University of California Press, London.

Cohen, A. P. 1994 *Self Consciousness: An Alternative Anthropology of Identity.* Routledge, London.

Davies, C. A., and S. Jones (editors) 2003 *Welsh Communities: New Ethnographic Perspectives.* University of Wales Press, Cardiff.

de Castro, E. V. 1998 Cosmological deixis and Amerindian perspectivism. *Journal of the Royal Anthropological Institute* 4(3):469–488.

de Saint-Exupéry, A. 1995 *The Little Prince.* Wordsworth Classics, London.

Descola, P., and G. Palsson (editors) 1996 *Nature and Society. Anthropological Perspectives.* Routledge, London.

Detienne, M., and J. P. Vernant 1989 *The Cuisine of Sacrifice among the Greeks.* University of Chicago Press, Chicago.

Douglas, M. 1966 *Purity and Danger: an Analysis of Concepts of Pollution and Taboo.* Routledge, Chicago.

Dundes, A. 1991 *The Blood Libel Legend: A Casebook in Anti-Semitic Folklore.* University of Wisconsin Press, Madison.

Ellen, R. F. 1986 What Black Elk Left Unsaid: on the Illusory Images of Green Primitivism. *Anthropology Today* 2(6):8–12.

Eriksen, T. H. 2001 *Small Places, Large Issues: An Introduction to Social and Cultural Anthropology.* Pluto Press, London.

Evans-Pritchard, E. E. 1969 *The Nuer: A Description of the Modes of Livelihood and Political Institutions of a Nilotic People.* Oxford University Press, Oxford.

Franklin, S. 2001 Sheepwatching. *Anthropology Today* 17(3):3–9.

Franklin, S. 2007 *Dolly Mixtures: The Remaking of Genealogy.* Duke University Press, Durham.

Girard, R. 1992 [1972] *Violence and the Sacred.* Johns Hopkins University Press, Baltimore.

Gupta, A. F. 2006 Foxes, Hounds, and Horses: WHO or Which. *Society & Animals* 14(1):107–128.

Haraway, D. 1991 *Simians, Cyborgs, and Women: The Reinvention of Nature.* Routledge, New York.

Hurn, S. 2009 Here Be Dragons? No, Big Cats! Predator Symbolism in Rural West Wales. *Anthropology Today* 25(1):6–11.

Ingold, T. 1980 *Hunters, Pastoralists, and Ranchers.* Cambridge University Press, Cambridge.

Ingold, T. 1987 *The Appropriation of Nature.* University of Iowa Press, Iowa City.

Ingold, T. (editor) 1994a [1988]. *What Is an Animal?* Unwin Hyman, London.

Ingold, T. 1994b From Trust to Domination: an Alternative History of Human-Animal Relations. In *Animals and Human Society: Changing Perspectives*, edited by A. Manning and J. Serpell, pp. 1–22. Routledge, New York.

Ingold, T. 2000 *The Perception of the Environment: Essays in Livelihood, Dwelling and Skill.* Routledge, London.

Kapferer, B. 1997 *The Feast of the Sorcerer. Practices in Consciousness and Power.* University of Chicago Press, Chicago.

Kohn, E. 2007 How Dogs Dream: Amazonian Natures and the Politics of Trans-Species Engagement *American Ethnologist* 34:3–24.

Krech, S. 2000 *The Ecological Indian. Myth and History.* W. W. Norton, New York.

Kruuk, H. 2002 *Hunter and Hunted: Relationships between Carnivores and People.* Cambridge University Press, Cambridge.

Lawrence, E. A. 1993 The Symbolic Role of Animals in the Plains Indian Sun Dance *Society & Animals* 1(1):17–37.

Leach, E. R. 1964 *Anthropological Aspects of Language: Animal Categories and Verbal Abuse.* MIT Press, Cambridge.

Lévi-Strauss, C. 1963 *Totemism.* Beacon, Boston.

Lindquist, G. 2000 The Wolf, the Saami, and the Urban Shaman: Predator Symbolism in Sweden. In *Natural Enemies: People-Wildlife Conflicts in Anthropological Perspective*, edited by J. Knight, pp. 170–188. Routledge, London.

MacDonald, D. W., and D. Johnson 1996 The Impact of Sport Hunting: A Case Study. In *The Exploitation of Mammal Populations*, edited by V. Taylor and N. Dunstone, pp. 160–207 Chapman and Hall, London.

Marvin, G. 2000 The Problem of Foxes: Legitimate and Illegitimate Killing in the English Countryside. In *Natural Enemies: People-Wildlife Conflicts in Anthropological Perspective*, edited by J. Knight, pp. 189–212. Routledge, London.

Marvin, G. 2001 Cultured Killers: Creating and Representing Foxhounds *Society & Animals* 9(3):273–292.

Marvin, G. 2006 Wild Killing: Contesting the Animal in Hunting. In Animal Studies Group, *Killing Animals*, pp. 10–29. University of Illinois Press, Chicago.

Miller, D. 1998 *A Theory of Shopping.* Polity Press, Cambridge.

Milton, K. 1996 *Environmentalism and Cultural Theory: Exploring the Role of Anthropology in Environmental Discourse.* Routledge, New York.

Milton, K. 2005 Anthropomorphism or Egomorphism? The Perception of Non-Human Persons by Human Ones. In *Animals in Person: Cultural Perspectives on Human-Animal Intimacies*, edited by J. Knight, pp. 255–271. Berg, New York.

Mitchell, J. P. 2001 *Ambivalent Europeans: Ritual, Memory, and the Public Sphere in Malta.* Routledge, London.

Moore, R. S. 1994 Metaphors of Encroachment: Hunting for Wolves on a Central Greek Mountain *Anthropological Quarterly* 67(2):81–88.

Morris, B. 2000 *The Power of Animals. An Ethnography.* Berg, Oxford.

Nadasdy, P. 2005 Transcending the Debate over the Ecologically Noble Indian: Indigenous Peoples and Environmentalism. *Ethnohistory* 52(2):291–331.

Nadasdy, P. 2007 The Gift in the Animal: The Ontology of Hunting and Human-Animal Sociality *American Ethnologist* 34(1):25–43.

Ortega y Gasset, J. 1972 *Meditations on Hunting.* Scribner, New York.

Page, R. 2004 *The Fox and the Orchid.* Swan Hill Press, Shropshire.

Pardo, I., and G. Prato 2005 The Fox-Hunting Debate in the United Kingdom: A Puritan Legacy? *Human Ecology Review* 12(2):143–155.

Rappaport, R. A. 2000 *Pigs for the Ancestors: Ritual in the Ecology of a New Guinea people.* Waveland Press, Illinois.

Scruton, R. 1998 *On Hunting.* Random House, London.

Serpell, J. A. 1999a Working out the Beast: An Alternative History of Western Humaneness. In *Child Abuse, Domestic Violence, and Animal Abuse: Linking the Circles of Compassion for Prevention and Intervention*, edited by F. Ascione and P. Arkow, pp. 38–49. Purdue University Press, West Lafayette, Indiana.

Serpell, J. A. 1999b Sheep in Wolves' Clothing? Attitudes to Animals among Farmers and Scientists. In *Attitudes to Animals: Views in Animal Welfare*, edited by F. L. Dolins, pp. 26–33. Cambridge University Press, Cambridge.

Serpell, J. A., and E. S. Paul 1994 Pets and the Development of Positive Attitudes to Animals. In *Animals and Human Society: Changing Perspectives,* edited by A. Manning and J. A. Serpell, pp. 127–144. Routledge, London.

Theodossopoulos, D. 2005 Care, Order, and Usefulness: The Context of the Human-Animal Relationship in a Greek Island Community. In *Animals in Person: Cultural Perspectives on Human-Animal Intimacy,* edited by J. Knight, pp. 15–36. Berg, Oxford.

Tuan, Y. 1984 *Dominance and Affection: The Making of Pets.* Yale University Press, London.

Turner, E. 1992 *Experiencing Ritual.* University of Pennsylvania Press, Philadelphia.

Turner, V. 1982 *From Ritual to Theatre: The Human Seriousness of Play.* PAJ Publications, New York.

Turner, V. 1995 *The Ritual Process: Structure and Anti-Structure.* Transaction, Aldine.

Van Gennep, A. 1960 *The Rites of Passage.* Routledge and Keegan Paul, London.

Vitebsky, P. 2005 *Reindeer People: Living with Animals and Spirits in Siberia.* Harper Collins, London.

Willerslev, R. 2007 *Soul Hunters: Hunting, Animism, and Personhood among the Siberian Yukaghirs.* University of California Press, Berkeley.

Woods, M. 1998 Researching Rural Conflicts: Hunting, Local Politics, and Actor Networks. *Journal of Rural Studies* 14(3):321–340.

PART II

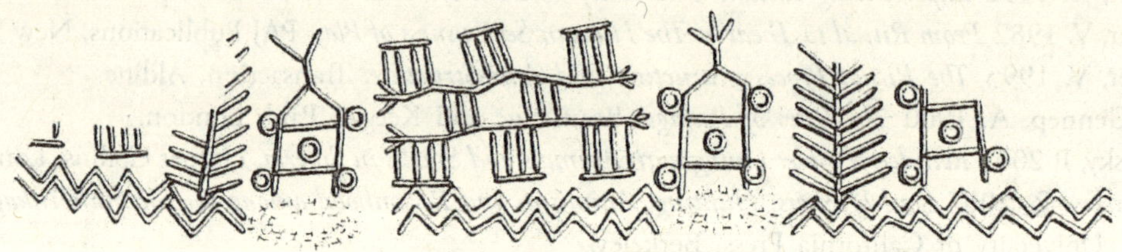

Sacrifice across the Mediterranean World

CHAPTER FIVE

Every Good and Pure Thing

Sacrifice in the Ancient Egyptian Context

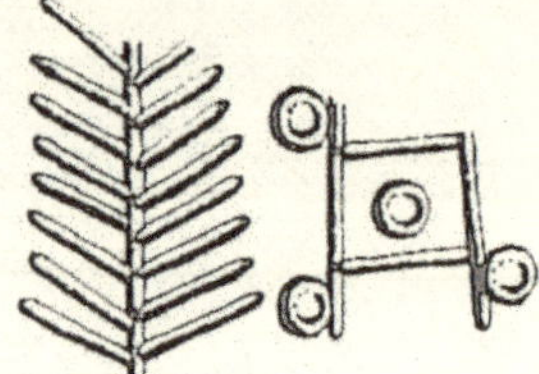

Mary-Ann Pouls Wegner

Abstract *Significant traces of sacrificial activity are preserved in the archaeo-logical and inscriptional record from ancient Egypt. While the evidence of such activity that derives from temple and tomb contexts has been studied extensively, however, the data from other kinds of contexts have received far less attention. In this cultural context ordinary people interacted with their deities primarily via processional festivals in which images of the gods were carried out of their dwell-ing-places in the temple sanctuaries and out into the surrounding villages. As a result, the peripheral areas around temple enclosures and the routes of processions that led through the adjacent landscapes form important loci of votive activity by both elite and nonelite sectors of the population. Depositions of material that comprised offerings to the gods within those extramural contexts replicate social structures in their spatial patterning, and also served as a mechanism for negotiat-ing an individual's place in society. This paper will examine the evidence relating to patterns in the deposition of material culture associated with sacrifices for the god Osiris as a means for understanding ancient social structures and the role of offerings in the construction of social identity.*

In his volume on Greek votive offerings, William Henry Rouse defined "sacrifices" as offerings of perishable commodities, in contrast to enduring memorials that were, in his view, more properly designated "votive objects" (1901:1). Material culture remains from ancient Egyptian contexts in fact reflect much more complex phenomena associated with offering behavior, in which both impermanent and enduring elements were combined in a single act of veneration. Perishable commodities were often presented to a divine or deceased recipient in pottery, wood, or stone containers designed to withstand the ravages of time, sometimes inscribed with the name of the donor, commemorating the gift and its accompanying prayer to a deity or intercessor, hence involving presentation of a stable material object (votive vessel), foodstuffs or unguents subject to short-term decay (sacrifice), and an even more fleeting set of utterances and actions that comprised the ritual involved in making the offering (performance). However, while Rouse's distinction between sacrificial and votive materials may be artificial, it is nonetheless useful in that it points to a significant feature of the archaeological record from Egypt: vessels can act as indicators of sacrificial activity, and their depositional contexts preserve information about the rituals associated with the presentation of offerings that is not accessible through the inscriptional or pictorial record. As Geraldine Pinch has noted, "A votive offering is not simply an artifact, it is the surviving part of an act of worship" (1993:339). Consequently, the analysis of sacrificial containers has immense potential to enrich the meager information we have about "personal piety" and the negotiation of social identity through votive behavior in the ancient Egyptian context.

ROYAL OFFERINGS: PATRONAGE

Scenes of the king offering sacrifices to the gods constitute the overwhelming majority of depictions in Egyptian temple contexts. The king was construed as the son of each deity with whom he interacted, and the depicted relationship thus forms a model for filial piety. In addition to commodities such as food and drink offerings, incense (as shown in Figure 5.1), linen cloth, jewelry, eye paint, and perfumed oils, which are replicated at the nonroyal level in tomb invocations, the king may also be depicted in such contexts surrendering a more abstract and intangible gift to the deities: the iconographic representation of *ma'at* (truth, justice, order). In the highly symbolic semiotic system of the temple, *ma'at* takes the form of a small statue of a seated goddess with an ostrich feather headdress (see Figure 5.2). In the Late Bronze Age temple of Seti I at Abydos, for example, the king presents *ma'at* to solar deities such as Amon-Re, Re-Horakhti, and Montu, as well as to Osiris (Calverley 1938:Pls. 4, 16, 21, 22; Calverley 1958:Pls. 10, 33B). In the accompanying texts associated with such representations of the offering of *ma'at*, the divine recipient is often said to "live on *ma'at*," a phrase that aligns cosmic order with other commodities providing nourishment to the deity (Helck 1980:1113; Teeter 1997).

In the reciprocal relationship between the king and the gods, which is expressed in visual iconography and formulaic texts in the decorative program of all known temples, the king provides offerings and in exchange receives divine legitimation: the power to rule the Egyptian state. The ruler could also be depicted providing offerings and veneration to ancestors, sometimes accompanied by his designated successor, as in the scene accompanying the famous kinglist from Abydos (Figure 5.3). This activity highlighted his genealogical relationship to all previous kings going back into primordial times. Within the semiotic system of the temple, then, sacrifice functions as the mechanism through which the king reaffirmed his position within the social order. Because the ruler was ultimately responsible for building temples and maintaining cult institutions, the king

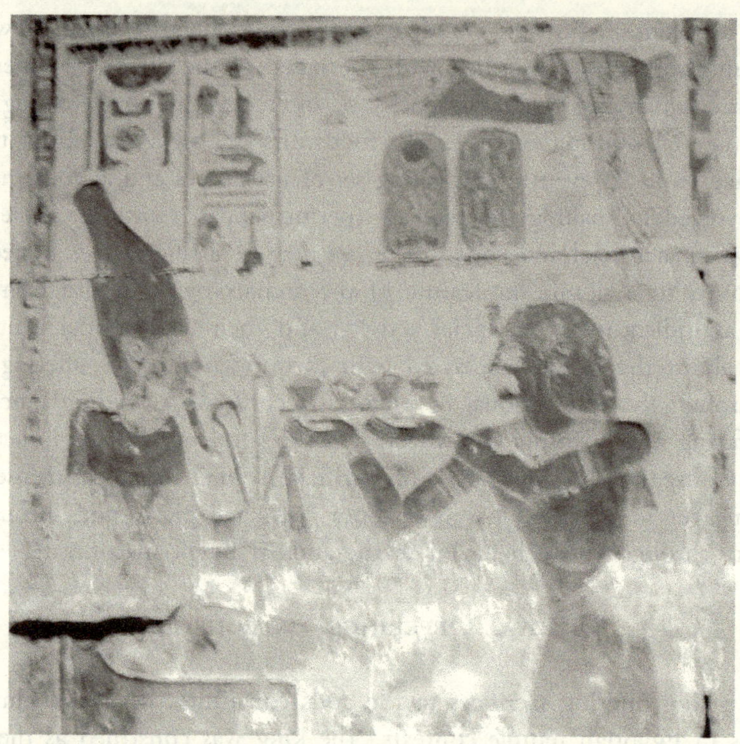

FIGURE 5.1 Seti I presenting offerings to the deity Osiris, temple of Seti I, Abydos *ca.* 1294-1279 B.C.E. (author's photo).

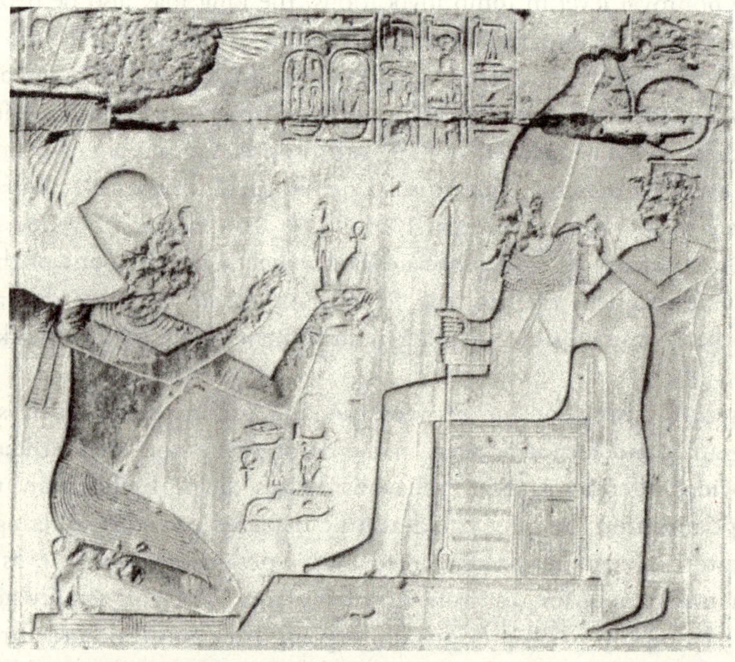

FIGURE 5.2 Seti I offering an image of *Ma'at* to the deity Osiris, temple of Seti I, Abydos *ca.* 1294-1279 B.C.E. (Calverley 1938: Pl. IV).

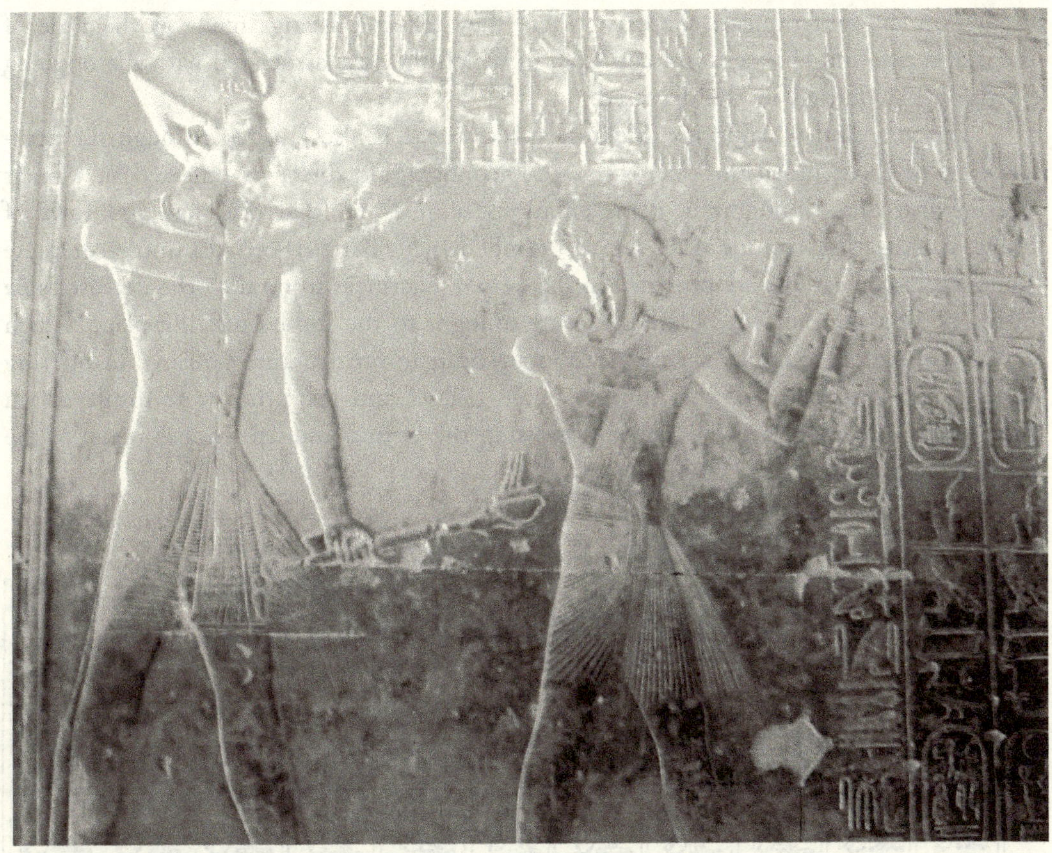

FIGURE 5.3 Seti I and Ramesses II offering before the names of preceding kings of Egypt, temple of Seti I, Abydos *ca.* 1294-1279 B.C.E. (author's photo).

was an active participant in the construction of these scenes through which he negotiated his social identity.

SACRIFICE IN THE MORTUARY CONTEXT

Just as the depictions of the ruler offering appropriate sacrifices to the gods legitimated his political authority and social preeminence, elites highlighted their contributions to social order as a means of reifying their own position. These deeds included providing offerings to the mortuary cults of their ancestors, as well as giving commodities such as food, drink, and clothing to the needy, and acting as useful administrators for the state. The setting for the provision of mortuary offerings was the tomb, the resting place for the *ka* or "spirit," rather than the temple, dwelling place of the god. Archaeological remains associated with burials provide evidence of ancient sacrifice in the form of faunal and botanical deposits that comprised offerings of food for the deceased. These depositions occur both in subterranean contexts, where they reflect offerings made at the time of the interment, and aboveground contexts, in which they are associated with the ongoing provision of offerings to the deceased.

The provision of offerings in elite tomb contexts is also enacted through the actualization of these provisions in textual and iconographic form, as reflected in tabular offering lists and iconographic representations of piles of food offerings and rows of individuals bearing commodities for the tomb owner (Barta 1963). Examples of these iconographic depictions are provided in Figure 5.4. Sacrifices to nourish the deceased's *ka* in the perilous journey to the afterlife were brought to the tomb's offering place, which could be a simple marker or a more elaborate built tomb structure housing an offering table as the focal point of the mortuary cult. Scenes and texts that were displayed on such monuments solicited sacrifices by stressing the virtues and accomplishments of the deceased.

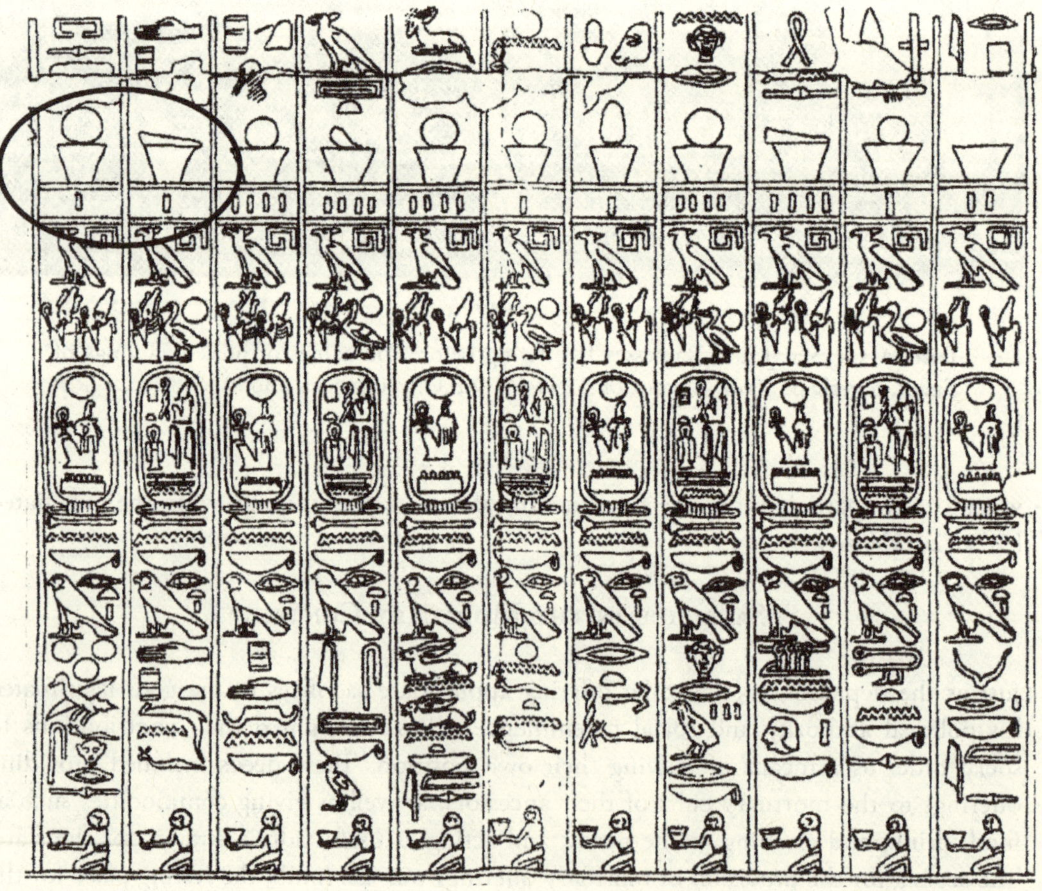

FIGURE 5.4 Tabular offering list, temple of Seti I, Abydos *ca.* 1294-1279 B.C.E. (Calverley 1935: Pl. 32).

The position of the tomb itself within the landscape, which was often closely circumscribed by the state, as well as the incorporation of royal gifts of architectural elements and statuary in the tomb structure, and the listing of administrative titles, could all provide tangible evidence of the deceased's social standing that might elicit the provision of offerings by the living. Conversely, the provision of offerings by family members and even passers-by actually enhanced the status of the deceased by affirming that he or she possessed the virtues described in the autobiographical text and concurrently providing him or her with the nourishment that ensured a successful postmortem transformation.

The Egyptian sources include funerary formulae and offering lists that specify and sometimes quantify the commodities to be given to the *ka* of the deceased in order to sustain it on the dangerous journey to the blessed afterlife. The formulae in their simplest form include one thousand units of each of the staples necessary for the *ka*: bread and beer, oxen and fowl, ointment and clothing, and every good and pure thing (Barta 1986). In some cases the inscriptions on the walls and other components of elite tombs explicitly enjoin anyone passing by the tomb to provide these offerings through verbal recitation (Müller 1975). An example of such an appeal to the living is preserved on the *verso* of the stele of Sehetep-ib-Re from Abydos (Cairo 20538, ca. 1835 B.C.E.):

> The prince, count, royal seal-bearer, temple-overseer Sehetep-ib-Re, he says: "O beloved of the king, favorite of his city-god, priests of Osiris Foremost of the Westerners in Abydos, hour-priests of this god, priests of King Nimaatre, may he live forever, and of Khakaure, justified . . . all people of Abydos, who shall pass by this monument . . . as you love your king, as you praise your city-gods, as your children remain in your place, as you love life and abhor death, may you say: 'A thousand of bread and beer, oxen and fowl, ointment and clothing, incense, unguent, and all kinds of herbs, and all kinds of offerings upon which a god lives, for the *ka* of the revered prince, count, royal seal-bearer . . . Sehetep-ib-Re.'" (Lichtheim 1976:128)

In the stele text, the invitation to invoke offerings is addressed to a hierarchically ordered list of individuals, namely: officials in the royal court, those who hold high priestly offices in their hometowns, then two levels of priests in the local temple institution of Osiris at Abydos, followed by priests of the reigning king and then those who serve in the mortuary cult of the deceased king, and finally any other members of the general local populace who might be able to read the inscription or hear it read aloud by a priest or official. Interestingly, the text addresses nonelites from the local Abydos area as well as courtiers and priests from a broader catchment area to participate in the invocation of offerings for the deceased.

The orality of the sacrificial performance is explicit in the text; the inscription encourages visitors to utilize recitation as the preferred vehicle for providing offerings for Sehetep-ib-Re's *ka*. The provision of offerings does not involve differential access to resources, since the means of supplying them is available to all. The receipt of such sacrifices furthers the deceased's goal of achieving eternal life through the ongoing repetition of his name and titles, and the act of invoking offerings for him highlights his fitness to attain the blessed afterlife and further enhances his status as a member of that realm. Through patronage of offerers from many different socioeconomic levels, the tomb owner's elite identity continues to be constructed and his possession of the virtues that will allow his *ka* to pass successfully through the final judgment into the eternal afterlife is reasserted on an ongoing basis.

In addition to its beneficial effect on the *ka* of the deceased, the stele text also conveys the underlying value of the sacrificial performance as a means of promoting the social standing of the offerer. The inscription cites the core values of elite culture as a means of motivating the intended audience to perform the invocation. The values specified include loyalty to the king and to local deities, the ability to bequeath administrative office (and its associated livelihood) to one's children, and even life itself. In explicitly invoking these characteristics the inscription simultaneously implies that the fulfillment of the invitation to invoke offerings for the deceased will demonstrate the offerer's commitment to king, local gods, children, and life, thereby highlighting his or her moral rectitude and justifying his or her own social standing, ultimately ensuring that the desired rights to succession and life are upheld.

In complying with the solicitation for sacrifice, the audience to whom the invitation in the stele text was addressed enacted a performative sacrifice consisting of a spoken invocation of offerings. There would also have been an audience for the invocation, whether composed of living individuals (as in the case of a priest reading the written text aloud to illiterate listeners) or divine observers (who might be in a position to judge the offerer at the divine tribunal that would take place after his or her death). The *ka* of the deceased was also envisioned as both present at the recitation and ultimate recipient of the invoked sacrifice. The sacrifice itself served to align the performer of the invocation with the elite recipient and by extension with the divinely sanctioned state administration in general, thereby enhancing his or her own socioeconomic status as well. It would even, the text implies, have a bearing on his or her own successful postmortem transformation.

Votive Behavior Associated with Temple Contexts

Pinch's 1993 study of votive offerings to Hathor, a goddess associated with love, fertility, music, and sensuality, represents the most sophisticated research carried out to date on the evidence relating to sacrifice and votive behavior in association with the worship of deities in the ancient Egyptian cultural context. She divides the actions of visitors to temples into three categories: prayer, sacrifice, and the dedication of votive offerings (1993:333). This division follows Rouse's notion of sacrifice involving perishable commodities, while votive offerings involve more enduring forms of material culture. In fact, votive monuments of elite individuals from New Kingdom temple contexts preserve evidence of the occurrence of a range of sacrificial activities carried out in association with temple deities, which included libation with wine, beer, milk, or water, burning of incense, and the presentation of bread and other foodstuffs, fruit, flowers, scented oils and unguents. Such perishable commodities leave only fugitive traces in the archaeological record. However, the transport of many types of sacrificial goods to the temple site, such as scented oils and liquids for libation, required the use of containers. These containers were most often made of pottery, as both the archaeological and iconographic evidence attests. While the contents of such containers were perishable, the containers themselves were not. Furthermore, in some cases the containers were inscribed with the name of a donor, commemorating the gift and accompanying prayer of an individual to the deity. Hence, while such vessels can be identified as votive objects, they also correlate directly with acts of sacrifice, and they provide an archaeologically recoverable marker of past sacrificial activity.

The process of making a sacrifice to the goddess Hathor is described in an engaging text preserved on the statue of Tjau (British Museum AN401576001), an elite official of the Ramesside Period who held the titles of Royal Butler and priest of Hathor. This individual was revered after his death as an intercessor or local "saint" in the area of Deir el-Bahari, where Hathor was especially venerated. The statue was positioned just inside the temple precinct of the mortuary complex of Nebhepetre Mentuhotep, an earlier king from the time of the Eleventh Dynasty. It bears the following inscription: "I am the ritual-priest of Hathor, who listens to the petitions of every young girl who weeps and who trusts in Hathor. Place perfumed oil upon my forehead, and beer for my mouth, bread and beer from what you offer, place offerings in front of [me]; then I shall speak to Hathor, [for] she has listened to what is repeated" (Naville 1913:pl. 9A; Pinch 1993:333).

In the statue text, the elite priest claims a share of the offerings brought to Hathor, and the placement of his statue within the temple precinct is a geographical marker of his privileged status as a priest and a member of the social elite. The statue effectively marked the boundary beyond which ordinary Egyptians could not pass. Furthermore, it is not likely that a young girl would have been able to read the inscription on the statue, since literacy rates for women were extremely low in Egypt during the pharaonic period (Baines 1983:384; Baines and Eyre 1983; Baines 2007:172–173). The assistance of a living priest of the temple would have been required for the petitioner to access the services of the intermediary Tjau. A priest would also have conveyed the offerings to the deity in the temple sanctuary, an area that the petitioner could not access. Both the priest and the statue owner mediated the process of offering sacrifice to Hathor, and both took a "cut" of the offerings that girls brought to the goddess. The visits of petitioners thus reinforced their social standing and provided direct material benefits in accordance with their relative importance in the intercessory process.

The lovesick young girls whom Tjau's text identifies as petitioners of Hathor are instructed in the presentation of liquid offerings (perfumed oil and beer) as well as solid commodities (bread) to the intercessor in exchange for his mediation with the goddess on their behalf. The sacrifices in liquid state would have been carried to the temple from the neighboring villages or perhaps purchased at the temple, but in either case they would have required pottery vessels for transportation. In fact, dense concentrations of small utilitarian ceramic containers have been found around the periphery of royal mortuary complexes from the Early Bronze Age through the Iron Age in Egypt, including the Early Dynastic tombs and enclosures at Abydos (O'Connor 2009:142–188), the pyramid complexes of the Old Kingdom at Giza (Petrie 1890:25; Reisner and Smith 1955:86–87), those of the Middle Kingdom at Dahshur and Kahun (Petrie 1890:25) and Abydos (Wegner 2007:231–287), and the New Kingdom royal mortuary complexes of Deir el-Bahari (Pinch 1993) and Abydos (Frankfort, de Buck, and Gunn 1933:24; Pouls Wegner 2011).

The Humble *Weskhet*-dish

Simple pottery votive dishes such as that shown in Figure 5.5, called *weskhet* in ancient Egyptian (Gardiner 1957:Signlist W10), statistically dominate the ceramic corpus of both temple and cemetery sites in Egypt. However, a systematic analysis of the vessels has not yet been undertaken. There are a number of reasons for this situation, including the static nature of the form, the coarse and utilitarian nature of the vessels, and their association with extramural contexts. The form itself remained remarkably consistent over

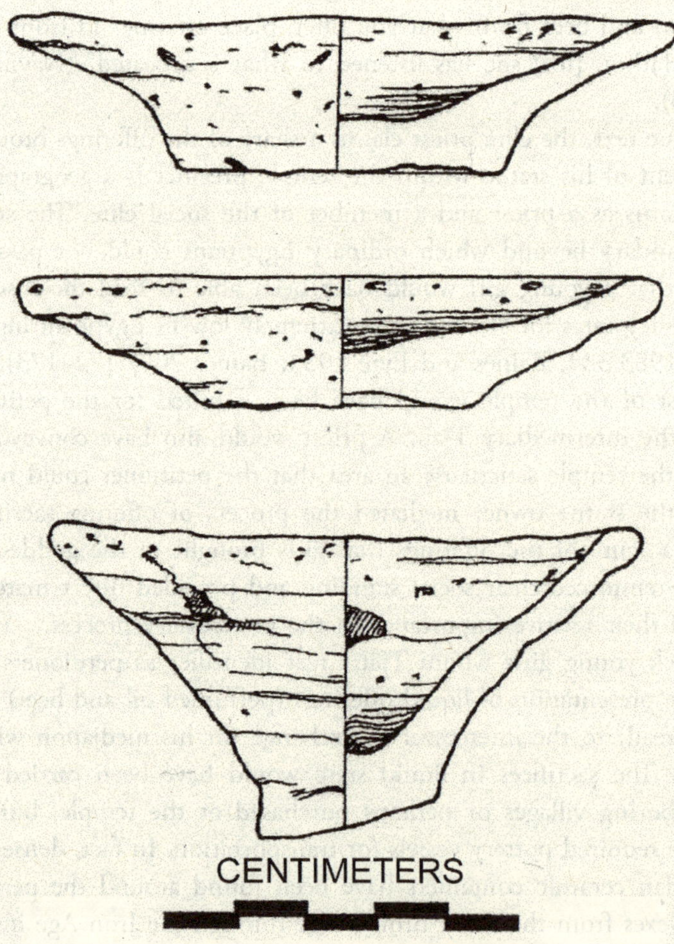

FIGURE 5.5 Excavated examples of *weskhet*-vessels from the Abydos Votive Zone site, New Kingdom/Late Bronze Age *ca.* 1550–1069 B.C.E. (drawings by author).

time, and hence does not display the clear morphological variability that would make it a useful chronological marker in archaeological depositions. Votive dishes were utilized for most of the pharaonic period, spanning more than 3,500 years, with only the most subtle changes of form evident over that time. Their manufacture reflects technological advances in ceramic production from hand-forming to the slow wheel and ultimately to the fast wheel, but these techniques were not accompanied by significant modifications to the vessel shape. The fact that the form remained static over time, despite changes in manufacturing technique, strongly suggests the deliberate retention of a form that came to signify "offerings." The standardized depiction of the vessel type in temple scenes and on mortuary monuments supports the interpretation of the form as an iconographic element charged with semantic power and inextricably linked with the offering ritual.

Another factor that may have played a role in the lack of attention devoted to the votive dish as an artifact type is the coarse, undecorated quality of the vessels themselves. They are made of Nile clay, tempered with chaff and fired at a low temperature. The wheel-made examples show no effort to smooth away rilling lines or the marks from the string that was used to cut them off the wheel. These characteristics indicate that the vessels were mass-produced and utilitarian in nature, and they have accordingly not been the subject of art-historical scrutiny. But it is perhaps the archaeological context of these humble vessels that has played the most significant role in their omission from the majority of discussions of sacrificial or votive activity in Egypt; they are found in greatest quantities outside the gateways of temple enclosures, in foundation deposits and rubbish dumps associated with cult structures, along processional routes, and around the superstructures of tombs and simple inhumation burials. Such extramural contexts have received far less attention than the temples and subterranean burial chambers that comprise the traditional foci of Egyptological interest.

The vessel type occurs in the Neolithic period (Eiwanger 1984:IV.53–56, 145, 166–168, 273–274, 352–353, 491–504; Randall-MacIver and Mace 1902:pl. VIII, R24), and it formed one of the main artifact types included in Early Dynastic royal burials of the nascent Egyptian state (Bestock 2009:Fig. 29). From at least the time of the Old Kingdom onward, the *weskhet*-vessel was closely associated with sacrificial offerings in general. The inscription of the formulaic list of offerings in tombs, which developed in the Fifth Dynasty (Barta 1963:710), was accompanied by the deposition of sets of small ceramic or stone vessels in the burial chamber. Junker first noted the correlation between the listed commodities and the vessel types associated with such mortuary contexts (1929:108–109). In fact, the offering lists themselves express the association of the votive dish form with sacrifice; in the tabular mortuary offering list illustrated in Figure 5.4, for example, a depiction of the *weskhet*-vessel occurs at the base of the vast majority of entries listing individual commodities to be supplied to the *ka* of the deceased. Its frequency of depiction in such contexts suggests that the vessel type was used to hold many different kinds of commodities, including offerings in both liquid and solid states. By the Middle Kingdom a depiction of the vessel alone could function as a signifier for offerings of all kinds. The sign would have been immediately recognizable to both literate and illiterate members of the population, and its use in the lunette of stele monuments such as Munich GL WAF 43, Florence 2590, and Berlin 7287 (Simpson 1974:ANOC 44.1, 44.2, 65.4), as shown in Figure 5.6, highlights the symbolic function of the vessel form and its general legibility.

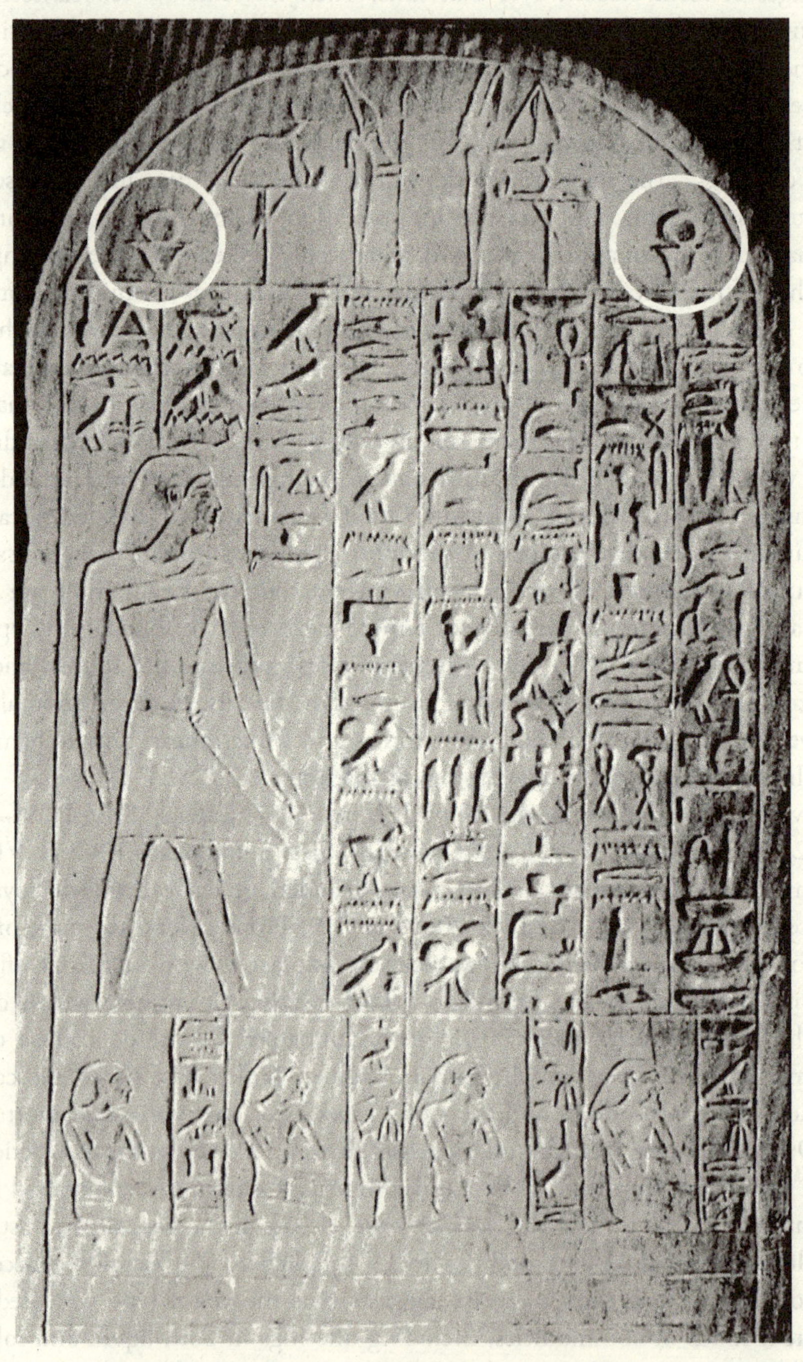

FIGURE 5.6 Stele from Abydos with *weskhet*-vessels in lunette, Middle Kingdom *ca.* 2055-1650 B.C.E. (adapted from Simpson 1974: ANOC 44.4, Pl. 63).

The association of the simple votive dish with sacrificial offerings was also retained in nonmortuary contexts. Specifically, the area where offerings were presented to the deity or deceased king in cult and royal mortuary temple complexes was designated by the term *weskhet,* often translated as "broad hall" or "outer court" (Spencer 1984:71–80). These areas are precisely the locations in which offerings contained in *weskhet*-vessels would have been presented to the deity. The earliest architecturally identifiable *weskhet* occurs in the temple of the Fifth Dynasty king Neferirkare at Abusir, which contained an altar upon which offerings were placed (Spencer 1984:73). Continuity of the term's correlation with the offering of sacrifice is attested in the references to the *weskhet n hwt Bnbn* ("offering-court of the temple of the Benben") in the Great Aten Temple that Akhenaten constructed at Amarna in the New Kingdom, an open courtyard that was filled with row after row of altars upon which offerings were heaped for the nourishment of the solar deity Aten (Spencer 1984:76).

ABYDOS: A CASE STUDY

Mortuary and cult practices intersected in the context of the major temple institution at Abydos. The site was the cult center of Osiris, Foremost of the Westerners, a god of death and resurrection, who became the archetype for the postmortem transformation to which all Egyptians aspired. Accordingly, his ceremonial center developed into a place of pilgrimage as well as royal patronage (Simpson 1974:3–13). An annual festival took place at the site in which the events of the god's death and regeneration were reenacted in the geographical landscape of Abydos (O'Connor 2009:70ff.). In the Middle Kingdom and subsequent periods, a procession in which an image of the god traveled up the path of a natural wadi or arroyo led from the divine "dwelling" in the temple into the desert. The murder of the god at the hands of his enemies was dramatically recreated along the course of the journey; then, at the site of the notional "tomb" of Osiris, the god was mystically regenerated and traveled back amid general rejoicing to the temple again.

The performative rituals associated with the Osiris festival provided a means for individuals from many different socioeconomic levels to interact with the deity. Inscriptional evidence indicates that these participants identified themselves as supporters of Osiris and followers of his son, the champion and rightful heir, Horus. They sought to participate in the festival and receive a share of the offerings presented to Osiris through the construction of offering chapels and the erection of inscribed stone stelae at the site (Simpson 1974:11–13).

Differential access to the procession is evident in the spatial patterning that exists among the monuments that visitors erected to establish an enduring presence at the site and ensure their eternal participation in the regenerative rituals enacted there. Elites constructed tomb-like offering chapels at the entrance to the processional route in the area adjacent to the Osiris temple temenos known as the "Votive Zone" (shown in Figure 5.7). Access to the processional route was carefully controlled by the state. The Middle Kingdom stele of Neferhotep, which was erected to mark a geographical boundary of the sacred space at the entrance to the processional route, provides evidence of the

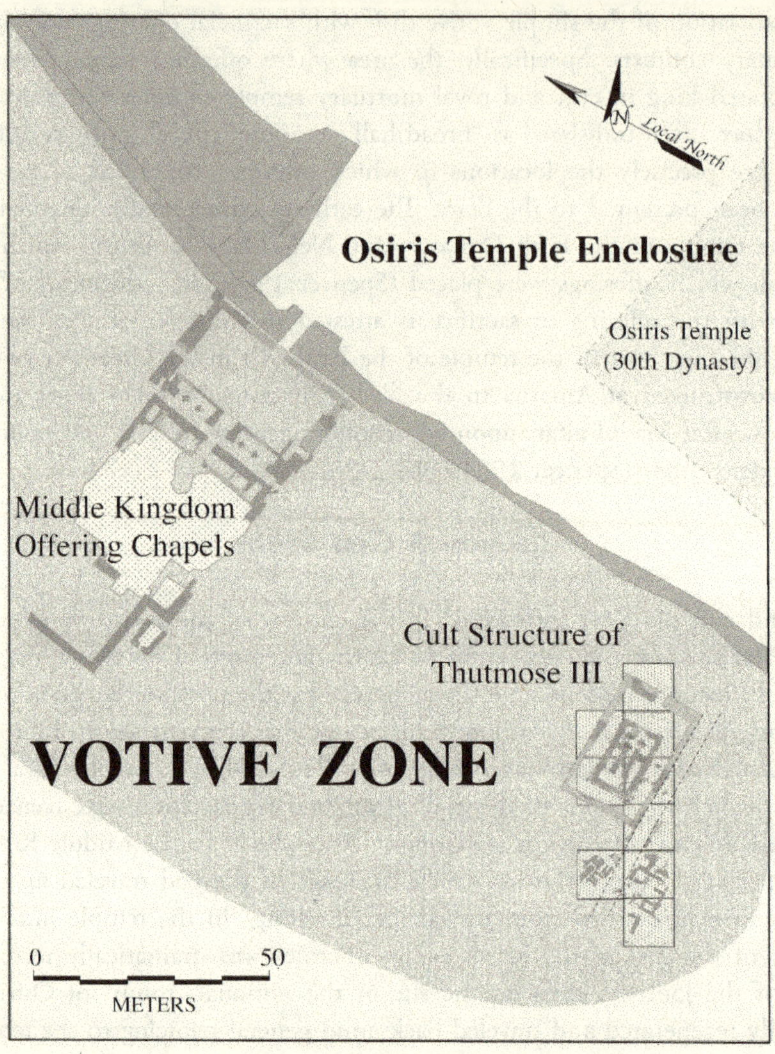

Figure 5.7 The Votive Zone Area in North Abydos (survey and graphics by author).

role of the state in the circumscription of space through the manipulation of the built environment of the site. The royal monument served to delimit circumscribed areas in which private construction activity was strictly prohibited and trespassing was punishable by death (Leahy 1989). The two chapels of Thutmose III, discovered at the site of the Votive Zone in the course of archaeological research under the auspices of the Pennsylvania-Yale-Institute of Fine Arts Expedition in 1996 and 1999, likely served a similar function in the New Kingdom (Pouls Wegner 2012:177–179).

Over time in the Votive Zone area, the core elite chapels situated in prime locations overlooking the processional route became surrounded by a dense accretion of smaller chapels belonging to family members, dependents, and associates of those elites

(O'Connor 2009:95–96). The hierarchical spatial organization of the built environment at the periphery of the Abydos Osiris Temple was replicated on the stone stelae that were erected there, in which elite owners are depicted in the upper registers, and subordinates who participate in the god's victory through the patronage of the dedicator are represented in lower registers. The monuments themselves thus clearly expressed and simultaneously enhanced the elite owner's status as a benefactor who enabled those of lesser resources to access the divine.

Alongside the inscriptional and architectural data relating to royal, elite, and subaltern activity at the site, material culture remains in the Votive Zone also preserve evidence of sacrifice in the form of pottery containers. Spatial patterning is also discernable in the accumulations of such containers, and in particular the votive *weskhet*-dishes so closely linked with the presentation of offerings. The densest deposits of these vessels, such as that associated with the Votive Zone chapel of Thutmose III (Pouls Wegner 2011), provide indications of the specific loci where offerings were presented by individuals from many different socioeconomic levels of society. Shifts in these localities occurred over time, indicating changes in the patterns of human movement through the landscape, variations in access to different areas, and perhaps also alterations to the festival itself.

CONCLUSIONS

In a culture in which ordinary people interacted with their deities primarily through participation in processional festivals, when images of the gods were carried from their dwelling-places in the temple sanctuaries out into the surrounding villages, the peripheral areas around temple enclosures and procession routes in adjacent landscapes became important loci of votive activity for both elite and nonelite sectors of the population. This paper has explored some of the ways in which performative activity associated with sacrifice served as a mechanism for negotiating an individual's place in ancient Egyptian society, based on textual and iconographic sources associated with major components of the built environment: temples and tombs. Material culture correlates can also be identified in the archaeological record, and the artifactual evidence provides a crucial component to our understanding of the function of sacrifice in the formation of social identity because it reflects the activity of individuals from a much broader range of socioeconomic levels. In conclusion, the study of patterning in the deposition of artifactual material associated with sacrificial offerings can provide significant information about ancient ritual landscapes and the routes by which individuals gained access to the deities they venerated.

REFERENCES CITED

Baines, J. 1983 Literacy in Ancient Egyptian Society. *Man*, New Series 18: No. 3:572–599.
Baines, J. 2007 *Visual and Written Culture in Ancient Egypt*. Oxford University Press, Oxford.
Baines, J., and C. Eyre 1983 Four Notes on Literacy, *Göttinger Miszellen* LXI:65–96.

Barta, W. 1963 *Die altägyptische Opferliste.* Münchner Ägyptologische Studien 3. Munich.

Barta, W. 1968 *Aufbau und Bedeutung der altägyptischen Opferformel.* Ägyptologisches Forschungen, Heft 24, J. J. Augustin, Glückstadt.

Bestock, L. 2009 *The Development of Royal Funerary Cult at Abydos: Two Funerary Enclosures from the Reign of Aha.* Harrassowitz, Wiesbaden.

Calverley, A. 1935 *The Temple of Sethos I at Abydos,* Vol. II. Egypt Exploration Fund, London, and University of Chicago Press, Chicago.

Calverley, A. 1938 *The Temple of Sethos I at Abydos,* Vol. III. Egypt Exploration Society, London, and the Oriental Institute of the University of Chicago, Chicago.

Calverley, A. 1958 *The Temple of Sethos I at Abydos,* Vol. IV. Egypt Exploration Society, London, and the Oriental Institute of the University of Chicago, Chicago.

Eiwanger, J. 1984 *Merimde-Benisalâme*: I. Von Zabern, Mainz.

Flinders Petrie, William, W. Matthew, and M. Flinders 1890 *Kahun, Gurob and Hawara.* Keegan Paul, London.

Frankfort, H., A. de Buck, and B. Gunn 1933 *The Cenotaph of Seti I at Abydos.* Egypt Exploration Fund Memoir, 2 vols. William Clowes & Sons, London.

Freed, R. 2008 The Tomb of Rekhmire. In *Valley of the Kings: The Tombs and the Funerary Temples of Thebes West,* edited by Kent Weeks, photographs by Araldo De Luca, pp. 385–388. White Star, Vercelli.

Gardiner, A. 1957 *Egyptian Grammar.* Third Edition, Revised. Oxford University Press, Oxford.

Helck, W. 1980 Maat. In *Lexikon der Ägyptologie,* vol. III, edited by Wolfgang Helck and Eberhard Otto, pp. 1110–1119. Otto Harrasowitz, Wiesbaden.

Ikram, S. 1995 *Choice Cuts: Meat Production in Ancient Egypt.* Orientalia Lovaniensia Analecta. Uitgeverij Peeters, Leuven.

Junker, H. 1929 *Vorläufigen Bericht über die sechste Grabungbei den Pyramider von Gizeh.* Akademie der Wissenschaft, Vienna.

Leahy, A. 1989 A Protective Measure at Abydos in the Thirteenth Dynasty. *Journal of Egyptian Archaeology* 75:41–60.

Lichtheim, M. 1976 *Ancient Egyptian Literature,* vol. I: *The Old and Middle Kingdoms.* University of California Press, Berkeley.

Müller, C. 1975 Anruf an Lebende. In *Lexikon der Ägyptologie,* vol. I, edited by Wolfgang Helck and Eberhard Otto, pp. 293–299. Otto Harrasowitz, Wiesbaden.

Naville, E. 1913 *The XIth Dynasty Temple at Deir el-Bahari* III. Egypt Exploration Fund Memoir 32, London.

O'Connor, D. 2009 *Abydos: Egypt's First Pharaohs and the Cult of Osiris.* Thames & Hudson, London.

Petrie, W., and M. Flinders 1890 *Kahun, Gurob, and Hawara.* Keegan Paul, London.

Pinch, G. 1993 *Votive Offerings to Hathor.* Griffith Institute, Oxford.

Pouls Wegner, M.-A. 2011 New Kingdom Ceramics associated with the Cult Chapel of Thutmose III at Abydos: Preliminary Analysis and Interpretation, *Cahiers de la Céramique Égyptienne* 9:367–414.

Pouls Wegner, M.-A. 2012 New Fieldwork at Abydos: The Toronto Abydos Votive Zone Project. *Near Eastern Archaeology* 75:3, 177–184.

Randall-MacIver, D., and A. Mace 1902 *El-Amrah and Abydos.* Egypt Exploration Fund, London.

Reisner, G., and W. S. Smith 1955 *A History of the Giza Necropolis II: The Tomb of Hetepheres the Mother of Cheops.* Cambridge University, Cambridge.

Rouse, W. H. 1901 *Greek Votive Offerings: an Essay in the History of Greek Religion*. University Press, London.

Simpson, W. K. 1974 *The Terrace of the Great God at Abydos: the Offering Chapels of Dynasties 12 and 13*. The Peabody Museum of Natural History of Yale University, New Haven, and the University Museum of the University of Pennsylvania, Philadelphia.

Spencer, P. 1984 *The Egyptian Temple: A Lexicographical Study*. Kegan Paul International, London.

Teeter, E. 1997 *The Presentation of Ma'at: Ritual and Legitimacy in Ancient Egypt*. Studies in Ancient Oriental Civilizations 57. University of Chicago Press, Chicago.

Wegner, J. 2007 *The Mortuary Temple of Senwosret III at Abydos*. The Peabody Museum of Natural History of Yale University, New Haven, and the University Museum of the University of Pennsylvania, Philadelphia.

CHAPTER SIX

The Mythology of Carthaginian Child Sacrifice

A Physical Anthropological Perspective

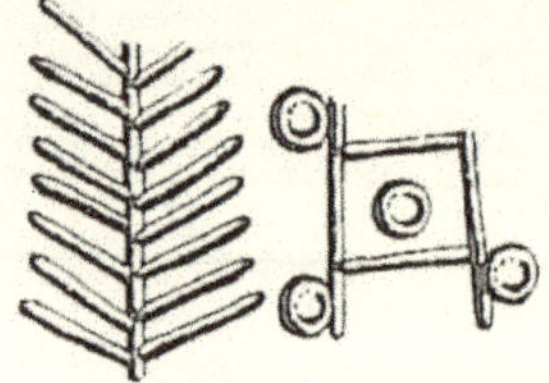

Jeffrey H. Schwartz

Abstract   *The claims of Kleitarchos, Diodorus, and others about the Carthaginians' ruthless and systematic practice of child sacrifice gave rise to the popular saga that hundreds upon hundreds of young humans met this fate until the Romans ended the Punic Wars in 146 B.C.E. Study of the largest sample ever of cremated bone–containing urns (348) from the sanctuary at Punic Carthage known as the Tophet challenges this portrayal of the Carthaginians: ca. 50 percent of the 540 human individuals identified were either prenatal ("unborn") or often did not survive more than a few postnatal days. Even without considering pathogenic insults to the mother and fetus or to the newborn due to poor sanitary conditions, the pre- and postnatal mortality profile of this sample parallels that of modern societies. Perhaps then, we might better interpret the Tophet at Carthage, and those at Carthaginian settlements, as a cemetery for the unborn and very young, regardless of a particular cause of death.*

THE FOUNDING OF CARTHAGE AND ITS TOPHET

The story of the founding of the most westerly Phoenician settlement, Carthage, is sufficiently well known to require but a brief overview. According to the Greek author Timaeus, Princess Elissa fled the Phoenician port city Tyre after her brother, King Pygmalion, killed for his wealth Acherbas, who was her uncle, husband, and high priest of the god Melqart (the equivalent of Hercules) (Harden 1963; Lancel 1995; Moscati 1965). Accompanied by a small band of aristocratic followers, Queen Dido (as Princess Elissa was then called) escaped to Cyprus, gained the support of the high priest of Juno and, with 80 girls to bear children in order to ensure the future of the her religion, eventually landed on the shores of North Africa (present-day Tunisia). Timaeus dated this event to 814/813 B.C.E. (Harden 1963).

In response to the native North African Berbers' accession to Queen Dido's request to settle in their land, but only as much land as an ox hide could cover, she supposedly cut the hide into thin strips, with which she encircled the primary hill overlooking the Mediterranean, called Byrsa (in Greek *byrsa* = ox hide and in Phoenician acropolis). Since Elissa and Pygmalion were actual historical figures, and Elissa's great-aunt Jezebel is believed to have married King Ahab ca. 875–850 B.C.E., Harden (1963) and other biblical scholars have typically accepted Timaeus's date for the founding of (Punic or western Phoenician) Carthage. Although Greek Geometric pottery, which was found at Carthage, indicates the city's founding is no earlier than 760 B.C.E., some radiocarbon dates based on bovid bones were slightly older than 800 B.C.E. (Docter et al. 2007), thereby providing potential support for Timaeus's suggestion.

After settlement, the Carthaginians established colonies throughout the Mediterranean in Sardinia, Sicily, and southern Spain, and also extended their North African domain beyond the Straits of Gibraltar to the Atlantic Ocean. Eventually, the center of Phoenician influence shifted from Tyre to Carthage. During this phase of geographic expansion, Carthage's attention was primarily on their Greek antagonists, and not on the rise of the new Roman Republic until such time as it became imperative to negotiate treaties with this emergent power (first in 348, then 306, and later 272 B.C.E.). Shortly after the last of these treaties, however, Rome attempted to control Carthaginian Sicily, which prompted a Carthaginian response and the beginning of the first Punic War (264–241 B.C.E.), which ended with a Roman naval victory off the island's coast. Carthaginian army general Hannibal initiated the second Punic War in 218 B.C.E. after the Romans assaulted a Carthaginian border town in Spain. Despite a series of successful military actions, including leading an army with its elephants across the French Alps and deep into Roman territory, Hannibal was defeated in 202 B.C.E. on the plains of Zama just west of Carthage by the young Roman general, Pontius Cornelius Scipio Africanus. The resultant treaty banned Carthage from engaging in warfare. Although the Romans then reduced the Carthaginian domain to the city itself, the Carthaginians nonetheless proceeded to outproduce the Nile Valley as the Mediterranean's "breadbasket." In 148 B.C.E. the Carthaginians defended themselves from a Libyan attack, which broke the treaty. The Romans attacked and, under the leadership of Scipio Africanus's grandson, Scipio Aemilianus, eventually broke through Carthaginian defenses at the mercantile harbor and razed the city to the ground (Appian *Roman History*).

But while Appian exaggerated the extent to which Rome destroyed Carthage (e.g., beyond the mercantile harbor area, ash layers are rather benign and the Roman rebuilding of Carthage, including the quay walls of the mercantile harbor, uncharacteristically exact in replication [Schwartz 1989; Schwartz 1993]), another aspect of Carthaginian history is true: separate from the primary cemetery, the cremated remains of very young humans and animals were buried in small urns in a place that biblical scholars have identified as a sanctuary dedicated to the female god Tanit or simply, in extrapolation from biblical association, as the Tophet (Benichou-Safar 1981; Harden 1963; Moscati 1965; Moscati

1987; Stager and Wolff 1984). Indeed, well before the mercantile and naval harbors were constructed, the Carthaginians cut a channel from the Mediterranean directly to their Tophet and in which a roughly hewn cippus was discovered that could only have been intended for use as a tombstone in this burial sanctuary (Stager and Wolff 1984).

A long-held interpretation of these cremated human and animal remains is that all represent the victims of ritualized and systematic sacrifice (Harden 1963), a notion that was popularized by Flaubert (1882) in his epic novel *Salammbô*. More recently, not-all-sacrifice interpretations of the Tophet human remains have been forthcoming (Agelarakis et al. 1998; Bartoloni 2006; Benichou-Safar 1981; Conte 2007; Fedele and Foster 1988; Harden 1963; Moscati 1987; Schwartz 1993; Schwartz et al. 2010; Stuckey 2009), the shared essence of which is that Tophets received the remains of the very young, regardless of how they died. In support of this clearly reasonable hypothesis and on the basis of circum-Mediterranean practice in general, Stuckey (2009) pointed out that sacrificial victims would likely have been individuals older than neonates, infants, and very young children.

Nevertheless, present-day advocates of the all-sacrifice theory tenaciously defend their position (Smith et al. 2011; Smith et al. 2013; Stager 1980; Stager and Greene 2000; Stager and Greene 2007; Stager and Wolff 1984). Alternative theories have even been labeled "revisionist" (Lancel 1995; Quinn 2011), as if the "all sacrifice" has and can actually be incontrovertibly demonstrated. Further, the "case" for an "all sacrifice" theory is typically based not on detailed study of the skeletal remains themselves, but on the notion that only all sacrifice can adequately explain historical and other evidence.

For example, first Smith et al. (2011) argued that since deforestation began with the founding of Carthage (van Zeist et al. 2001) nothing less profound than sacrifice-related cremation could have justified using increasingly scarce wood when it was most needed for building ships and habitation. Subsequently, they claimed that only sacrifice could justify the expense of cremation and urn internment (Smith et al. 2013). In reality, however, only thin branches were used in Tophet funeral pyres (Schwartz 1993; Schwartz et al. 2010) and these would not have been suitable for the construction of structures of substance, whether ship or dwelling. Further, as Docter et al. (2003) describe in detail, the primary wood sources were cultivated plants (small trees, e.g., *Prunus,* and bushes, e.g., *Ligustrum*); when used, *Quercus* was the largest plant but likely only scraps left over from large-scale construction (e.g., the Carthaginian harbors) were used to fuel cremation pyres.

Given the claims and assertions over the years upon which the all-sacrifice theory has been constructed, it would seem useful and appropriate to review what we do and do not know about the osseous remains interred in the Carthaginian Tophet as well as the assumptions that have informed their interpretation.

The Case for Carthaginian Child Sacrifice

Written Evidence

According to Brown (1991) and Mosca (1975), the first classical note on Carthaginian infant/child sacrifice was likely drafted by Sophocles (fifth century B.C.E.): "For among foreigners, it has been the custom, from the beginning to require human sacrifice to [the god] Kronos" (translations from Mosca [1975]). A century or so later, Pseudo-Plato constructed a conversation between Socrates and himself that mentioned Carthage by name: "With us, for instance, human sacrifice is not legal, but unholy, whereas the Carthaginians perform it as a thing they account holy and legal, and that too when some of them sacrifice even their own sons to Cronos."

The Greek Kleitarchos (third century B.C.E.) provided the first detailed and often subsequently paraphrased description of this presumed Carthaginian ritual, in which the victims were cremated alive:

> Out of reverence for Kronos, the Phoenicians, and especially the Carthaginians, whenever they seek to obtain some great favour, vow one of their children, burning it as a sacrifice to the deity, if they are especially eager to gain success. There stands in their midst a bronze statue of Kronos, its hands extended over a bronze brazier, the flames of which engulf the child. When the flame falls upon the body, the limbs contract and the open mouth seems almost to be laughing, until the contracted [body] slips quietly into the brazier. Thus it is that the "grin" is known as "sardonic laughter," since they die laughing. (*Scholia* to Plato's *Republica* 337A in Allen et al. 1939)

Diodorus Siculus (*Library of History* XIII. 86, ca. 54 B.C.E.) told of an even more vivid story of child sacrifice. In 406 B.C.E., during the siege of Acragas, the Carthaginian general Himilco "supplicat[ed] the gods after the custom of his people by sacrificing a young boy to Cronus," and then in 310 B.C.E. and under siege the Carthaginians sacrificed children to appease the gods, who they believed had caused their problems (Brown 1991; Mosca 1975; Stager and Wolff 1984):

> They also alleged that Cronus had turned against them inasmuch as in former times they had been accustomed to sacrifice to this god the noblest of their sons, but more recently, secretly buying and nurturing children, they had sent these to the sacrifice; and when an investigation was made, some of those who had been sacrificed were discovered to have been supposititious. When they had given thought to these things and saw their enemy encamped before their walls, they were filled with superstitious dread, for they believed that they had neglected the honors of the gods that had been established by their fathers. In their zeal to make amends for their omission, they selected two hundred of the noblest children and sacrificed them publicly; and others who were under suspicion sacrificed themselves voluntarily, in number not less than three hundred. There was in their city a bronze image of Cronus, extending its hands, palms up and sloping toward the ground, so that each of the children when placed thereupon rolled down and fell into a sort of gaping pit filled with fire. Also the story passed down among the Greeks from ancient myth that Cronus did away with his own children appears to have been kept in mind among the Carthaginians through this observance. (Diodorus Siculus *Library of History* XX. 14)

During Roman occupation of Northern Africa after the fall of Carthage, Plutarch (ca. 46–120 C.E.) (Pearson and Sandbach 1960) wrote that well-to-do Carthaginians without children to sacrifice would buy surrogates from the poor. The throats of these children were cut prior to their being offered to the statute of Ba'al; if the mother uttered anything during this ritual, she forfeited payment. Plutarch also remarked that flutes and drums were played loudly in order to mask from others (onlookers?) the "cries of wailing." Questions, however, arise. Who was wailing? Who was being prevented from hearing it? And how would Plutarch have known these details centuries after Carthage and, like the Library of Alexandria, all Carthaginian documentation of their history, had been destroyed by the Romans? Plutarch's contemporary, the North African Tertullian, also referred to the practice of child sacrifice, but in this case it was presumably practiced by the Romans, who hung their victims alive on crosses (Brown 1991; Stager and Greene 2007; Stager and Wolff 1984).

Biblical Evidence

Although Carthaginian domination of the western Mediterranean varied over time and geographical extent, Carthaginian roots were Phoenicia (Canaan). After restricting Phoenicia to the eastern coastal fringe of the Mediterranean, the invading Israelites adopted various aspects of Phoenician culture, most notably the alphabet, and some Israelite factions even came to worship the god Ba'al (Harden 1963; Moscati 1965). Citing this history, some biblical scholars continue to seek in the Old Testament support of the speculation that the Carthaginians were predisposed toward a practice of human sacrifice that could then have developed into the frequent and ritualized killing of infants and children (Mosca 1975; Stager and Greene 2007; Stager and Wolff 1984; Xella et al. 2013).

In specific reference to the Old Testament, some scholars have also maintained that these sacrificial victims were first-born males. For instance, Chronicles 27 states that King Ahaz "made molten images for the Ba'als . . . and burned his sons as an offering, according to the abominable practices of the nations whom the Lord drove out before the people of Israel." And in 29–30 Exodus 22 we read: "Thou shalt give me the first-born of their sons. . . . The first-born shall be left seven days with its mother and then, on the eighth, thou shalt hand it over to me."

But an alternative, nonliteral interpretation of "hand it [the first-born child] over" may also refer to a "passage by fire," which is an interpretation that emphasizes a symbolic and not actual taking of a life (Brown 1991; Schwartz 1989; Stuckey 2009). That is, rather than signifying specifically that cremation in restricted to and only associated with a ritual of sacrifice, "passage by fire" may more simply refer to an infant or child's "kiss with smoke and flames" as it was moved swiftly over a ritual fire (perhaps by a priest or a parent?).

Whether generically human or specifically infant or child, the Old Testament contains numerous allusions to, or threats of, committing violent acts of sacrifice, which continue to be cited as concrete evidence of an ongoing and rampant Carthaginian practice of infant sacrifice (Xella et al. 2013). Of these, perhaps the most widely known passages of potential sacrifice are those that relate the near-killing by Abraham of his first-born son Isaac (Genesis 22:1–19), including Abraham's constructing a funeral pyre and unsheathing his knife in anticipation of cutting his son's throat. But the sacrifice was never consummated. At the last moment, God intervened and commanded Abraham to sacrifice a ram that was hiding in nearby bushes. Indeed, virtually all accounts do not portray actual sacrifice, and the potential victim was neither infant nor child. There is only one reported instance of sacrifice being enacted and the victim was female and likely young adult.

Probably the least-known passage in the Old Testament referring to human sacrifice tells of a vow that Jephtah, leader of an Israelite clan in Gilead, made to God to sacrifice the first thing he saw if he won an upcoming battle with the Ammonites (Judges 11:1–11, 29–40). Upon Jephtah's victorious return home after this encounter, his (unnamed) daughter rushed to greet him. In keeping his vow to God, but with supreme remorse, Jephtah told her of his pledge. She then spent two months in the mountains with friends reflecting on her fate, returned home, and was sacrificed by her father.

Inscriptions and Iconography on Grave Markers

Although identification of the Carthaginian Tophet was originally based on the discovery of displaced and unassociated grave makers, subsequent excavations uncovered many in situ, with some bearing inscriptions (Brown 1991; Harden 1927; Harden 1963; Stager and Wolff 1984). Inscriptions have generally been translated as referring to an "offering" that parents (?) of high status (?) made to the female god Tanit (the counterpart of the Egyptian/Assyrian Astarte, Greek Hera, and Roman Juno), and the male god of the sun, heavens, and fire, Ba'al Hammon (Greek Kronos/Cronus and Roman Saturn), or to both. Tanit has often been taken as Egyptian in origin (Brown 1991; Harden 1927; Harden 1963; Stager and Wolff 1984), which would appear to be consistent with the Ankh-like representation of her as a round, often unfilled, "head" atop two short, laterally extended, often sticklike "arms," atop a triangular, outlined body. Recently, however, Stuckey (2009) has convincingly argued that Tanit's origins are strictly Phoenician. She reasons further that a more plausible interpretation of the relationship between Tanit and the sanctuary dedicated to her is that she was a benevolent god who, rather than demanding their sacrifice to her, would have embraced perinates, infants, and children who had died naturally. The icon of Ba'al Hammon is believed to be a crescent-shaped outline hovering above a circular object that is easily mistaken for an eye, most likely because the tool (somewhat like a compass) that circumscribed the spherical object created a depression in the center. When the two gods' symbols were depicted together, the one believed to be Ba'al Hammon was situated (as if floating) above Tanit. Occasionally the "eye" of Ba'al "floated" above the image of an urn (Figure 6.1).

Two types of grave markers were excavated at Carthage (Brown 1991; Harden 1927; Harden 1963; Stager and Wolff 1984): limestone stelae and sandstone cippi. The thick, chunky, and typically "L"-shaped cippi were more prevalent during the earlier phases of Tophet usage (ca. eighth–fifth century B.C.E.) and were apparently adorned on one side with stucco and paint. Over time, cippi became larger and more square, and could bear inset carvings of the images of one or both gods, an urn, an urn set on a platform, or just a platform, which has been interpreted as a sacrificial platform. Although cippi do not preserve engraved inscriptions to Tanit and/or Ba'al, Brown (1991) has speculated that their icons were likely represented in paint.

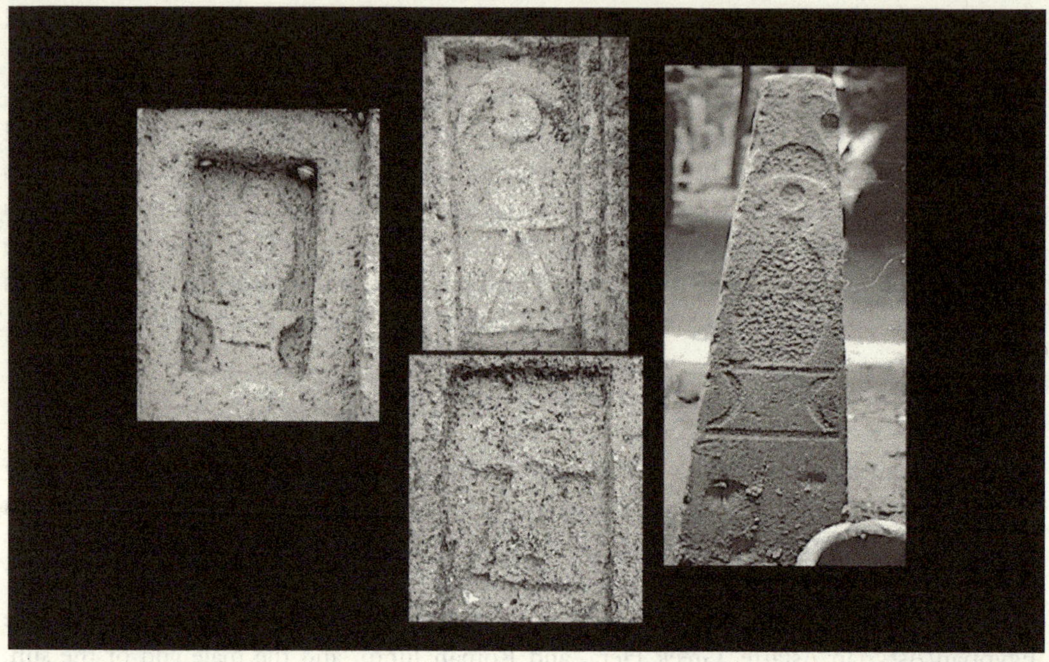

FIGURE 6.1 Examples of stelae with an urn (left), image of Ba'al Hammon above image of Tanit (middle top), image of Tanit (middle bottom), and image of Ba'al Hammon above an urn (right). Not to scale. Copyright © Jeffrey H. Schwartz.

Stelae began to replace cippi in the latter part of the fifth century B.C.E. and did so increasingly until Roman conquest in 146 B.C.E. (Brown 1991; Harden 1927; Harden 1963; Stager and Wolff 1984). Similar to cippi, stelae were decorated on one side, typically and (compared to the more regimented stylistic motifs of cippi) more variably with symbols, figures, and scenes incised in bas-relief. Although some stelae were adorned in the style of cippi, as an assemblage, they typically bore representations of rosettes, palm trees, a hand raised with palm facing outward, part of a boat or only an oar, an animal (not only lamb, but adult sheep, bull, cow, fish, bird), or an adult human. Indeed, one stela, which advocates of the all-sacrifice theory consistently cite as incontrovertible evidence of this practice (Smith et al. 2011; Stager and Wolff 1984), is incised with the image of what is interpreted as an adult male priest holding in the crook of his left arm a small, amorphous figure that is interpreted as a living child on its way to being sacrificed (Figure 6.2).

Of note is that the adult is presented in some detail: for instance, his fingers are depicted individually and his left ear (his left side is shown in profile) is clearly delineated, and he appears to be animated, in motion. His right arm, which is forwardly placed, is bent at the elbow with the lower arm upturned, and his right leg, which is slightly bent at the knee, is placed well in front of the left. In stark contrast, the small figure,

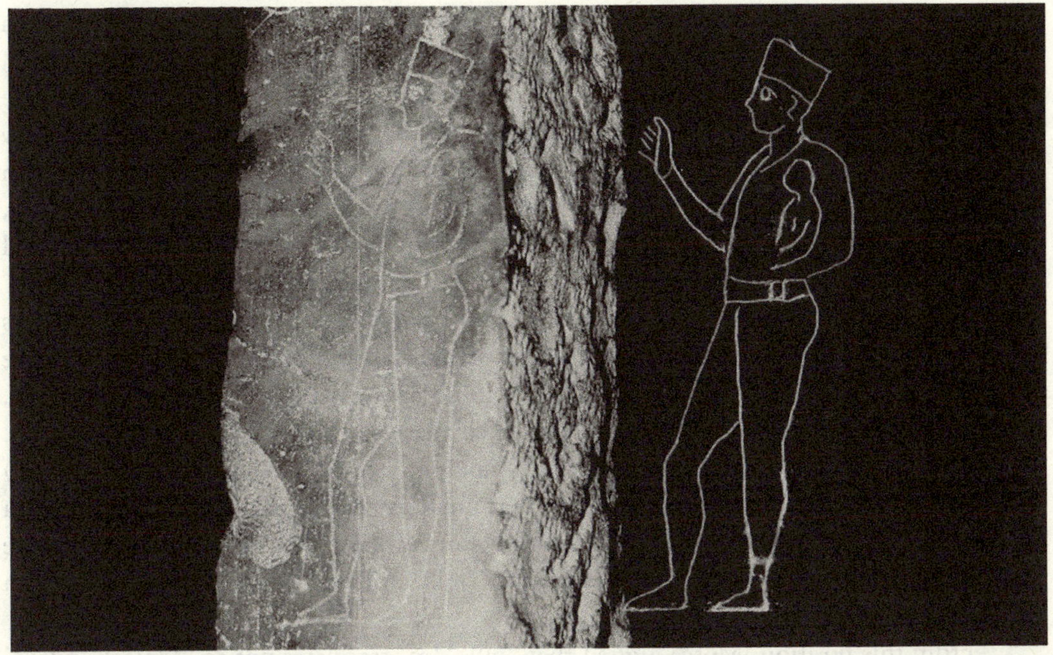

FIGURE 6.2 The Bardo stela depicting adult carrying small individual (right: tracing of image). Not to scale. Copyright © Jeffrey H. Schwartz.

which could be human, is slumped over and appears motionless, its dangling "arms" are sketchily depicted, and the head and face are featureless (Schwartz et al. 2012).

From an interpretatively neutral perspective, it is reasonable to infer that the small figure might have been drugged or simply, and perhaps more sensibly, dead. Since no one defending the all-sacrifice hypothesis has taken into consideration the extremely relevant fact that perinatal and infant mortality would have been high at Carthage, as it was at other major Mediterranean cities (Scobie 1986), conceiving Tophets as sanctuaries for the remains of those whose death was premature is consistent with the distribution of infant mortality we achieved for the Carthaginian Tophet sample, which, significantly, mirrors that of the present (Richard 1961; Schwartz et al. 2010). But for a priori conviction, it is thus a mystery why those who insist that infant sacrifice alone accounts for the presence of humans in Carthaginian Tophets continue to deny natural causes of perinatal and infant death (Smith et al. 2011; Smith et al. 2013; Xella et al. 2013). For, even if the studies identifying high percentages of pre- and perinates in their samples are incorrect (Docter et al. 2003; Richard 1961; Schwartz et al. 2010), and Smith et al.'s (2013) determination of no prenates and a predominance of one- to two-months-old infants is, disease and dehydration (primary or disease related), as is the case today (Behrman and Shiono 1997) would be a likely cause of death.

Stelae also differed from cippi in sometimes bearing an inscription that is often identified as the individual or individuals who dedicated the grave marker (male, female, or male/female couple), as well as the god/s to whom the dedication was made. Some biblical scholars interpret the more detailed dedications as reflecting parents making a vow of sacrifice, to Tanit or Tanit and Ba'al (Brown 1991; Mosca 1975; Xella et al. 2013). In contrast, Stuckey (2009) has convincingly argued that since Tanit was a beneficent god, the most reasonable interpretation of these inscriptions is that parents are dedicating and turning over to Tanit's care the remains of their prematurely deceased offspring.

The more detailed of these inscriptions may contain the consonants transcribed as "mlk," which for decades was accepted by most biblical scholars as referring to a male individual ("Molech" or "Malik"), which, in combination with other consonants (e.g., "mlk 'mr"), signified a god or king of a particular place (e.g., mlk 'mr = King of Omar). However, Mosca (1975) and Lancel (1995), among others, have revived Harden's (1963) interpretation of stelae-borne inscriptions that "mlk" refers to the actual sacrifice of a living organism, which was based on a single Roman stela that described the sacrifice of a ram to the Roman god Saturn. From this "mlk 'immor" was extrapolated to mean sacrifice of a lamb or kid.

From this position, Mosca argued that "mlk 'dm" translates not as "Molech 'Adam" or "King of Men" (i.e., someone making a sacrificial offering), but as the act itself (i.e., "sacrifice of a human"). Invoking a more specific translation of these inscriptions, Mosca further speculated that stelae inscriptions actually identify the social status of the victim: that is, "mlk 'dm" specifies the sacrifice of a commoner while "mlk b'al" denotes the sacrifice of an elite individual. Although one would expect in a culture that purportedly engaged in wanton sacrifice of its newborns and infants that one or more religious or other circumstance-dictated rituals would require participation of citizens of every social rank, Mosca bolstered his inferences with Plutarch's assertion (*Moralia* 171-C-D; see Pearson and Sandbach [1960]) that couples of the elite without infants or children to sacrifice could purchase the offspring of the poor. Quinn, for example, has since endorsed Mosca's inferences in defense of the all-sacrifice theory (Quinn 2011; Xella et al. 2013).

Mosca's assumptions beg the following questions: Could childless elite couples purchase a commoner's offspring to sacrifice? Does Plutarch's comment impact, even falsify, Stager and Wolff's (1984) contention that upper-class Carthaginians sacrificed their infants as a means of population control in order to perpetuate their elite status via a mechanism-turned-institutionalized ritual that kept their numbers low? Assuming that the remains of human infants and children interred in the Carthage (or any Carthaginian) Tophet resulted solely from the taking of a life and not, as was common then and now, from expected infant mortality, and that, if sacrifice, these acts as estimated would have numbered in the tens of thousands over Carthage's history (Harden 1927; Harden 1963; Xella 2010), it strains the bounds of credulity to take seriously the claim that this ritual was practiced only by a small and select group that would have remained extant and politically and socially dominant for almost 600 years.

Archaeological and Osteological Evidence

Tophet burial urns containing burnt bone were unearthed first in 1860 and then in 1911 at a Carthaginian site known only by its Latin name, Hadrumentum (modern-day Sousse) (Harden 1963). Before then, excavations in the 1870s of the Carthaginian Tophet itself had yielded only grave markers (stelae and cippi) that were not associated with burial urns (Harden 1963). The possibility that urns containing burnt bone might constitute evidence of acts of sacrifice was not entertained until Whitaker (1921) recovered 150 of them during his excavation of the Sicilian Carthaginian colony Motya. Since subsequent analysis of only 50 of these urns identified animal (dog, cat, lamb, kid, calf, and one monkey) but no human bone, Whitaker concluded that animals had been the sacrificial surrogates for humans.

The accounts of child sacrifice by Kleitarchos, Diodorus, and Plutarch were not considered validated until 1922, when de Prorok, Gielly, and Icard discovered at the Carthage Tophet urns containing burnt bones, most of which their colleague, Pallary, identified as human infant or child (Stager and Wolff 1984). In 1923, Poinssot and Lantier (1923) excavated what Icard called the "Sanctuary of Tanit" and demonstrated that the most recent urns were associated with stelae, the next oldest with stelae and cippi, and the earliest with piles of common stone (see also review by Quinn [2011]). Poinssot and Lantier's colleague Henry determined that most of the burnt bones in these urns were those of human infants and children.

In 1925, Kelsey (1926) renewed excavation of the Sanctuary of Tanit. Although more than 1,000 urns were unearthed, he had the contents of only 36 analyzed because he assumed that most urns would contain only the burnt bones of human infants and children. Nevertheless, neither Kelsey nor his pottery expert Harden (1927) was willing to claim unreservedly that the Carthaginians had engaged in the rampant and institutionally sanctioned sacrifice of human infants and children.

A different picture of Carthaginian human sacrifice emerged from Chabot and Lapeyre's 1934 to 1936 excavations of the "Sanctuary of Tanit," during which they exhumed more than 1,000 urns (Lapeyre and Pellegrin 1942). Beyond speculating that all urns in the vicinity of a stela or cippus represented sacrifice by one or a few related family members or families (there were many fewer burial monuments than urns), and reiterating that most burnt bone represented human infants and children, Chabot and Lapeyre believed that urns could contain the remains of a single human, two humans, or a human and an animal. Even more spectacular was their assertion that some bones were those not of infant, but adolescent humans.

Charles-Picard and Cintas's 1944–45 excavations confirmed Poinssot and Lantier's interpretation of the stratigraphic context of and association between urns and grave markers (Charles-Picard 1945). They also sent the contents of 42 urns to J. Richard for analysis, which he included in his medico-legal doctoral thesis (Richard 1961). Unfortunately, Richard (1961) combined as one sample the Carthaginian remains and those from 138 urns from Hadrumentum and identified the remains of one or more humans in 88, human and "os d'agneaux" in 59, and only "os d'agneaux" in 29 urns; he considered the bones from four urns too fragmentary for study. Based on his assessment, Richard concluded that the ratio of humans to animals had reversed during Carthaginian times from more humans than animals to more animals than humans. Stager and Wolff (1984) subsequently embraced Richard's speculation as demonstrating that, as Carthaginian culture "matured," animals were increasingly substituted for humans as sacrificial entities. However, study of the contents of 348 urns from the Carthage Tophet documents the scarcity of animal remains (kid or lamb) alone in an urn; indeed, although still rare, the more frequent situation was the interment of a few animal bones with those of humans (Schwartz et al. 2010). Since animal remains are so infrequently represented in this sample from the Carthage Tophet, it seems reasonable to suggest that, since the number of urns from Hadrumentum represents 70 percent of Richard's sample, the abundance of animal remains derives from the Hadrumentum, not Carthage, component of his sample.

LONG BONES

Curiously, Smith et al. (2011, 2013) cite Richard's study as demonstrating the absence of prenates and the prevalence of infants in Tophet urns. In fact, however, based on long bone measurements representing 41 individuals, Richard identified five (12.2%) as prenatal (one being 7.5, and four between 8 and 9 fetal months), 20 (48.8%) as term, and 16 (39%) as postnatal (nine between ≤ 1 month, three between 1 and 3 months, and four 2-to-3 years of age). He suggested that the uppermost limit of error would be one prenatal, 33 perinatal, and seven postnatal individuals.

TOOTH FORMATION

From study of relative states of tooth formation—dental remains indicating 126 individuals—Richard concluded that 16 were prenatal, 118 perinatal, and 13 postnatal, of which six were only a few months and seven between three and six years of age. In considering potential error, he maintained that 13 individuals were postnatal, between two and 16 individuals prenatal, and the rest perinatal. His summary interpretation was that 5 percent of the sample was prenatal, 75 percent perinatal, and 20 percent postnatal, which, he commented, was consistent with pediatric expectation. Smith et al. (2013) also cite Gejvall's (1949) analysis of a small sample Carthage Tophet remains as verifying the prevalence of very young infants, but even a cursory review of his dental aging criteria reveals they were not precise.

Most recently, Smith et al. (2011, 2013) argued that the predominant age group represented by human remains in the Carthage Tophet fell within one to two postnatal months. In their first publication, they used petrosal bone length as well as tooth crown length, which they corrected by 0.6 mm for shrinkage—a figure they derived from comparison of one study on uncremated deciduous tooth measurements with another that sampled a different population for calcined tooth length metrics. Based on petrosal and tooth length, they (Smith et al. 2011) identified at least three individuals as prenatal. Based on tooth length alone, they concluded that the majority of individuals were four to six postnatal weeks. In their attempt to rule out neonatal line (NL) analysis as a reliable test of the likelihood an individual was either prenatal or had not survived extrauterine life long enough for this imprint to be established in its tooth enamel (see discussion below), Smith et al. (2011) published (Figure 3d) microphotographs of sections of a non-cremated upper molar crown they thought presented an NL and of a similarly formed cremated crown from the Carthage Tophet they thought did not. Critically, the magnification they used was insufficient to capture the detail of enamel prism architecture necessary to determine presence/absence of NLs. In reality, the "line" visible in the non-cremated molar is the normal juncture between the enamel of the crown and the dentine that underlies it. In their second publication, and although they used the same crown lengths, Smith et al (2013) claimed there were no prenates and that the majority of individuals were one to two postnatal months. Nevertheless, beyond Smith et al.'s (2011, 2013) incorrect assumption of tooth lengths in populations disparate in both time and place as being sufficiently similar they can be used comparatively, their study relies on only once source of information to estimate age at death. As is well known, however, it is imperative that one uses a multifactorial approach, using multiple indicators of age at death, in order to avoid bias that only one criterion often introduces (Fazekas and Kósa 1979; Krogman and Iscan 1986; Lovejoy et al. 1985; Schwartz 2007; Ubelaker 1989).

THE CARTHAGINIAN TOPHET: 1976–79 EXCAVATIONS

URNS AND URN CONTENTS

In the mid-1970s and in response to increasing construction along Tunisia's northern coast, including the region of Carthage (Salammbó), UNESCO sponsored a multinational effort to excavate in five or so years as much as possible of the major Punic and later occupational phases of the region. The mercantile harbor and the Tophet were allocated to one of two teams from the United States. At the invitation of this team's director, L. E. Stager, I undertook in-field sorting and preliminary analysis as well as subsequent detailed laboratory analysis of the human and animal skeletal remains from both areas (1976–79).

The Tophet was difficult to excavate because the now-high water table required the constant use of sump pumps in order to keep surfaces and finds visible. The submersion of burial urns for approximately two millennia had caused silt and other extraneous items to seep into urns (especially if they were cracked and/or their lids broken or ajar), and dissolved calcium carbonate had solidified and cemented everything together, which made it impossible to excavate their contents once they dried out (Schwartz 1989). This was what I encountered upon arriving at the site in 1976, the first season after excavation had begun. Trying to "excavate" these solid blocks with dental picks was useless—which would explain why so little bone had been salvaged, for instance, during Kelsey's excavation.

Fortunately, the solution to the calcium carbonate problem was simple: keep urns wet. This was accomplished by placing each urn into a bucket of water after it was excavated. Stored thereafter in the shade, an urn and its contents were protected until I processed them (Schwartz 1989). At first, I transferred each urn from its bucket to a vat of water, gently removed its contents and then emptied the vat's contents onto plastic mosquito mesh supported on a wire cot. Soon thereafter, I decided it would be safer and more expeditious to use a gentle stream of water from a hose to flush out an urn's contents directly onto the mesh and then immediately rinse away silt and calcium carbonate; while doing this I carefully spread urn contents into a single layer to keep them separated. For the remaining field seasons, this was the technique I used to process an eventual total of 348 urns (Schwartz et al. 2010).

In addition to osseous remains and silt, an urn always presented evidence of both a lid (many of which were intact or represented by easily reconstructed fragments that had fallen inside the urn) and a clay stopper (Schwartz 1989). A lid was constructed of the same clay as its urn and fired. Lids were red and individually configured (potentially painted and three-dimensional, even dome-like) in the earlier, and pale yellow, disc-like, and more thoroughly fired in the later Tophet phases; in all cases, lids were essentially the same diameter as urns' mouths. Stoppers were also molded from the same clay as the urn but were unfired. The stiff, pale yellow-clay stoppers were better preserved than the red, which were often represented as unformed lumps of soft, slimy clay in an urn's belly.

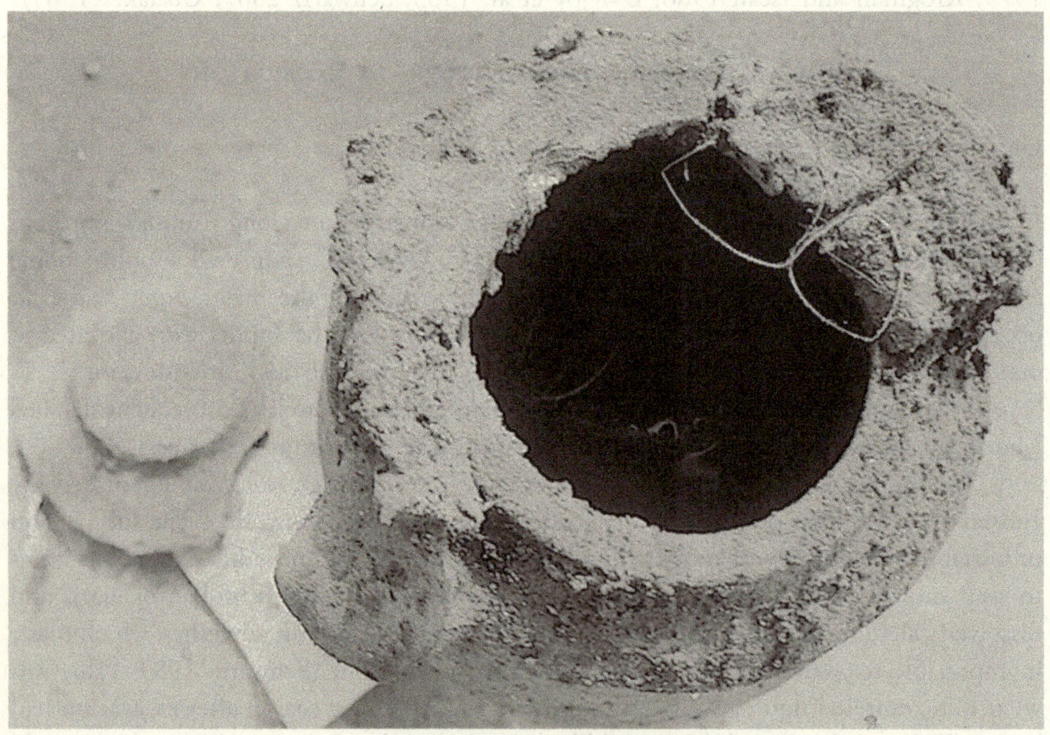

FIGURE 6.3 Top: A yellowish clay urn representative of the later Tophet phases with unfired clay adherent to the rim with partial rim; the stopper had fallen into the urn. Bottom: Fragmentary red clay stopper and fragment of poorly fired red clay lid retrieved with the lamb or kid bones from within the urn; note the depressions in the clay. Not to scale. Copyright © Jeffrey H. Schwartz.

Occasionally, thin patches of unfired clay clung to an urn's rim (Figure 6.3). Presumably, a lid was pressed onto an approximately 2 cm sheet of clay that stretched across an urn's mouth, which squeezed the clay between lid and urn while maintaining the thickness of the stopper's "body" within the margin of the mouth. Over time, the weight of the clay spanning an urn's mouth and its softening due to the rising water table, caused the stopper's body to separate from the part squeezed between lid and rim. Intriguingly, some stoppers or stopper fragments preserved finger- and/or thumbprints (Schwartz 1989).

After bone, the most numerous urn contents consisted of variably small chunks of charred wood that retained sufficient organic structure to be identified not as substantial pieces of wood sufficient to construct ships or building (contra Smith et al. [2011]), but as thin branches of olive tree and other small, predominantly domesticated, small trees and bushes (Docter et al. 2003; Schwartz 1989); the only large tree represented is oak, of which small pieces (likely waste from large construction) were used as fuel (Docter et al. 2003). Urns also contained amulets (from a few to several dozen, most frequently as a representation of the "eye of Horus"), as well as some beads. A few urns contained small gold ornaments (e.g., a tiny representation of Tanit) or carvings (e.g., figures of Egyptian influence and animals) (Schwartz 1989).

In order to avoid mildew and other problems during preanalysis storage, I sorted and separately bagged urn contents only after they had dried thoroughly. Prior to bagging skeletal material, I recorded whether it was human, animal, or a comingling of both and also whether any skeletal elements (especially the most frequently preserved basicranial petrosal bones and often tooth crowns rather than complete teeth) were represented in duplicate, triplicate, or more of the same bony element (Schwartz 1989). The assumption among faunal analysts is that replicates of the same bone or tooth are a direct reflection the number of complete individuals that had been butchered or otherwise manipulated because one would not expect to recover every skeletal element of each individual (Hesse and Wapnish 1985). Since the majority of preserved bone was extremely fragmentary, I initially thought that it was reasonable to infer MNI (minimum number of individuals) in the Tophet sample from number of duplicated skeletal elements (Schwartz 1993). Ultimately, however, the MNI approach proved misleading (Schwartz et al. 2010).

The bias that was introduced using the MNI approach began to become evident when more than two individuals were indicated by that number of duplicated skeletal elements (e.g., petrosal bones [Figure 6.4]), but there was insufficient osseous corroboration of that many complete, or even relatively complete, skeletons. Further re-scrutiny of all osseous elements from an urn presenting MNI of multiple individuals also failed to produce additional examples of skeletal duplication. Repeated instances of incongruity between MNI and the details of an urn's skeletal contents led to a multiple re-analyses— fragment by fragment—of the Tophet sample, which proved insightful.

When one individual was identified on the basis of teeth and target bones (that is, bones most frequently preserved intact or nearly intact, e.g., petrosals), the spectrum of preserved and identifiable skeletal material indicated the presence of an essentially complete individual (this appears to be the case in another study [Docter et al. 2003]). When two individuals could be identified, duplicate bones and teeth often differed in formative

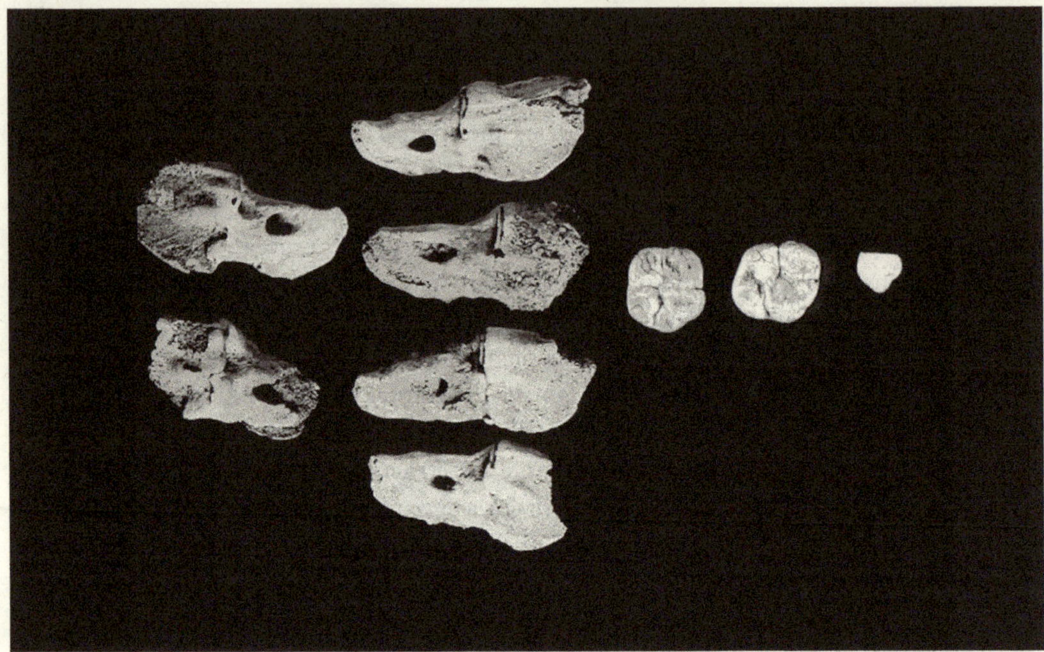

Figure 6.4 Left: Isolated petrosal bones, two on the left and four on the right; MNI would lead to the erroneous conclusion that four individuals had been placed in the same urn. Right: Similarly developed crowns of upper and lower first permanent molars of child (left and middle) and a developing crown of a deciduous upper canine of a perinate (far right). Not to scale. Copyright © Jeffrey H. Schwartz.

stage and size (Figure 6.4), which indicated individuals of different ages (Schwartz et al. 2010). In these cases as well, there was sufficient, skeletally representative bone to warrant concluding that the remains of two, relatively complete individuals had been placed in the same urn (this also appears to be true of Docter et al's [2003] material). When, however, three or more individuals were identified on the basis of MNI, other instances of skeletal-element duplication were lacking and there was insufficient bone to justify the assumption that three or more (relatively) complete skeletons had been placed in the same urn (Schwartz et al. 2010). (I suspect this was the case in Docter et al.'s [2003] identification of three newborns in an urn, since they specify this number only for three right petrosal bones.)

Analysis and Interpretation of the Human Remains

Although most bone, whether animal or human, had been exposed to heat, the degree of carbonization or calcination was not uniform, not only across the sample but also, and with the rare exception, among bones from the same urn (Schwartz et al. 2010). Indeed, in a number of instances, reassembled pieces of the same bone were so disparately burned that one fragment could be well calcined and the piece adjoining it barely singed (Figure 6.5). These observations are consistent with a crematory pyre made up of ash and small, unevenly burning branches, with voids in between into which bones would fall randomly as they separated, burst due to heat, and/or were prodded by the pyre tender working to keep the fire alive (Gejvall 1969; McKinley 1989; McKinley 1994). This kind of nonuniform pyre is also suggested by the charred remnants of small trees and bushes present in every urn analyzed (Schwartz 1989; Schwartz 1993).

At the other end of the taphonomic spectrum, but consistent with the use of a loosely constructed pyre into which bones and teeth could scatter and avoid severe incineration, was the occasional discovery of human as well as lamb or kid bones that were in anatomical position, being held together by either solidified matrix or oxidized hemoglobin (Figure 6.6) (Schwartz et al. 2010). Although suggesting there had been other instances of bones-in-articulation that may have been dissociated during rinsing of urn contents, the examples that did survive indicate that not all Tophet individuals were sufficiently exposed to heat to become fully skeletonized. Thus, in an unknown number of cases, some post-cremation remains were still invested in soft and connective tissue when, along with burned, isolated bones, they were placed in urns.

With specific regard to human remains, the contents of the 348 urns analyzed provided evidence of 540 individuals. Given the cautionary note above about taking MNI

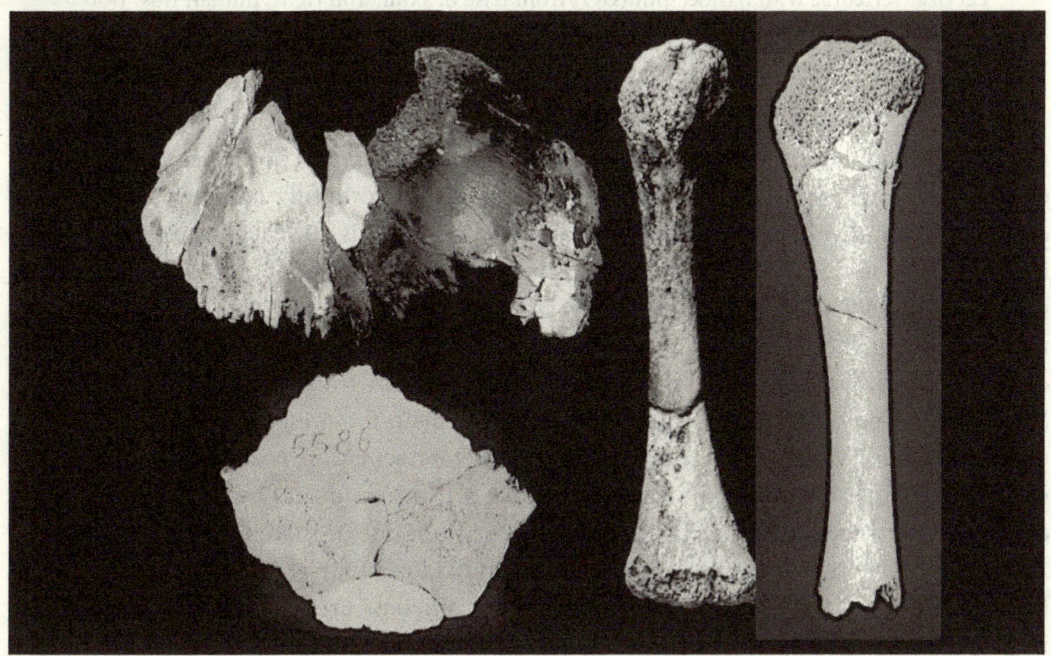

FIGURE 6.5 Reassembled pieces of the same bone showing disparate degrees of burning. Left: parts of crania; middle: a right humerus; left: a right femur. Not to scale. Copyright © Jeffrey H. Schwartz.

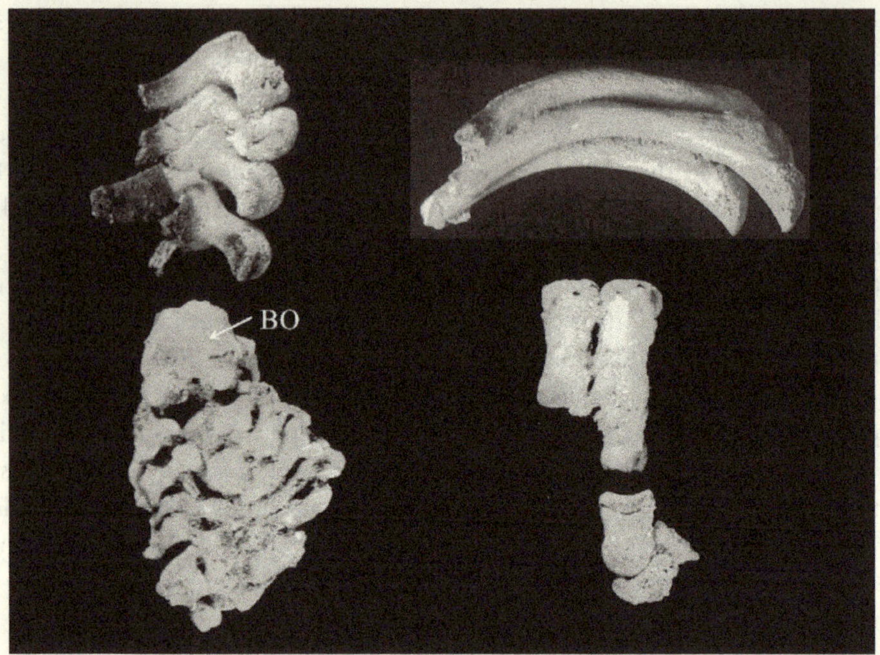

FIGURE 6.6 Bones in anatomical position with minimal burning. Top left: human cervical vertebrae, note charring primarily on the spines (posteriorly). Bottom left: human cervical vertebrae with basiocciput (BO) from base of skull. Top right: human ribs. Bottom right: bones from the foot of a lamb. Not to scale. Copyright © Jeffrey H. Schwartz.

at face value without considering all factors that could impact interpretation, we can conclude for this Tophet sample that, if not initially anatomically complete, some parts of these 540 individuals had been cremated. Since there is sufficient skeletal evidence in single and double internments to reconstruct these numbers of relatively completely preserved individuals, we can reasonably conclude that once ash and charcoal cooled, those retrieving the remains of these one or two individuals were not concerned about collecting all skeletal elements, much less separating them from charred plants remains. Such "sloppy" post-crematory cleanup may partly explain the presence of duplicated skeletal elements for which indication of full skeletal representation is lacking. In turn, this suggests that repeated use of the same crematory platform and that bones and teeth from one cremation were randomly collected with those from one or more previous cremations. Alternatively, the skewed sampling of multiple individuals may reflect a group cremation from which bones were randomly divided among different urns. The general scenario of incomplete retrieval of cremated osseous remains also implies that some (perhaps many) bones and teeth did not end up in the Tophet.

Estimation of age-at-death of the human remains was based on determination of relative states of tooth formation, including discriminating between deciduous and permanent teeth, and intra-individual sequences of tooth formation, supplemented with analyses of relative states of development of cranial and postcranial elements (particularly changes in the petrosal bone, such as closure of the subarcuate fossa and fusion to the squamosal, and basisphenoid, such as shape of the optic foramina and shape and closure of the fissure in the external surface), and measurements of cranial (basisphenoid, basiocciput, petrosal) and postcranial (pubis, ischium) elements. The age distribution of the sample is significant: ca. 23 percent were prenatal, ca. 30.7 percent perinatal, and ca. 11.1 percent between one and two postnatal months, with numbers of individuals diminishing rapidly after ca. six months (Schwartz et al. 2010) (Figure 6.7). In appreciation of potential bone shrinkage due to exposure to heat, we "enlarged" the cranial and postcranial metrics incrementally to 25 percent (representing 25% shrinkage), with the result that significant numbers of individuals were still classified as prenatal.

In consideration of the possibility that infants of low birth weight (LBW) would be incorrectly classified as prenatal, a survey of the literature revealed that while the mortality rate of these < 2500 gram neonates is ca 40 percent higher than infants of normal (N)BW (> 2500 gram) (Behrman and Shiono 1997), long bone lengths of LBW and NBW individuals are similar (Jaya et al. 1995). The latter is of potential interest with regard to the Carthaginian Tophet sample in light of ailments that could have afflicted pregnant women and thus potentially impacted their fetuses, resulting in LBW neonates. Given their high mortality rate, it is likely that some LBW infants are represented in the Tophet sample.

In order to test the reliability of developmentally and metrically based estimates of age-at-death, teeth from 50 individuals that were identified as being perinatal were subjected to neonatal line (NL) analysis.

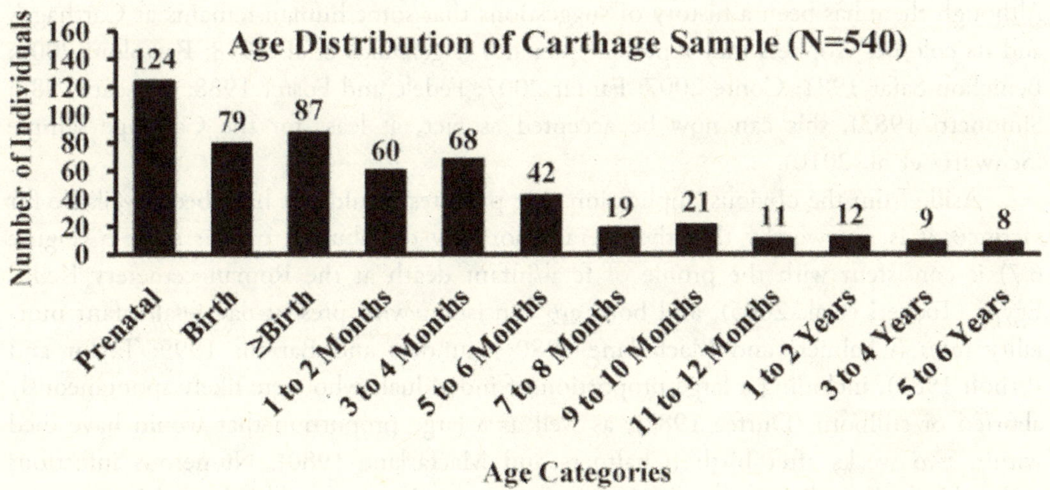

Figure 6.7 Age distribution of the Carthage Tophet sample [from Schwartz et al. (Schwartz et al. 2010)].

An NL is observed histologically as a disruption of prism formation in the crown's enamel near its juncture with underlying dentine. It typically emerges within a few days after a fetus leaves the uterine environment and reflects the traumatic physiological impact of this event. Significantly, of the 50 specimens chosen for NL analysis because their ages-at-death had been estimated as being perinatal (based on tooth and cranial bone development as well as shrinkage-corrected measurements of these bones), 26 lacked an NL (Schwartz et al. 2010), which means that if not prematurely aborted or stillborn, these individuals had not survived beyond the few days during which an NL forms. In turn, the latter suggests that these individuals would not have been available or even deemed suitable for sacrifice.

Since all Tophet urns bearing human remains yielded at least some intact tooth crowns, we based our age estimates first and foremost on relative states of tooth-crown formation (Schwartz et al. 2010). Thus, even if the assertion (Smith et al. 2011) of heat inducing extreme tooth-crown shrinkage were true, the *relative* states of tooth formation would not be affected (i.e., teeth would just be smaller, not morphologically altered).

Lastly, our Tophet sample included 70 pelvic ilia sufficiently intact to permit estimation of sex (Schwartz et al. 2010). Using Schutkowski's morphological sexing criteria (Schutkowski 1993) based on a sample of known-age male and female children, and consistent with the predictability of correctly allocating specimens to sex, we identified 38 ilia as probably and two as possibly female, and 26 as probably and one as possibly male; three ilia could not be allocated, even tentatively, to sex. Given the likelihood that at least some individuals we identified as female were indeed female, it is obvious that males were not the focus of any Tophet-related activity.

Conclusion

Although there has been a history of suggestions that some human remains at Carthage's and its colonies' Tophets may represent prenates (Agelarakis et al. 1998; Bartoloni 2006; Benichou-Safar 1981; Conte 2007; Fantar 2007; Fedele and Foster 1988; Moscati 1987; Simonetti 1983), this can now be accepted as fact, at least for the Carthage sample (Schwartz et al. 2010).

Aside from the obvious implication that prenates would not have been available for sacrifice, it is noteworthy that the overall mortality distribution of this sample (Figure 6.7) is consistent with the profile of fetal/infant death at the Roman cemetery Kellis, Egypt (Tocheri et al. 2005), and both are consistent with present-day fetal/infant mortality rates (Chalmers and Macfarlane 1980; Saunders and Barrans 1999; Taylor and Pernoll 1987), including a large proportion of individuals who were likely spontaneously aborted or stillborn (Durfee 1987), as well as a large proportion that would have died within two weeks after birth (Chalmers and Macfarlane 1980). Numerous infectious and noninfectious diseases can lead to spontaneous abortion, stillbirth, and prematurity (Behrman and Shiono 1997; Taylor and Pernoll 1987). Further, numerous ailments that result from poor water management and disposal of human and animal waste, which were apparently significant vectors of disease at the Carthage-like cities Pompeii, Rome, and Ostia (Scobie 1986) lead to severe dehydration, which is still a common cause of infant death (Behrman and Shiono 1997).

Although it may be more spectacular to imagine heartless Carthaginians dispatching their offspring with ritualized regularity than to attribute fetal and infant/child death to common and prevalent diseases, the latter is the simpler and more plausible explanation of the data. This is not to say that the cremated bones of animals in Tophet urns, albeit rare, do not attest to some kind of sacrifice. But it might also be worth considering that when only a portion, often an extremity, of a lamb or kid is present in an urn and comingled with human remains (Schwartz, unpublished data), the animal had been "killed" both for consumption and as an offering to the gods via the smoke of cremation (Detienne 1989).

Did the Carthaginians never sacrifice a human? This study cannot completely rule out that possibility. Yet one cannot always assume that the only focus of sacrifice was a healthy individual. Would we think the Carthaginians cruel for the taking the life of a congenitally ill or malformed infant or child, and thus sparing this son or daughter a terrible life? Are the barely charred bones and examples of bones in anatomical position reflective of a benign sense of the meaning of "passing through fire"? Unfortunately, bones and teeth cannot provide answers to these questions. But they do suggest that the Tophets at Carthage and its colonies were at base cemeteries for the cremated remains of the very young, regardless of how they died. As Stuckey (2009) has eloquently argued, Tophets represented a special place into which Tanit welcomed those whose death was unfortunately premature.

ACKNOWLEDGMENTS

I thank Carrie Murray for inviting me to participate in this stimulating workshop and IEMA for sponsoring it, Frank Houghton for years of collaboration analyzing and re-analyzing the Tophet bones, Roberto Macchiarelli and Luca Bondioli for undertaking the neonatal line analysis, and Bruno Marsca for translating sources in Italian. Thanks also to the Department of Antiquities, Tunisia, for permission to study the human and animal remains from various excavations at Carthage.

REFERENCES CITED

Agelarakis, A. P., A. Kanta, and N. Stampolidis 1998 The Osseous Record in the Western Necropolis of Amathous: An Archaeo-anthropological Investigation. In *Eastern Mediterranean Cyprus-Dodecanese-Crete 16th–6th cent. B.C.*, edited by V. Karageorghis and N. Stampolidis, pp. 217–232. University of Crete, Heraklion.

Allen, F. D., J. Brunet, W. C. Greene and C. P. Parker 1939 *Scholia Platonica*. American Philological Association, Haverford.

Bartoloni, P. 2006 Il Tophet: un pietoso rito offuscato da troppo miti. *Darwin Quaderni* 1:68–75.

Behrman, R. E., and P. H. Shiono 1997 Neonatal Risk Factors. In *Neonatal-Perinatal Medicine: Diseases of the Fetus and Infant*, edited by A. A. Fanaroff and R. J. Martin, pp. 3–12. Mosby, St. Louis.

Benichou-Safar, H. 1981 A propos des ossements humains du *tophet* de Carthage. *Rivista di Studi Fenici* 5:5–9.

Brown, S. 1991 *Late Carthaginian Child Sacrifice and Sacrificial Monuments in their Mediterranean Context*. JSOT Press, Sheffield.

Chalmers, J., and A. Macfarlane 1980 Interpretation of Perinatal Statistics. In *Topics in Perinatal Medicine*, edited by B. A. Wharton, pp. 1–11. Pitman Medical, Tunbridge Wells.

Charles-Picard, G. 1945 Le sanctuaire dit de Tanit à Carthage. *Comptes-rendus des séances de l'Academie des Inscriptions et Belles-Lettres* 89e année:443–452.

Conte, S. 2007 Child Sacrifice: Children of Phoenician Punic Carthage Were Not Sacrificed to the Gods. http://phoenicia.org/childsacrifice.html, 4–6.

Detienne, M. 1989 Culinary Practices and the Spirit of Sacrifice. In *The Cuisine of Sacrifice among the Greeks*, edited by M. Detienne and J.-P. Vernant, pp. 1–20. University of Chicago Press, Chicago.

Docter, R. F., R. Chelbi, B. M. Telmini, H. G. Niemeyer, and A. de Wulf 2007 Punic Carthage: Two Decades of Archaeological Investigations. In *Las ciudades fenicio-púnicas en el Mediterráneo Occidental*, edited by J. L. López Castro, pp. 85–104. Editorial Universidad de Almería, Almería.

Docter, R. F., E. Smits, T. Hakbijl, I. L. M. Stuijts, and J. van der Plicht 2003 Interdisciplinary Research on Urns from the Carthaginian Tophet and Their Contents. *Paleohistoria* 43–44 (2001–02):417–433.

Durfee, R. B. 1987 Obstetric Complications of Pregnancy. In *Topics in Perinatal Medicine*, edited by B. A. Wharton, pp. 255–278. Pitman Medical, Tunbridge Wells.

Fantar, M. H. 2007 Child Sacrifice: Children of Phoenician Punic Carthage Were Not Sacrificed. http://phoenicia.org/childsacrifice.html, 2–4.

Fazekas, I. G., and F. Kósa 1979 *Forensic Fetal Osteology*. Akademiai Kiado, Budapest.

Fedele, F., and C. Foster 1988 Tharros ovicaprini sacrificiali e rituale del Tofet. *Rivista di Studi Fenici* 16:29–42.

Flaubert, G. 1882 *Salammbó*. Michel Leve, Paris.

Gejvall, N.-G. 1949 Determination of Cremated Bones from Carthage. *Report for the Ashmolean Museum*. Ashmolean Museum, Oxford.

Gejvall, N.-G. 1969 Cremations. In *Science in Archaeology*, edited by D. Brothwell, E. Higgs, and G. Clark, pp. 468–479. Thames and Hudson, London.

Harden, D. 1927 Punic Urns from the Precinct of Tanit at Carthage. *American Journal of Archaeology* 31: 297–310.

Harden, D. 1963 *The Phoenicians*. Frederick A. Praeger, New York.

Hesse, B., and P. Wapnish 1985 *Animal Bone Archaeology: From Objectives to Analysis*. Taraxacum, Washington, D.C.

Jaya, D. S., N. S. Kumar, and L. S. Bai 1995 Anthropometric Indices, Cord Length, and Placental Weight in Newborns. *Indian Pediatrics* 32:1183–1188.

Kelsey, F. W. 1926 *Excavations at Carthage, 1925: a Preliminary Report*. Macmillan, New York.

Krogman, W. M., and M. Y. Iscan 1986 *The Human Skeleton in Forensic Medicine*. Charles C. Thomas, Springfield.

Lancel, S. 1995 *Carthage: A History*. Oxford University Press, Oxford.

Lapeyre, R. P., and A. Pellegrin 1942 *Carthage Punique (814–146 avant J.-C.)*. Payot, Paris.

Lovejoy, C. O., R. S. Meindl, R. P. Mensforth, and T. J. Barton 1985 Multifactorial Determination of Skeletal Age at Death: A Method and Blind Tests of Its Accuracy. *American Journal of Physical Anthropology* 68:1–14.

McKinley, J. I. 1989 Cremations: Expectations, Methodologies, and Realities. In *Burial Archaeology: Current Research, Methods and Developments*, 211, edited by C. A. Roberts, F. Lee, and J. Bintliff, pp. 65–76. BAR British Series, London.

McKinley, J. I. 1994 *The Anglo-Saxon Cemetery at Spong Hill, North Elmham. Part VIII: the Cremations*. Field Archaeology Division, Norfolk Museums Service, Dereham.

Mosca, P. G. 1975 *Child Sacrifice in Canaanite and Israelite Religion*. Unpublished PhD Dissertation, Harvard University, Cambridge.

Moscati, S. 1965 *The World of the Phoenicians*. Weidenfeld and Nicolson, London.

Moscati, S. 1987 Il sacrificio punico dei fanciulli: realtà or invenzione? *Quaderni dell'Accademia Nazionale dei Lincei* 261:4–15.

Pearson, L., and F. H. Sandbach 1960 *Plutarch Moralia*. Harvard University Press, Cambridge.

Poinssot, L., and R. Lantier 1923 Un sanctuaire de Tanit à Carthage. *Revue dd l'Histoire des Religions* 1923:32–66.

Quinn, J. 2011 The Cultures of the Tophet. Identification and Identity in the Phoenician Diaspora. In *Cultural Identity in the Ancient Mediterranean*, edited by E. S. Gruen, pp. 388–413. Getty Research Institute, Los Angeles.

Richard, J. 1961 *Etude Médico-Légale des Urnes Sacrificielles Puniques et de leur Contenu*. Ph.D., Lille.

Saunders, S. R., and L. Barrans 1999 What Can Be Done about the Infant Category in Skeletal Sample? In *Human Growth in the Past*, edited by R. D. Hoppa and C. M. Firzgerald, pp. 183–209. Cambridge University Press, Cambridge.

Schutkowski, H. 1993 Sex Determination of Infant and Juvenile Skeletons I. Morphognostic Features. *American Journal of Physical Anthropology* 90: 199–205.

Schwartz, J. H. 1989 The Tophet and "Sacrifice" at Phoenician Carthage: An Osteologist's Perspective. *Terra* 28:16–25.

Schwartz, J. H. 1993 *What the Bones Tell Us*. Henry Holt, New York.

Schwartz, J. H. 2007 *Skeleton Keys: An Introduction to Human Skeletal Morphology, Development, and Analysis*. Oxford University Press, New York.

Schwartz, J. H., F. Houghton, L. Bondioli, and R. Macchiarelli 2012 Bones, Teeth, and Estimating Age of Perinates: Carthaginian Infant Sacrifice Revisited. *Antiquity* 86:738–745.

Schwartz, J. H., F. Houghton, R. Macchiarelli, and L. Bondioli 2010 Skeletal Remains from Punic Carthage Do Not Support Systematic Sacrifice of Infants. *PLoS ONE* 5:1–12.

Scobie, A. 1986 Slums, Sanitation, and Mortality in the Roman World. *Klio* 2: 399–433.

Simonetti, A. 1983 Sacrifici umani e uccisioni rituali nel mondo Fenicio-Punico: il contributo delle fonti letterarie. *Rivista di Studi Fenici* 11:91–111.

Smith, P., G. Avishai, J. A. Greene, and L. E. Stager 2011 Aging Cremated Infants: The Problem of Sacrifice at the Tophet of Carthage. *Antiquity* 85:859–875.

Smith, P., L. E. Stager, J. A. Greene, and G. Avishai 2013 Age Estimations Attest to Infant Sacrifice at the Carthage Tophet. *Antiquity* 87:1191–1199.

Stager, L. E. 1980 The Rite of Child Sacrifice at Carthage. In *New Light on Ancient Carthage*, edited by J. G. Pedley, pp. 1–11. University of Michigan Press, Ann Arbor.

Stager, L. E., and J. A. Greene 2000 An Odyssey Debate: Were Living Children Sacrificed to the Gods—Yes. *Archaeological Odyssey* 2:29–31.

Stager, L. E., and J. A. Greene 2007 Child Sacrifice: Yes, Children of Phoenician/Punic Carthage Were Sacrificed to the Gods. http://phoenicia.org/childsacrifice.html, 2–3.

Stager, L. E., and S. R. Wolff 1984 Child Sacrifice at Carthage: Religious Rite or Population Control. *Biblical Archaeology Review* 10:31–51.

Stuckey, J. 2009 Tanit of Carthage. *MatriFocus* 8–4:1–12.

Taylor, C. M., and M. L. Pernoll 1987 Normal Pregnancy and Prenatal Care. In *Current Obstetric & Gynecologic Diagnosis & Treatment 1987*, edited by M. L. Pernoll and R. C. Benson, pp. 161–177. Appleton and Lange, Norwalk.

Tocheri, M. W., T. L. Dupras, B. P. Sheldrick, and J. E. Molto 2005 Roman Period Fetal Skeletons from the East Cemetery (Kellis 2) of Kellis, Egypt. *International Journal of Osteoarchaeology* 15:326–341.

Ubelaker, D. H. 1989 *Human Skeletal Remains*. Taraxacum, Washington, D. C.

van Zeist, W., S. Bottema, and M. van der Veen 2001 *Diet and Vegetation at Ancient Carthage: The Archaeological Evidence*. Gröningen Institute of Archaeology, Gröningen.

Whitaker, J. I. S. 1921 *Motya: A Phoenician Colony in Sicily*. G. Bell and Sons, London.

Xella, P. 2010 Per un "modello interpretativo" del *tofet*: il *tofet* come necropoli infantile? In *Tiro, Cartagine, Lixus: nuove acquisizioni. Atti del convegno internazionale in onore di Maria Giulia Amadasi Guzzo*, Quaderni di Vicino Oriente 4, edited by P. Bartoloni, P. Matthiae, I. Nigro, and L. Romano, pp. 259–279. Università di Roma <<La Sapienze>>, Rome.

Xella, P., J. Quinn, V. Mechiorri, and P. van Dommelen 2013 Phoenician Bones of Contention. *Antiquity* 87:1199–1207.

Chapter Seven

The Art of Ancient Greek Sacrifice

Spectacle, Gaze, Performance

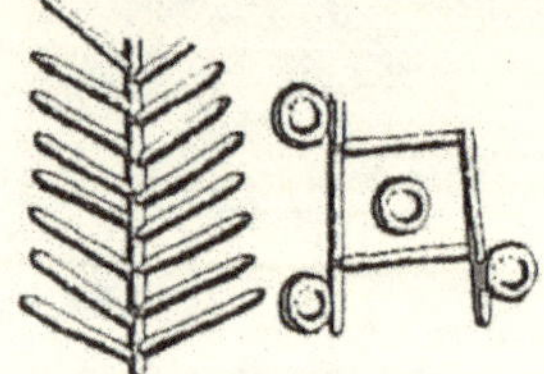

Tyler Jo Smith

Abstract   *The iconography of religious practices in ancient Greek art has received a certain amount of attention from scholars in recent years. On the subject of animal sacrifice in particular, a key starting place remains Folkert van Straten's book published in 1995. Therein, the author gathers a large amount of archaeological data, namely, painted vases and sculpted reliefs, and presents these according to the deities they represent or honor. Using van Straten as a starting point, this paper revisits the evidence he collected and the manner in which he approached it. Here it is suggested that the time is ripe for a discussion of Greek sacrificial iconography within its broader cultural and artistic contexts. Two separate, yet related modern concepts—"the Gaze" and "Performance"—are applied to examples on vases in hopes of demonstrating alternative methods of visual analysis. In a number of instances, their unified iconographic programs place "the art of ancient Greek sacrifice" directly in conversation with the festival and performance cultures of archaic and classical Greece.*

The publication of Folkert van Straten's *Hiera Kala: Images of Animal Sacrifice in Archaic and Classical Greece* in 1995 opened up a new chapter in the study of ancient Greek religion. Cataloguing and discussing some 674 artifacts, the author assembles ancient Greek vases into "broad iconographical groups" and sculpted votive reliefs "according to recipient deities and sanctuaries of provenance" (van Straten 1995:193). Using van Straten as the starting point, this paper revisits the evidence for animal sacrifice in Greek art and the ways in which van Straten, among others, has collected the evidence and approached it. The focus will be limited to a single object category—ancient Greek vases—and one chunk of time—the archaic and classical periods (sixth-fifth century B.C.E.). By way of introduction, the key literature on the subject of sacrificial iconography will be summarized, beginning with but not confined to van Straten. One question should be kept in mind: Twenty-five years on, what has changed with regard to our understanding of this subject? In light of new evidence and alternative methodologies, how has our thinking about the iconography of sacrifice on Greek vases made during the sixth and fifth centuries B.C.E. evolved? It should readily become clear that identifying a scene as "sacrifice" is not as straightforward as it may seem, and scholars have not always been consistent in their selection criteria. In an effort to steer the discussion in a new direction, I shall then apply two modern but related approaches to visual culture to the ancient Greek vase corpus: the gaze and performance. By reframing depictions of sacrifice on vases in these particular terms, it is hoped that we may better understand the spectacle of sacrifice as portrayed by the vase painter on the one hand, and the experience of sacrifice on the part of actual participants on the other. Furthermore, some of the visual methods employed by vase painters to direct the outside viewer's attention will be revealed. In this way, and on more than one level, art and life might be better related and more clearly understood. Finally, it is suggested that we should be speaking in terms of "sacrificial" imagery—a necessarily broad category—comprised of many stages and multiple participants.

In Search of Sacrifice

Prior to van Staten, much scholarship on ancient Greek sacrifice was concerned with the question of origins, a problem regarding which art and archaeology informs us little (Bowie 1995; *ThesCRA* 2004:1:60–61; van Straten 1995:2–3). Based on surviving literary and epigraphic sources, the vocabulary of sacrifice has been established and applied by archaeologists and classicists alike. When we turn to van Straten's book *Hiera Kala* (literally "the holy things are beautiful"; cf. Xenophon, *Anabasis* I.8.16), we find a clearly laid out iconographic approach and an unapologetic understanding of the limitations of his evidence. The chapters are structured both temporally and thematically with regard to the practice of animal sacrifice (there is minimal artistic or archaeological evidence for human sacrifice; cf. Bremmer 2007; Hughes 1991). Rather than dividing the material by technique or painter (i.e., for vases), the author carries the reader through three ritual stages: "pre-kill," "the killing," and "post-kill." In the case of the first, he is able to further subdivide the archaeological evidence into categories of "vase paintings" and "votive offerings" (pinakes, reliefs, etc.), thus following his catalogued data. Though fully integrating abundant textual and inscriptional evidence, the imposed layout of the book calls for careful, sometimes literal, readings of the images themselves. There are frequent attempts to match the written record with the visual one, and to contextualize the images in an ancient mindset. To quote the author himself: "[I]t is not wise to try to identify the object by establishing what it looks like *to us*. We should try to recognize it, taking the visible world as *we* know it as our frame of reference. The Greek vase painters painted these scenes with their contemporary compatriots in mind. It is *their* frame of reference we must try to reconstruct" (van Straten 1995:120). It should be emphasized that *Hiera Kala* was not van Straten's initial foray into this subject. In several shorter publications the same scholar dealt with similar or related subject matter and evidence in much the same manner, as is seen in "Gifts for the Gods," a section of H. S. Versnels's 1981 edited volume entitled *Faith, Hope and Worship*, and again in two volumes of conference proceedings from the late 1980s (van Straten 1981, 1987, 1988). Throughout these publications, van Straten incorporates information about the sacrificial "ceremony" or "ritual" (1988:51, 1995:161), and the details that vase painters or artists working in other media include, among them tables, altars, animals, and personnel.

A second substantial book on the subject of sacrifice and Greek art appeared in 2002. Jörg Gebauer's *Pompe und Thysia* (literally: "Procession and Sacrifice") is a lengthy tome based on a 1999 doctoral dissertation. Unlike van Straten, Gebauer isolates vases as iconographic evidence. Though largely concerned with animal sacrifice, much of the book is devoted to procession, as the title indicates, with 138 Athenian vases catalogued under this heading, and another 10 non-Athenian examples, among them Boeotian, Corinthian, and South Italian (Gebauer 2002:161–165). The author further catalogues the successive stages: preparation for sacrifice (23 examples), killing (28 examples), the aftermath (butchering [39], reading the entrails/hieroscopy [22], cooking [83], consuming [48])—each phase followed by a discussion and analysis based on the catalogued evidence, and an appendix of even more examples (Gebauer 2002:550–582). Discussions of wider cultural aspects, such as religious personnel, gods and heroes, and equipment are also included. Like van Straten, the analyses are sequential and catalogue derived. Also in both books, the authors are driven by theme rather than by the artists or groups to which the vases have been previously assigned. Similarly, Laxander's *Individuum und Gemeinschaft im Fest* (2000), explores our theme with relation to other individual and group rituals, including funerary evidence, and again uses vases as the primary iconographic evidence.

Other contributors to the discussion of Greek sacrifice on vases are less substantial but no less significant. A chapter authored by Durand and Schnapp in the seminal *Cité des images* of 1984 (appearing in English as *A City of Images* [Bérard et al. 1989]), as well as various chapters in Detienne and Vernant's *La Cuisine du sacrifice en pays grec*, published a decade earlier in 1979 (appearing in English as *The Cuisine of Sacrifice among the Greeks* [1989]), look to vases as at once the most informative and most enigmatic pieces of evidence in the puzzle of ancient Greek sacrificial ritual. The approach amongst this "Paris (or Francophone) School" of scholars is more overtly iconological than iconographical—i.e., more concerned with unlocking meanings than creating typologies, generating definitions, or describing scenes (Bérard 1983; Bérard et al. 1989). Similarly, Sarah Pierce's "Death, Ritual and Thysia," a 1993 article appearing in *Classical Antiquity*, ventures to "shed light on what Greeks thought and felt about the ritual" (220). In more recent years the images of sacrifice on black- and red-figure vases, as well as other cultic activities have found their way into various discussions focused on figure-decorated pottery in particular, among them an article by Borgers (2008) on "religious citizenship" in Athens, an essay by Blok (2009) on private versus public sacrifice and procession, and the recently published doctoral thesis of the late Eleni Hatzivassiliou on later Athenian black-figure iconography (2010:esp. 48–53). Unfortunately, S. Bundrick's article (2014) appeared too late for consideration in this essay. Two articles have dealt with the subject in the context of festivals and with a certain amount of attention to non-Athenian evidence: Scheffer's 1992 contribution to the *Iconography of Greek Cult*, and my own essay in *Games and Festivals of Antiquity* published in 2004. Such presentations only confirm the importance of vases in the discussion of Greek religion, and the special, if complex, role of sacrificial imagery at the convergence of mortal and mythical realms.

One final publication that must be mentioned with regard to our joint subjects of sacrifice and Greek art is the *Thesaurus Cultus et Rituum Anitquorum* (*ThesCRA*), the sequel to the better-known *Lexicon Iconographicum Mythologiae Classicae* (*LIMC*). The format of these encyclopedic volumes necessitates a selective cataloguing of evidence under specific cultic or religious categories, including archaeological evidence, texts, and testimonia. The two multiauthored entries that concern us here are the one on "Sacrifices" and another on "Processions," both appearing in Volume 1 (2004). The treatment of Greek animal sacrifice divides the subject by deities and heroes, furnishings and victims, circumstances and location, participants and implements, pre-kill, killing, holocaust, butchering, and cooking. The authors also incorporate a section on archaeozoology. Similarly, in the entry on "Processions," much of the evidence is listed according to deity. Such an approach in both instances, prioritizes the gods and cults themselves, and also considers the function of deities who are sometimes included in the scenes as observers or as active participants.

Such is the case on an Athenian black-figure band cup (Figure 7.1) of c. 550 B.C.E., and now in a private collection, where a partially preserved Athena is situated behind a burning altar (van Staten 1995:203, V55). Before her stands a female figure, perhaps a priestess, prepared to greet a crowded multifigure sacrificial procession (perhaps led by a

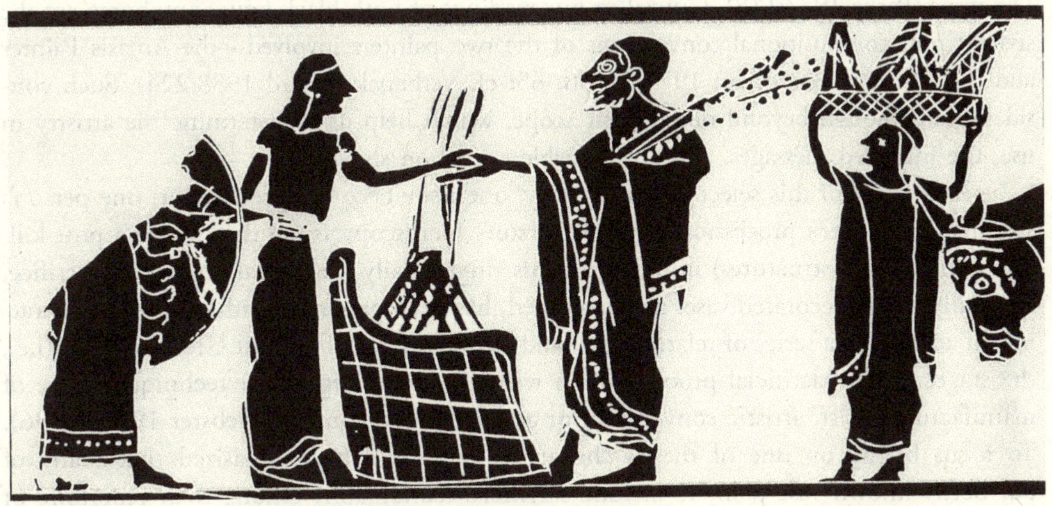

FIGURE 7.1 Detail of Athenian black-figure band-cup. c. 550 B.C.E. Niarchos Collection A 031. Drawing by D. Weiss, after Laxander 2000: pl. 1.

priest, according to van Straten) complete with victims, basket bearer (*kanephoros*), branch bearers (*thallophoroi*), and musicians. Sadly, the goddess herself is only partially preserved. But, as we shall see shortly, her presence is probably not the intended focal point of this crowded composition. *ThesCRA* lists and illustrates this cup under the category of Processions (2004:1:78, no. 105). Meanwhile, in the *ThesCRA* chapter on "Sacrifices" we find another Athenian black-figure vase of about the same date, an amphora in Berlin (F 1690) attributed to the Amasis Painter, listed under the subcategory of "processions to the altar" (2004:1:113, no. 450). Five figures, at least three of whom are draped and bearded males carrying branches, walk uniformly to the right. One of the males carries a piglet, the figure at the front balances a basket, and the figure bringing up the rear holds a jug and perhaps a wineskin. On the opposite side of this vase is a dancing scene (van Straten 1995:197, V22, "komos"). An Attic black-figure vase of slightly later date (Munich 1441), attributed to a painter known as the Affecter, is also listed as a procession (*ThesCRA* 2004:1:114, no. 452). The sacrificial procession in this example is less subtle thanks to the inclusion of the altar; but the placement of the altar beneath the handle is a more than a little puzzling, as is the diminutive priestess who tends it. Although no god or goddess is present at the sacrifice, I would suggest that the placement of the altar and of important religious personnel beneath the handle, and thus at the juncture of the two sides, encourages us (the outsider viewer) to have a look at the divine Dionysos who is represented on the other side, accompanied by (according to some scholars) Ikarios, the bringer of wine to Athens (Carpenter 1986:44–47; van Straten 1995:165–167). A comparison can be made with Attic black-figure skyphoi attributed to the Theseus Painter, an artist who sometimes places a goat beneath the handles in, arguably, a similar manner and for a similar purpose (Borgers 1999; van Straten 1995:52–53). In other words, the altar is not hidden from sight, but functions as a unifying element. And, if that is in fact its role, the procession would be suggestive of a specific festival, the Anthesteria, to honor a specific god, namely Dionysos (Parke 1977:118). Crucial to our readings of both black-figure amphorae are the stylistic and compositional conventions of the two painters involved—the Amasis Painter and the Affecter (Boardman 1974:54–56, 65; cf. Verbanck-Piérard 1988:224). Such considerations, though beyond our present scope, would help us to determine the artistry in use, the intended messages, and any possible events on show.

As a result of this select historiography, one issue becomes pretty clear: one person's sacrifice is another's procession; or, one person's hieroscopy is another person's post-kill. The structure (or structures) imposed on this single "daily life" ritual, known as sacrifice, especially where decorated vases are concerned, has been presented with a view to illustrating an activity or a series of related ones, and as documents of ancient Greek religion (i.e., the stages of the sacrificial process) often without careful regard for technique, place of manufacture, artist, artistic convention, or archaeological context (Webster 1969:74–96). To focus briefly on one of these—the artist—it should be emphasized that many of our better known vase painters include sacrificial iconography among their repertoire of scenes, among them the black-figure painters: Lydos, the Amasis Painter, Elbows Out, Swing Painter, the Antimenes, Gela and Theseus Painters; and the red-figure painters: Eucharides, Brygos Painter, Nikosthenes, Polygnotos, Pan, Makron, Oltos, Douris, and the Meidias Painter (Boardman 2001). There is even some evidence to suggest that a few of these painters "specialized" in sacrificial images and should be assessed for their greater contribution to religious iconography in general (Boardman 1989:221; Borgers 1999:88; Hatzivassiliou 2010:48–51).

THE SACRIFICIAL GAZE?

"The Gaze" (with a capital g) has been applied very little to the history of Greek art or ancient Greek culture, and is a relative methodological newcomer (Cairns 2005; Frontisi-Ducroux and Vernant 1997). The term has wider art historical applications and has found its way into the corpus of writings about the ancient Romans and their visual culture (Jay 1993:esp. ch. 1; Fredrick 2002). Gaze is related to *viewing* and *spectatorship* and implies an *audience* concerned with *watching, looking,* even *staring.* To quote Margaret Olin: "The term 'gaze' is . . . emblematic of the recent attempt to wrest formal discussions of art from the grasp of linguistic theory, to focus on what is visual about a work of art and yet addresses wider issues of social communication . . . there must be someone to gaze and there may be someone to gaze back" (2003:319). Our attempt to apply the term to ancient Greek vases, with their preference for multi- and especially human-figure compositions, seems an obvious idea. While it might in some ways appear almost simplistic (i.e., who stares at whom, or who's looking at what), it is a powerful tool for understanding the images and the way that the painter intends us as outside or external viewers to experience them.

In black-figure vase painting the gaze best applies to, and perhaps originates in, scenes with erotic or sympotic content (Frontisi-Ducroux 1996). That is not to say that figures in mythological scenes never look at one another within the context of their wars or births or heroic exploits, but the function of the gaze in certain daily life categories seems somehow more meaningful when we consider that the ancient viewer would have been able to share the experience of such everyday events as dancing, drinking, or lovemaking, procession, libation, or sacrifice. In scenes of revelry or *komos,* we find the precursors to both processional and sacrificial iconography. On an Athenian black-figure skyphos of c. 580 B.C.E. we see that lightly clad male figures hold drinking cups and walk in single file, each facing the same direction (Athens 640; Smith 2010: Plate 6a). The figures focus on an undisclosed destination: perhaps an *andron* (literally "men's room") to attend a *symposion,* or (less likely) a sanctuary to leave offerings. The same types of figures can be seen on vases of the same shape, decorated by the same group of painters, but in these instances the pair have set down their drinks and taken up the dance (e.g., Athens 528; Smith 2010: Plates 6c-d, and pp. 52–56). Although scholars before me have suggested that "komast dancers" such as these, are performing in honor of a god, probably Dionysos, in the context of a religious festival, I have specified elsewhere that there is little or no evidence to suggest that this is the case (Smith 2007). These are performers of a different stage: the private drinking party, associated with the Greek word *symposion.* The extreme eye contact the dancers make is overt, as they kick their legs, slap their bottoms, sometimes even snap their fingers. When a third dancer is added to a scene, the problem of gaze becomes more complicated, but the artists develop and implement a simple solution: the outer figures face toward the center, and so we the viewer are enticed to do so as well (e.g., Paris, Louvre E 742; Smith 2010: Plate 8a). Painters of another group of black-figure dance scenes, those belonging to the so-called Tyrrhenian Group increase the use of the gaze as well as the erotic content of the scenes. The male dancers may form gazing pairs (London 1897.7–27.2; Smith 2010: Plate 14b), pairs that gaze (Boston 98.916; Smith 2010: Plate 13a), a male-female gazing couple (Tokyo, Kurashiki-Ninagawa 22; Smith 2010: Plate 13b), and (my personal favorite) the human-animal gaze (Louvre E 840; Smith 2010: Plate 14d). Painters of this group, and indeed others will add a wine-mixing bowl used at a *symposion,* such as a dinos or krater, and redirect the gaze, and often the action, toward that object (e.g., Berlin 1966.17; Smith 2010: Plate 9c, and pp. 46–49). The large mixing vessel defines the scene and situates it in a specific location. Not only is such an object an indispensable element of the event (much like the altar in a scene of sacrifice), but the viewers—be they ancient or modern—are encouraged to step inside or "enter" the imagery, and to communicate on some level with these dancer-drinkers (Bérard et al. 1989:23). Related to these are scenes of homosexual courtship where an older man may stare directly into the eyes of a younger man, while performing the ritualistic "up-and-down-position" or exchanging animal love-gifts (e.g., Cyprus, Nicosia Museum C 440; Smith 2010: Plate 16c, and pp. 108–117). Here the gaze is unambiguous and potent.

Returning to sacrificial iconography, we may recognize and observe the use of the gaze as, again, a way of directing the viewer's attention toward a specific action or moment. If we look again at the black-figure band-cup mentioned above (Figure 7.1), we have a scene that has been labeled as both procession and pre-kill (*ThesCRA* 2004:1:78, no. 105; van Staten 1995:14). While both descriptions are correct—we note a large group of figures and animals moving uniformly in a single direction, with a lit altar as their destination—if we look more carefully at the figures situated immediately on either side of the altar, we witness the gaze in use. It is a shame that the face of the goddess Athena is not preserved; however, the priest and priestess figures, who join hands next to her or in front of her, are also staring at each other, and thus directing the spectacle toward a fundamental and immovable element: the altar itself. Such an intentional use of the gaze is not always utilized by black-figure painters of sacrificial scenes, who oftentimes prefer the fanfare of the moving procession to the static moment of the kill itself. In other examples, eyes meet over the altar, and the parties involved can be human, animal, or divine (e.g., van Straten 1995: Plates 4, 5, 8, and 12). Black- and red-figure painters manipulate these details, be they mobile and immobile, to create a variety of combinations, all of which still say "sacrifice" to the viewer. Among the most interesting, for our purposes, are those where one of the gazing pair is a stone statue of a phallic Herm who, though displayed at an altar, both stares out at—and is stared at by—a basket-bearer or the sacrificial victim itself (Gebauer 2002: Figure 63; *ThesCRA* 2004:1:86–87; van Straten 1995:27–30, Plates 23–27). Whether the Herm is an object of worship, a participant in the ritual, or a simple indicator of place, or some combination of these, is a matter for further discussion. In at least one example, on one side of an Athenian red-figure pelike in Berlin attributed to the Pan Painter (Figure 7.2), the Herm

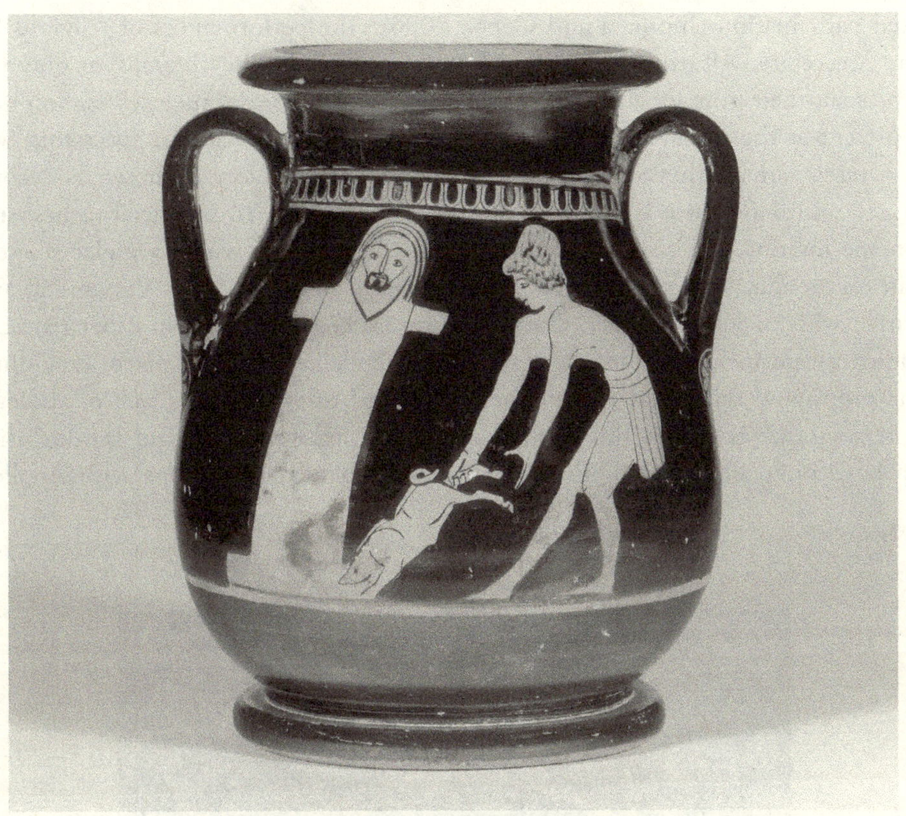

FIGURE 7.2 Athenian red-figure pelike, Pan Painter. c. 460 B.C.E. Berlin, Staatliche Museen 1962.62.© Antikensammlung—Staaliche Museen zu Berlin.

is positioned frontally, thus engaging an external viewer, rather than the young boy, an internal participant, who holds awkwardly onto the leg of a pig and lunges toward the base of the statue (*ThesCRA* 2004:1: 86, no. 194). Regardless, it seems there "must be someone to gaze" (audience-viewer-us) and, at least on this occasion "someone to gaze back" (the Herm).

PERFORMING SACRIFICE

If gaze indicates what vase painters wish us to observe, performance tells us why and how to observe, or, put another way, "the consequences of looking" (Olin 2003:329). The idea of Performance with a capital 'p' has entered the discussion of ancient Greek culture, from the literal performances of dance and drama to the figurative contexts of athletics, festivals, funerals, or religious rituals (Wiles 2000, 2003). Any performance, as in the theatrical variety, requires actors, costumes, props, stage or set, and of course an audience. It also requires a prescribed set of activities: a particular order, certain words, expected participation (Inomata and Coben 2006). The performances of religious life in ancient Greece are well expressed in Greek vase painting; be they literally or only figuratively present, their primary audiences are the gods and goddesses themselves. Secondarily, those present at the ritual, be they as direct participants or as distant spectators (we see both on vases), are another audience. Once the religious imagery is chosen as decoration on a vase, a third audience is created—the user of the vessel. In sacrificial scenes, such as one on the interior of a red-figure cup in Paris (Figure 7.3), where a piglet is about to be slain on an altar, two male figures are involved: a boy who holds the animal and an older man who wields the knife (*ThesCRA* 2004:1:117, no. 487). No other participants (or audience) are included, but other performative elements are in place, including the set, the props, and the actors. We might be tempted to explain this lack of audience in literal terms—that is to say, this is a domestic or private sacrifice. But the inclusion of such a large built altar, and of the palm tree, which has associations with Apollo and

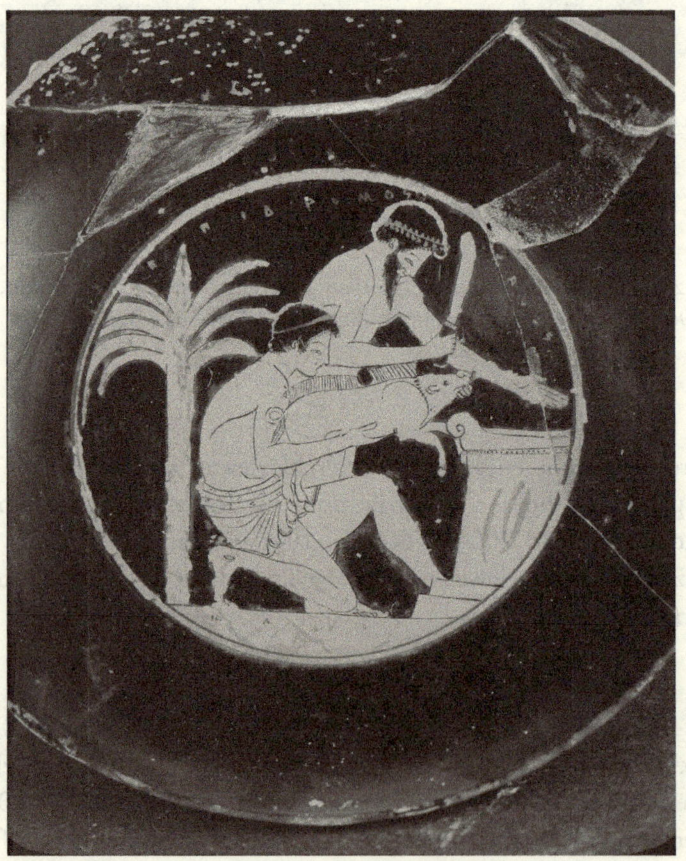

FIGURE 7.3 Athenian red-figure cup interior, Epidromos Painter. c. 500 B.C.E. Paris, Louvre G. 112.4.© Musée du Louvre. Image Source: Erich Lessing, Art Resource, New York.

Artemis, suggests otherwise (Lissarrague 2001:137–141). Similarly, on a red-figure cup by Makron, a young man pours a libation over an altar in total isolation (Paris, Louvre G 149; Lissarrague 2001: Figure 109). The painter is confined to decorating the round interior space, or tondo. Nonetheless, his only audience is the outside viewer; as such, we as spectators must imagine a grander occasion with more participants, as well as the other known stages of a religious ceremony. A final example is found on the detail of an Athenian red-figure krater of about 420 B.C.E., where four men, three youthful and one more mature as indicated by his beard, are engaged in the post-kill phase of a sacrifice (Figure 7.4). The detailed and complex scene is described by François Lissarrague as follows:

> On the krater . . . the sacrificial scene is constructed around the altar. Behind it, a laurel tree occupies a central place in the axis of the image. This altar, itself stained with blood, supports a series of regularly spaced planks of wood, seen from their ends and sides, in two layers. A fire is lit, indicated by the white markings. Above these flames, the meats are roasting on long iron spits (*oveloi*), held by a young assistant to the left of the scene. Near the altar a bearded priest wearing a crown holds in his hand an object which is difficult to identify, and about which opinions diverge. It is a round irregular mass taken out of the fire, which one interprets as a flour cake (*pelanos*) or as part of the entrails (*splanchna*). . . . To the right a young assistant . . . holds a tray with three branches (*kanoun*) and a wine jug (*oinochoe*), the contents of which he seems to pour on the altar. All the gestures of these three actors are concentrated on the altar. (2001:141–142)

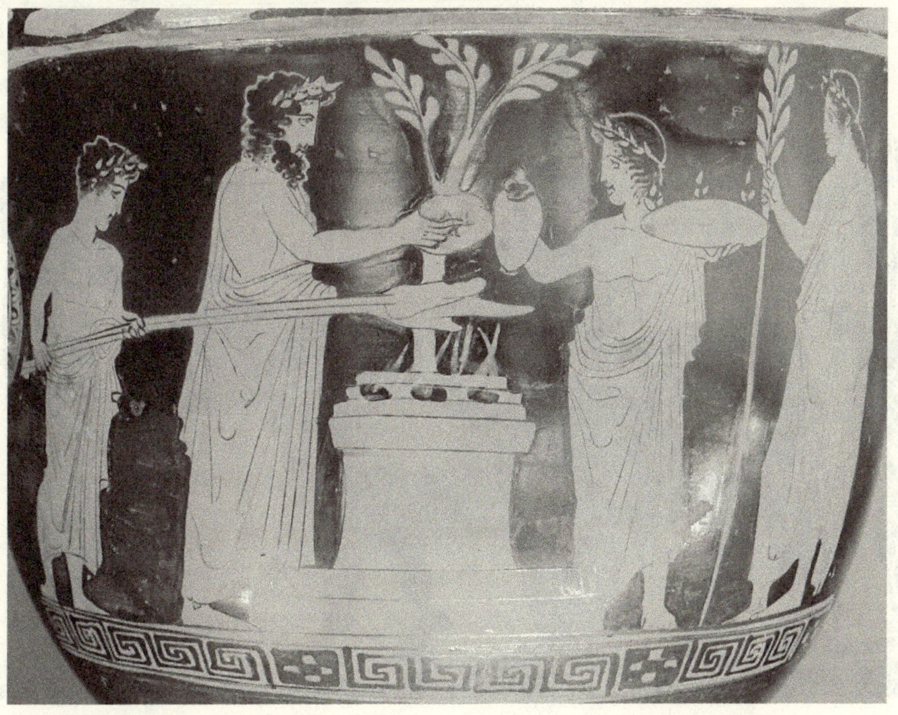

FIGURE 7.4 Athenian red-figure krater, Pothos Painter. c. 420 B.C.E. Paris, Louvre G 496. © RMN (Musée du Louvre) / Les frères Chuzeville.

Following this last description and indeed using our own eyes, it becomes clear that in such an example as this one, performance and gaze converge. The figures look toward the center (with the exception of the boy holding roasting spits), and the two immediately on either side of the altar are particularly intent on one another. That being said, the situation is complicated by the presence of a beardless male figure standing to the far right, holding a long laurel branch in one hand. It is possible that this is the god Apollo attending and even, on some level, taking part in the event (*ThesCRA* 2004:1:128, no. 573; Lissarrague 2001:142). The role of the Greek gods in scenes of ritual has been debated for several decades. These divine actors have been interpreted with regard to myth, cult, ritual, psychology, symbolism, agency, and "divine reflexivity" (Patton 2009, with bibliography). The most recent discussion posits that the gods are aiding mortals in ritual acts by taking an active role (Deschodt 2011). The deities not only assist, they instruct in religious matters as well. As one scholar so appropriately explains, in reference to the phenomenon of viewing: "They [the Greek gods] were conceived as avid spectators of human actions, as well as willing to provide the occasional spectacle themselves. The perfection of idealized visible form in the Greek's art accorded well with their love of theatrical performance" (Jay 1993:23).

Returning to our own set of images, it is worth noting that some vase painters take a more obvious approach to performance and sacrificial imagery than others. Such is the case on a fifth-century black-figured kantharos from the Boeotian Kabirion sanctuary (Figure 7.5 [van Staten 1995:213, V112]), where the heavy exaggerated faces on all the figures, including the Herm, resemble theatrical masks. The vases of this group

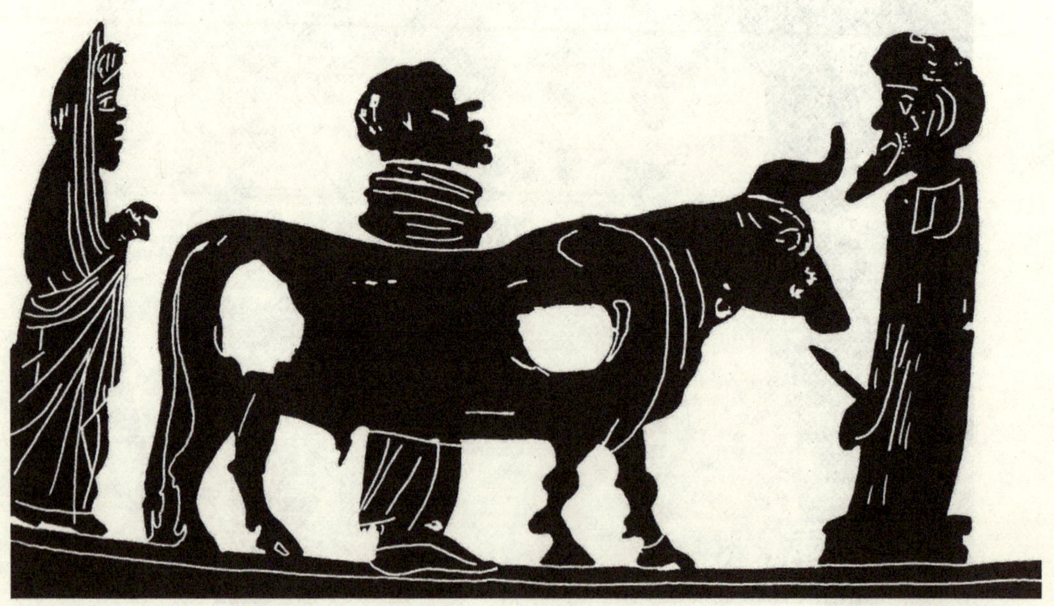

FIGURE 7.5 Boeotian black-figure kantharos, Kabirion Group. 5th c. B.C.E. Cassel, Staatliche Kunstsammlungen. Drawing by D. Weiss, after van Straten 1995: pl. 26.

are frequently described as comic and their figures viewed as grotesque; and they have been connected with "dramatic performances" held at the Kabirion sanctuary near Thebes (Walsh 2009:15). On some Athenian red-figure vases from the middle years of the fifth century, such as an amphora now in the British Museum, women are shown literally "dressing up" the willing sacrificial victims, as if to prepare them for their public spectacle (Figure 7.6 [*ThesCRA* 2004:1:112, no. 439; cf. Petropoulou 2008:40–42; Parker 2011:134–135]). But let us conclude with one of the most enigmatic and pleasing examples of all. On the interior of a red-figure cup in Vienna, attributed to the Epidromos Painter and dated to the early fifth century (Figure 7.7 [*ThesCRA* 2004:1:86, no. 193]), the god Hermes walks an eager sacrificial victim toward an altar. But do look more closely. What is actually being portrayed is a domestic dog dressed up like a pig, which begs the question: Is this Hermes or a mortal disguised as a god (cf. Hipponax fr. 3a.1)? Regardless, this element of disguise or trickery or costuming—whatever we choose to

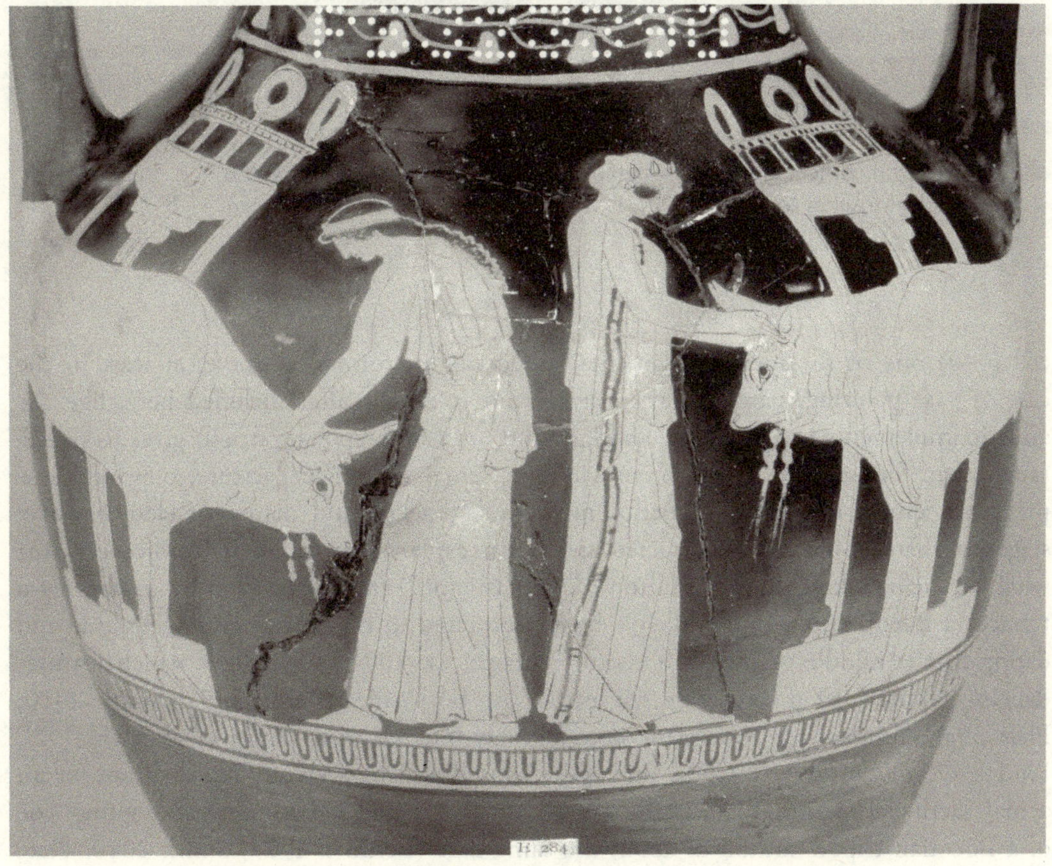

FIGURE 7.6 Athenian red-figure amphora, Nausicaa Painter. c. 440–430 B.C.E. London, British Museum E 284. © Trustees of the British Museum.

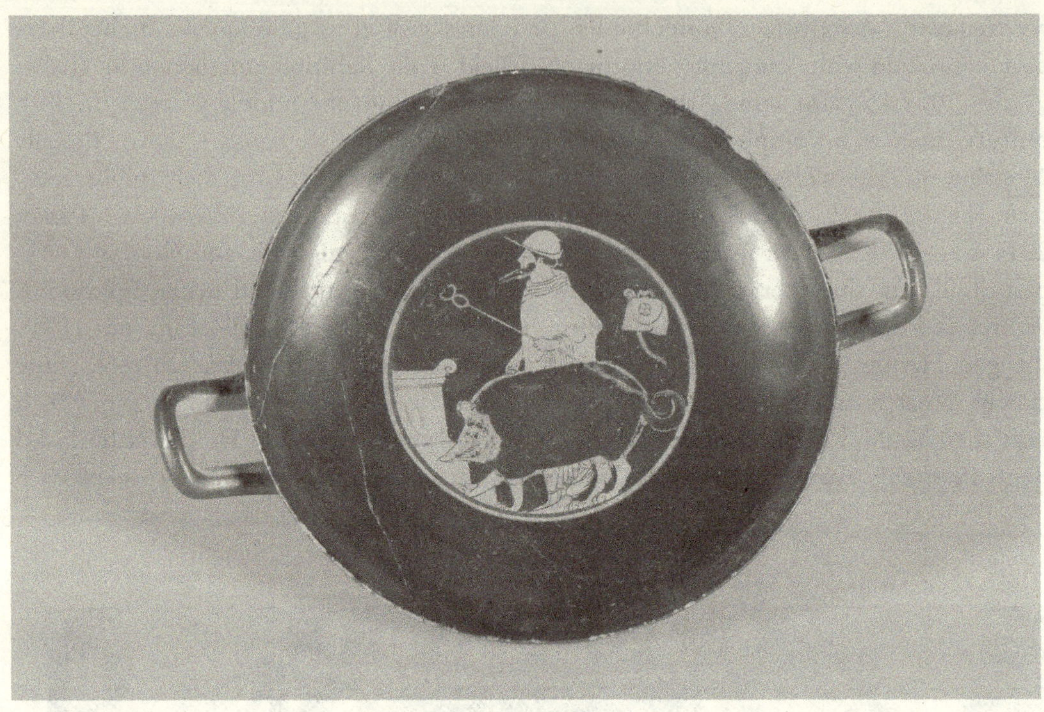

FIGURE 7.7 Athenian red-figure cup interior, Epidromos Painter. c. 500 B.C.E. Vienna, Kunsthistorisches Museum IV 3691. © Kunsthistorisches Museum Wien.

call it—is one of the most fundamental aspects of performance where, at least in the case of vase painting, parody plays a significant role. The altar included here, like the athletic implements hanging in the background (aryballos, sponge, strigil) gives us pause; rather than focusing the scene, or providing a center of activity, gesture, or gaze, these props are almost incidental—functioning more as background matter or elements of a stage set than as indicators of sacred space. An explanation for such "tomfoolery" (or what we might jokingly term "mutton dressed as lamb") might be found by comparing a terracotta Boeotian pig (more likely a boar) decorated in the black-figure technique and dating to the middle of the sixth century (hence, ca. 100 years earlier), which features dancing komasts, of the type we saw earlier, on both sides (Berlin 3391; Smith 2010: Plate 30a). Although the Boeotians were jokingly referred to in antiquity as "swine" (cf. Pindar, *Olympian Ode* 6.89–90), this figure should also be seen as the substitute for an actual sacrificial victim. In fact, the same animal is being led to sacrifice on one side of a Boeotian tripod-kothon of about the same date (Berlin F 1727; Smith 2010: Plate 28d). This intriguing vessel, which may in itself have served a ritual function, is decorated with a sacrifice, a row of dancers, and reclining banqueters or symposiasts on each of its three sides (Smith 2004:15–18).

SACRIFICIAL SPECTACLE

In his succinct and informative introduction to *Greek Religion*, Jan Bremmer stated that "future studies of sacrifice will be satisfactory only if they are based on literary, epigraphical, iconographical, and archaeological evidence" (1999:43). Although this is indeed true, it remains the case that some categories of evidence continue to require evaluation in their own right and on their own terms. While the time is ripe for a discussion of Greek sacrificial iconography, on vases and in other arts, within its broader cultural context, the archaeological setting of votive reliefs and dedications, including those with relevant imagery, might supplement our knowledge of the rites and rituals. Painted vases, such as those presented above, should also be discussed in light of their shapes, artists, places of manufacture, and archaeological find-spots. In a number of instances, their unified iconographic programs place "the art of ancient Greek sacrifice" in direct conversation with the festival cultures of archaic and classical Greece on the one hand, and with the visual (and material) cultures on the other. The relationship between mythological setting or story and actual real-life cult practice remains an important area of inquiry. Analyzing visual materials relegated to a specific time period or periods in relation to descriptive textual accounts belonging to distant ones is yet another thorny area. And finally, the difficulty, even impossibility, of matching scenes on vases, reliefs, or other arts with known contemporary events or documented cults is problematic and tenuous. By reframing the iconographic evidence on vases in relation to both gaze and performance it is hoped that new ways of seeing might be applied to such a dynamic corpus of images. To be sure, these phenomena are not unique to images of sacrifice—or as I would prefer to term them, "sacrificial imagery"—but their meaning as spectacle is specific to their times, places, events, and creators.

ACKNOWLEDGMENTS

For assistance with this paper I wish to thank Veronica Ikeshoji-Orlati, Elizabeth Molacek, Alan Shapiro, Daniel Weiss, and of course Carrie Murray.

REFERENCES CITED

Bérard, C. 1983 *Iconographie*-Iconologie-iconologique. *Etudes de Lettres* 4:5–37.

Bérard, C., and C. Bron (editors) 1989 *A City of Images: Iconography and Society in Ancient Greece.* Translated by D. Lyons. Princeton University Press, Princeton.

Bérard, C., Ch. Bron, J.-L., Durand, F. Frontisi-Ducroux, F. Lissarrague, A. Schnapp, and J.-P. Vernant 1989 *A City of Images: Iconography and Society in Ancient Greece.* Translated by D. Lyons. Princeton University Press, Princeton.

Blok, J. 2009 Sacrifice and Processions on Attic Black- and Red-Figure Pottery: Reflections on the Distinction Between "Public" and "Private." In *Shapes and Images: Studies on Black Figure and Related Topics in Honour of Herman A.G. Brijder,* edited by E. M. Moormann and V. V. Stissi, pp. 127–135. Peeters, Leuven.

Boardman, J. 1974 *Athenian Black Figure Vases*. Thames and Hudson, London.

Boardman, J. 1989 *Athenian Red Figure Vases: The Classical Period*. Thames and Hudson, London.

Boardman, J. 2001 *The History of Greek Vases*. Thames and Hudson, London.

Borgers, O. 1999 Some Subjects and Shapes by the Theseus Painter. In *Proceedings of the 15th International Congress of Classical Archaeology, Amsterdam, July 12–17, 1998. Classical Archaeology towards the Third Millennium: Reflections and Perspectives*, edited by R. F. Docter and E. M. Moormann, pp. 87–89. Allard Pierson Series 12. Allard Pierson Museum, Amsterdam.

Borgers, O. 2008 Religious Citizenship in Classical Athens: Men and Women in Religious Representations on Athenian Vase-Painting. *BABESCH* 83:73–98.

Bowie, A. M. 1995 Greek Sacrifice: Forms and Functions. In *The Greek World*, edited by A. Powell, pp. 463–482. Routledge, London and New York.

Bremmer, J. N. 1999 *Greek Religion*. 2nd ed. *Greece & Rome:* New Surveys in the Classics 24. Oxford University Press, Oxford.

Bremmer, J. N. 2007 Myth and Ritual in Greek Human Sacrifice: Lykaon, Polyxena and the Case of the Rhodian Criminal. In *The Strange World of Human Sacrifice*, edited by J. N. Bremmer, pp. 55–79. Peeters, Leuven.

Bundrick, S. D. 2014 Selling Sacrifice on Classical Athenian Vases. *Hesperia* 83:653–708.

Cairns, D. 2005 Bullish Looks and Sidelong Glances: Social Interaction and the Eyes in Ancient Greek Culture. In *Body Language in the Greek and Roman Worlds*, edited by D. Cairns, pp. 123–155. The Classical Press of Wales, Swansea.

Carpenter, T. H. 1986 *Dionysian Imagery in Archaic Greek Art: Its Development in Black-Figure Vase Painting*. Clarendon Press, Oxford.

Deschodt, G. 2011 Modes de figurations des dieux en Grèce ancienne. Le Cas du sacrifice. *Images Revues* 8 (http://imagesrevues.revues.org/).

Detienne, M., and J.-P. Vernant 1989 *The Cuisine of Sacrifice among the Greeks*. Translated by P. Wissing. University of Chicago Press, Chicago.

Durand, J.-L., and A. Schnapp 1989 Sacrificial Slaughter and Initiatory Hunt. In *A City of Images: Iconography and Society in Ancient Greece*, edited by C. Bérard and C. Bron, translated by D. Lyons, pp. 53–70. Princeton University Press, Princeton.

Fredrick, D. (editor) 2002 *The Roman Gaze: Vision, Power, and the Body*. The Johns Hopkins University Press, Baltimore and London.

Frontisi-Ducroux, F. 1996 Eros, Desire, and the Gaze. In *Sexuality in Ancient Art: Near East, Egypt, Greece, and Italy*, edited by. N. B. Kampen, pp. 81–100. Cambridge University Press, Cambridge and New York.

Frontisi-Ducroux, F., and J.-P. Vernant 1997 *Dans l'oeil du miroir. Odile Jacob, Paris*.

Gebauer, J. 2002 Pompe und Thysia: Attische Tieropferdarstellungen auf Schwarz- und rotfigurigen Vasen. UGATERIT-Verlag, Münster.

Hatzivassiliou, E. 2010 *Athenian Black Figure Iconography between 510 and 475 B.C.* Tübinger Archäologische Forschungen 6.Verlag Marie Leidorf GmbH, Rahden.

Hughes, D. D. 1991 *Human Sacrifice in Ancient Greece*. Routledge, London.

Inomata, T., and L. S. Coben 2006 Overture: An Invitation to the Archaeological Theater. In *Archaeology of Performance: Theaters of Power, Community, and Politics*, edited by. T. Inomata and L. C. Coben, pp. 11–44. AltaMira Press, Oxford.

Jay, M. 1993 *Downcast Eyes: The Denigration of Vision in Twentieth-Century Thought*. University of California Press, Berkeley.

Laxander, H. 2000 *Individuum und Gemeinschaft im Fest: Untersuchungen zu attischen Darstellungen von Festgeschehen im 6. frühen 5. Jahrhundert v. Chr.* Scriptorium, Münster.

LIMC = *Lexicon Iconographicum Mythologiae Classicae*, 9 volumes (1981–1999) Artemis, Zurich and Munich.

Lissarrague. F. 2001 *Greek Vases: The Athenians and their Images.* Riverside, New York.

Olin, M. 2003 Gaze. In *Critical Terms for Art History*, edited by R. S. Nelson and R. Shiff, pp. 318–329. The University of Chicago Press, Chicago and London.

Parke, H. W. 1977 *Festivals of the Athenians.* Thames and Hudson, London.

Parker, R. 2011 *On Greek Religion.* Cornell University Press, Ithaca and London.

Patton, K. C. 2009 *Religion of the Gods: Ritual, Paradox, and Reflexivity.* Oxford University Press, Oxford.

Petropoulou, M.-Z. 2008 *Animal Sacrifice in Ancient Greek Religion, Judaism, and Christianity 100 B.C.–A.D. 200.* Oxford University Press, Oxford.

Pierce, S. 1993 Death, Ritual, and Thysia. *Classical Antiquity* 12:219–266.

Scheffer, C. 1992 Boeotian Festival Scenes: Competition, Consumption, and Cult in Archaic Black Figure. In *The Iconography of Greek Cult in the Archaic and Classical Periods: Proceedings of the First International Seminar on Ancient Greek Cult, organised by the Swedish Institute at Athens and the European Cultural Centre of Delphi (Delphi, 16–18 November 1990), edited by R. Hagg, pp. 117–141. Kernos Supplement 1.* Centre d'Étude de la Religion Grecque Antique, *Athens.*

Smith, T. J. 2004 Festival? What Festival? Reading Dance Imagery as Evidence. In *Games and Festivals in Classical Antiquity: Proceedings of the Conference held in Edinburgh 10–12 July 2000*, edited by S. Bell and G. Davies, pp. 9–23. BAR International Series 1220. Archaeopress, Oxford.

Smith, T. J. 2007 The Corpus of Komast Vases: From Identity to Exegesis. In *The Origins of Theater in Ancient Greece and Beyond: From Ritual to Drama*, edited by E. Csapo and M. C. Miller, pp. 48–67. Cambridge University Press, Cambridge.

Smith, T. J. 2010. *Komast Dancers in Archaic Greek Art.* Oxford University Press, Oxford.

THesCRA = *Thesaurus Cultus et Rituum Anitquorum*, 5 volumes (2004–05) J. Paul Getty Museum, Los Angeles.

van Straten, F. T. 1981 Gifts for the Gods. In *Faith, Hope and Worship: Aspects of Religious Mentality in the Ancient World*, edited by H. S. Versnel, pp. 65–151. Studies in Greek and Roman Religion. Brill, Leiden.

van Straten, F. T. 1987 Greek Sacrificial Representations: Livestock Prices and Religious Mentality. In *Gifts to the Gods: Proceedings of the Uppsala Symposium 1985*, edited by T. Linders and G. Nordquist, pp. 159–170. BOREAS, Uppsala Studies in Ancient Mediterranean and Near Eastern Civilizations 15, Uppsala.

van Straten, F. T. 1988 The God's Portion in Greek Sacrificial Representations: Is the Tail Doing Nicely? In *Early Greek Cult Practice: Proceedings of the 5th International Symposium at the Swedish Institute at Athens, 26–29 June, 1986*, edited by R. Hagg, N. Marinatos, and G. C. Nordquist, pp. 51–68. Acta Instituti Atheniensis Regni Sueciae, Series In 4°, 38, Stockholm.

van Straten, F. T. 1995 *Hiera Kala: Images of Animal Sacrifice in Archaic and Classical Greece.* Religions in the Graeco-Roman World 127. Brill, Leiden.

Verbanck-Piérard, A. 1988 Images et piété en Grèce classique: la contribution de l'iconographie céramique à l'étude de la religion grecque. *Kernos* 1:223–234.

Versnel, H. S. (editor) 1981 *Faith, Hope, and Worship: Aspects of Religious Mentality in the Ancient World. Studies in Greek and Roman Religion.* Brill, Leiden.

Walsh, D. 2009 *Distorted Ideals in Greek Vase-Painting: The World of Mythological Burlesque.* Cambridge University Press, Cambridge.

Webster, T. B. L. 1969 *Everyday Life in Classical Athens.* Batsford, London.

Wiles, D. 2000 *Greek Theatre Performance: An Introduction.* Cambridge University Press, Cambridge.

Wiles, D. 2003 *A Short History of Western Performance Space.* Cambridge University Press, Cambridge.

CHAPTER EIGHT

Etruscan Human Sacrifice

The Case of Tarquinia

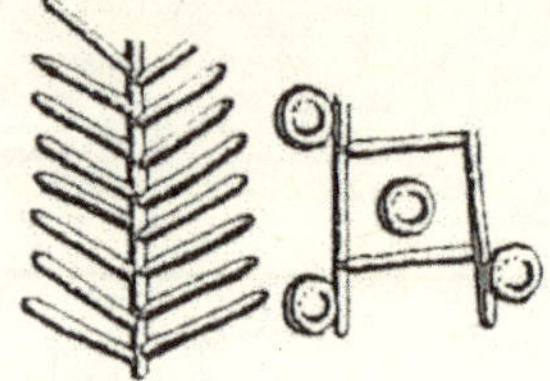

Nancy T. de Grummond

Abstract   *Up until recently, opinions have been divided as to whether the Etruscans practiced human sacrifice (Di Fazio 2001; Bonghi Jovino 2007–08:781–782). Many of the clear references in written sources and in artistic representations have at one time or another been minimized or dismissed as not sufficient for determining if the Etruscans did in fact engage in this practice. Recent excavations, however, in the monumental sacred area on the Pian di Civita at Tarquinia by the University of Milan (Università degli Studi di Milano), directed by M. Bonghi Jovino, have proven that human sacrifice was indeed practiced by the Etruscans, through the discovery of a number of burials, in this nonfunerary context, of infants, children, and adults. The first part of this article reviews the astonishing discoveries made at Pian di Civita. In the second part, I attempt to show the larger context for understanding this ritual at Tarquinia and in the region around it.*

THE SPECIAL CASE OF TARQUINIA

Excavations on the plateau of habitation at Tarquinia are revealing a remarkable complex of sacred structures, features, and offerings, beginning from the earliest Etruscan periods, the Proto-Villanovan and Villanovan, in the tenth century B.C.E. A prominent cavity in the ground (diam. ca. 80 cm.) and a burial of an epileptic child nearby, both in "Area Alpha," seem to have been the focal point of ritual activities in this area of the Pian di Civita. Bonghi Jovino (2007–08:779) has stressed the likelihood that the cavity is a key ritual element in the perceived history of Tarquinia, relating to its foundation and its destiny as indicated through prophecy. Further, the combination of cavity and child evokes in an uncanny way the famous Etruscan myth about the revelation of the *etrusca disciplina,* which is described by Cicero and others as taking place when a farmer at Tarquinia drove his plow deep into the ground, and a child named Tages, a newborn in one version, popped out of the furrow and recited or sang out the principles for worshipping the gods. The hero founder of the city, Tarchon, interpreted the mysterious messages for the Etruscans who gathered around; in one version they are the leaders of the Twelve Peoples of Etruria (de Grummond 2006:23–26). The cavity also suggests comparisons with rituals followed by the Romans and other people of early Italy according to which a sacred pit served as a conduit for communication between the lower world and the upper world. Referred to in Latin as a *mundus,* the pit was thought of as being formed by the First Furrow (*sulcus primigenius*) ploughed at the time of the establishing of a settlement. Such an underground installation could be entered by a child who would emerge with prophetic information, as happened at the sanctuary of Fortuna at Praeneste and at Rome (Marcattili 2005). Near the cavity at Pian di Civita was erected in the early seventh century B.C.E. a structure, Edificio (Building) Beta, surely religious in nature, out in front of which were two pits where a surprising secular/political offering was made, consisting of a bronze axe head, a bronze folded shield, and a curved ceremonial trumpet or *lituus,* along with sacrificed animals and an assemblage of ceramics indicating a special meal had taken place (Bonghi Jovino 2010a:168). The building featured, inside, a stone bench, or better, altar, which had a channel next to it leading to the cavity behind the building. It is almost certain that here sacrifices took place and the blood was allowed to run through the channel and into the cavity.

From the area around Edificio Beta a total of 10 human burials have been published to date, a truly amazing assemblage for a nonfunerary site in the middle of the plateau of habitation. In addition, the burials were almost completely lacking in grave goods and often the bodies were laid directly on the ground rather than in a trench, which would not be the case if they were buried by customary Etruscan practices. All burials were inhumation, a rite that was unusual at the time of the earliest burials in the ninth and eighth centuries B.C.E., though it later became normal. Bonghi Jovino has demonstrated how the sacred area evolved, beginning with the cavity in the tenth century, then following with the first individual burial in the ninth century, then with others, all the way down to the sixth century B.C.E. (Figure 8.1). The results of anthropological examination have been provided by Gino Fornaciari and Francesco Mallegni of the University of Pisa and the Scuola Normale Superiore di Pisa. The individuals have received numbers from 1 to 10, not according to chronology, but rather according to the sequence in which they were recognized. (See the Appendix for a systematic listing, including bibliography.)

Individual no. 1 is the most remarkable of all. Buried in Area Alpha in the ninth century, it is a child aged between seven and eight years, probably male, showing a deformation of the skull that anthropologists have analyzed as causing pressure on the nervous system that could result in seizures. The irregularities are the basis for the diagnosis of the child as epileptic. The excavators and others have noted that epilepsy was regarded in

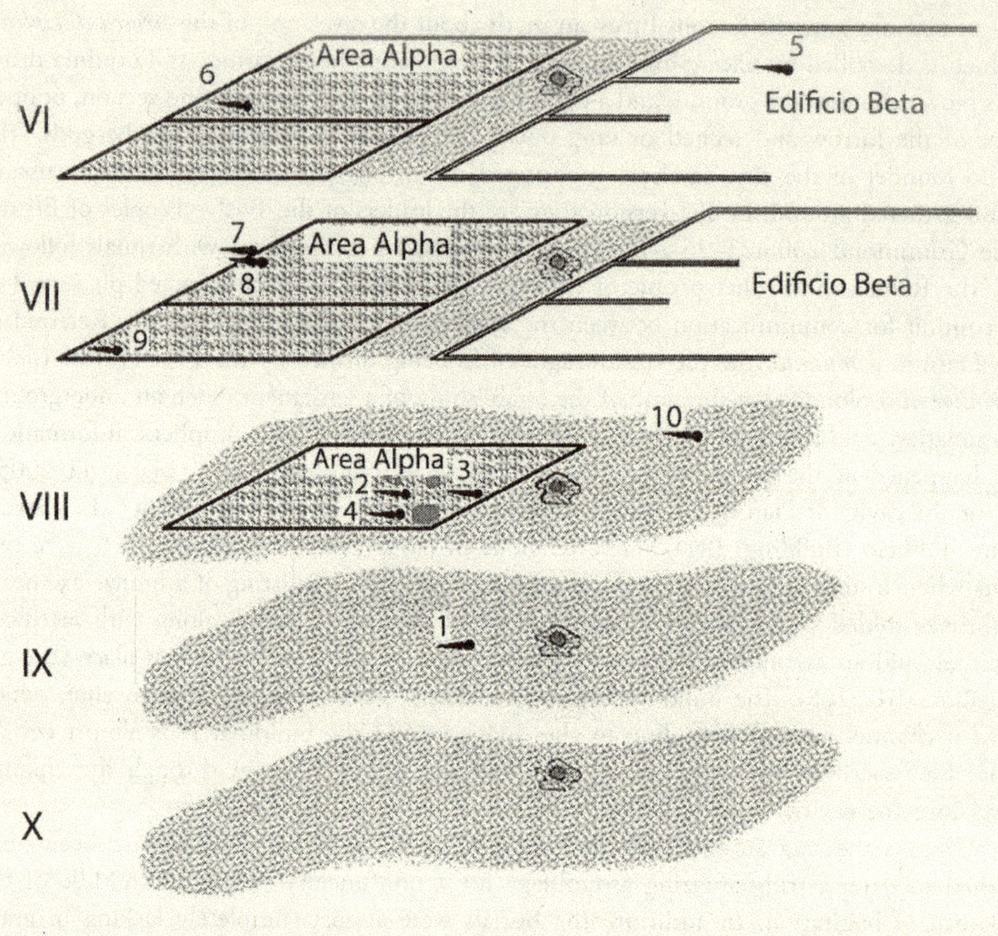

FIGURE 8.1 Diagram of the ten burials at Pian di Civita (indicated by Arabic numerals), with indications of the century in which they were interred (indicated by Roman numerals). After Bonghi Jovino 2007–2008, fig. 3.

antiquity as a sacred disease, and that it was also seen as a prodigy. There is no evidence that the special child was executed; rather, it is hypothesized that after years of health problems, he died of an aneurism. It is easy to see how the moaning or crying out that might occur during a seizure (cf. Lucretius, *de Rerum Natura*, 3.487–509; Aretaeus of Cappadocia, ed. Hude, I.5 passim) suggests a connection with the sacred story about Tages and the *etrusca disciplina*. The actual life and death of the epileptic child may have validated or even given rise to the fundamental Etruscan myth about the revelation of the basic tenets of Etruscan religion. As Bonghi Jovino notes, the situation "could have favored a symbiosis between perception and reality that elevated the status of the child and afforded it this rather unusual burial" (Bonghi Jovino 2010:165).

Next, in the eighth century there were interred near to the cavity and near Individual no. 1, again in Area Alpha, the remains of three newborn infants, of which the number of surviving parts varies greatly. Individual no. 2, the best preserved, lacked hands and feet. No. 4 lacked the head, but most of the postcranial skeleton was recovered. Of no. 3 very little was found. The bones were scattered and not connected with one another in a way to suggest that the corpses were laid out whole on the ground; one may suspect acts of dismemberment. Segments of deer antler (discussed below) were also found scattered within the strata that contained the infant bones.

In the same century, to the north of Area Alpha was buried an adult male (Individual no. 10), who had suffered blows and injuries in various parts of his body, which had already healed or begun to heal before his death. He then died from a blow to the right side of his head. Anthropological analysis showed bone spurs and erosive action on his feet that may have resulted from constantly standing on a slippery surface, hence the deduction that he may have been a sailor. There is a temptation to expand his biography—as a foreigner, because of his long skull differing from Etruscan ones, and because he was buried with a sherd of Euboean Greek pottery on his chest. The pottery helps to date the burial rather precisely, to ca. 770–740 B.C.E., the time of the earliest Greek settlement in Italy, at the Euboean outpost of Pithekoussai.

In the next century occur two more adult burials. The only female identified so far in the sacred complex at Tarquinia is a woman aged ca. 40, whose body did not reveal any evidence of trauma (Individual no. 7). The excavators and anthropologists describe this as a "natural death," showing no evidence that she was executed. Still, there was an unusual feature of the burial in that a slab of limestone was jammed up against the right side of the head. Nearby was a male (Individual no. 8), close in age, who presented evidence of having well-developed musculature, but also a stooped posture suggesting that he habitually carried heavy loads. He has been described as a "laborer." His skeletal remains did include fractured and healed bones, though there is no evidence of any blow that may have killed him, and his death has also been described as "natural." We may well ask whether other means of execution, such as smothering or strangling, could have occurred and left no physical evidence.

Also in the seventh century belongs a quite special case, a child of ca. eight years, who was decapitated and placed with the feet extending under a wall in Area Alpha (Individual no. 9). Of the ten individuals, the head was missing from five (nos. 3, 4, 5, 6, and 9), but only in the case of no. 9 was it possible to confirm that the head was deliberately cut off. Mallegni was able to document the point of the decapitation and was even able to ascertain the trajectory of the blow, showing that the head was pulled back. Most of the hands and feet were lacking, as well as various joints in the body. The child fits the pattern of a human sacrifice known in a number of cultures (Bremmer 2007), where the individual is placed under a wall as a foundation offering, and perhaps the same is true of a newborn found underneath the north wall of Edificio Beta (Individual no. 5; sixth century B.C.E.). Its head was missing, too, though in this case, the anthropologists did not report an act of decapitation. The descriptions of the burial of no. 5 do not indicate that the bones were laid out in a regular burial.

The important point about Individual no. 6 (Area Alpha, sixth century B.C.E.) is that the infant in this case was not a newborn, but could be identified as a child that was nursing. There is the possibility that the newborns were actually stillborn and thus appropriate for deposit, with no need to make reference to human sacrifice. But this infant, as a child that certainly lived and thus may have died in a ritual act, clearly does not fit in that pattern. Again, it may be significant that only a portion of the skeleton was found, a tibia (or femur) fragment.

In sum, there are many reasons to believe that Pian di Civita shows cult practice of human sacrifice: the number and variety of the individuals, the lack of grave goods, the identification of decapitation and dismemberment and of probable physical abuse in the case of the "foreign sailor" and the "laborer," all within the astonishing context of the first burial of the diseased child, combined with the ritual cavity, the altar and the channel, connected with a building that showed an overarching framework of political authority.

Cult Activity

What was the nature of the deity (or the deities) of the cult? Just to look at the offerings, apart from the human sacrifice or sacrifices, there is evidence of a female deity, since the offerings immediately around the cavity and the newborns included weaving implements and parts of necklaces (Bonghi Jovino 1997, 2010a, 2010b). Numerous offerings of animals (pig, sheep/goat, and cow) and of vegetation are consistent with the excavators' identification of a goddess with concerns of earth and agriculture. In Area Gamma, about 15 meters southwest of Area Alpha and the burial of the epileptic child, a sequence of four superposed deposits (a *deposito reiterato*) was made, containing an array of vegetation, including seeds of poppies (most numerous of all), camelina, figs, grape, celery, parsley, melon or possibly cucumber, and various grains and legumes. In addition, there were unusual faunal remains: mollusks, mammals, birds, fish. The dates of the deposits are highly problematic since the artifacts showed a reverse chronology, but in general they were dated to the seventh, sixth, and early fifth century B.C.E. (Bagnasco Gianni, 2001b and 2005; Rottoli 2001).

Near the cavity and the epileptic child, 16 fragments of tortoise shells were found within one (but only one) deposit. Most notable and abundant are the antlers of deer, either whole or fragmented, or cut into precise shapes from the sliced cross-section of the horn; these were found in many contexts, from as early as the ninth century and as late as the fifth century B.C.E. (Figures 8.2 and 8.3; more than 300 specimens of antler are referenced in Bedini 1997:105, pl. 113 and 115; Bonghi Jovino 1986:87; 2010b). The cross-sections are consistently ca. 4 mm thick. Some are hexagonal or octagonal, some are oval, and some have a lunate shape (conjectured to be a sickle). Others are rectangles cut out of the horn longitudinally. A good many are made from the tips of antlers, carefully cut. These are not accidental forms, nor is there evidence that they are discards from making tools or working of horn for some other purpose. Clearly they are key ritual items.

Why were all of these segments of deer horn used at Pian di Civita through the centuries? What rituals could consistently require such items? It seems that the suggestion

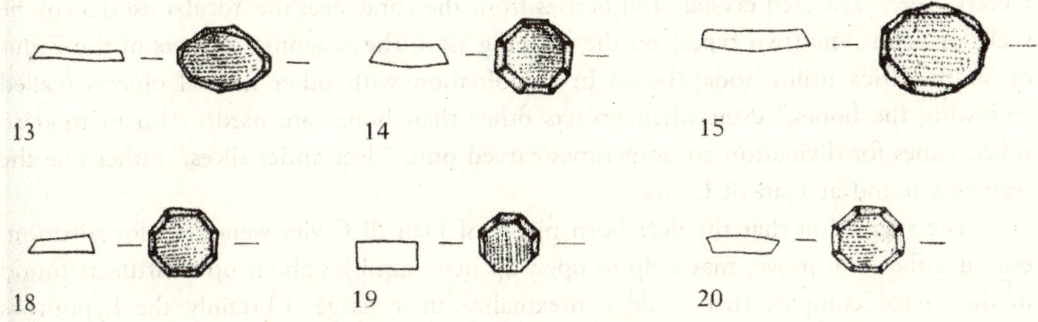

FIGURE 8.2 Examples of segments of the horn of deer found at Pian di Civita. Octagonal type. After Bonghi Jovino and Chiaramonte Treré 1997: Pl. 115, 13–15, 18–20.

has not yet been made that the pieces made from horn could be elements in divination, that is lots, or, to use the Latin term, *sortes*. The use of *sortes* by the Etruscans has recently been reviewed (Bagnasco Gianni 2001a; Maras 2009:37–40); unfortunately, no direct *comparanda* for *sortes* made of deer horns have yet been noted. Numerous similar cuttings from deer antler have been found at Poggio Civitate di Murlo, but these are incompletely published and have not been interpreted beyond questions relating to artistry (Nielsen 1995).

Etruscan *sortes* made of lead, bronze, iron, and stone in circular and quadrangular shapes have been identified. At Pyrgi just to the south of Tarquinia, *sortes* in the shape of a leaf, made of bronze or iron, have been unearthed and from the sanctuary of Menerva at nearby Punta della Vipera comes a perforated lead disc (Colonna 2006:137, 139; Maras 2009:283). Very likely the Etruscans used knucklebones in divinatory practice (especially from sheep) and dice made of bone or ivory, commonly attested in ancient Greece and Italy. The *sortes* from Praeneste were described as made of oak wood and with writing upon them. Comparisons from non-Mediterranean cultures indicate that many different kinds of material may be used for lots. The Chinese "oracle bones" are well known, with their messages interpreted from the cracks on tortoise shells and bones (smeared first with

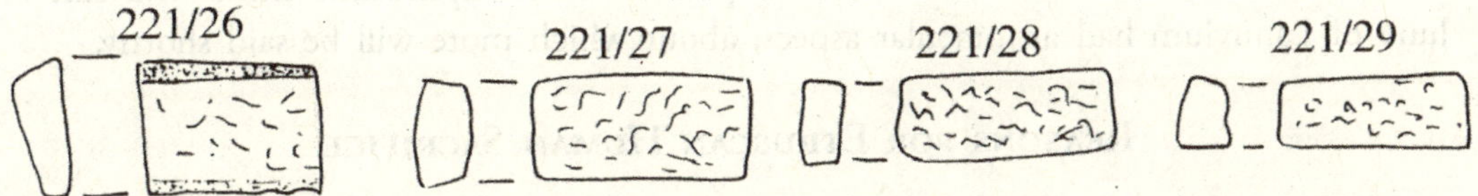

FIGURE 8.3 Examples of segments of the horn of deer found at Pian di Civita. Rectangular type. Bonghi Jovino and Chiaramonte Treré 1997: Pl. 113, 3–14.

blood). The Maya used crystals and berries from the coral tree; the Yoruba use 16 cowrie shells or palm nuts (two types) on the divining tray. The sangoma diviners of the Zulus of South Africa utilize today bones in combination with other natural objects (called "throwing the bones," even when objects other than bones are used). Also in modern times, runes for divination are sometimes carved onto "deer antler slices," rather like the segments found at Pian di Civita.

The suggestion that the deer horn pieces of Pian di Civita were used for sortition, even if difficult to prove, may help to open up new inquiries about other artifacts found in the sacred complex that could contextualize their usage. Certainly the hypothesis fits in with the idea that the central cavity at Pian di Civita may be oracular. It also suggests a ritual that would be effective as part of civic cult (so clearly present at Pian di Civita), which often supports a randomizing mechanism such as liver divination or augury, guiding and providing counsel to officials and other inquirers into the will of the gods and allowing citizens to come to an agreement.

As to the name of the deity there is actually an inscription with a dedication to Uni (second half of the seventh century B.C.E.), the principal Etruscan goddess, and there are also other *graffiti* that seem to refer to this name in a variant form (Bagnasco Gianni 1996:163–167). Uni herself is a multidimensional deity controlling fertility and protecting cities (de Grummond 2006:78–84), who was syncretized with various other great nature goddesses of the Mediterranean. At Pyrgi, the port city of Cerveteri, her name is translated as Astarte in the Phoenician text of the famous gold tablets. At Rome, she was equated with Juno and her iconography in art sometimes recalls her Greek homologue Hera, who was worshipped under that name at Gravisca, the port city of Tarquinia, frequented by both Greeks and Etruscans.

Many Etruscan sanctuaries show a multiplicity of deities, and it is possible, even likely, that other gods shared cult with Uni at the Pian di Civita. So far no other inscriptions have been published that may reveal the names of divinities, but excavations continue and new insights are likely. Meanwhile, scholars have not been slow to bring up Greek comparisons, such as Artemis, who has a particular and well-known connection with deer (Bonghi Jovino 2010a:164); Aphrodite Ourania, who, it was argued, could be associated with tortoises and the burial of children (Torelli 1987), and Demeter or Roman Ceres, who would have been an appropriate recipient of the *deposito reiterato* (Bagnasco Gianni 2005). Chiaramonte Treré (1987) notes comparisons with the Latin goddess Juno Sospes of Lanuvium, 32 km. southeast of Rome, whose cult involved the horns of the goat and whose sacrificial animal was the goat, as well as Juno Regina of Rome, who was involved in a ritual to dispose of a hermaphroditic child. The cult of Juno of Lanuvium had an oracular aspect, about which more will be said shortly.

Reasons for Etruscan Human Sacrifice

Why were the humans sacrificed at Pian di Civita? A number of aspects of human sacrifice outlined by Jan Bremmer (2007) for the context of human sacrifice can be recognized in the Etruscan material. He noted that human sacrifice should by no means be regarded as having only a single purpose, and reviews the possibilities. Frequently, the victims were marginal in their society, and this criterion would certainly cover most if not all of the individuals at Tarquinia—babies, children, a woman, a foreign adult. Further, such sacrifice is said to be common among agrarian, advanced cultures more than primitive ones; at Tarquinia we see that the cult of human sacrifice, while possibly originating in a pre-urban society, nevertheless continued to be operative as political organization became more complex. At the same time, the cult offerings indicated a continuous interest in agriculture and fertility.

But to consider the burials case by case it is important to state first of all that Individual no. 1 is regarded by the excavators as not having been sacrificed. Even though an argument could be made that the child was considered an ill omen because of his deformity, deserving to be put to death, in fact there is no evidence that he was killed; rather, all indications are that he died from his disease. Further, his placement in the earliest burial, the location of the grave by the cavity, and all of the overtones of the oracular cult come into focus if we conclude that he was in fact a (or the) central feature of the cult. The infants, nos. 2, 3, 4, 5, and 6, could all have been offerings to and recapitulations of this special oracular child. (This is not to say that they could not have had other meanings as well.) Individual no. 5, buried not in Area Alpha but next to Edificio Beta, may have been sacrificed at the time of the foundation of Beta, with the purpose of providing extra strength to the building. Bremmer notes that the "construction sacrifice" is attested from Russia to France and from Scandinavia to Greece, with special popularity in the Balkans. Individual no. 9 is most likely a second example of this kind of ritual, with his feet going under the wall in Area Alpha.

Individual no. 10, if understood as a foreigner, may well have been a prisoner of war, who was beaten and then killed in an act of retaliation. There are several literary references that refer to human sacrifice—or perhaps better, ritual killing—of prisoners of war by the Etruscans—one from nearby Cerveteri (Caere) and one from Tarquinia. The famous passage in Herodotus (1.166–167) concerning the stoning of prisoners after the battle between the Phokaian Greeks who had settled at Alalia and the combined forces of the Etruscans from Cerveteri and Carthaginians may not qualify as human sacrifice, for when the Etruscans killed the prisoners, no deity was invoked or targeted. The episode may be seen, as it was in antiquity, as a particularly gruesome murder of prisoners of war. That event took place in the sixth century, thus overlapping with the latest of the burials at Pian di Civita. Another instance relates to the wars between Tarquinia and Rome, told by Livy (7.15.10), in which he notes that the Tarquinians immolated 307 Roman troops in the *forum* of Tarquinia in 358 B.C.E. He subsequently tells of the Roman retaliation, with whipping and the use of the axe, evidently to decapitate (7.19.2–4). Even though he specifically refers to both vicious acts as taking place in a civil context, it is interesting that he uses the word *immolare* to describe the actions of the Tarquinians. Again, no deity is mentioned and so a better designation may be "ritual killing."

Yet another instance of human sacrifice associated with Tarquinia and Rome is related by Macrobius (*Saturnalia* I.7.35). Though writing much later, in the early fifth century C.E., he records a quite relevant detail of cult in Archaic Rome when it was ruled by Etruscan kings. For a long time under Tarquinius Superbus and evidently his predecessors of this dynasty that came out of Tarquinia, there was a practice of sacrificing children for the *sospitas* (welfare) of families to the goddess Mania, mother of the Lares and also mother or grandmother of the Manes (she is the "Good Lady," not "Madness"; Scullard 1981:59; Radke 1965). Thus, the sacrifice sanctioned by the Etruscan king in this case was made as an act of propitiation to secure prosperity and well-being and it could be that the sacrifices at Pian di Civita had similar significance. Another interesting detail relates to how Brutus put a stop to the ritual. He advised the substitution of "heads" for "heads," that is instead of human heads he ordered that the heads of poppy plants and garlic be offered. The poppy seeds from the *deposito reiterato* in Area Gamma immediately come to mind, but perhaps also worth noting is that the plant camelina produces heads both before it flowers, and in its final stage of maturity. The seed coat has been described as having a garlic-like flavor. Could the *deposito reiterato* be construed as a ritual of substitution?

Another purpose for human sacrifice is that the sacrifice may have been like that of an animal, in which the victim, as he died, might provide information for divination; possibly the body or parts of the body were relevant for the divination. Tacitus (*Annales* 14.30) tells us that the Celts of Britain practiced human sacrifice so that they could perform divination over the corpse, drenching their altars with the blood and consulting their gods by means of the human entrails. Diodorus Siculus (5.31.3) reports other details: after the victim was stabbed, the priest would prophesy from the manner in which the victim fell, how much blood gushed out and whether there were involuntary movements that might come after the victim was already dead. From quite a different source comes evidence of divination from human sacrifice even in late antiquity, reported by Ammianus Marcellinus (29.2.17). This time, it involves infanticide. The emperor Valens pardoned a tribune for having practiced divinatory rites concerning the fate of the empire by extracting a fetus from its mother's belly (cf. Chiaramonte Treré 1987:85, n. 19). Regarding older children, Elagabalus was said to have sacrificed boys of noble birth and inspected children's entrails (Augustan History, *Life of Elagabalus* 8). Why indeed would children be in the majority in the burials made in this area at the Pian di Civita? A great deal has been written about child sacrifice, often with the assumption that a child was considered particularly valuable and therefore its life was the greatest sacrifice one could offer to the gods. But another important aspect is evident, for example, in the Inca custom of *capacocha,* in which a child was sent to the gods because children were seen as especially effective communicants with the gods (Kamp 2001:22). Certainly in the ancient classical world children were commonly believed to have a special ability in divination because of their purity and lack of preconditioning experiences (Johnston 2001). As noted earlier, the *sortes* at Praeneste were managed by a child who descended into an underground cavern. A significantly similar ritual was that at the temple of Juno Sospita at Lanuvium, where girls descended into a grotto to feed a great serpent; if the serpent accepted their offering, the maidens were deemed chaste and the ritual was considered prophetic for a favorable future for the community. That the Etruscans participated in this kind of belief in the oracular relevance of children is suggested by the Tages myth itself, and other themes in which a child or youth participates in divination (de Grummond 2006:27–28, 186).

The execution of a child, young man, or warrior, probably a scene of human sacrifice, is included in a curious and amazing series of Etruscan gemstones; the earliest in the series dates to the fifth century B.C.E., and shows a bearded man, next to a *thymiaterion* indicating a sacrificial context, carrying a small human—most likely a child—and a sacrificial knife (Figure 8.4). Other, later examples of the theme show other stages of the killing, often showing an adult rather than a child as the victim. The scenes may include dismemberment and decapitation with the executing figure manipulating the limbs or the head (Figures 8.5–8.7; Martini 1971). One example

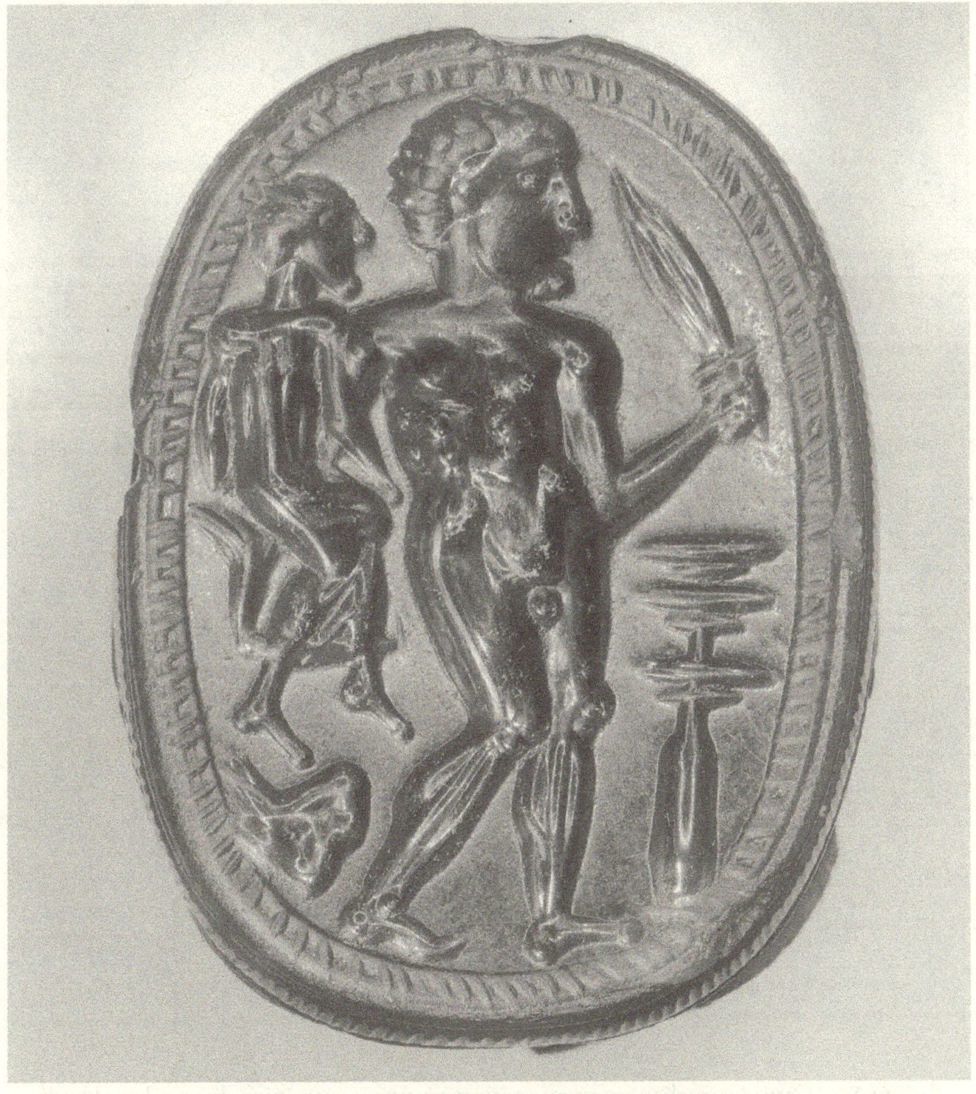

FIGURE 8.4 Carved cornelian scarab with image of sacrifice of a child (?). Munich, Staatliche Münzsammlungen. Middle of the 5th century B.C.E. Photo: Staatliche Münzsammlung München. Photographer Nicolay Kästner.

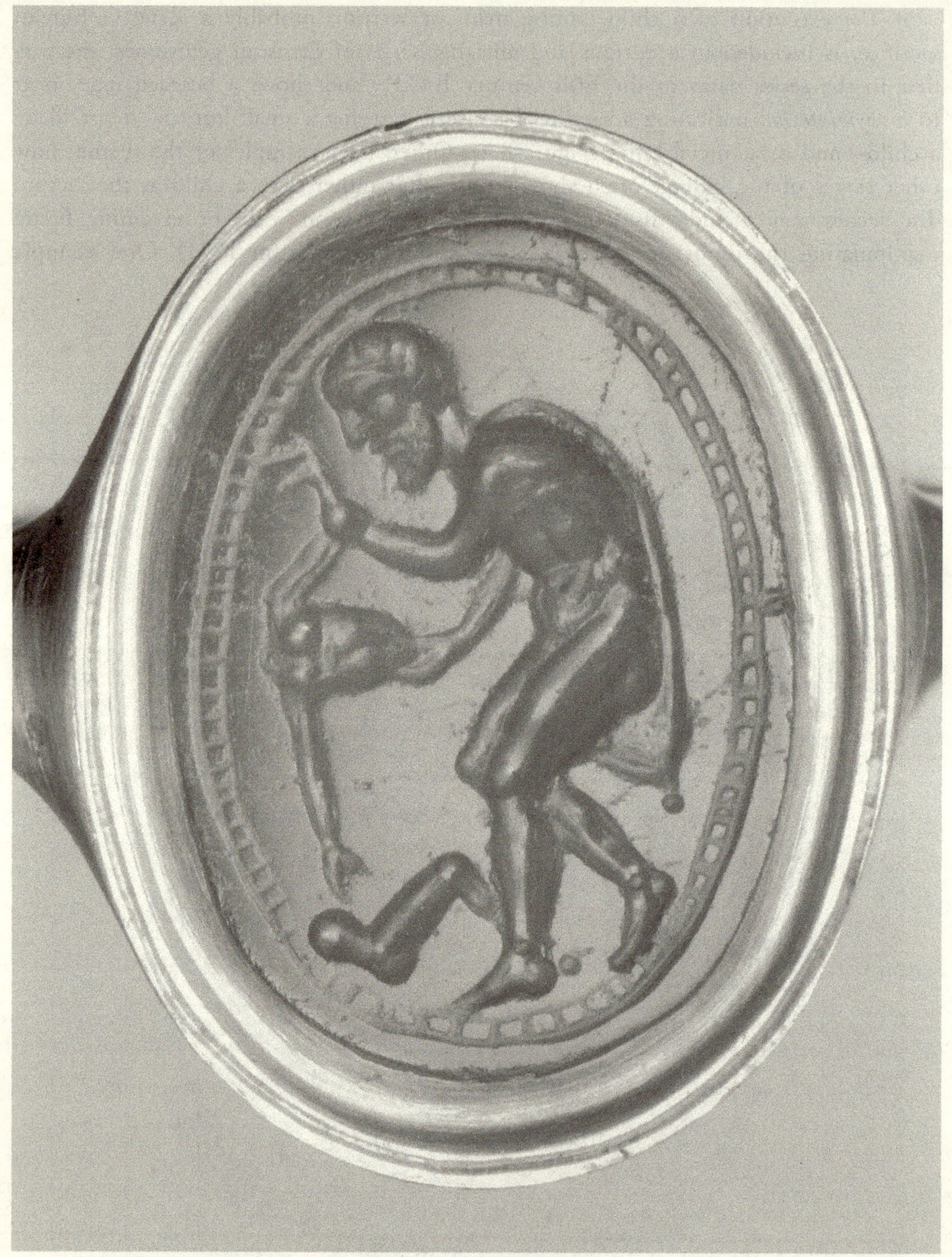

FIGURE 8.5 Carved cornelian ring stone with executioner examining dismembered body (of child?). Berlin, Staatliche Museen, Antikenabteilen FG 469. First half of 3rd century B.C.E. Photo: bpk, Berlin, Staatliche Museen, Antikenabteilung, Art Resource, NY.

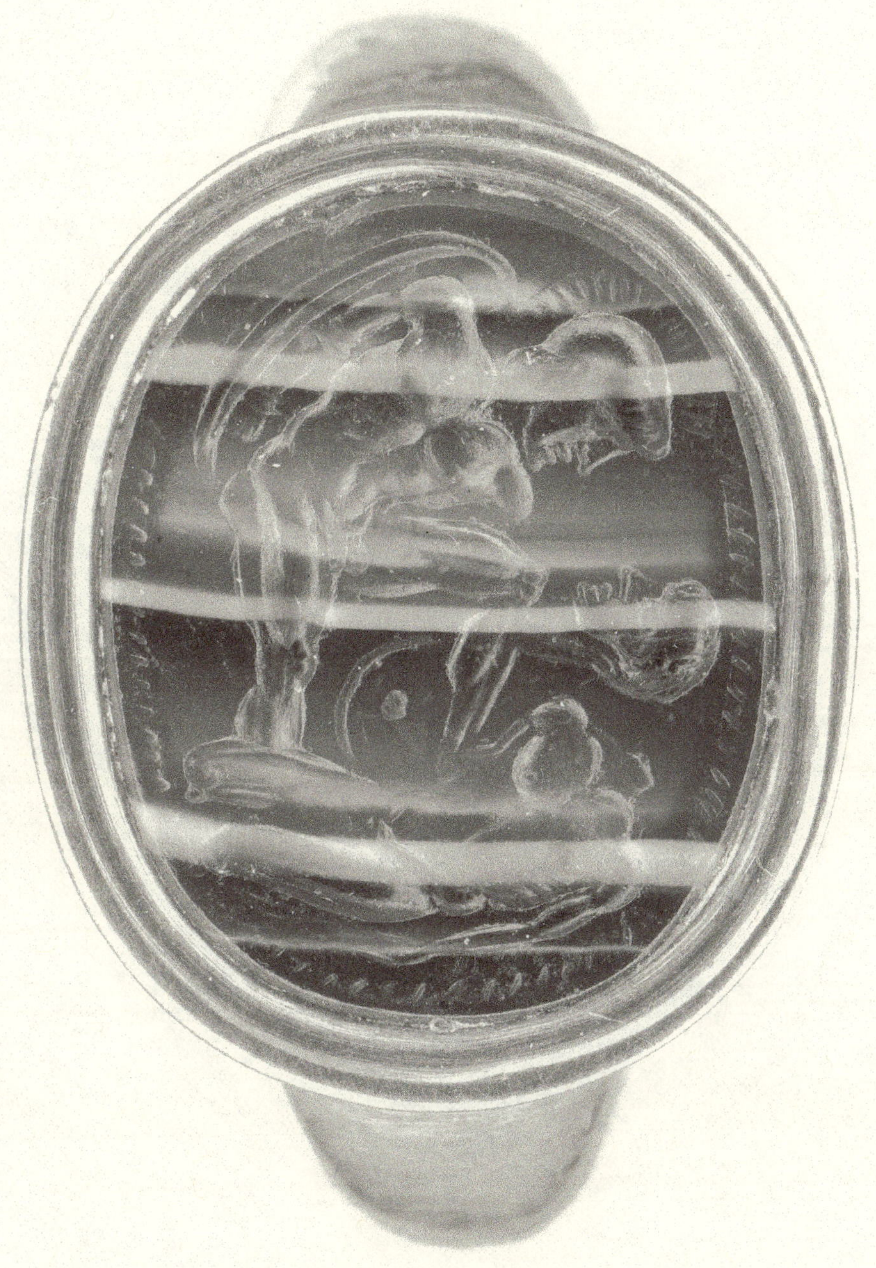

FIGURE 8.6 Carved sardonyx ring stone with image of warrior examining decapitated head. Florence, Archaeological Museum 15552. By permission of the Soprintendenza per i Beni Archeologici della Toscana-Firenze.

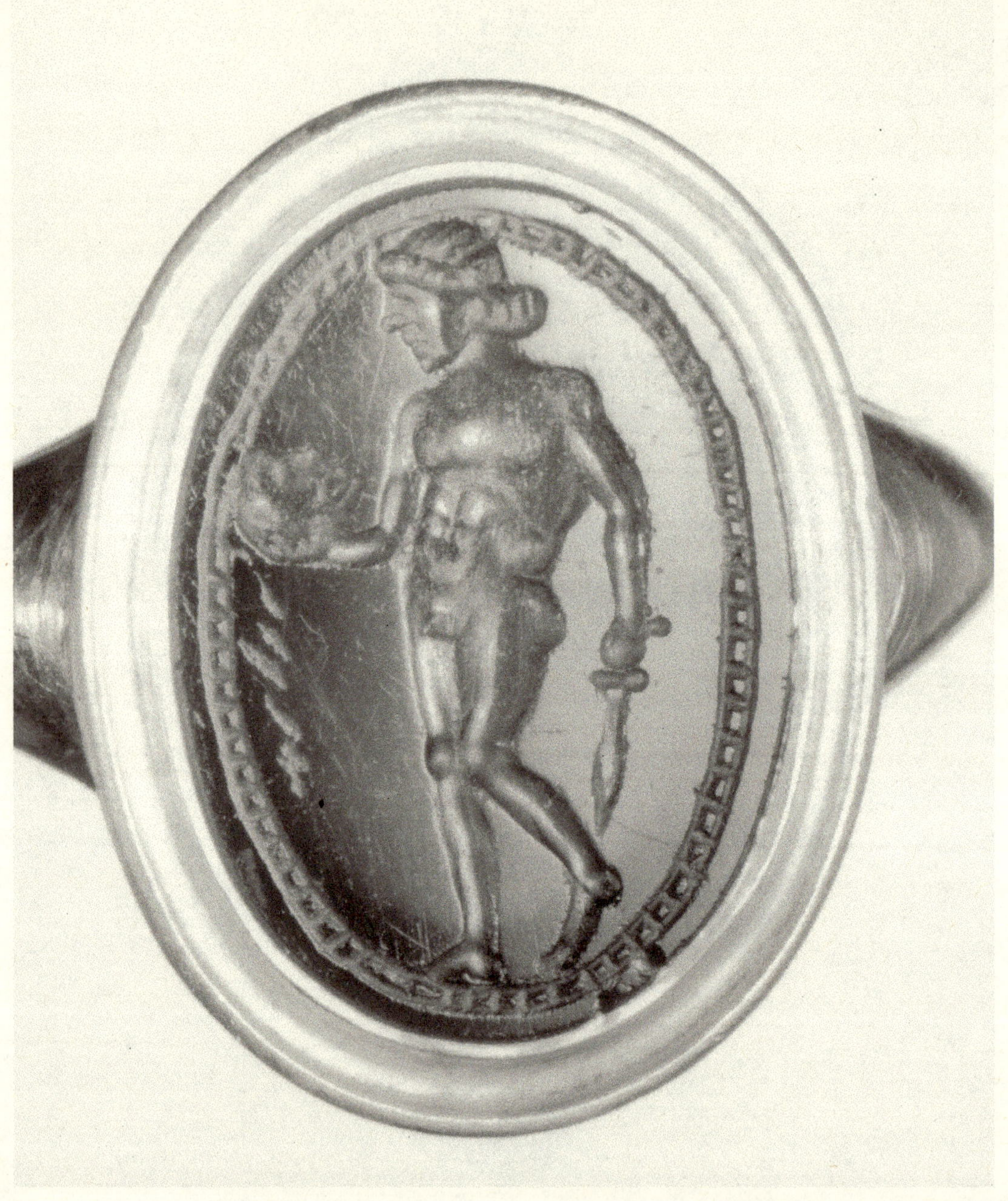

FIGURE 8.7 Carved gem with image of young executioner with decapitated head. Berlin, Staatliche Museen, Antikenabteilen, FG 472. First half of 3rd century B.C.E. Photo: bpk, Berlin, Staatliche Museen, Antikenabteilung, Art Resource, NY.

shows two men decapitating and dismembering a body; the head lies on the ground and seems to look up and watch as the limbs are cut off (Figure 8.8). Since the executioner is always nude, the theme is certainly mythological, but attempts to identify the child as Troilos killed by Achilles (Giudice 2006) are blunted by the fact that the iconographical parallels for that subject are not convincing, and that the scene with the child seems to have the same subject as the gems that show an adult victim. Since the executioner is sometimes armed, the myth may at times have to do with warfare and the ritual killing of an enemy or prisoner. While the theme as a whole suggests a mytho-ritual similarity to the activities at Pian di Civita, particularly striking is the way in which the executioner seems to study the body parts, and especially the head of the victim. In fact the decapitated head is seen to interact with the executioner. One example shows a nude youth with a sacrificial knife, gazing intently at the decapitated head, represented with the blood still dripping from it (Figure 8.7). Another example

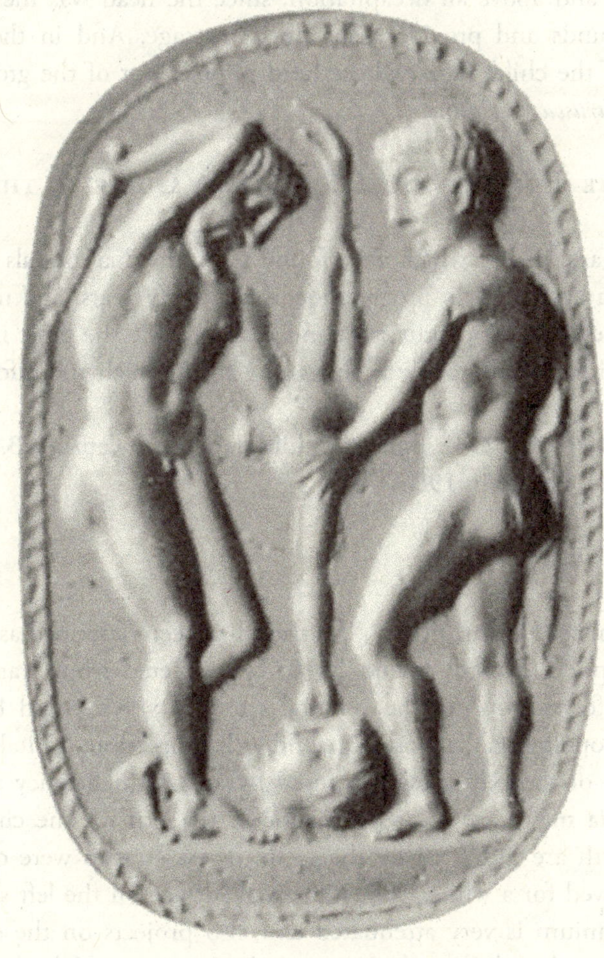

FIGURE 8.8 Carved sardonyx gem with image of decapitation and dismemberment. Formerly Rome, art market (cast). After Martini 1971: Pl. 13.5.

includes a Latin inscription, as on a few other examples of the Etruscan *Ringsteinglyptik,* and it tells us something interesting. The word FAUSTA seems to mean that the head tells "favorable omens" (Martini 1971:139, no. 91). The conclusion seems unavoidable: there must be prophecy associated with the human sacrifice on these gemstones (for further discussion, see de Grummond, forthcoming).

Thus, something remarkable appears in these Etruscan gems, dating from the fifth century and later, that actually may reflect back on the ensemble of associations with human sacrifice discussed in regard to Pian di Civita. It is not argued that the gems necessarily show an actual practice from the later centuries of Etruscan civilization, but rather that they may record a mytho-ritual tradition of human sacrifice associated with divination in which the decapitation of a head might yield the oracle. Thus, to the possible reasons for human sacrifice at Pian di Civita discussed here—propitiation, foundation, and retaliation—I suggest the addition of another possibility, that sometimes the human sacrifice may have been carried out for purposes of divination, with a special emphasis on dismemberment and above all decapitation, since the head was the part of the body that could utter sounds and provide a sustained message. And in that case, we circle back to the story of the child Tages, whose head popped out of the ground at Tarquinia and sang out the *Etrusca disciplina.*

Appendix: The Ten Individual Burials: A Guide to the Evidence

The excavations at Tarquinia in which were found ten individual burials in the sacred area of the Pian di Civita have been in progress for nearly thirty years, and numerous publications have been issued. This appendix is intended to provide the basic information about each burial along with a guide to the bibliography from which the information is taken.

1. No. 566 (also C 189; also 293). Epileptic child, late ninth century B.C.E. (Early Villanovan/Iron Age). Found in 1985.

Anthropological Data

Age 7–8. Probably male. Height ca. 1m. The child has been described as "albinic, encephalopathic and epileptic" (Bonghi Jovino 2010a). It suffered from cranial abnormalities ("arteriovenous malformations" of the cerebral cortex), which could have caused poor coordination. Anthropologists diagnose the child as having cribra orbitalia (porotic hyperostosis of the orbits of the eyes), lesions caused by an iron deficiency anemia. The condition of sideropenia may have created a pallor in the skin of the child. Three phases of interrupted growth are indicated by the teeth. These stresses were overcome and the child's health improved for a while. The endocrinal surface on the left side presents three depressions. The cranium is very attenuated and also projects on the exterior. It would have contained enlarged and twisted veins and the brain would have suffered pressure. These probably caused epilepsy. He may have suffered from multiple aneurisms and a massive hemorrhage causing death.

DETAILS OF BURIAL

Found in Area Alpha. The inhumed body was placed in supine position on a thin layer of grainy clay that contained fragments of proto-Villanovan and Villanovan pottery. The clay also covered over the body (stratum 293 in Bonghi Jovino 1986). The head was on the east end. The hands were placed under the thighs. The associated artifacts included a bronze pendant and part of a bronze pin (or needle?), as well as two pieces of lead roughly resembling a ring, though not joining.

A cache of fragments of tortoise carapaces (*Testudo sp*, the Mediterrranean tortoise, a land animal), listed as 16 in Sorrentino, 1986:202; listed as 13 in Torelli 1987:135, from multiple individuals, all came from the same sector, C 180, closely associated with the burial, but later in date. Torelli's link of child sacrifice with Aphrodite Ourania is now undermined by evidence that the well of Kolonos Agoraios, Athens, with numerous child burials (between 100 and 200 according to Torelli, but 450 according to the latest count reported by Susan Rotroff) is no longer thought to be connected with a sacred area of Aphrodite Ourania (Rotroff personal communication, 2011). Also from C 180 came 25 fragments of deer horn, some worked, and one fragment of deer bone. There were also faunal remains from C 180 of ox, sheep/goat, pig, and dog (2 bones). In addition, there was a curved strip of bronze (19.5 cm; a *lituus?*). The burial and C 180 were closely associated with the large ritual cavity, numbered 263.

BIBLIOGRAPHY

Bedini, E. 1997:esp. 105–110. Bonghi Jovino, M. 1986:89–92. Bonghi Jovino, M. 2007–08:776–779. Bonghi Jovino M. 2009. Bonghi Jovino 2010a:165. Bonghi Jovino, M. 2010b (deer antlers). Fornaciari and Mallegni 1986. Fornaciari and Mallegni 1987. Fornaciari and Mallegni 1997. Leighton 2004:40. Sorrentino 1986. Torelli 1987:137 and 138.

2. No. 562 (also C 180-A). Fetus or newborn, eighth century B.C.E. (Villanovan/Iron Age). Found in campaigns of 1982–88.

ANTHROPOLOGICAL DATA

Fetus at term, or newborn possibly of several months. Gender not known. Height ca. 51.5 cm. Skeleton almost complete. Hands and feet lacking.

DETAILS OF BURIAL

Found in Sector E1, Area Alpha, buried near individual 1, to the northwest. It was not possible to ascertain the original position of the bones, which were found in a mixed earth deposit including tips of deer horns as well as cross-sections of deer horns in geometric shapes. There was no evidence of any kind of standard burial receptacles or of a trench to contain the body, or any evidence of an attempt to protect the burial.

BIBLIOGRAPHY

Bonghi Jovino 1997:40–41. Bonghi Jovino 2010a. Fornaciari and Mallegni 1986. Fornaciari and Mallegni 1987. Fornaciari and Mallegni 1997.

3. No. 563 (also C 180-B). Fetus or newborn, eighth century B.C.E. (Villanovan/Iron Age.). Found in campaigns of 1982–88.

ANTHROPOLOGICAL DATA

Fetus at term or newborn. Gender not known. Height ca. 49 cm. Little preserved; only the right shoulder, a part of the left shoulder, and a fragment of a radius.

DETAILS OF BURIAL

Found in Sector E1, Area Alpha, buried near individual 1, to the northeast.

BIBLIOGRAPHY

Bonghi Jovino 1997:40–41. Fornaciari and Mallegni 1986. Fornaciari and Mallegni 1987. Fornaciari and Mallegni 1997.

4. No. 564 (also C 180 C). Fetus or newborn, eighth century B.C.E. (Villanovan/Iron Age). Found in campaigns of 1982–88.

ANTHROPOLOGICAL DATA

Fetus at term or newborn. Gender not known. Height ca. 51 cm. Postcranial skeleton almost complete. Head lacking.

DETAILS OF BURIAL

Found in Sector E1, Area Alpha, buried near individual 1, to the southwest. It was not possible to ascertain the original position of the bones, which were found in a mixed earth deposit including tips of deer horns and cross-sections of deer horns in geometric shapes. There was no evidence of any kind of standard burial receptacles or of a trench to contain the body, or any evidence of an attempt to protect the burial.

BIBLIOGRAPHY

Bonghi Jovino 1997:40–41. Fornaciari and Mallegni 1986. Fornaciari and Mallegni 1987. Fornaciari and Mallegni 1997.

5. 226A. Newborn, sixth century B.C.E. (Archaic). Found in campaigns of 1982–88.

ANTHROPOLOGICAL DATA

Newborn. Gender not known. Height 51 cm. From both sides of the body came ribs, shoulders, radii, ulnae, femurs, and tibias. No evidence of the head has been reported.

DETAILS OF BURIAL

Found against the exterior of the north wall of Edificio Beta (Sector D, against wall 29B), above a pit of the seventh century B.C.E. A deposit of burnt earth (351) contained the bones (not burned) of the newborn along with a small votive chalice of bucchero and fragments of impasto jars, thought to be from whole vessels. According to Bonghi Jovino, Individual 5 died a violent death.

BIBLIOGRAPHY

Bonghi Jovino 2010:171. Chiaramonte Treré 1987:85. Chiaramonte Treré 1997:68. Fornaciari and Mallegni 1997:101.

6. No. 565 (also C 59-60; also 59A). Nursling Infant, sixth century B.C.E. (Archaic). Found in campaigns of 1982–88.

ANTHROPOLOGICAL DATA

Infant. Gender not known. Height not known. Only tiny fragments of bone and the diaphysis of a tibia or femur, slightly robust, survive. It is enough to indicate that the child was not a fetus or newborn, but was nursing.

DETAILS OF BURIAL

Found in Sector E1 in the southwest corner of Area Alpha, with a bronze fibula and worked horns of deer. There was no trench for the burial, nor was it covered over. Nearby was a deposit (301) of vessels for drinking and eating, including several miniatures, and at least two with *sigla* (so-called *graffiti*), as well as the bones of pig, sheep/goat, and cow.

BIBLIOGRAPHY

Bonghi Jovino 1997:37–38 (*diafisi femorale*). Chiaramonte Treré 1997:190. Fornaciari and Mallegni 1986 (*diafisi tibiali*). Fornaciari and Mallegni 1987 (*diafisi femorale*). Fornaciari and Mallegni 1997 (*Diafisi incompleta di tibia*).

7. Adult female, seventh century B.C.E. (Orientalizing). Found in 1997.

ANTHROPOLOGICAL DATA

Age, ca. 40 years. Female. Height ca. 162 cm. Almost all the body was preserved, and no evidence of violence was found.

DETAILS OF BURIAL

Found in Area Alpha, Sector M, in the northwest part of the monumental complex, buried in supine position with the head toward the east. The elbows were bent and the hands were laid upon the pelvic area. The feet overlapped one another. The burial area was not in a trench but a hollow in the bedrock, with a stratum of earth partially supporting the burial. Two small bronze objects were found with the skeleton: a part of a needle or pin, perhaps from a fibula, and a minute decorative element. Close by was found a votive deposit of a wall foundation dating between the late seventh and full sixth century B.C.E., including two impasto jars containing grains set underneath the wall, which, running in a north-south direction, closed off Area Alpha on the west. The proximity of the offering to Individuals 7 and 8 (below) suggests observation of the existence of those burials from a previous time.

Even though the body showed no evidence of violence, it is noteworthy that a squared block of white limestone, approximately the size of the head itself, was found lodged against the proper right side of the head. The head was slightly out of line.

BIBLIOGRAPHY

Bonghi Jovino 2007–08:775, 780. Chiesa 2001. Mallegni 2001:59. Mallegni and Lippi 2007–08:799–801.

8. Adult male "laborer," seventh century B.C.E. (Orientalizing). Found in 2003.

ANTHROPOLOGICAL DATA

Age ca. 45. Male. Height 1.63. The body was whole and complete, showing no evidence of violence. The skeleton was gracile, but showing attachments for powerful musculature, suggesting that the individual habitually undertook strenuous physical tasks, extending and withdrawing his arms. Bone spurs on the vertebrae suggest that he carried heavy burdens on his shoulders. His upper teeth showed signs of excessive use for some task and related gum disease. His right hip had been broken but was healed, and his ribs (healed) and the third metacarpal of his right hand also had been fractured.

DETAILS OF BURIAL

The body was buried in a low ditch tightly cut to fit his measurements, next to Individual 7. His head may have been propped up on an item of perishable material. He had no grave goods.

BIBLIOGRAPHY

Bonghi Jovino 2007–08:780. Mallegni and Lippi 2007–08:801–803.

9. Decapitated child, early seventh century B.C.E. (Orientalizing). Found in 2005.

ANTHROPOLOGICAL DATA

Age ca. 8 years. The head, not found, was decapitated; indications of the cutting occur at the sixth and seventh cervical vertebrae. Besides the head, most of the hands and feet were lacking, as well as the knees, one elbow, and one hip.

DETAILS OF BURIAL

Found in Area Alpha. Buried supine, on bare ground, with feet under a wall (TP 740). The body was oriented in such a way that the head (not present) would have been on the eastern end. There were no grave goods and no associated deer horns.

BIBLIOGRAPHY

Bonghi Jovino 2007–08:784. Mallegni and Lippi 2007–08:800–801.

10. 545/1. "Foreign sailor," 770–740 B.C.E. (Villanovan/Iron Age). Found in 1991.

ANTHROPOLOGICAL DATA

Age 30–35 years. Male. Height not known. The skeletal remains indicate that the body was robust and muscular. The typology of the head, dolicocranial and with elongated face, was not Tarquinian, but rather recalls south Italian (i.e., Greek) features. Bone spurs on the soles of the feet are interpreted to indicate that the subject stood frequently on a slippery surface, while granules of bone formed in the auditory canal support the idea that the individual had extensive contact with water, that is, that he was a sailor. The body shows evidence of beating, with numerous areas of wounds and fractures that had partially healed before death. The' left side of the head sustained a severe blow, from which it had healed, when, several months later, the subject died from a mortal blow to the right side of the head.

Details of Burial

The body was found in a part of the site north of the sacred cavity and Area Alpha. It was placed supine in a low ditch (USS 540) cut out of the bedrock. Inhumation burials were still rare at this time. The head was on the northeast, with the burial going from northeast to southwest. The body was covered over by a stratum of red-brown clay (USS 540/1), in a manner similar to other burials at the complex. But no evidence of burning as is frequent in other cases. The burial predates the use of stone monuments in the complesso. Fragments of a Greek geometric ("Euboean," not Pithekoussan, according to D. Ridgway) jug were found around the head; also on the breast.

Bibliography

Bonghi Jovino 2004. Bonghi Jovino 2010:166. Bonghi Jovino, Mallegni, and Usai 1997. Mallegni and Lippi 2007–08:797–799. Mallegni, Usai, and Ragghianti: 1994.

Note

In observing the conventions for length and style of documentation for the papers from the conference, I have decided to focus on the case of Tarquinia and leave aside for now some other fascinating aspects of Etruscan human sacrifice, such as other sites in early Italy where burials have occurred in a habitation context and thus may be sacrificial (cf. Backe Forsberg 2005; Bartoloni and Bendettini 2007–08); the problem of Etruscan ritual murder and early gladiatorial games; and the general subject of representations of human sacrifice in Etruscan art (cf. Bonfante 1984; Steuernagel 1998). To facilitate the flow of text I have created an Appendix of the ten burials so far published on Pian di Civita, which I hope will be helpful in drawing together basic data and bibliography for each burial, since the information is distributed in a number of publications not easily accessible in most American libraries. For help with my research I thank Maria Bonghi Jovino and Giovanna Bagnasco Gianni, now director of the excavations of the University of Milan at Pian di Civita, for patiently answering my questions, and Ingrid Edlund-Berry, Lora Holland, Trevor Luke, and Stephen Dyson for suggestions that have helped me in understanding certain aspects of the rituals and lines of research to pursue further.

References Cited

Backe-Forsberg, Y. 2005 *Crossing the Bridge, An Interpretation of the Archaeological Remains in the Etruscan Bridge Complex at San Giovenale, Etruria.* Reproenheten, Swedish Institute of Agricultural Sciences, Uppsala.

Bagnasco Gianni, G. 1996 *Oggetti iscritti di epoca orientalizzante in Etruria*. Leo S. Olschki Editore, Florence.

Bagnasco Gianni, G. 2001a *Le sortes etrusche*. In *Sorteggio pubblico e cleromanzia dall'antichità all'età moderna, Atti della Tavola Rotonda, Università degli Studi di Milano, Dipartimento di Scienze dell'Antichità, 26–27 gennaio 2000*, edited by F. Cordano and C. Grottanelli, pp. 197–220. Università degli Studi di Milano, Milan.

Bagnasco Gianni, G. 2001b L'Area Gamma: Recenti interventi. In *Tarquinia etrusca, Una nuova storia, Catalogo della Mostra*, edited by A. M. Moretti Sgubini, pp. 41–42. "L'Erma" di Bretschneider, Rome.

Bagnasco Gianni, G. 2005 *Tarquinia: Il deposito votivo reiterato. Una preliminare analisi dei comparanda*. In *Offerte dal regno vegetale e dal regno animale nelle manifestazioni del sacro, Atti del Incontro di Studio, Milano 26–27 giugno 2003*, edited by M. Bonghi Jovino and F. Chiesa, pp. 91–97. Tarchna/Supplementi I. "L'Erma" di Bretschneider, Rome.

Bartoloni, G., and M. G. Bendettini 2007–08 *Sepolti tra i vivi/ Buried Among the Living. Evidenza ed interpretazione di contesti funerari in abitato. Atti del Convegno Internazionale, Roma, 26–29 Aprile 2006 (Scienze dell'Antichità 14)*. Quasar, Rome.

Bedini, E. 1997 I resti faunistici. In *Tarquinia, Testimonianze archeologiche e ricostruzione storica, scavi sistematici nell'abitato, 1982–1988, Tarchna I*, edited by M. Bonghi Jovino and C. Chiaramonte Treré, pp. 103–144. "L'Erma" di Bretschneider, Rome.

Bonfante, L. 1984 Human Sacrifice on an Etruscan Funerary Urn. *AJA* 88:531–539.

Bonghi Jovino, M. 1986 L'orizzonte protovillanoviano; La Prima Età del Ferro. In *Gli Etruschi di Tarquinia*, edited by M. Bonghi Jovino, pp. 83–92. Edizioni Panini, Modena.

Bonghi Jovino, M. 1997 Settore E. Lo scavo dell'Area Alpha. In *Tarquinia, Testimonianze archeologiche e ricostruzione storica, scavi sistematici nell'abitato, 1982–1988, Tarchna I*, edited by M. Bonghi Jovino and C. Chiaramonte Treré, pp. 33–43. "L'Erma" di Bretschneider, Rome.

Bonghi Jovino, M. 2004 A proposito di un'olla "Euboica" rinvenuta nell'abitato di Tarquinia. *Annali Faina* 11: 31–46.

Bonghi Jovino, M. 2005 Offerte, uomini e dei nel "complesso monumentale" di Tarquinia: dallo Scavo all'interpretazione. In *Offerte dal regno vegetale e dal regno animale nelle manifestazioni del sacro, Atti del Incontro di Studio, Milano 26–27 giugno 2003*, edited by M. Bonghi Jovino and F. Chiesa, pp. 73–84. Tarchna/Supplementi I. "L'Erma" di Bretschneider, Rome.

Bonghi Jovino, M. 2007–08 L'ultima dimora. Sacrifici umani e rituali sacri in Etruria. Nuovi dati sulle sepolture nell'abitato di Tarquinia. In *Sepolti tra i vivi/ Buried Among the Living. Evidenza ed interpretazione di contesti funerari in abitato. Atti del Convegno Internazionale, Roma, 26–29 Aprile 2006 (Scienze dell'Antichità 14)*, edited by G. Bartoloni and M. G. Bendettini, pp. 771–793. Quasar, Rome.

Bonghi Jovino, M. 2009 A proposito del bambino epilettico di Tarquinia, una revisitazione. *Athenaeum* 97(2):471–476.

Bonghi Jovino, M. 2010a The Tarquinia project: A Summary of 25 Years of Excavation. *AJA* 114:161–180.

Bonghi Jovino, M. 2010b Tarquinia. Types of Offerings, Etruscan Divinities, and Attributes in the Archaeological Record. In *Material Aspects of Etruscan Religion, Proceedings of the International Colloquium, Leiden, May 29 and 30, 2008*, edited by L. B. van der Meer, pp. 5–16. *Babesch* Supplement 16. Peeters, Leuven.

Bonghi Jovino, M., and C. Chiaramonte Treré 1997 *Tarquinia, Testimonianze archeologiche e ricostruzione storica, scavi sistematici nell'abitato, 1982–1988*, edited by M. Bonghi Jovino and C. Chiaramonte Treré. "L'Erma" di Bretschneider, Rome.

Bonghi Jovino, M., F. Mallegni, and L. Usai 1997 Una morte violenta, Sul rinvenimento di uno scheletro nell'area del "complesso sacro-istituzionale" della Civita di Tarquinia. In *Aspetti della cultura di Volterra etrusca fra l'età del Ferro e l'età ellenistica e contributi della ricerca antropologica alla conoscenza del popolo etrusco* (*Atti del XIX Convegno di Studi Etruschi ed Italici, Volterra 15–19 ottobre 1995*), edited by G. Maetzke, pp. 489–498. Leo S. Olschki, Florence.

Bremmer, J. N. 2007 Human Sacrifice: A Brief Introduction. In *The Strange World of Human Sacrifice*, edited by J. Bremmer, pp. 1–8. Peeters, Leuven.

Chiaramonte Treré, C. 1987 Altri dati dagli scavi alla Civita. Sugli aspetti cultuali e rituali. In *Tarquinia: Ricerche, scavi e prospettive. Atti del Convegno Internazionale di Studi La Lombardia per gli Etruschi, Milano 24–25 giugno, 1986*, edited by M. Bonghi Jovino and C. Chiaramonte Treré, pp. 79–89. "L'Erma" di Bretschneider, Milan.

Chiaramonte Treré, C. 1997 Considerazioni sulla stratigrafia e ipotesi interpretative dall'Orientalizzante recente ad età ellenistica. In *Tarquinia, Testimonianze archeologiche e ricostruzione storica, scavi sistematici nell'abitato, 1982–1988, Tarchna I*, edited by M. Bonghi Jovino and C. Chiaramonte Treré, pp. 183–216. "L'Erma" di Bretschneider, Rome.

Chiesa, F. 2001 Il Settore M: La deposizione femminile e il deposito delle olle. In *Tarquinia etrusca, Una nuova storia, Catalogo della Mostra*, edited by A. M. Moretti Sgubini, pp. 38–40. "L'Erma" di Bretschneider, Rome.

de Grummond, N. T. 2006 *Etruscan Myth, Sacred History, and Legend.* University of Pennsylvania Museum of Archaeology and Anthropology, Philadelphia.

de Grummond, N. T. 2014 The Cult of Lur: Prophecy and Human Sacrifice. In *Atti del Simposio Internazionale in ricordo di Francesca Romana Serra Ridgway, Tarquinia 24–25 settembre 2010*, edited by M. D. Gentili and L. Maneschi, *Mediterranea* 11. Rome. 141–52.

Di Fazio, M. 2001 Sacrifici umani e uccisioni rituali nel mondo etrusco. *Rendiconti della Accademia Nazionale dei Lincei, Classe di scienze morali, storiche e filologiche.* Series 9.3, pp. 435–505.

Fornaciari, G., and F. Mallegni 1986 I resti scheletri umani. In *Gli Etruschi di Tarquinia*, edited by M. Bonghi Jovino, pp. 197–199. Edizioni Panini, Modena.

Fornaciari, G., and F. Mallegni 1987 Il bambino della Civita: Un caso di probabile aneurisma venoso del IX secolo a.C. In *Tarquinia: Ricerche, scavi e prospettive, Atti del Convegni Internazionale di Studi La Lombardia per gli Etruschi, Milano, 24–25 giugno, 1986*, edited by M. Bonghi Jovino and C. Chiaramonte Treré, pp. 95–98. Edizioni ET, Milan.

Fornaciari, G., and F. Mallegni 1997. I resti paleoantropologici. In *Tarquinia, Testimonianze archeologiche e ricostruzione storica, scavi sistematici nell'abitato, 1982–1988*, edited by M. Bonghi Jovino and C. Chiaramonte Treré, pp. 100–102. "L'Erma" di Bretschneider, Rome.

Giudice, E. 2006 Postilla in margine ad uno scarabeo etrusco di Monaco. In *Gli eroi di Omero* (*Atti del Convegno Internazionale—Taormina, Giuseppe Sinopoli Festival, 20–22 ottobre 2006*), edited by I. Colpo, I. Favaretto, and F. Ghedini. *Iconografia* 8:241–248. Edizioni Quasar, Rome.

Johnston, S. I. 2001 Charming Children: The Use of the Child in Ancient Divination. *Arethusa* 34:97–117.

Kamp, K. A. 2001 Where Have All the Children Gone? The Archaeology of Childhood. *Journal of Archaeological Method and Theory* 8:1–34.

Leighton, R. 2004 *Tarquinia, An Etruscan City.* Duckworth, London.

Mallegni, F., and B. Lippi 2007–08 Considerazioni antropologiche sugli inumati nell'Area Sacra dell'abitato di Tarquinia. In *Sepolti tra i vivi/Buried among the Living: Evidenza ed interpretazione di contesti funerari in abitato. Atti del Convegno Internazionale, Roma, 26–29*

Aprile 2006, Scienze dell'Antichitá 14, edited by G. Bartoloni and M. G. Benedettini, pp. 795–804. Quasar, Rome.

Mallegni, F., U. Ragghianti, and L. Usai 1994 Traumatic Events, of Which One Was Perhaps Lethal, in a Skeleton of an Individual of Etruscan Culture of the Eighth Century B.C.E. from the Civita of Tarquinia. *Journal of Paleopathology* 6(2):93–101.

Maras, D. 2009 *Il dono votivo, gli dei e il sacro nelle iscrizioni etrusche di culto*. Biblioteca di "Studi Etruschi" 46. Fabrizio Serra Editore, Pisa and Rome.

Marcattili, F. 2005 Mundus. *ThesCRA* 4:282–283.

Martini, W. 1971 *Die Etruskische Ringsteinglyptik*. F.H. Kerle Verlag, Heidelberg.

Nielsen, E. 1995 Aspetti della produzione artigianale a Poggio Civitate. In *Preziosi in oro, avorio, osso e corno: arte e techniche degli artigiani etruschi: atti del seminario di studi ed esperimenti, Murlo, 26 settembre-3 ottobre, 1992*, edited by E. Formigli, pp. 19–24. Nuova Immagine, Siena.

Radke, G. 1965 Mania. In *Die Götter Altitaliens*, p. 198. Verlag Aschendorff, Münster.

Rottoli, M. 2001 Analisi botaniche. In *Tarquinia etrusca, Una nuova storia, Catalogo della Mostra*, edited by A. M. Moretti Sgubini, pp. 59–61. "L'Erma" di Bretschneider, Rome.

Sorrentino, C. 1986 La Fauna. In *Gli Etruschi di Tarquinia*, edited by M. Bonghi Jovino, pp. 200–202. Edizioni Panini, Modena.

Steuernagel, D. 1998. *Menschenopfer und Mord am Altar, Griechische Mythen in etruskischen Gräbern*. Dr. Ludwig Reichert Verlag, Wiesbaden.

Torelli, M. 1987 Appunti per una storia di Tarquinia. In *Tarquinia:Ricerche, scavi e prospettive. Atti del Convegno Internazionale di Studi La Lombardia per gli Etruschi, Milano 24–25 giugno, 1986*, edited by M. Bonghi Jovino and C. Chiaramonte Treré, pp. 129–140. "L'Erma" di Bretschneider, Rome.

PART III

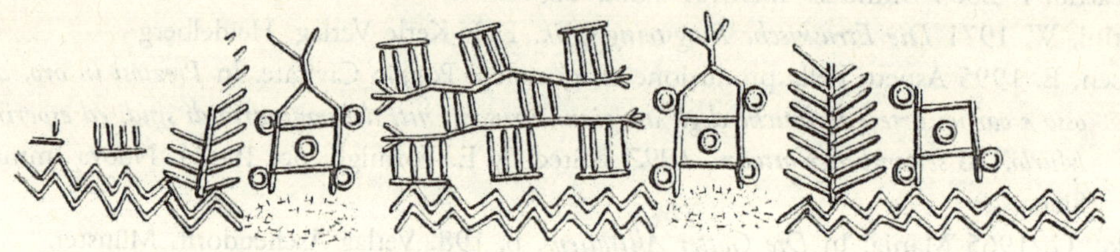

Exploring Exceptional Cases of Sacrifice

CHAPTER NINE

Human Sacrifices as "Crisis Management"?

The Case of the Early Neolithic Site of Herxheim, Palatinate, Germany

*Andrea Zeeb-Lanz, Rose-Marie Arbogast,
Silja Bauer, Bruno Boulestin, Anne-Sophie Coupey,
Anthony Denaire, Fabian Haack, Christian Jeunesse,
Dirk Schimmelpfennig, Rouven Turck*

Abstract *The early Neolithic site of Herxheim has revealed extraordinary remains of a unique ritual, comprising the sacrifice of more than 500 human individuals. The site consists of a settlement area of the Linear Bandkeramik Culture, surrounded by an earthwork constructed of a double ring of overlapping pits. The sacrificed individuals were butchered like animals, their bones in most cases smashed into small fragments. The leitmotif of the site, intentional destruction of all kinds of material, comprises high quality pottery as well as stone and flint tools or grinding stones. The smashed human bones were found in concentrations of varying size in the pit enclosure of the settlement. A lot of questions accrued during the scientific analysis of the site. The examination of the human bones revealed cut marks and traces of scraping. One of the hypotheses for the normed and repeated treatment of the human bodies calls for cannibalism as an important part of the strange rituals, which do have neither tradition nor analogies in the 650 years of the Linear Pottery culture. Various ideas concerning the ritual, its motivation, and the identity of the sacrificed persons are advanced in this article.*

THE BACKGROUND

From roughly 5500 to 4950 B.C.E., the first sedentary, full-fledged tillers in Middle Europe, the bearers of the so called Linear Bandkeramik culture (LBK), seem to have lived rather peaceably in small farming communities spread over the loess-covered plains extending from the Paris Basin to the borders of the Black Sea (Figure 9.1). But as aggression is a deeply rooted streak in human nature (Mitscherlich 1969; Wahl 2009), naturally violent encounters between individuals as well as different communities of the Bandkeramik also occurred. Proof of murderous conflicts are rare for the whole of this culture—until now, there are only two sites known that bear witness to inner cultural conflicts resulting in the deaths of multiple individuals. One of them is the mass grave of Talheim in Baden-Württemberg, where the skeletons of 38 persons, obviously killed in one event and showing deathly head traumata were found unceremoniously thrown into a large pit (Wahl and König 1987; Wahl and Strien 2007).

The other example for an obviously violent conflict is the large settlement site of Asparn in Austria. In the entrance area of a ditch system surrounding the village and at various other places in the ditch, the dislodged skeletal elements of 67 humans were detected (Teschler-Nicola et al. 2006; Windl 1996, 1999, 2001). Many of the individuals showed mortal head injuries caused primarily by the transverse hafted adze, the characteristic Bandkeramik stone tool (Teschler-Nicola et al. 1996). Both sites date to the latest phase of the LBK-culture around 5000 B.C.E.

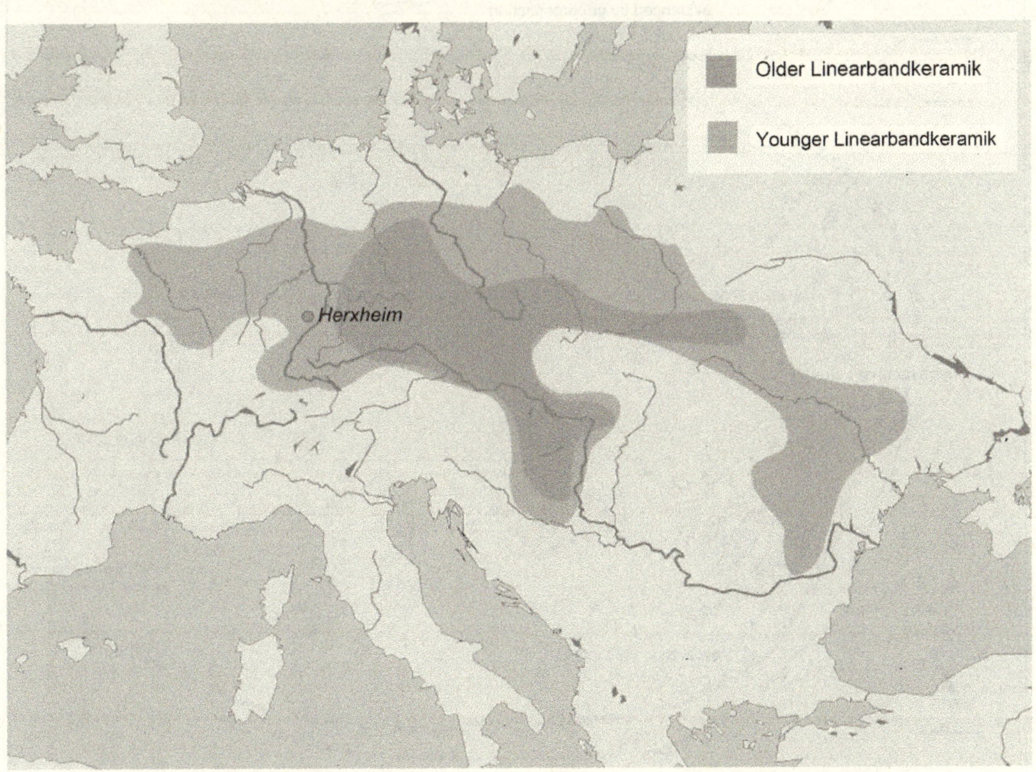

FIGURE 9.1 Geographical distribution of the Linear Pottery Culture (5600–4950 B.C.E.) from the Paris Basin to the borders of the Black Sea (GDKE Rheinland-Pfalz, Dir. Landesarchäologie—Speyer).

Although initially considered as evidence of warlike context, the features and findings from Herxheim soon revealed a pattern that must have resulted from something entirely different than a "normal" interpersonal aggressive conflict.

The Site of Herxheim

The Bandkeramik site of Herxheim, consisting of a settlement area surrounded by a double earthwork, lies at the western periphery of the modern village of Herxheim in the southwest of the Palatinate (southwest Germany). Approximately half of the complex was excavated during two campaigns (Figure 9.2), the first representing a rescue excavation from 1996 to 1998, the second being a research enterprise from 2005 to 2008 (Zeeb-Lanz and Haack 2006).

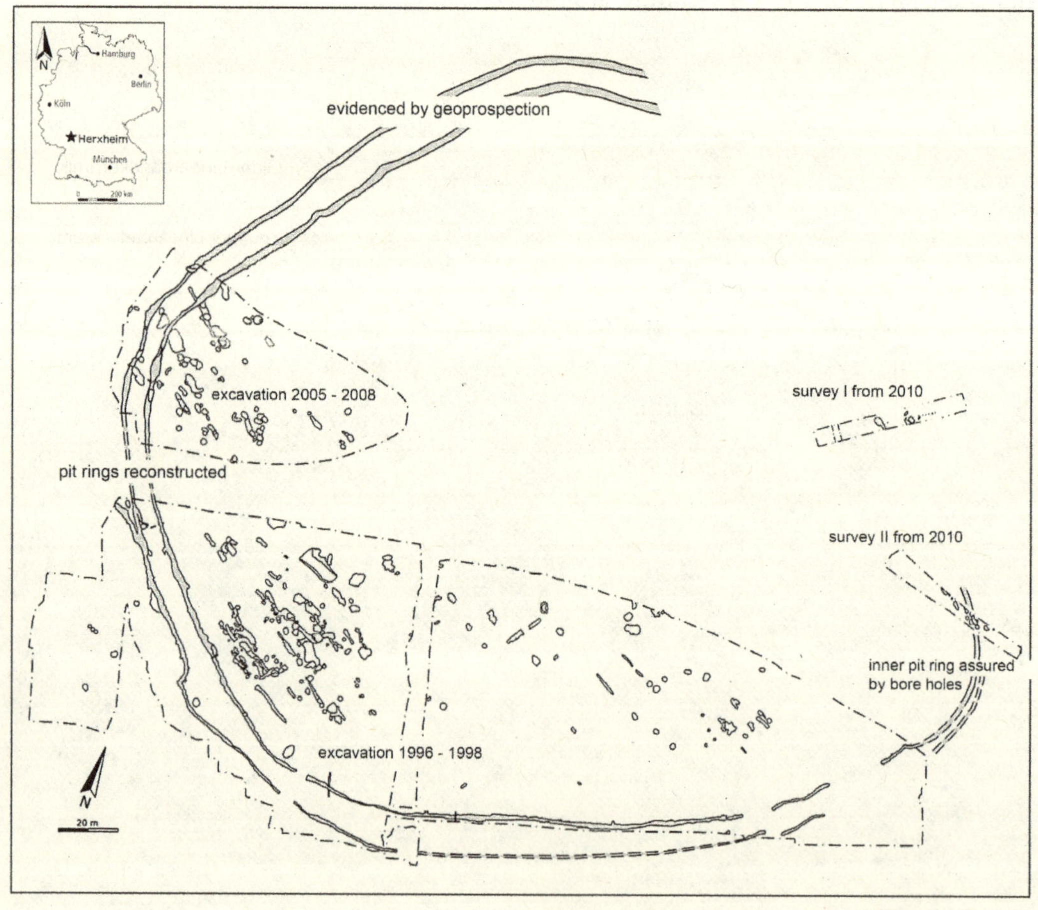

FIGURE 9.2 Plan of the excavated and prospected areas of the settlement and double pit enclosure of Herxheim. (GDKE Rheinland-Pfalz, Dir. Landesarchäologie–Speyer)

While we initially thought the earthwork to be a sort of "pseudo-ditch," consisting of overlapping pits dug out and filled over a long period of time, the analysis of the excavation executed by F. Haack (2014) revealed that in fact the earthwork consists of long stretches of pits dug at the same time that resulted in long ditch segments. All of these were obviously dug in a rather short period of time not long before the "ritual phase" of the site. Only a few pits were actually dug into already refilled parts of the ditch system, thus creating overlapping features.

In many parts of the ditch system, extraordinary find compositions could be documented (Zeeb-Lanz et al. 2007). They consisted mainly of heavily fragmented human skeleton elements of more than 500 individuals. From the age distribution of the dead, they were intentionally sacrificed here, as they do not represent a naturally deceased community.

Concentrations of Human Remains and Artifact Groups in the Ditches

The Human Remains

The smashed body parts of the dead were lying in concentrations, which could also incorporate torsi such as spinal columns with still-adhering pelvis, upper or lower halves of skeletons, and more or less whole limbs (Figure 9.3). The concentrations could contain

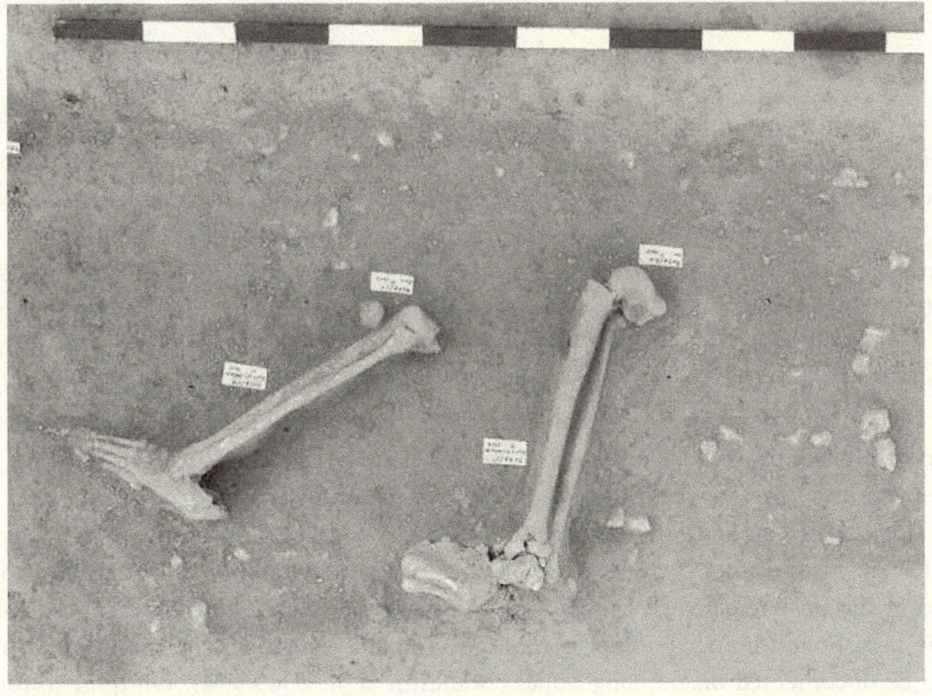

Figure 9.3 Lower legs with feet from the inner pit ring of the enclosure.

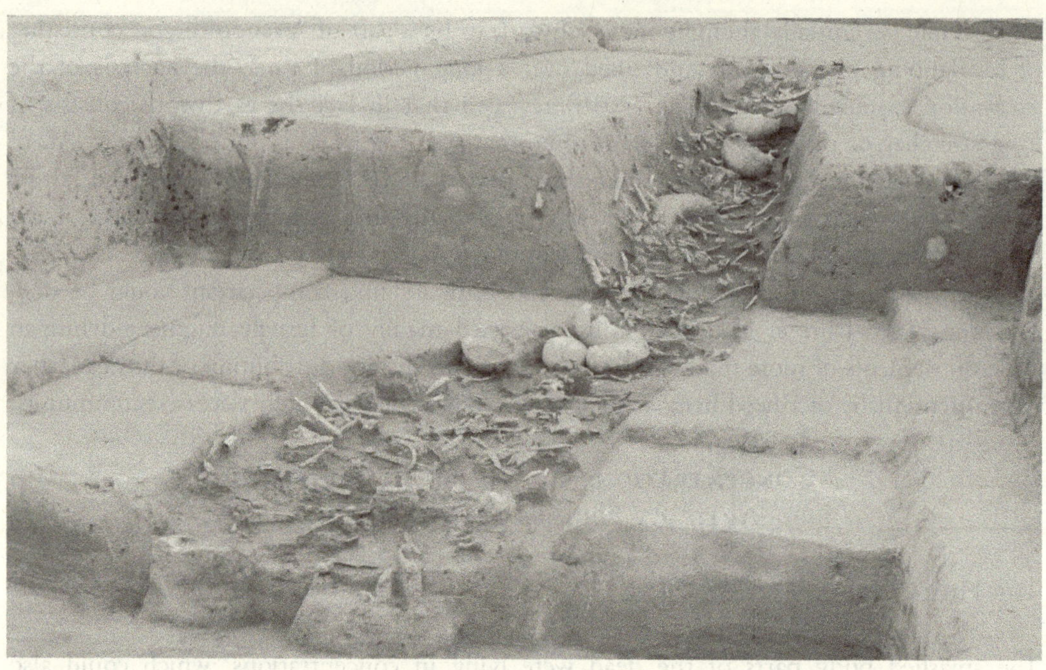

Figure 9.4 Concentration N° 9 of the research excavation, dug out in "negative technique," shows the scattering of human bone fragments, animal bones and cattle horn cores as well as a number of human calottes, the ones in the foreground forming a sort of nest.

human bone fragments up to approximately 4,000 pieces (Figure 9.4). But the different skeleton elements present in each concentration did not represent whole individuals, as various parts such as ribs or vertebrae and also long bones were missing as a rule. Also, the number of skulls in one concentration of fragmented human individuals was inconsistent with the postcranial rests in the same complex of bone rests (Boulestin et al. 2009:976f.). Furthermore, most of the skulls had been manipulated in a very special way (Orschiedt and Haidle 2001:147f.), leaving only the skullcaps or "calottes" intact. Fragments of the facial parts of the skulls were also found in all the concentrations, but they were not as frequent as the skullcaps themselves. The calottes in several cases were observed arranged together positively in "nests" (Figure 9.5), but in most cases, they were unsystematically mixed with other fragments of human skeletons.

Close observation of the human skulls, bones, and bone fragments revealed quite a number of traces of specific, unequivocally anthropogenic manipulations of the dead: the bones of the postcranial skeleton show distinctive cut marks, especially on the diaphysis of the long bones or the shoulder blades. Subtle parallel shallow cuts or scraping marks could be documented on the long bones (Boulestin et al. 2009:974). On quite a number of the calottes, fine long cuts from flint knives stretch from the root of the nose over the whole skullcap to the nape of the neck. Beyond that, some entirely preserved spinal

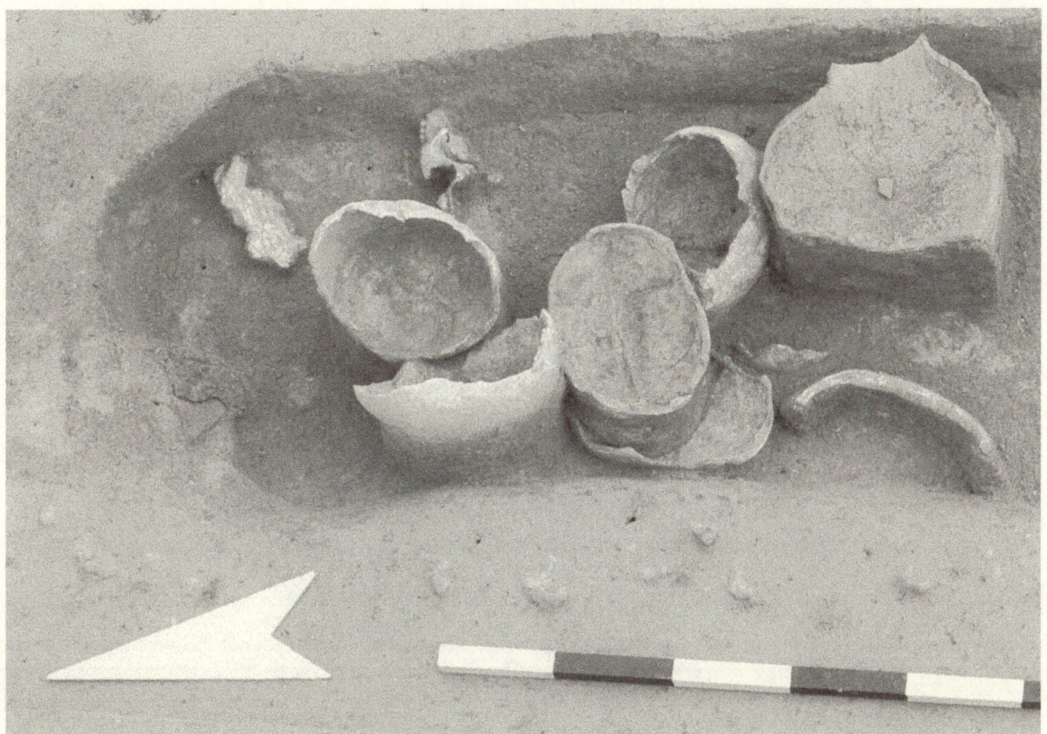

FIGURE 9.5 All in all thirteen human calottes had been stacked together in the form of a "nest" in this concentration in the inner pit ring.

columns revealed the absence of the transverse processes of the thoracic vertebrae; the mutilation of the vertebrae suggests ribs were cut off from the spinal column.

OTHER ARTIFACTS IN THE CONCENTRATIONS

The concentrations, however, did not exclusively contain the rests of manipulated human bodies. They also revealed a spectrum of decorated pottery, which is surprising in various aspects. On the one hand, it is the largest amount of ornate pottery found at an early Neolithic site. On the other hand, the pottery from Herxheim is characterized by its extraordinary quality in ornamentation, design, and fabrication (Zeeb-Lanz et al. 2009a:212–214, 2009b:117–120). The embellishment is especially accurately designed and contains a captivating variety. Most of the pottery had been highly polished, and the polish is still visible on the potsherds today. Among the forms of the decorated pots, the bulbous bottle plays a dominant role.

As many sherds could be restored to whole or nearly whole vessels (Figure 9.6), it can be concluded they had been smashed directly on site and then scattered in the concentrations. Around 20 miniature pots had not been smashed; of these only the handles had been cut of intentionally.

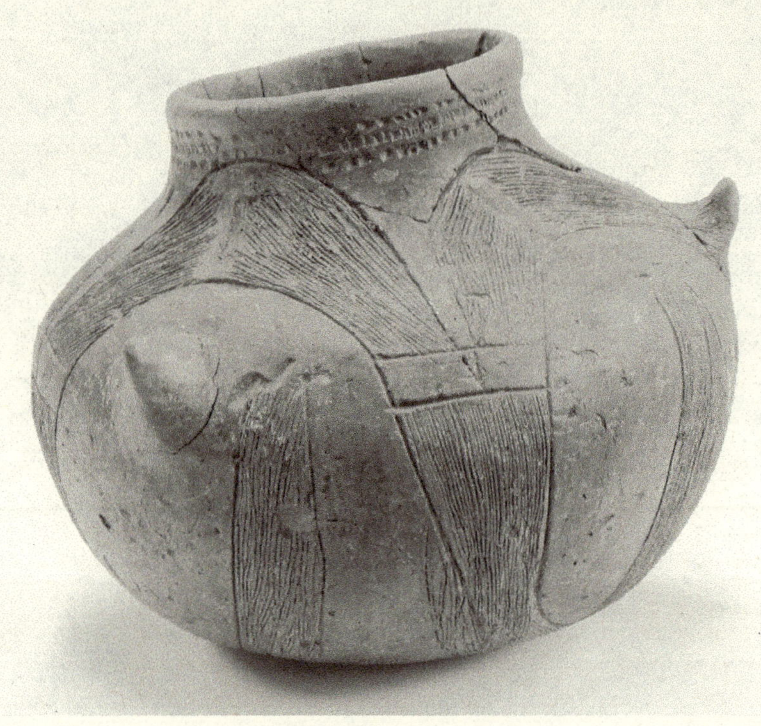

Figure 9.6 Example of a high quality ornamented vase from the pit enclosure of Herxheim.

A surprising feature was the stylistic analysis of the pottery decoration: the vessels that consistently date to the younger and youngest phase of the Bandkeramik do not all bear the expected regional decoration style of the Palatinate. Moreover, nearly half of the vessels revealed regional Bandkeramik ornamentation styles from areas as far away as Bohemia (approximately 400 km east of Herxheim) (Figure 9.7). In all, eight different non-local styles of decoration were detected in the ceramic spectrum deriving from the concentrations with smashed human skeleton elements. Whether the vessels were actually made in the respective regions cannot be said with total certainty, but clay analyses proved that they were not created from local clay of the Palatinate. Quite a number of undecorated pots, ranging from flat bowls to huge storage vessels, the latter in some cases decorated with clay bands, were also found in association with human bones and other findings in the concentrations of the pit enclosure.

Destruction can be monitored in other artifact categories as well, namely stone and flint tools or grinding stones (Zeeb-Lanz et al. 2009a:207–209). Stone adzes were destroyed by smashing them in half, flint blades—usually those from high quality raw materials—were broken, while grinding stones were found shattered into many small fragments. The wide variety of bone and antler artifacts found in the pit enclosure (Figure 9.8) were sometimes broken, but the degree of destruction cannot be distinguished from

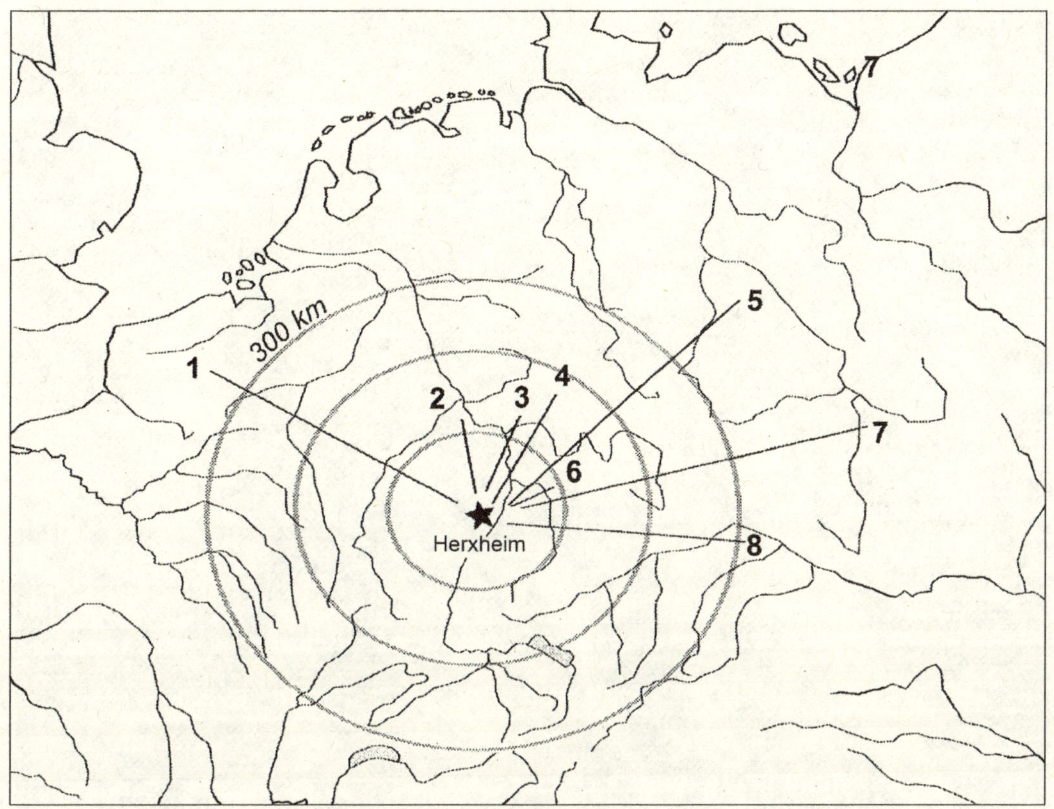

FIGURE 9.7 Distribution of the origins of the pottery ornamentation styles found on the vases in the concentrations of the pit enclosure. 1=Blicquy; 2=Rhine-Moselle; 3=Rhine-Main hatched style; 4=Nordhessen (style of Leihgestern); 5=Elster-Saale; 6=Neckar; 7=Bohemia (style of Šarka); 8=Bavaria.

that of comparable artifacts from normal refuse pits in LBK settlements (Zeeb-Lanz et al. 2007:225).

A further category in the concentrations consists of animal bones. A special selection found its way into the respective complexes of human bones and other artifacts. Domestic animals such as cattle, pig, sheep, and goat are represented by certain extremities that cannot be denoted as butchering decay (Arbogast 2009). We found forelegs and hind legs, as well as the horn cores of cattle and aurochs—all of the mentioned parts depict the respective animal without doubt and might perhaps be interpreted as *pars pro toto* depositions of the particular animal. Wild animals, especially small carnivores such as fox, wild cat, or marten are represented by mandibles or maxillae; around thirty of these jaws were found in a singular deposition in the inner pit ring. A striking feature is the presence of around 200 dog bones representing parts of the animals or even whole cadavers (Zeeb-Lanz et al. 2007:211). The bones belong to at least six individuals and the number of dog bones is greater than the quantity of rests of this animal in all other known Bandkeramik settlements in Europe. In summary, the animal bones in the pit

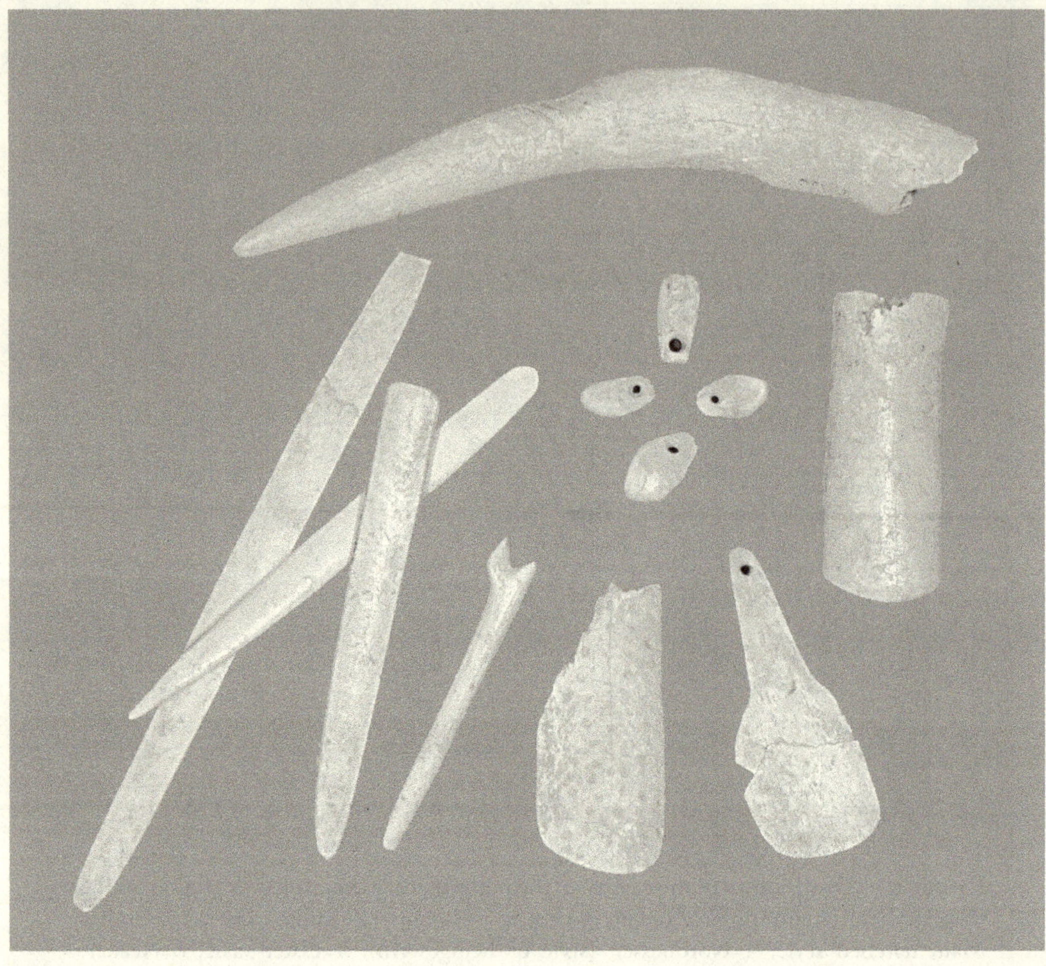

Figure 9.8 Assortment of animal bones, teeth and antler artifacts from the pit enclosure.

enclosure constitute a selection of animal species and parts that underline the special character of the features in the earthwork of Herxheim.

Interpretative Approaches to the Anthropological and Archaeological Research Results

Anthropological Interpretation of the Human Remains

What can at first sight be deduced from an overview of the composition of findings of Herxheim is the highly ritual character of the concentrations in the pit enclosure. The leitmotif of the site, violent destruction of objects of all kinds and the deposition of the shattered rests in concentrations in the pit enclosure, shows a recurrent, repetitive, and normative pattern (Boulestin et al. 2009:979). Close observation and analysis of the human rests revealed, furthermore, that the dead were treated in a systematic way which strongly resembles the technique and procedure of butchering animals with the aim of gaining nutrition. The cut marks on diaphysis, shoulder blades, or on the ramus mandibulae (Figure 9.9) suggest the cutting through of muscles and fibers to sever the extremities from the trunk, the separation of the mandible from the head and the "levée de l'échine" (detachment of the spinal column) as the first part of the special treatment of the human bodies. In a second step, the bones were freed from all flesh and tissue, allocated by the parallel scraping marks found especially on the long bones and on skeleton parts that hold a considerable amount of soft tissue. All the described actions were obviously undertaken on the fresh bone, relatively soon after the death of the victims. This is proved by the characteristic form and length of the long bone fragments as well as the appearance of the fracture outlines (Boulestin et al. 2009:974). After the excision of all meat and fat, the cleaned skeleton elements, especially massive long bones, were smashed into small fragments. Assumedly, this action was undertaken for marrow extraction. A conspicuous fact remains that quite a number of skeleton elements rich of marrow and fat, such as vertebrae bodies and epiphysis, are often missing in the compositions of human remains. These observations have led to the hypothesis that cannibalism may

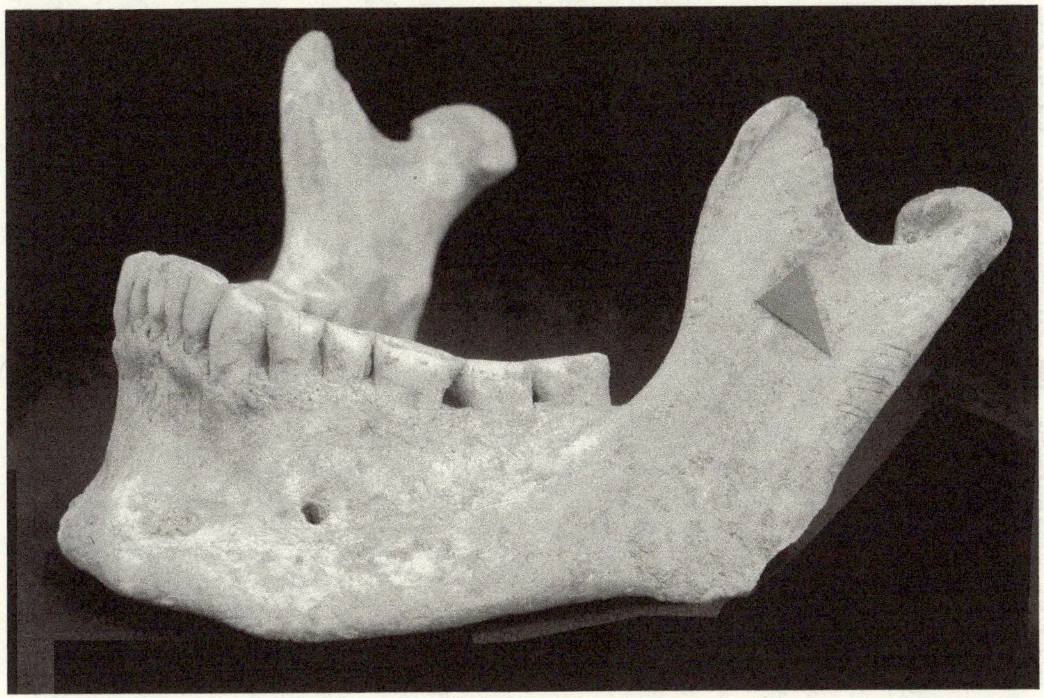

FIGURE 9.9 Example for cut marks on a ramus mandibulae of a human individual from one of the concentrations.

have taken place at Herxheim as a potential part of the approved rituals (Boulestin et al. 2009). This hypothesis cannot be proved directly, but it is supported by a number of arguments: the treatment of the human sacrifices is comparable to butchering methods for animals, as well as the heavy fragmentation of the long bones which can be observed in animal butchering remains. Furthermore, there is a distinctive overrepresentation of skulls whereas patella and vertebrae bodies, for example, are relatively underrepresented. The treatment of the human bodies, especially the destruction of marrow-rich long bones and other spongy bone parts, can be interpreted as a nutritionally motivated exploitation of the killed individuals.

Not really consistent with the assumption of ritual cannibalism is the special treatment of the skulls of the deceased. The distinctive cut marks on the crania (Figure 9.10) suggest the ablation of the scalp before the sculls were treated in a special way with stone adzes, leaving only the skullcap intact. As most of the heads of the deceased were treated in the same manner, it is obvious that the production of calottes was an intended part of the ritualistic actions. Their abundance in the pit enclosure, as well as in some cases the observed placement of the calottes in the form of "nests" show that they must have had a special meaning for the participants of the strange rituals in Herxheim. The edges of the calottes are not processed any further, negating an interpretation of the manipulated

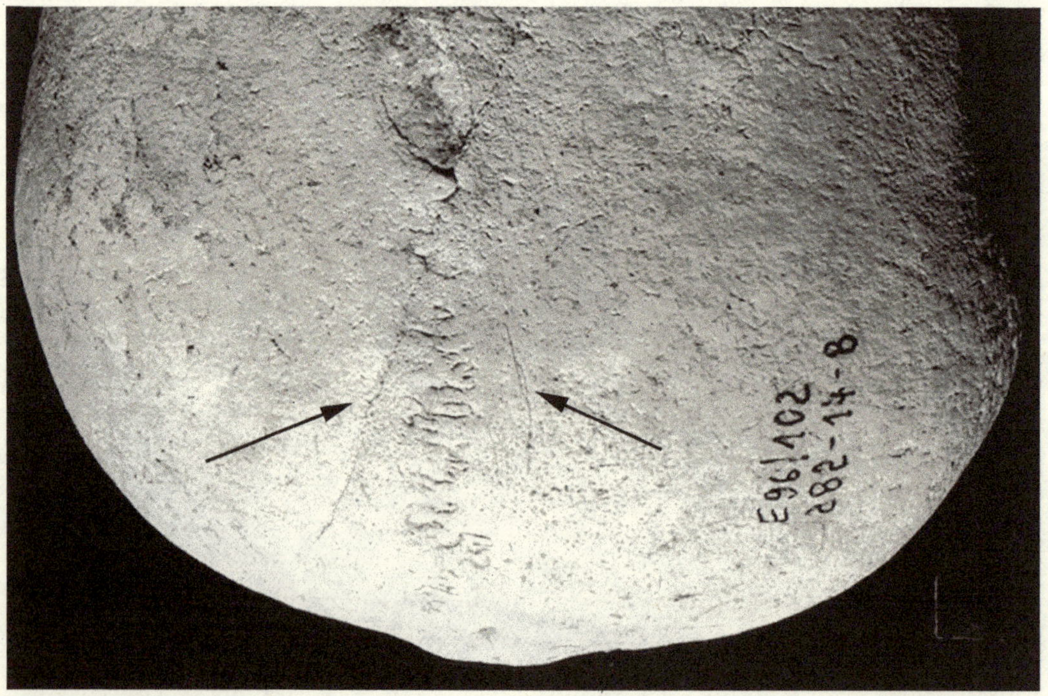

Figure 9.10 Human calotte from Herxheim with the characteristic cut marks crossing the middle of the skullcap.

crania as drinking cups suggested recently in a popular science journal (Schulz 2011). But it cannot be totally excluded that the skullcaps were used during the assumed rituals as eating bowls containing special food—no traces of fare were found inside any of them, though.

Although the treatment of human bodies using butchering methods without the aim of gaining nutrition but rather for religious reasons is well known (e.g., the "sky burials" in Tibet; see Lo Blue 2009), the arguments for cannibalism in a ritual context are the most plausible explanation for the fate of the human victims from Herxheim. Nevertheless, the supposed cannibalization of the human individuals would have been part of a complex ceremony and has to be seen in the context of a larger ritual whose main purpose is the destruction of precious objects, human lives being the most valuable ones among the selection of findings in the concentrations in the pit enclosure.

For the accomplishment of the strange and violent rituals in Herxheim, a maximum time span of 50 years is given by the pottery in the concentrations, which as a whole belongs to the latest phase of the Bandkeramik culture (approximately 5000 to 4950 B.C.E.). But the amount of refitting pottery sherds derived from different pits/concentrations of the enclosure (Denaire 2009) suggests a much shorter time frame. Quite a number of pottery fragments belonging to the same pot were found in different concentrations. In one case, several fitting pottery sherds were found in concentrations lying 120 meters apart, one situated in the inner pit ring, the other in the outer pit ring (Denaire 2009:81). These refitting pottery sherds show fresh breaklines indicating that the sherds did not lie around on the ground for a long time after the destruction of the respective pot but were filled in into different concentrations simultaneously or in the course of a short time span. Quite a number of bone refittings from diverse concentrations underline the observation that the rituals took place in a shorter rather than longer time span.

The huge number of approximately 500 human individuals, counted by excavated skullcaps and intact crania, must be amplified as only half of the enclosure has been examined so far. But even 500 individuals could not have lived and died in a small village like the Herxheim site in the short period of 50 years. The first hypothesis deduced from the various pottery styles present in the concentrations assumed that delegations from a number of communities, some of them originating rather far from Herxheim, came with slaves, prisoners, or other persons selected for sacrifice to Herxheim and participated in the ritual actions.

ISOTOPE ANALYSES

Strontium isotope analyses from the first and third molars of a representative random sample of eighty individuals from the pit rings were executed for the verification of the above-mentioned thesis. The sample included children, as well as juveniles and adults from both sexes. To our great surprise it turned out that the majority of the tested individuals did not grow up on loess soils representing the typical residence of the earliest European farmers. In contrary, the teeth showed rather high radiogenic ratios, which proved that the origin for most of the people was from mountainous regions with granite or gneiss bedrock (Turck et al. 2012). As there is not a single Bandkeramik settlement in Europe known to lie in a low or high mountain range, the isotope analyses present a further mystery in the enigmatic features of the Herxheim site. DNA analyses from teeth of the isotope-tested individuals are under way to answer the question of whether the human sacrifices of Herxheim perhaps represent a late Mesolithic population.

For the whole area of the Palatinate, until now there has been one site that revealed artifacts dating to the latest phase of the Mesolithic: the Weidentalhöhle near Wilgartswiesen in the southernmost part of the Palatinate (Cziesla 1992). A similar situation can be stated for Rhine-Hesse; following the research to date, it seems there was a very scarce late Mesolithic population in the regions directly west of the Rhine. Even if the DNA tests hint at Mesolithic people, this would still pose a problem concerning the identity of the many sacrificed individuals from the double pit enclosure at Herxheim. Besides, until now there are no DNA samples of the latest Mesolithic hunter-gatherers of Middle Europe available, making the identification of the dead from Herxheim still more complicated.

Human Sacrifices in Herxheim—A Special Case

Human Sacrifices—Some General Remarks

The term *sacrifice* comprises a whole world of different settings. Even in theology, notions such as "cult," "sacrifice," "magic," "sacred operation," or "ritual" are often used nonspecifically and within a variety of contexts. Archaeology has adopted these terms without defining them with regard to their usage in explaining archaeological features (Beilke-Voigt 2007:18). Therefore, the term *sacrifice* encompasses quite a number of different acts, ideas, and likewise many varying sceneries. A general definition (Malina 2000:23ff.) or a general theory of sacrifice has not yet found comprehensive acceptance in the scientific community (Beilke-Voigt 2007:18; Janowski and Welker 2000). A "pragmatic and open" definition of the term *sacrifice* is offered by B. Gladigow: sacrifice is generally an integrated part of complexes of ritual actions; the symbolic value of the latter relies on the "logic of social relations" (Gladigow 2000:88). The author sees sacrifices as a dialectical act of giving and taking, of participation and distribution; the ritual meal also plays an important role in this context. Notwithstanding his "pragmatic and open" general determination of the term *sacrifice,* Gladigow states that an unambiguousness of the concept of sacrifice does not exist (2007:93). He rather tries to focus on the complexity of the rituals that include sacrifices to connect these rituals with the respective cultures in which they are practiced. Gladigow discusses the routines of sacrifices, the circumstances of their occurrence, and their connection with economical as well as rational factors. Further, the economical, political, and social interconnections of the respective rituals and the included sacrifices have to be accounted for in deciding on the definite nature of each variation of sacrifice (see Gladigow 2007:103f.). A shorter and more general formula for the concept *sacrifice* is given by H. Hubert and M. Mauss: They state: "La sacrifice est un acte religieux qui, par la consécration d'une victime, modifie l'état de la personne morale qui l'accomplit ou de certains objets auxquel elle s'intéresse" (Hubert and Mauss 1968:205). The authors, whose essay about the nature and function of sacrifice, first published in "L'Année sociologique 2" from 1899, can still be counted as one of the most important works about sacrifice, concentrate on the traits that connect the different types of sacrifice with a special view of the relation between the sacrificial person and the victim that is sacrificed. The victim personifies the agent between the person who sacrifices (profane world) and the addressee of the sacrifice (sacred world)—and the victim always has to be destroyed during the ritual to fulfill its destination (Hubert and Mauss 1968:302). The victim thus plays the most important part in the sacrifice, acting as a connection between profane and divine (Hubert and Mauss 1968:304f.). The sacrifice has an important social function as it always alludes to social affairs (Hubert and Mauss 1968:306).

As Burkert (1972) has assessed in detail, the origin of sacrifice in human societies already in prehistoric times comprises the act of killing—then, usually a wild animal—and the sacrificial meal afterward (Burkert 1972:20ff.). He emphasizes the relevance of the consumption of the meat of the sacrificed animal, the meal representing an important part of the sacrificial ceremony.

Not all cases of sacrifice are dedicated to the gods—there are also examples of sacrifice where the act itself unfolds a magical power. The release of this power is the ultimate reason for the sacrifice, not the appeasement or invocation of a divine force (Bertholet 1942:5f.). It is generally a great difficulty to comprehend the motives and reasons for sacrifices in an archaeological context—moreover, there are often problems in defining the nature of a sacrifice.

Human sacrifices are attested for a variety of prehistoric and historic peoples. Recent investigations (Bremmer 2007a), but also older literature on the topic, have shown that human sacrifice is found in prehistoric agrarian societies, as well as in larger and more complex societies such as kingdoms or empires (Bremmer 2007b:3). A question that has not yet been answered is whether there exists a correlation between the general degree of violence in a society and the practice of human sacrifice (Bremmer 2007b:7). If a correlation of this kind could be proved, it could shed new light on a number of prehistoric and historic societies.

Sometimes human sacrifices are also combined with cannibalism, the most prominent example being the Aztec sun cult, where the heart of a sacrificed human individual was offered to the sun god and the other parts of the body were consumed by the ceremonial community (Graulich 2007).[1] This consumption was believed to represent a symbolic absorption of the god himself. In rituals comprising human sacrifice we again find the combination of killing the victim and the following consumption as already found in early prehistoric communities.

THE SPECIAL CASE OF HERXHEIM

In Herxheim, it is vital to account for the violent destruction of precious things—the most precious being a human life—as the main streak that defines the extraordinary actions revealed by the archaeological and anthropological analyses. These actions are characterized by repetition, standardization, and normative succession of working steps relative to the treatment of the human bodies. The ritualistic character of the actions is defined by the latter attributes, the overall destructive nature of the treatment of both humans and artifacts and the nature of the destroyed objects.

If we look at the variety of examples for human sacrifices in different societies, it becomes obvious that the social identity of the victims generally ranges within a low level. Slaves or prisoners of war are as a rule were the main sources for human sacrifice (e.g., Graulich 2007:29, for the Aztec human sacrifices). There is also the custom of retainer sacrifices, well attested for the Egyptian early pharaohs (Van Dijk 2007), although the social status of the retainers in ancient Egypt, often young men, cannot be verified.

Neither are we able to decide the place or position in the social hierarchy for the individuals found in the ditch rings at Herxheim. In this special case, the chronological aspect has to be taken into account as well. The concentrations were—following the dating of the pottery and roughly attested by C14 analyses of human bones—deposited in the ditch structures in the latest phase of the Bandkeramik. The whole culture came to a rather sudden end around 4950 B.C.E., an end which the Neolithic research community has assumed to result from a general crisis at least in parts of the LBK-territory. The crisis in some places obviously resulted in local violent aggression between individuals, groups, or whole communities, as shown by the mass grave of Talheim in Germany (Wahl and König 1987; Wahl and Strien 2007) or the enclosed settlement of Asparn in Austria (Windl 1996, 1999, 2001). But actual theatres of war, which could prove "increasingly violent warfare against each other, culminating in an intense struggle in the area of western and central Europe"—as can be read in a recent publication about the end of the Bandkeramik (Golitko and Keeley 2007:332)—are still missing in the archaeological record. Herxheim has revealed by far the largest number of killed persons known in a Neolithic context in Europe, albeit the site cannot be interpreted as a theatre of war. In fact, it rather has to be interpreted as a central place where extraordinary rituals—with human sacrifices that perhaps were consumed as part of the ceremonies—had been accomplished. These rituals have to be seen in close relation to the impending end of the Bandkeramik culture, its traditions and sociocultural norms. The drastic and extreme treatment of the human bodies in Herxheim—probably including even the ritual consumption of their flesh and marrow—might be interpreted as a reaction to the doom that seems to have hovered over the Bandkeramik world in the latest phase of the culture. Actually, there are a number of especially late Bandkeramik sites where corpses were treated in ways unusual to the norms of burial rites, indicating a deep crisis in the sociocultural, economic, and ritual foundations of the culture. Herxheim might well be interpreted as a mirror of this crisis, which eventually led to the disappearance of the Bandkeramik all over Europe. The definite nature of this crisis can at the moment not yet be defined, any more than the question why these strange rituals took place in Herxheim, and what directly triggered them.

There are a number of examples both in ethnology and in prehistory showing that people resorted to human sacrifice when the life, the culture, or the general well-being of their communities was in danger (Bremmer 2007:6, with annotation 28). The victims were chosen out of specific classes, prisoners of war or slaves representing the prevalent choice (Graulich 2007:24f.). Nevertheless, sacrificing people is the elimination of the most precious value there is—human life. In this regard, the killing of so many individuals of Herxheim could reasonably be interpreted as a reaction to an enormous threat to the culture of the LBK—extreme situations often require extreme measures. This desperate reaction would still be accentuated by the consumption of the sacrificed persons and the ultimate destruction of the skeletons, as well as quite a number of precious artifacts.

ACKNOWLEDGMENTS

Our thanks go to the German Research Foundation (DFG) for providing the necessary financial means to realize the research project of the very special site of Herxheim. We also want to thank the community of Herxheim, which financed the majority of the research excavation from 2005 to 2008.

NOTE

1.   In contrast, P. Hassler denies the existence of human sacrifice in the Aztec culture, interpreting its descriptions and graphic representations as misinterpreted by Western researchers (see Hassler 1992: esp. 246ff.).

REFERENCES CITED

Arbogast, R.-M. 2009 Les vestiges de faune associés au site et structures d'enceinte du site rubané de Herxheim (Rhénanie-Palatinat, Allemagne). In *Krisen—Kulturwandel—Kontinuitäten. Zum Ende der Bandkeramik in Mitteleuropa. Beiträge der internationalen Tagung in Herxheim bei Landau (Pfalz) vom 14.–17.06.2007*, edited by Andrea Zeeb-Lanz, pp. 53–60. Internationale Archäologie. Arbeitskreis, Tagung, Symposium, Kongress Bd. 10. Marie Leidorf Verlag, Rahden/Westfalen.

Beilke-Voigt, I. 2007 *Das "Opfer" im archäologischen Befund. Studien zu den sog. Bauopfern, kultischen Niederlegungen und Bestattungen in ur- und frühgeschichtlichen Siedlungen Norddeutschlands und Dänemarks.* Berliner Archäologische Forschungen 4. Marie Leidorf Verlag, Rahden/Westfalen.

Bertholet, A. 1942 *Der Sinn des kultischen Opfers.* Abhandlungen der Preußischen Akademie der Wissenschaften Jahrgang 1942. Philosophisch-historische Klasse Nr. 2. Preußische Akademie, Berlin.

Boulestin, B., A. Zeeb-Lanz, Ch. Jeunesse, F. Haack, R.-M. Arbogast, and A. Denaire 2009 Cannibalism in the Linear Pottery Culture at Herxheim (Palatinate, Germany). *Antiquity* 83: 968–982.

Bremmer, J. N. 2007a *The Strange World of Human Sacrifice*, edited by Jan N. Bremmer. Peeters, Leuven, Belgium, Paris, Dudley.

Bremmer, J. N. 2007b Human Sacrifice: A Brief Introduction. In: *The Strange World of Human Sacrifice*, edited by Jan N. Bremmer, pp. 1–8. Peeters, Leuven, Paris, Dudley.

Cziesla, E. 1992 *Jäger und Sammler. Die Mittlere Steinzeit im Landkreis Pirmasens.* Linden Soft, Aichwald.

Denaire, A. 2009 Remontage de la céramique des fossés / Zusammensetzungen von Keramik aus den Grubenringen. In *Krisen—Kulturwandel—Kontinuitäten. Zum Ende der Bandkeramik in Mitteleuropa. Beiträge der internationalen Tagung in Herxheim bei Landau (Pfalz) vom 14.–17.06.2007*, edited by Andrea Zeeb-Lanz, pp. 79–85. Internationale Archäologie. Arbeitskreis, Tagung, Symposium, Kongress Bd. 10. Marie Leidorf Verlag, Rahden/Westfalen.

Gladigow, B. 2000 Opfer und komplexe Kulturen. In *Opfer. Theologische und kulturelle Kontexte*, edited by Bernd Janowski and Michael Welker, pp 86–107. Suhrkamp, Frankfurt am Main.

Golitko, M., and L. H. Keeley 2007 Beating Ploughshares back into Swords: Warfare in the Linearbandkeramik. *Antiquity* 81:332–342.

Graulich, M. 2007 Aztec Human Sacrifice as Expiation. In *The Strange World of Human Sacrifice*, edited by Jan N. Bremmer, pp. 9–30. Peeters, Leuven, Paris, Dudley.

Haack, F. 2001 Die Knochen- und Geweihgeräte der bandkeramischen Siedlung von Herxheim bei Landau. In *Archäologie in der Pfalz. Jahresbericht 2000*, edited by Helmut Bernhard, pp 189–193. Archäologische Denkmalpflege Amt Speyer, Speyer.

Haack, F. 2009 Zur Komplexität der Verfüllungsprozesse der Grubenanlage von Herxheim: Zwei Konzentrationen aus Menschenknochen, Keramik, Tierknochen und Steingeräten der Grabungen 2005 bis 2008. In *Krisen—Kulturwandel—Kontinuitäten. Zum Ende der Bandkeramik in Mitteleuropa. Beiträge der internationalen Tagung in Herxheim bei Landau (Pfalz) vom 14.–17.06.2007*, edited by Andrea Zeeb-Lanz, pp. 27–40. Internationale Archäologie. Arbeitskreis, Tagung, Symposium, Kongress Bd. 10. Marie Leidorf Verlag, Rahden/Westfalen.

Haack, F. 2014 Die frühneolithische Grabenanlage von Herxheim bei Landau: Architektur, Verfüllungsprozesse und Nutzungsdauer (unpublished thesis University of Berlin).

Hassler, P. 1992 *Menschenopfer bei den Azteken? Eine quellen- und ideologiekritische Studie*. Europäische Hochschulschriften Reihe XIX Volkskunde/Ethnologie, Abt. B: Ethnologie, Bd. 30. Bern, Frankfurt a. M., New York, Paris, Wien.

Haidle, M. N., and J. Orschiedt 2001 Das jüngstbandkeramische Grabenwerk von Herxheim, Kreis Südliche Weinstraße: Schauplatz einer Schlacht oder Bestattungsplatz? Anthropologische Ansätze. In *Archäologie in der Pfalz. Jahresbericht 2000*, edited by Helmut Bernhard, pp 147–153. Archäologische Denkmalpflege Amt Speyer, Speyer.

Hubert, H., and M. Mauss 1968 Essai sur la nature et la fonction du sacrifice. In Marcel Mauss, *Œuvres. 1. les fonctions sociales du sacré (1899)*, pp 193–324. Les Éditions de Minuit, Paris.

Janowski, B., and M. Welker 2000 Einleitung: Theologische und kulturelle Kontexte des Opfers. In: *Opfer. Theologische und kulturelle Kontexte*, edited by Bernd Janowski and Michael Welker, pp 9–20. Suhrkamp, Frankfurt a.M.

Kaiser E., J. Burger, and W. Schier 2012 *Population Dynamics in Prehistory and Early History. New Approaches Using Stable Isotopes and Genetics*. TOPOI. Berlin Studies of the Ancient World 5. De Gruyter, Berlin.

Lo Blue, E. 2009 Notes on Sky Burial in Indian, Chinese, and Nepalese Tibet. In *Mountains, Monasteries, and Mosques*, edited by John Bray, pp 221–238. Proceedings of the 13th colloquium of the International Association for Ladakh Studies. Istituti Ed. e Poligrafici Internazionali, Pisa, Rome.

Malina, B. J. 2000 Rituale der Lebensexklusivität. Zu einer Definition des Opfers. In: *Opfer. Theologische und kulturelle Kontexte*, edited by Bernd Janowski and Michael Welker, pp 23–57. Suhrkamp, Frankfurt a.M.

Mitscherlich, A. 1969 *Bis hierher und nicht weiter: ist die menschliche Aggression unbefriedbar?* Pieper, München.

Schulz, M. 2011 Der Kelch der Kannibalen. *Der Spiegel* 9/2011:127–128.

Teschler-Nicola, M., F. Gerold, F. Kanz, K. Lindenbauer, and M. Spannagel 1996 Anthropologische Spurensicherung—Die traumatischen und postmortalen Veränderungen an den linearbandkeramischen Skelettresten von Asparn/Schletz. In *Rätsel um Gewalt und Tod vor 7000 Jahren*, edited by Helmut Windl, pp 47–64. Katalog des Niederösterreichischen Landesmuseums N.F. 393. Amt der NÖ Landesregierung Abt. III/2, Asparn a.d. Zaya.

Teschler-Nicola, M., T. Prohaska, and E. M. Wild 2006 Der Fundkomplex von Asparn/Schletz (Niederösterreich) und seine Bedeutung für den aktuellen Diskurs endlinearbandkeramischer Phänomene Zentraleuropas. In *Frühe Spuren der Gewalt—Schädelverletzungen und Wundversorgung an prähistorischen Menschenresten aus interdisziplinärer Sicht*, edited by Joachim Piek and Thomas Terberger, pp 61–76. Workshop in Rostock-Warnemünde vom 28.–30. November 2003 (= Beiträge zur Ur- und Frühgeschichte Mecklenburg-Vorpommerns Bd. 41) Schwerin 2006.

Turck, R., B. Kober, J. Kontny, F. Haack, and A. Zeeb-Lanz 2012 "Widely Travelled People at Herxheim? Sr Isotopes as Indicators of Mobility." In *Population Dynamics in Prehistory and Early History. New Approaches Using Stable Isotopes and Genetics*, edited by E. Kaiser, J. Burger, and W. Schier, pp. 149–163. TOPOI. Berlin Studies of the Ancient World 5. De Gruyter, Berlin.

Van Dijk, J. 2007 Retainer Sacrifice in Egypt and in Nubia. In *The Strange World of Human Sacrifice*, edited by Jan N. Bremmer, pp. 135–155. Peeters, Leuven, Paris, Dudley.

Wahl, K. 2009 *Aggression und Gewalt: ein biologischer, psychologischer und sozialwissenschaftlicher Überblick*. Heidelberg Spektrum, Heidelberg.

Wahl, J., and H. G. König 1987 Anthropologisch-traumatologische Untersuchung der menschlichen Skelettreste aus dem bandkeramischen Massengrab bei Talheim, Kr. Heilbronn. *Fundberichte Baden-Württemberg* 12:65–186.

Wahl, J., and H.-Ch. Strien 2007 *Tatort Talheim. 7000 Jahre später. Archäologen und Gerichtsmediziner ermitteln.* Katalog zur Ausstellung Archäologie-Museum Heilbronn 22.09.07–27.01.08. museo 23. Städtische Museen Heilbronn, Heilbronn.

Windl, H. 1996 Archäologie einer Katastrophe und deren Vorgeschichte. In *Rätsel um Gewalt und Tod vor 7000 Jahren*, edited by Helmut Windl, pp 7–39. Katalog des Niederösterreichischen Landesmuseums N.F. 393. Amt der NÖ Landesregierung Abt. III/2, Asparn a.d. Zaya.

Windl, H. 1999 Makabres Ende einer Kultur? *Archäologie in Deutschland* 1999/1:54–57.

Windl, H. 2001 Erdwerke der Linearbandkeramik in Asparn an der Zaya/Schletz, Niederösterreich. *Preistoria Alpina* 37:137–144.

Zeeb-Lanz, A., and F. Haack 2006 Zerhackt und begraben: Herxheims rätselhafte Tote. *Archäologie in Deutschland* 5/2006:8–13.

Zeeb-Lanz, A., F. Haack, R.-M. Arbogast, M. N. Haidle, Ch. Jeunesse, J. Orschiedt, and D. Schimmelpfennig 2007 Außergewöhnliche Deponierungen der Bandkeramik—die Grubenanlage von Herxheim. *Germania* 85:199–274.

Zeeb-Lanz, A. F. Haack, R.-M. Arbogast, M. N. Haidle, Ch. Jeunesse, J. Orschiedt, D. Schimmelpfennig, and S. van Willigen 2009(a) The LBK Settlement with Pit Enclosure at Herxheim near Landau (Palatinate). In *Creating Communities. New Advances in Central Europe Neolithic Research*, edited by Daniela Hofmann and Penny Bickle, pp 199–215. Oxbow, Oxford.

Zeeb-Lanz, A., B. Boulestin, F. Haack, and Ch. Jeunesse 2009 Außergewöhnliche Totenbehandlung—Überraschendes aus der bandkeramischen Anlage von Herxheim bei Landau (Südpfalz). *Mitteilungen der Berliner Gesellschaft für Anthropologie, Ethnologie und Urgeschichte* 30:115–126.

CHAPTER TEN

Dog Sacrifice at the Protohistoric Site of Mas Castellar (Pontós, Spain)

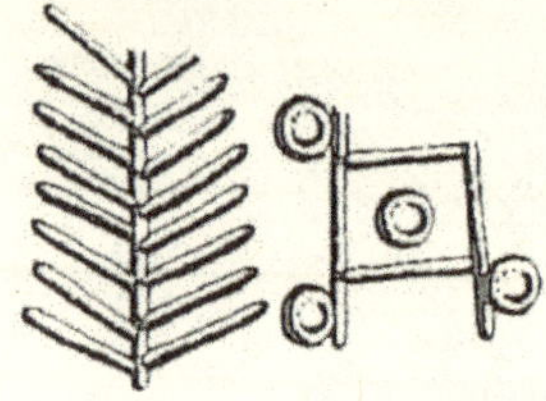

Enriqueta Pons,
Lídia Colominas, Maria Saña

Abstract   *The dog played a marginal role in the meat diet of Iberian people if we compare it with that of other domestic animals; moreover, it did not play a predominant role in sociopolitical practices either, despite offerings of canids being documented in funeral contexts and habitat settings. The prominent presence of dog remains (Canis familiaris) at the farmstead of Mas Castellar de Pontós (225–180 B.C.E.), in the northeast of the Iberian Peninsula, is an important and a unique item of documentation in Catalonia. Skeletal remains of dogs, showing cut marks of dismemberment and thermo-alterations, together with votive items, have been documented in special deposits as well as in sacrificial spaces. Reports of these data sets in consideration with the animal husbandry strategy normally implemented at the site has led to an emphasis on the special nature of these remains, as confirmation that dogs were used for blood offerings, social prestige, and commensality.*

Mas Castellar is located at the western end of the Empordà Plain, in an interfluvial position, 17 km from the coast and at an equal distance from the Greek colonies of Rhode and Emporion (Figure 10.1). This position between two rivers shaped a peculiar geomorphology formed by two stepped terraces, conditioning the topography of the archaeological site, in two different areas: *Camp de Dalt* (High field) and *Camp de Baix* (Low field) (Figure 10.2). The archaeological excavations (1990–2011) carried out in the *Camp de Dalt* area revealed two architectonic units associated with a field of silos and two ditches. They comprise a fortified settlement in the south (late fifth and early fourth centuries B.C.E.) and a farmstead of Hellenistic influences (third to early second centuries B.C.E.) (Figure 10.2). The *Camp de Baix* sector probably comprises a similar

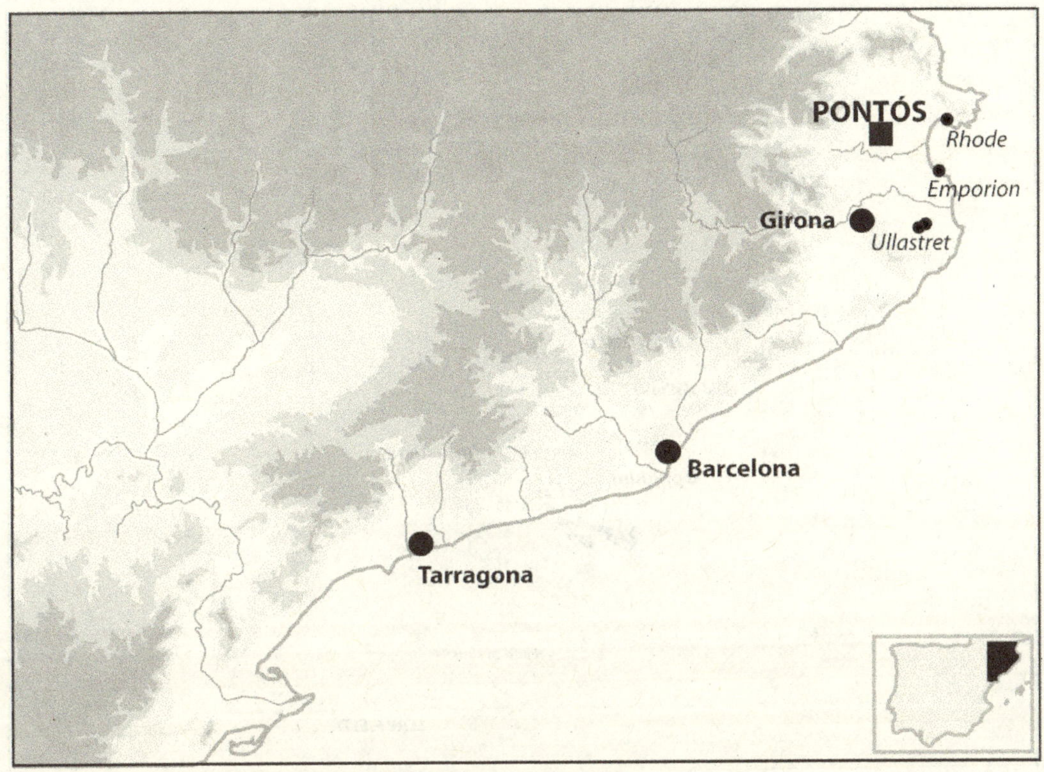

FIGURE 10.1 The location of the site of Pontós in the northeast of the Iberian Peninsula (Museum of Archaeology of Catalonia).

sequence, although it is less well known, as no large-scale excavations have been carried out in this area. The only data available come from test excavations and surveying. It has been estimated that, in the land around the two areas, there may be about 2,500 silos, dispersed over a surface area of 2.5 ha, dated from the seventh to the early second century B.C.E. This suggests that the settlement acted as a place for the concentration, distribution, and trading of agricultural surpluses (Asensio et al. 2007; Pons et al. 2010).

RITUAL TREATMENT OF CANIDS AT THE SITE OF MAS CASTELLAR

The ritual practices documented at Mas Castellar include animal sacrifices and offerings of agricultural products (Pons and Rovira 1997). The most common acts involving animals are the so-called foundational offerings. In this case, the animal species are usually domestic, and mainly adult sheep have been documented (Colominas 2008). Animals or parts of animals were deposited in small pits. These parts, mostly the head and limbs, are usually found in anatomical connection and often exhibit processing marks (dismembering and defleshing). At Mas Castellar, these foundational offerings are located in the Hellenistic farmstead (250–180 B.C.E.) and are generally found inside the houses (both

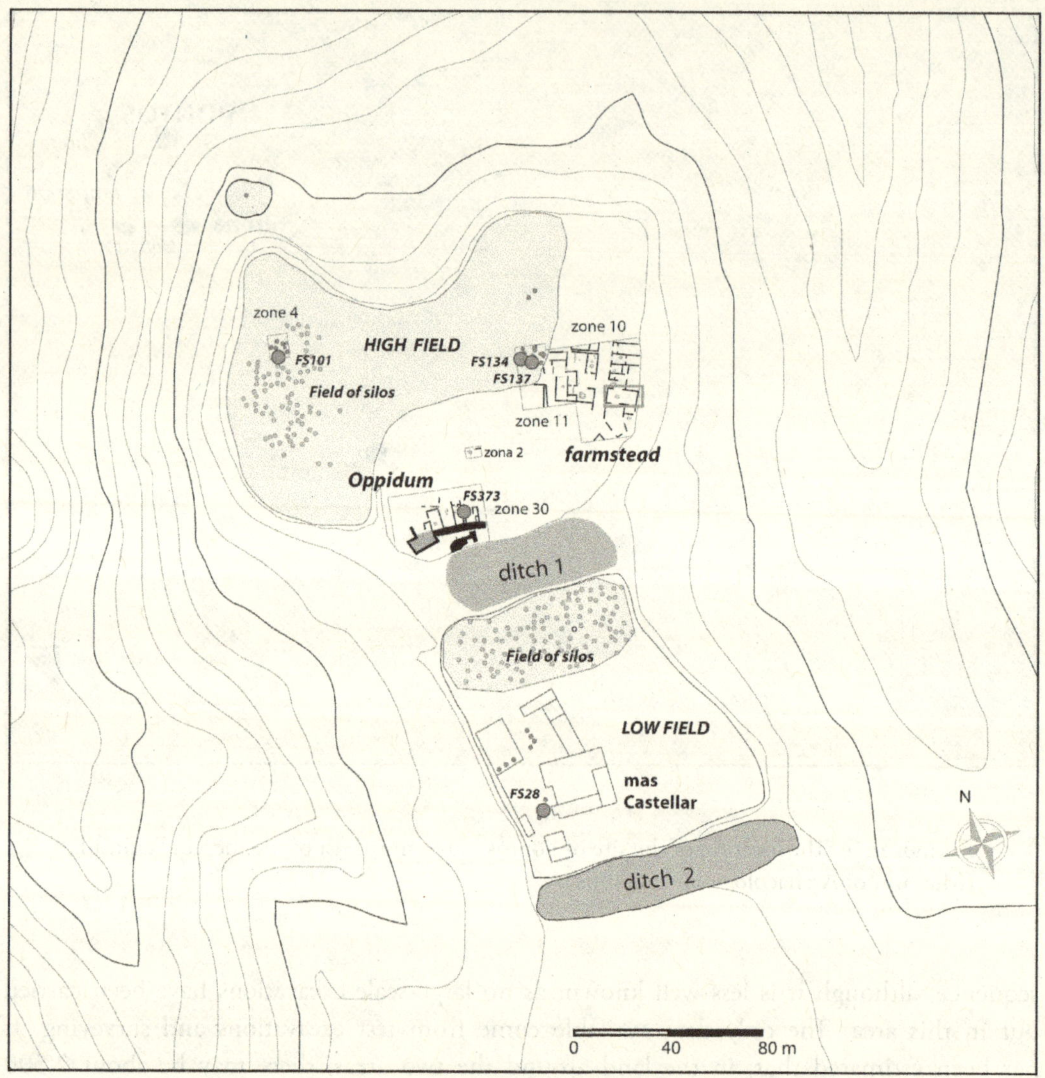

Figure 10.2 Plan of the site, located on two terraces (high field and low field) surrounded by two ditches on the south (Museum of Archaeology of Catalonia).

simple and complex buildings), in one of the main rooms of the house, next to an internal door near the ante-hall, vestibule, or courtyard (Colominas 2008; Pons et al. 2011).

The offerings of agricultural products are usually burnt. Given the kind of material involved, they are more difficult to identify archaeologically. It is their spatial context and association with certain other elements that suggest that they are offerings. The remains of carbonized plants are associated with blood sacrifices, votive elements, terracotta figures with female faces, ointment vessels, miniature perfume containers, imported luxury drinking wares, amphorae with valuable products such as wine, beer, oil, or salted fish, important iron farm tools, bronze objects and jewelry (Pons and Rovira 1997; Pons and Vargas 2002; Pons et al. 2011).

However, one of the peculiarities at the site of Mas Castellar, throughout the different phases of occupation, is the direct involvement of dogs in the various ritual practices.

RITUAL DEPOSITS OF CANIDS

The first type of deposit consists of canids placed in pits dug in the ground that were primarily used as storage silos, mainly for agricultural products. Once they became obsolete, they were filled with waste. After a relatively short amount of time, some of these pits were partly emptied and refilled with objects that were not of everyday use: large amounts of food remains, ceramics, and sometimes also entire animals or certain parts of animals. In most cases, the pits also contain the remains of a hearth and abundant burnt waste.

At Mas Castellar, three pits have been excavated exhibiting the results of these types of actions. In all of them, dogs played an important role. These are Pit 137, with a whole dog buried in it; Pit 134, where the head of a dog was deposited as a blood offering; and Pit 373, where the recovered dog bones displayed cut marks showing the means of processing and consumption.

INTENTIONAL BURIAL OF A DOG

A whole skeleton of a dog was recorded in Pit 137 (Figure 10.3a). The pit contained a very varied fill, with two different kinds of deposits. The dog skeleton was found in the

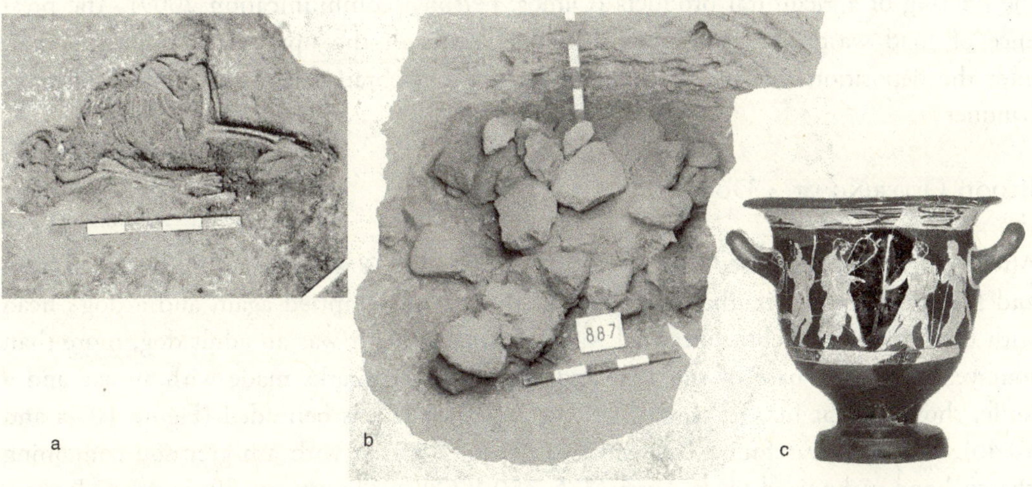

FIGURE 10.3 Details of the remains recovered in Pit 137, where a) shows the dog burial, b) shows the pieces of basalt swing mill that covered the dog and c) shows the bell-shaped crater with red figures showing a symposium scene (Museum of Archaeology of Catalonia).

lower deposit. The animal was placed on its left side, with its head facing northeast and against the wall of the pit. It was completely covered by a pile of millstones, mostly made of basalt, all of which had been used, broken, and affected by fire (Figure 10.3b). Above this burial, forming the second deposit, there were large amounts of organic remains (carbonized seeds, charcoal, and domestic fauna) together with inorganic items, such as potsherds, remains of building material, and fragments of bronze and iron objects. All of this archaeological material was broken up and badly affected by fire (Asensio and Pons 2004–05; Colominas 2007).

Of the 6,156 carbonised seeds, 78.4 percent are cereals. The main species are millet (*Panicum milliaceum*), a spring cereal, and barley (*Hordeum vulgare*), a spring and autumn cereal. Among the rest, there were legumes (14.40 percent) and synanthropic plants (7.20 percent). The 404 faunal remains mainly belong to sheep or goats (66.21 percent), pigs (17.93 percent) and cattle (15.86 percent). In general, they are animals slaughtered at a young age for consumption.

The numerous ceramic vessels are containers for transport (*amphorae*) and luxury imported drinking wares; 23.8 percent of the latter are Greek. Particularly interesting is the red figure bell-shaped crater, with a representation on the front of a symposium scene where four devotees of *Komos* are walking and dancing happily (Figure 10.3c).

A total of 152 skeletal elements from a dog were recovered. It is an adult dog, older than four years, of medium-large size (55 cm tall at the withers) and probably a female. These remains contained no signs of any butchering, thermo-alterations, or other kinds of anthropic modifications.

Considering the large amount and variety of seeds and pottery vessels that have been found, it is possible that the fill of this silo corresponds to the waste from a ritual related to an offering of gratitude to a god, involving the sacrifice of a dog and the offering of agricultural products (Olmos, personal communication 2009). The presence of food waste and numerous drinking vessels in the upper layer indicates that, after the depositions of the offerings, there was a celebration consisting of a collective banquet.

Blood Offering of a Dog

After Pit 134 had been used as a silo (450–425 B.C.E.), it was filled with waste, rubbish, and food remains. Later, the upper half of the pit was emptied again and a dog's head with the first two vertebrae attached was deposited in it. It was an adult dog, more than four years old. The base of the atlas and axis displayed marks made with an axe and a knife, showing that first its throat was cut and then it was beheaded (Figure 10.4a and 10.4b). The skull was found between two deposits, mixed with ash-grey soil containing charcoal and carbonized seeds. Later (375–350 B.C.E.), the pit was filled with sediment, food remains, and other waste.

The find could seem banal, but the intentionality of the deposit, which involved emptying the waste from the upper half of the pit before depositing the canid's head, might be related to the practice of sacrificing dogs followed by an underground ritual

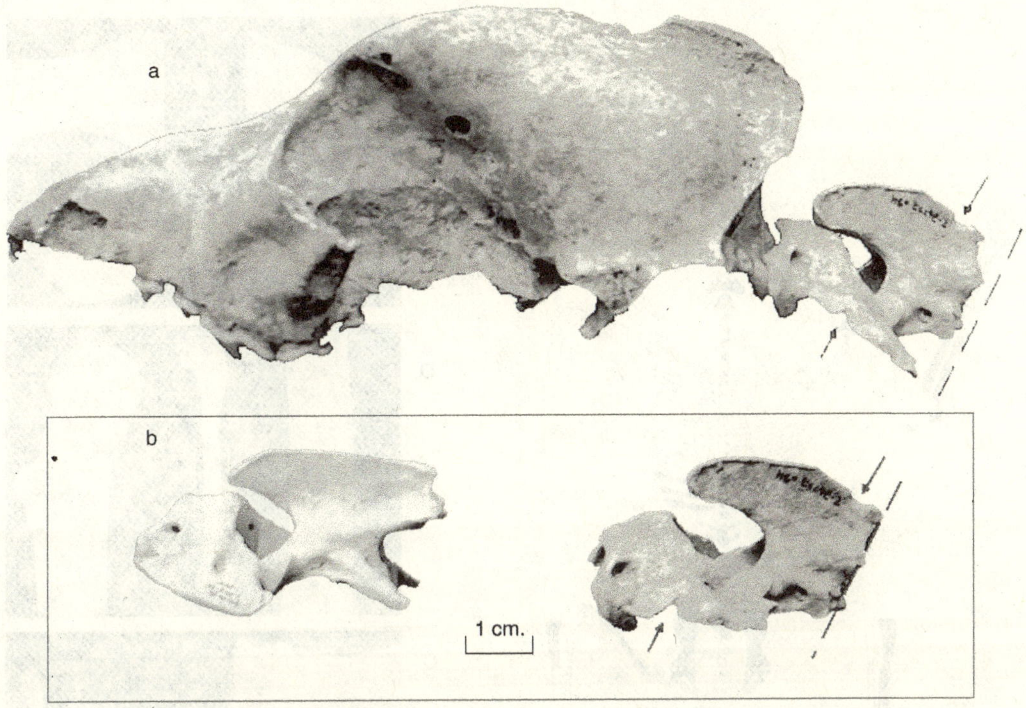

FIGURE 10.4 Dog's head documented in Pit 134: a) shows the chop marks documented at the back of its atlas and the axis cut. Figure 4b) comparison of a dog reference atlas and axis with the archaeological remains of pit 134 showing the area cut of the beheaded the dog (Universitat Autònoma of Barcelona).

called *bothros*. This practice is widely documented around the Mediterranean in classical times (Adroher et al. 1993; Olmos 1996; Pons 2004).

DEPOSIT OF FOOD WASTE

Pit 373 was excavated over the ruins of the fortified settlement 200 years after its deliberate destruction, and was filled in the late third century B.C.E. The contents of the pit consisted of potsherds and food waste (mainly debris of domestic mammals). Archaeozoological studies have shown the presence of sheep, goats, cattle, and pigs, together with a few bones of *Canis familiaris* (3.3 percent of the ensemble).

The dog remains were found in the top part of the pit and at the bottom. A total of 33 skeletal elements had been found belonging to an individual over 18 months old, with a height of 53.45 cm at the withers (Figure 10.5). Some of these remains (pelvis, proximal epiphysis of the tibia, proximal and medial part of the femur, neck of the scapula and axis) exhibit anthropic marks and fractures caused by the processing and probably the consumption of the meat (Figure 10.5a, b and c) (Colominas 2011).

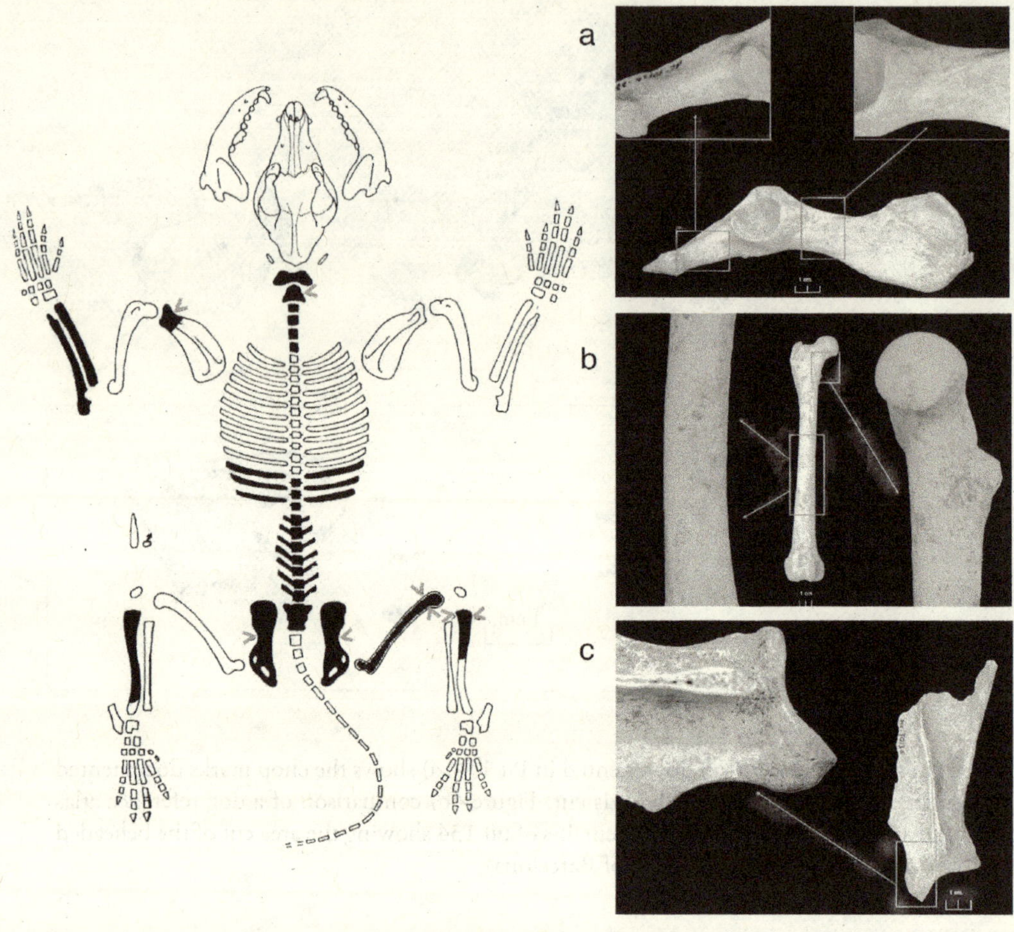

Figure 10.5 Image of a schematic dog showing the skeletal elements documented in Pit 373 and those elements with cut marks: a) pelvis, b) femur, c) scapula (Universitat Autònoma of Barcelona).

The documentation of this silo with canid remains showing evidence of human consumption is unique at the site. The silos are often filled with meat food waste, but the animal species found are usually sheep, goats, pigs, and cattle.

Ritual Sacrifice of Canids

The second type of material evidence of ritual acts involving dogs is associated with areas of worship. In House 1 of the Mas Castellar farmstead, part of the domestic area appears to have been used for cult rituals related with dog sacrifices. This hypothesis can be corroborated by a number of elements, as described below (Pons 1977).

House 1, with a Hellenistic style, has a surface area of 432 m², seven internal compartments, and two courtyards as a result of joining together two old houses; one courtyard is at the main entrance and joins the two parts (Pons et al. 2010:110–114). Room 3 in House 1, the largest in the whole enclosure, has a surface area of 75 m². To the north, it adjoins the courtyard at the main entrance, and to the south, it connects with an arched vestibule open to the other courtyard, to which it has access through a secondary door (Pons 1997) (Figure 10.6).

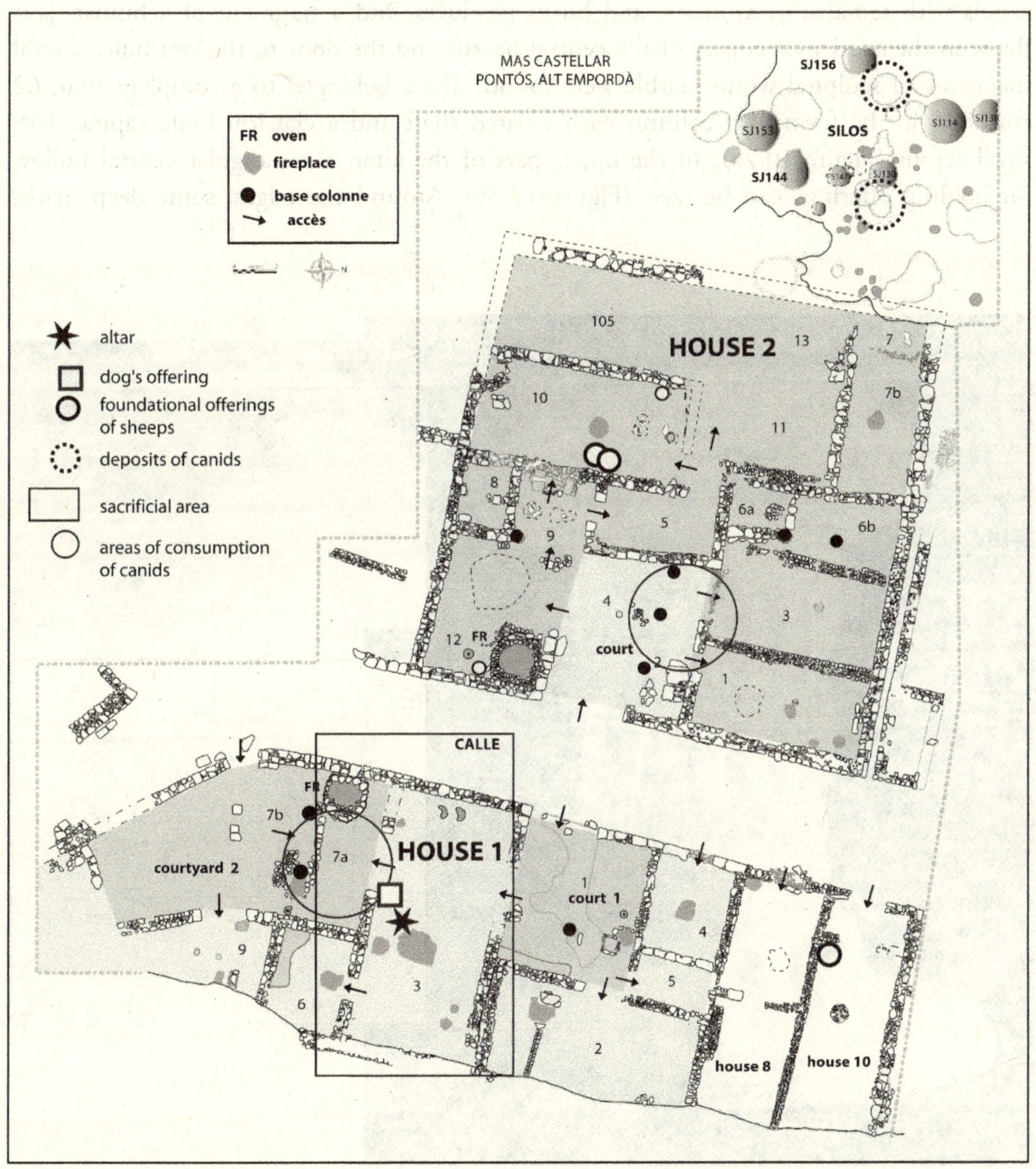

FIGURE 10.6 Location of the sacrificial area (square) and special deposits (round) documented in the two houses of Mas Castellar farmstead (Museum of Archaeology of Catalonia).

In the central longitudinal axis of the eastern part of Room 3, a large quadrangular hearth was built, made by several layers of different materials and covered by a layer of refractory clay, which was raised a little above the level of the pavement. Symmetrically toward the west, a small container was excavated in the pavement, with lined walls, and it was probably used to hold water. An oil lamp was found inside it. Another four smaller fireplaces were built around the sides of the room.

Dispersed around the room, there were a large number of drinking vessels, miniature vessels with remains of aromatic and burnt products, and a fragment of a human jaw. Between the southwest corner of the central hearth and the door to the vestibule, several fragments of sculpted white marble were found. These belonged to a complete altar, 62 cm high, in the form of a column with striated shaft and a classical ionic capital with small scrolls (Figure 10.7a). In the upper part of the altar, a rectangular central hollow for holding offerings can be seen (Figure 10.7b). Around the edges, some deep marks

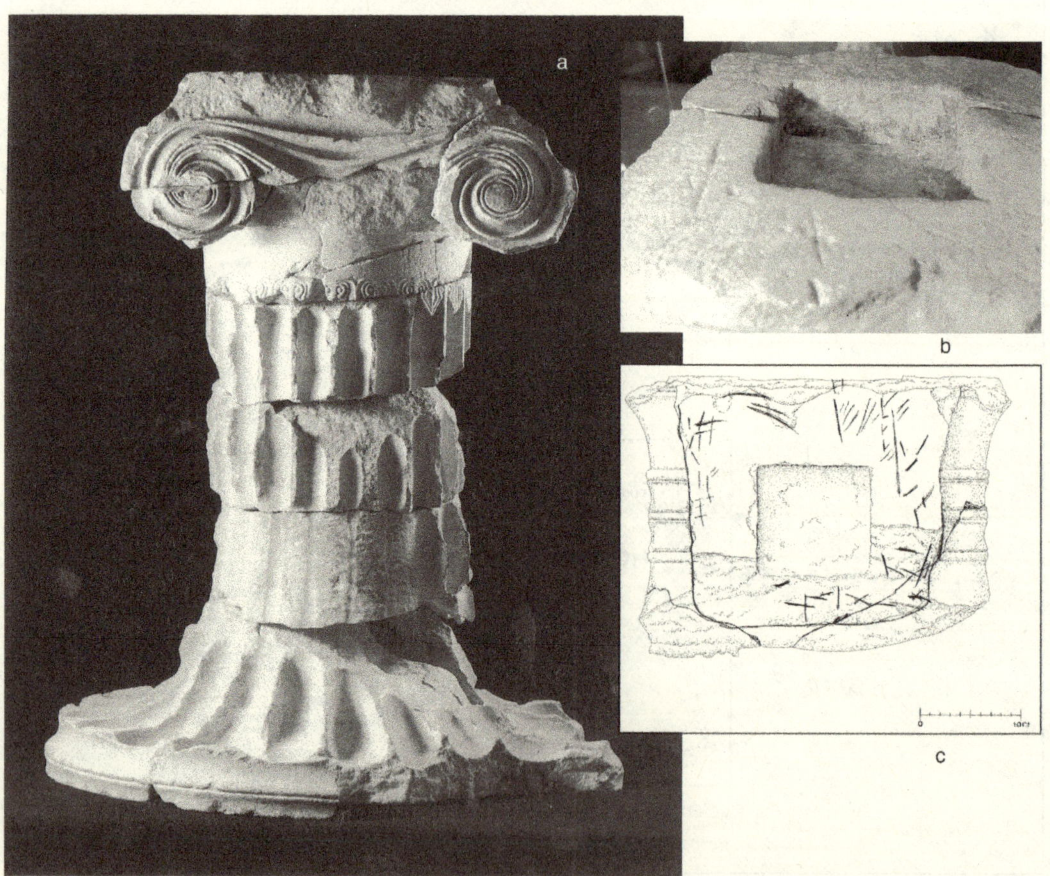

FIGURE 10.7 Altar in a form of a column with an Ionic capital documented in Room 3 of House 1: b and c) show respectively a photo and a drawing of the upper part where deep marks were documented (Museum of Archaeology of Catalonia).

made with an axe and knife, have been documented; some parts were affected by fire (Figure 10.7c). The petrographic study of the marble has shown that the stone came from a quarry at Mount Pentelicus in Greece (Alvarez 2002:557).

Very near the door to the vestibule, next to one of the small fireplaces, a deposit with 258 remains of fauna was excavated (Figure 10.8). Most of the remains were badly fragmented and some had been affected thermally (Figure 10.8b). A total of 98 remains belonged to *Canis familiaris*; they came from a minimum number of three adult canids; all skeletal parts were present (Figure 10.8). The absence of penile bones suggests that these individuals were females (Casellas 1995). By applying Clark's index (1995), the height at the withers of two of the dogs has been calculated as 50.31 cm and 52.86 cm.

The spatial association between all these elements allows us to propose that this room could have been an area for ritual practices, involving purification ceremonies (evidenced by a water container and lamp), libations (suggested by the presence of miniature vessels with remains of aromatic products), and sacrifices (indicated by the hearth, the dog remains, and the altar for sacrifices).

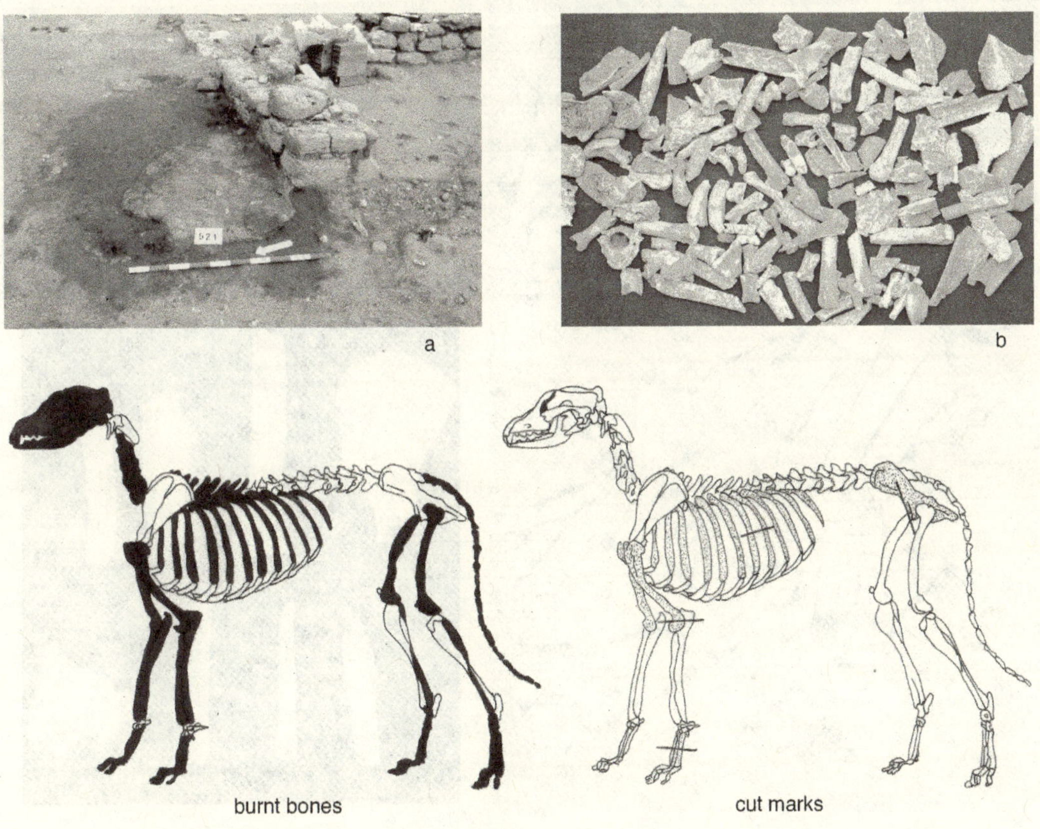

FIGURE 10.8 Dog skeletal elements with thermo-alterations and cut marks recovered in the court of House 1: a) shows a detail of this assemblage during excavation and b) the assemblage itself (L. Colominas, E. Pons).

Ritual Consumption of Canids

A third type of material evidence indicates collective acts involving the consumption of dog meat. Shortly before the settlement of Mas Castellar was finally abandoned (about 200 B.C.E.), at a time when the Roman occupation achieved economic control over the area, a banquet was held in the settlement where large amounts of meat and drinks were consumed. The excavation documented numerous remains of food and broken pottery vessels abandoned in the courtyards and vestibules of Houses 1 and 2. Mixed among the remains of domestic animals (sheep, goats, cattle, and pigs,), remains of dogs were also found in significant proportions (Figure 10.9).

In House 2, the dog remains (63.5 percent of the total faunal assemblage) were found only in the arched vestibule, and belonged to a minimum of four adult individuals, one with a height at the withers of 49.13 cm (according to Clark's Index 1995). Some remains displayed cut marks, fractures and thermo-alterations identical to the ones identified on the remains of the other domestic species (Figure 10.9a).

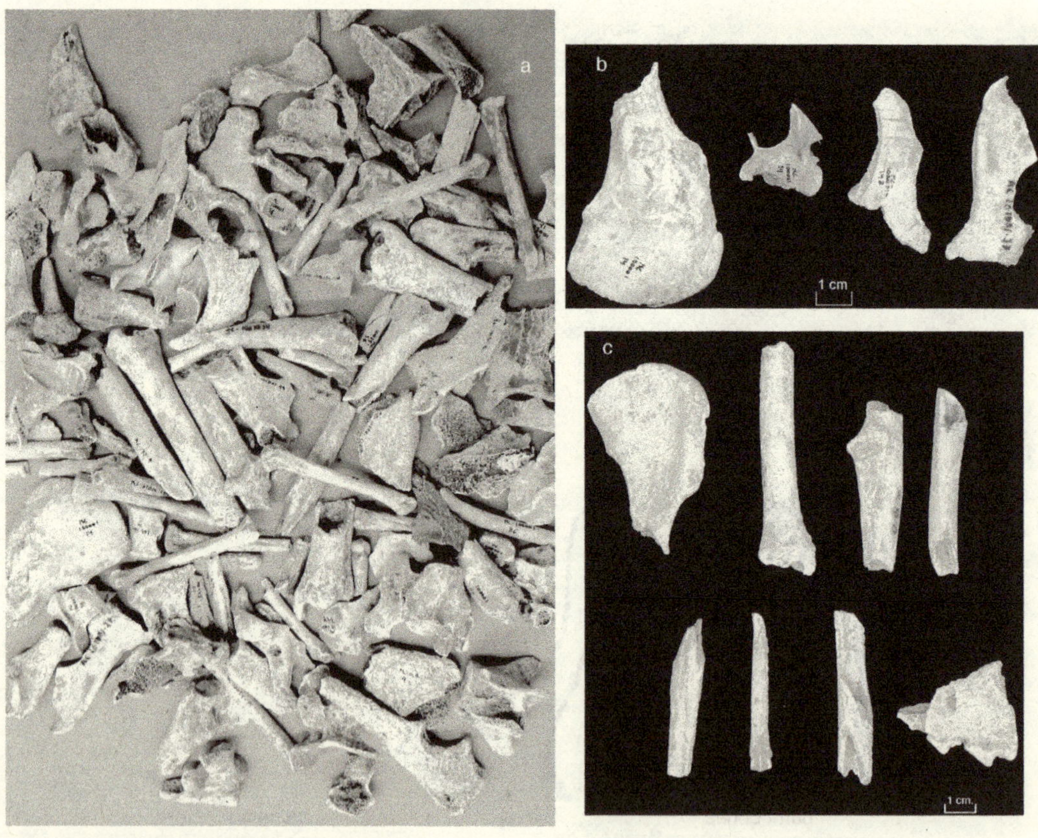

FIGURE 10.9 Dog skeletal elements documented in the porch halls of Houses 1 and 2: a) shows some fragmented remains with chop marks from House 2 and b) from House 1 (Universitat Autònoma of Barcelona).

In House 1, the dog remains come from Room 3 and were dispersed around the sacrifice area, in the two courtyards, inside the water container, and also near the side entrance. The archaeozoological study identified the remains of at least five animals. The estimates of the height at withers of these dogs, as in House 1, were medium-sized, with heights of 51.18 cm, 50.61 cm, 49.7 cm, and 47.21 cm for four of the five canids. The remains also exhibited cut marks of processing and thermo-alterations (Figure 10.9b).

Shortly after the rural establishment had been abandoned, it was visited again (190–180 B.C.E.) to repeat the ritual carried out a few years earlier. During the excavation of House 1, some waste with the remains of building materials and food were documented above the earlier occupational levels. One of these features contained numerous potsherds and faunal remains with abundant anthropic modifications. Of the total of 271 remains of fauna that were recovered, 85.2 percent belong to dogs, with a minimum number of five adult individuals: all skeletal parts were represented. The height at withers calculated with Clark's Index (1995) reveals a significant variety in size (47.43 cm, 60.69 cm, 50.12 cm, 52.34 cm, and 58.12 cm). It is important to highlight the existence of a large number of skeletal elements in anatomical connection, particularly the distal part of the limbs. The rest of the faunal assemblage consists of cattle (MNI = two), sheep (MNI = one), pig (MNI = one), and horse (MNI = one), with percentages much lower than those of the canids.

The waste studied in other nearby areas of the site, also formed after the settlement had been abandoned, contained a much smaller number of dog remains without human alterations, which emphasizes the exceptional nature of the assemblage described above.

SELECTION CRITERIA OF THE CANIDS INVOLVED IN RITUAL PRACTICES

At Mas Castellar, dogs were not only involved in ritual practices. At the farmstead, they were also associated with hunting and livestock activities, as shown by the documentation of remains of this species with no anthropic manipulations or any particular connections with other elements or structures.

To study the use and function of this animal in the different occupations at the site in greater depth, one of the first questions to be posed refers to the selection criteria of the canids sacrificed as part of ritual practices. Among the variables that can be taken into account are age, sex, and general size and shape of the animals.

The bones of all the canid individuals documented at Mas Castellar, whether or not they were associated with ritual practices, were fused at the time of death. Therefore, no possible selection according to age has been documented.

The absence of penile bones suggests that the individuals recovered whole from the pit in House 1 were females. The individual documented in Pit 137 is similarly thought to be a female. The sex of the other individuals could not be determined.

The biometric analysis was used to compare the sizes of the dogs that had been involved in ritual practices with those of the dogs employed in other functions (maintenance, guarding, and hunting, herding, and so on). As most of the remains are highly fragmented, this study was based on the comparison of the heights at withers of the different individuals.

The results obtained (Figure 10.10) show some significant trends, but the small number of specimens in the calculations means that this analysis can only be considered as a first approach. As can be seen, the dogs at Mas Castellar that are not associated with ritual practices (PER = individuals) exhibit different heights, from 49 cm (PER 3) to 52.9 cm (PER 2) and 56.3 cm (PER 1). These differences can be compared with those that currently exist between a spaniel (small hunting dog) and a boxer (guard dog) (de Grossi and Tagliacozzo 2000). In contrast, the heights at the withers of the individuals associated with the rituals documented in House 1 (C1.1, C1.2, C1.3, C1.4, F.1, and F.2) and House 2 (C2) are very similar (between 47.2 cm and 52.9 cm) and no taller individuals have been found. The dogs documented from the silos 137 (s.137) and 373 (s.373) have heights at the withers that are between medium and large, in contrast with the individuals involved in the rituals in Houses 1 and 2, which are around 50 cm tall. The canids associated with the banquet that took place after the settlement had been abandoned vary in size and include individuals with a height of 60.7 cm (S14.1), 58.12 cm (S14.2), 52.3 cm (S14.3), 50.12 (S14.4,), and 47.4cm (S14.5). Therefore, in this last case, dogs were not selected according to their height. However, this criterion might have been applied in the selection of the dogs chosen for the rituals in Houses 1 and 2, of a medium-small height in comparison with other individuals present at the farmstead.

It is also important to consider that at other contemporary sites near Pontós, canids have not been linked to any ritual practices, and quite varied heights at the withers have been recorded. At Saus (Girona, Spain), 20 km away, individuals 61–62 cm tall and 48 cm tall were documented (Colominas and Saña 2012). At the site of Bosc del Congost (Girona, Spain) 25km away, there was an individual 52.5 cm tall (Colominas and Saña 2009).

Therefore, the results of the biometric analysis seem to show that individuals with a medium size (about 50 cm) were possibly selected for the ritual practices carried out in

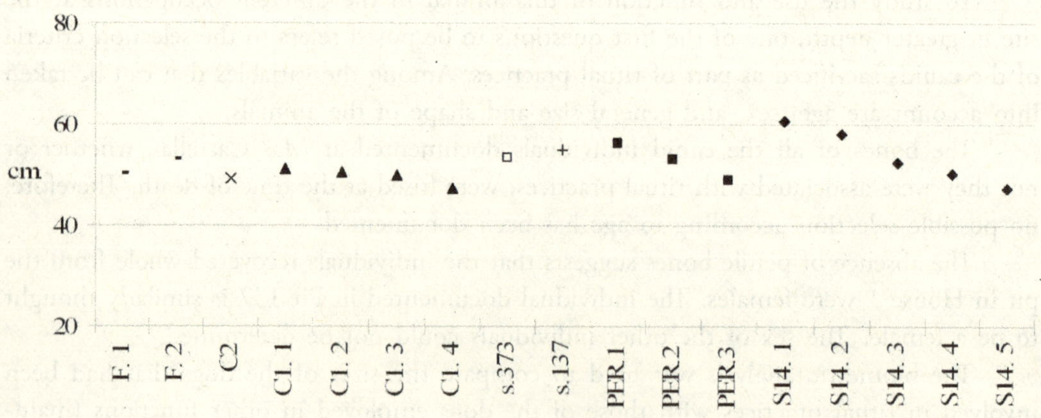

FIGURE 10.10 Comparison of heights at withers of different dog remains recovered at Mas Castellar. Legend explained in the text (L. Colominas, M. Saña).

Houses 1 and 2. This documented selection of height could be the result of a possible selection of a "type" of dog.

SACRIFICE AND CONSUMPTION OF DOGS IN PREHISTORY AND PROTOHISTORY

The acceptance of dogs as a source of food is very rare in the western Mediterranean, apart from a few particular moments in history when their consumption became more common (sixth to third centuries B.C.E., coinciding with the arrival of the first Phoenician and Punic colonizers, or in the world wars in the twentieth century) (Friesch 1987:71). Although they are thought of as "man's best friend" and are regarded as one of the most prestigious animals after horses (Meniel 1992), dogs have also been disparaged and ill-treated (Sergis 2010). However, there is increasing evidence that shows that at certain times during our history this species played an important sociopolitical role as an element of social cohesion and prestige.

Canids are generally represented in low percentages at Iron Age settlements, and their presence is usually documented indirectly by the marks that they leave on the bones of other animals while gnawing them. However, the number of burials or intentional deposits of dogs in pits documented at Bronze Age and Iron Age sites in the Iberian Peninsula is significant (Albizurri 2011; Colominas and Saña 2009). Recent data derived from the study of Iberian Bronze Age sites have also shown that dogs were often buried in graves as part of the grave goods, and dispersed remains of this species are frequently recovered around the edges of the necropolis (Albizurri 2011). Although cases are rare, there is also evidence of the sacrifice and consumption of dogs in the Bronze Age. Examples are the remains of dogs with anthropogenic marks documented at Lloma de Betxi, Pics dels Corbs, and Cabezo Redondo (all in Valencia, Spain), and at Cerro de la Encina (Granada, Spain), where fractures and cut marks have been associated with the consumption of their meat (Sanchis and Sarrion 2004; Driesch and Boessneck 1969; Friesch 1987). This type of evidence becomes more common in the middle-late Iron Age, above all at sites with Punic influences, such as the Phoenician necropolis at Cádiz (Andalucía, Spain) (Niveau 2004), the site of Hort d'en Xim (Balearic Islands) (Saña 1994), and the orientalized necropolis of La Joya (Andalucía, Spain) (Garrido, Orta 1978). Increasing numbers of middle-late Iron Age Iberian sites are also documented with canid remains displaying processing marks and links to ritual practices, such as the votive deposit of Amarejo IV-III-II (Albacete, Spain) (Iborra 2003), the necropolis of La Serreta, and the necropolis of El Molar (Valencia, Spain). Dog remains with processing marks have also been documented in other parts of the Mediterranean basin. In Italy, at the necropolis of Osteria dell'Osa, a pit containing dog skulls was found (de Grossi and Tagliacozzo 1997). In France, at the necropolis of Acy-Romance (Ardennes), dogs had been incinerated, accompanying humans, and others had been butchered and interpreted as offerings of meat (Meniel 2001).

Therefore, while the sacrifice of dogs was not a common practice, it is known above all in the first millennium B.C.E. and among protohistoric societies very near the Iberians, such as Celtic societies (Meniel 1992), those in contact with Phoenician-Punic formations (Niveau and Ferrer 2004), and even the classic civilizations in Greece and Italy (Zinder and Klippel 2003).

From the data described in this paper, we consider that the sacrifice of dogs has also been proven at the site of Mas Castellar. This is especially the case of the individual documented in Pit 134, which was beheaded. It is possible, although there is no direct evidence, that the canids associated with the altar were also sacrificed. The altar has cut marks made with an axe and the animals were undoubtedly processed, as were those in House 2 and Silo 373. The other individuals exhibit the same processing pattern, along with other medium-sized domestic animals, such as the sheep, goats, and pigs (Casellas 2002; Colominas 2011). It should be recalled that remains of these domestic animals, with marks, fractures, and thermo-alterations, were also recovered with the dog remains in Houses 1 and 2, and in Pit 373. Therefore, there is no reason to believe that the meat from these canids was not consumed. The fact that, in Houses 1 and 2, all anatomical parts were documented suggests that once these products had been processed, distributed, and consumed, the waste was abandoned in the same place. The canid remains from the deposit in House 1, in contrast, were not mixed with the remains of other animals usually consumed and were deposited in a particular place, separated and protected. This may indicate that these dogs were processed but not consumed.

Conclusions

The settlement of Mas Castellar is currently one of the few sites in which it has been possible to document archaeologically the variety of uses and functions that dogs had in protohistory. Above all, it has been possible to document the great variability in the ritual practices in which this animal was involved. However, it is difficult to determine the purpose for which each of these rituals was carried out. The context of the recovery, the spatial associations, the taphonomic history, and the composition of the assemblages containing dogs are the most commonly used aspects to define and corroborate these rituals.

In general, the structured deposits tend to be interpreted as funerary, foundational offerings or sacrifices dedicated to certain divinities. A clear dichotomy is established between assemblages formed by domestic waste and those resulting from actions to which a special character is attributed, generally classified as rituals. The exhaustive recording method used during the excavation at the site of Mas Castellar and the meticulous taphonomic study enabled researchers to differentiate between waste from normal and exceptional consumption and also between casual and patterned deposits. The latter usually pursue very precise objectives and are perceived as acts of cohesion and/or control. The position and characteristics of the structures where the remains of *Canis familiaris* have been found suggest that they were collective actions concerning the community as a whole or an elite part of it. An individualized equitable practice by all the members of the community can be ruled out.

The repetition observed in Mas Castellar with the presence of dog remains of a certain size and age shows that not all of the individuals of this species were equally likely to be involved. However, other criteria, most of which are difficult to characterize in an archaeozoological study, may have influenced the selection, such as the color of the dog's coat, the docility, or their access and availability. If we take into account that these rituals were occasional events, it is unlikely that animals were bred especially for ritual practices, although the sacrifice and consumption of exclusively adult animals shows certain interest in keeping the animals until an adult age.

The reason for the choice of this species, the dog, is another often-discussed topic. Frequently implicated in cult and funerary ceremonies and in rituals of fecundity, fertility, and healing, the dog's role in the economic sphere of society should not be ignored. It is one of the most eclectic animal species at a productive level, and covers basic needs ranging from defense to consumption. In this line, Rouse (1975) has proposed that the use of these animals as sacrificial offerings might have been precisely to avoid wasting other animals that were usually consumed.

In recent years, a large number of papers have been published emphasizing the important role of dogs in ritual practices during prehistory and protohistory, covering significantly distant places and times. As the present study has shown, the identification and differentiation of ritual practices is a complex task that can only be approached through integrated studies that take into account the condition of the remains and their spatial distribution. As it is an animal that is not often consumed, the deposition and distribution of the remains at a site may condition the differential patterns that it exhibits in comparison with other animals, although this will not necessarily involve its association with specific ritual practices. Given the diversity that has been noted in this paper, it is important to avoid reductionism that could lead to an excessive homogenization of the interpretations, and, in each case, recurrences and singularities should be respected. The site of Mas Castellar has shown that *Canis familiaris* played a transcendental role in different kinds of events, many of which are hard to explain without referring to all of the actions that coincided at a certain time and place and that generated the materiality that can give meaning to its presence.

ACKNOWLEDGMENTS

The authors wish to thank Anna R. Fanck (Girona-Spain), Leslie Feldballe (Buffalo), and Peter Smith (Cantabria-Spain) for helping with and translating the text, and Paco Morgado (Girona-Spain) for selecting images in this paper.

REFERENCES CITED

Adroher, A., E. Pons, and J. Ruiz de Arbulo 1993 El yacimiento de Mas Castellar de Pontós y el comercio del cereal ibérico en la zona de Emporion y Rhode. (s. IV-II a.C.) *Archivo Español de Arqueologia* 66: 31–70.

Alvarez, A. 2002 Anàlisi petrogràfica de l'ara, In *Mas Castellar de Pontós (Alt Empordà). Un complex arqueològic d'època ibèrica (Excavacions 1990–1998)*, edited by E. Pons, pp. 557. Sèrie Monogràfica *21*, Museu d'Arqueologia de Catalunya-Girona, Girona.

Albizurri, S. 2011 *La ofrenda animal durante el Bronce Inicial en Can Roqueta II (Sabadell, Vallès Occidental). Arqueozoología del ritual funerario.* PhD dissertation, Universitat de Girona, Girona.

Asensio, D., and E. Pons 2004–05 La troballa d'un crater àtic de figures roges en el jaciment de Mas Castellar (Pontós, Alt Empordà). *Quaderns de Prehistòria i Arqueologia de Castelló* 24: 199–211.

Asensio, D., E. Pons, and M. Fuertes 2007 La darrera fase d'ocupació del Mas Castellar de Pontós (Alt Empordà, Girona), In *De Kerunta a Gerunda. Els orígens de la ciutat*, edited by L. Palahí, J.Mª Nolla, and D. Vivó, pp. 97–131. Col·lecció Història de Girona 41. Girona.

Cabrera Díez, A. 2010 *El ritual del sacrificio de animales en la cultura ibérica: una perspectiva arqueológica.* PhD dissertation, Universidad Complutense de Madrid, Madrid.

Cardoso, J. L., and M. V. Gomes 1997 O consumo de cao, em contextos fenício-púnicos, no territorio português. In *Estudos Orientais* VI:89–117. Instituto Oriental, Lisboa.

Casellas, S. 1995 Dipòsits faunístics no subsistencials a la Catalunya prehistòrica, in *Cota Zero* 11:89–93. Eumo editorial, Vic, Barcelona.

Casellas, S. 2002 Els macromamífers i la dieta càrnia. In *Mas Castellar de Pontós (Alt Empordà). Un complex arqueològic d'època ibérica (Excavacions 1990–1998)*, edited by E. Pons, pp. 483–506. Sèrie Monogràfica 21. Museu d'Arqueologia de Catalunya-Girona, Girona.

Chenal-Velarde, I., and J. Studer 2003 Archaeozoology in a Ritual Context: the Case of a Sacrificial Altar in Geometric Eretria. In *Zooarchaeology in Greece: Recent Advances*, edited by E. Kotjabopoulou, Y. Hamilakis, P. Halstead, C. Gamble, and P. Elefanti, pp. 215–220 Papers of the British School at Athens 9. The Council of the British School of Athens, Athens.

Clark, K. M. 1995 The Later Prehistoric and Protohistoric Dog: the Emergence of Canine Diversity. *Archaeozoologia* VII(2):9–32.

Codina, F., A. Martín, J. Nadal, G. de Prado, and S. Valenzuela 2009 Étude et interprétation des dépôts fauniques sous pavement identifiés au Puig de Sant Andreu (Ullastret, Catalogne). In *Du Materiel au spirituel. Realités archéologiques et historiques des "dépôts" de la Prehistoire à nos jours,* edited by S. Bonnardin, C. Hamon, M. Lauwers, and B. Quilliec, pp. 267–274. Éditons APDCA, Antibes.

Colominas, L. 2007 Estudi arqueozoològic de les restes de fauna recuperades a la sitja 137 del jaciment de Mas Castellar de Pontós. Laboratori d'Arqueozoologia, Universitats Autònoma de Barcelona, Barcelona.

Colominas, L. 2008 Els animals en el conjunt de les pràctiques socials desenvolupades a l'establi-ment rural de Mas Castellar (Pontós, Girona). *Cypsela* 17:219–232.

Colominas, L. 2011 Anàlisi arqueozoològica de les restes de fauna recuperades a la sitja 373 del jaciment de Mas Castellar de Pontós. Laboratori d'Arqueozoologia, Universitats Autònoma de Barcelona, Barcelona.

Colominas, L., and M. Saña 2009 Dinàmica de formació i variabilitat dels conjunts de restes de fauna recuperats al jaciment del Bosc del Congost: gestió animal entre el 325 aC. i el 100 aC. In *Excavacions Arqueològiques a la muntanya de Sant Julià de Ramis 3, Els sitjars,* edited by J. Burch and J. Sagrera, pp. 155–179. Universitat de Girona, Diputació de Girona, Girona.

Colominas, L., and M. Saña 2012 Dinámica de formación y variabilidad de los conjuntos de restos de fauna recuperados en los silos del yacimiento de Saus. In *El Asentamiento Rural Ibérico de Saus (Girona). Un Ejemplo de Explotación Agrícola en el territorio de Emporio,* edited by J. Casas and V. Soler, pp. 114–125. BAR International Series 2390. British Archaeological Reports, Oxford.

De Grossi Mazzorin, J. 2008 L'uso dei cani nel mondo antico nei riti di fondazione purificacione e passaggio. In *Uomini, piante e animali nella dimensione del sacro*, edited by F. Adria, J. de Grossi, and G. Fiorentino, pp. 71–82. Edipuglia, Bari.

De Grossi, J., and A. Tagliacozzo 1997 Dog Remains in Italy from the Neolithic to the Roman Period. *Anthropozoologica* 25-26:429–440.

De Grossi, J., and A. Tagliacozzo 2000 Morphological and Osteological Changes in the Dog from the Neolithic to the Roman Period in Italy. In *Dogs Through Time: An Archaeological Perspective*, edited by I. Crockford, pp. 141–161. *BAR International Series* 889. British Archaeological Reports, Oxford.

Driesch A., and J. Boessneck, 1969 Die fauna des Cabezo Redondo bei Villena (prov. Alicante). *Studien über frühe Tierknochenfunde von der Iberischen Halbinsel* 1:43–95.

Friesch K. 1987 Die Tierknochenfunde von Cerro de la Encina bei Monachil, Provinz Granada (Grabungen 1977–1984). *Studien über frühe Tierknochenfunde von der Iberischen Halbinsel*. 11:5–8.

Garrido, J. P., and E. M. Porta 1978 Excavaciones en la necrópolis de "La Joya," Huelva. II (3ª, 4ª y 5ª campañas), *Excavaciones Arqueológicas en España* 96, Ministerio de cultura, Madrid.

Iborra, Mª P. 2004 *La ganadería y la caza desde el Bronce Final hasta el Ibérico Final en el territorio valenciano*. In Servicio de Investigación Prehistórica 103, Diputación Provincial de Valencia, Valencia.

Miró, C., and N. Molist 1990 Elements de ritual domèstic al poblat ibèric de la Penya del Moro, *Zephyrus* XLIII:311–319. Ediciones Universidad de Salamanca, Salamanca.

Meniel, P. 1992 *Les sacrifices d'animaux chez les Gaulois*. Editions Errance, París.

Meniel, P. 2002 Le chien en Gaule. In *Animali tra uomini e dei*, edited by A. Curci and D. Vitali, pp. 45–52. *Archaeozoologia del mondo prerromano. Studi e scavo* 14. Ante Quem, Bologna.

Niveau, A. M., and E. Ferrer 2004 Sacrificios de cánidos en la necrópolis púnica de Cádiz, *Huelva Arqueológica* 20:63–88.

Olmos, R. 1996 Metáforas de la eclosión y del cultivo: Imaginarios de la agricultura en época ibérica. *Archivo Español de Arqueologia* 69: 3–6.

Pons, E. 1997 Estructures, objectes i fets cultuals en el jaciment protohistóric de Mas Castellar-Pontós (Girona). In *Espacios y lugares cultuales en el mundo ibérico. Quaderns de Prehistòria i Arqueologia de Castelló* 18:71–89.

Pons, E. 2004 Agrarian Worship in Iberian Catalonia. In *Tasks and Tools in Rural Catalonia: The Study of Agriculture through Archaeology*, directed by R. Buxó, 173–174. Museu d'Arqueologia de Catalunya-Girona, Girona.

Pons, E. (editor) 2002 *Mas Castellar de Pontós (Alt Empordà). Un complex arqueològic d'època ibèrica (Excavacions 1990–1998)*, Sèrie Monogràfica 21, Museu d'Arqueologia de Catalunya-Girona, Girona.

Pons, E., D. Asensio, M. Fuertes, and M. Bouso 2010 El yacimiento del Mas Castellar de Pontós (Alt Empordà, Girona): un núcleo indígena en la òrbita de la colonia focea de *Emporion*. In *Grecs et indigènes de la Catalogne à la Mer Noire*, edited by H. Tréziny, pp. 105–118. *Actes des rencontres du programme européen Ramses* (2006–08), Bibliothèque d'Archéologie Méditerranéenne et Africaine—3. Éditions errance-Centre Camille Jullian, Paris.

Pons, E., L. Colomina, M. Saña, and A. Vargas 2011 Mas Castellar, Pontós, Gérone. In *Des Rites et des Hommes. Les pratiques symboliques des Celtes, des Ibères et des Grecs, en Provence, en Languedoc et en Catalogne*, directed by L. Pernet and R. Roure, 183–188. Éditions errance, Paris.

Pons, E., and L. Garcia (editors) 2008 *Prácticas alimentarias en el mundo ibérico. El ejemplo de la fosa FS362 de Mas Castellar de Pontós (Empordà-España)*. BAR International Series 1753. British Archaeological Reports, Oxford.

Pons, E., and M. C. Rovira 1997 *El dipòsit d'ofrenes de la fossa 101 de Mas Castellar de Pontós: un estudi interdisciplinari*. Estudis Arqueològics, 4, Universitat de Girona, Girona.

Pons, E., and A. Vargas 2002 Religió i creences. In *Mas Castellar de Pontós (Alt Empordà). Un complex arqueològic d'època ibèrica (Excavacions 1990–1998)*, edited by E. Pons, pp. 533–560. Sèrie Monogràfica 21. Museu d'Arqueologia de Catalunya-Girona, Girona.

Rouse, W. H. D. 1975 *Greek Votive Offerings*, Arno Press, New York.

Saña, M. 1994 Análisis zooarqueológico del Pozo HX-1. El Pozo Púnico del "Hort d'En Xim" (Eivissa), *Trabajos del Museo Arqueológico de Ibiza* 32:71–81.

Sanchis, A., and I. Sarrión 2004 Restos de cánidos en yacimientos valencianos de la edad del bronce, *Archivo de Prehistoria Levantina* 25:161–198.

Sergis, M. G. 2010 Dog Sacrifice in Ancient and Modern Greece: From the Sacrifice Ritual to Dog Torture (kynomartyrion). *Folklore: Electronic Journal of Folklore* 45:61–88.

Snyder, L. M., and W. E. Klippel 2003 From Lerna to Kastro: Further Thoughts on Dogs as Food in Ancient Greece; Perceptions, Prejudices, and Reinvestigations. In *Zooarcheology in Greece. Recent Advances*, edited by E. Kotjabopoulou, Y. Hamilakis, P. Halstead, C. Gamble, and P. Elefanti, pp. 221–231. Papers of the British School at Athens 9. The Council of the British School of Athens, Athens.

CHAPTER ELEVEN

Understanding the Death and Burial of Northern European Bog Bodies

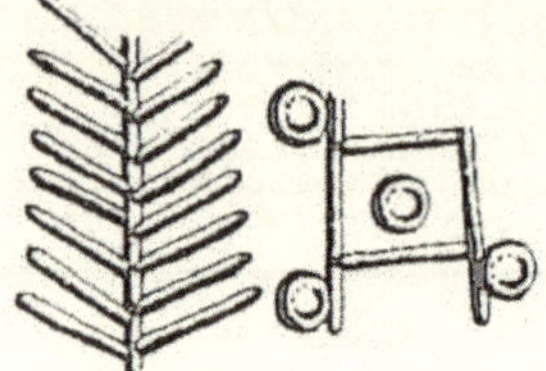

Guinevere Granite

Abstract *Several theories have been posited to explain the use of Northern European bogs as internment sites where bodies have been discovered. The first (Practicality Theory) is practical; dead bodies are heavy and awkward to move. Carrying them downhill and submerging them is easier, rapid, and effectively removes the body from view without cremation or underground internment. Other theories, such as Social Ritual Theory, are more complex and often involve the conduct of social rituals, such as human sacrifice, to appease various deities. The circumstances of death may indicate the need to appease a single deity or a combination of rituals to appease several deities. Often, there is evidence of pre-, peri-, and postmortem violence to bog bodies, which may indicate human sacrifice through strangulation or intentional traumatic injury. Such individuals may vary widely in age and have unique or unusual physical characteristics, such as physical deformities. Other bog bodies, discussed in terms of Dehumanization Theory, may have been criminals, scapegoats, or captives "dehumanized" during their deaths. The final theory, Accidental Death or Suicide Theory, includes any bog body death that may have been accidental (drowning, natural causes, etc.) or suicide. My research involves using x-ray fluorescence spectroscopy to compare the elemental strontium concentration levels of the cranial/post-cranial skeletal bone and the dental remains of twelve bog bodies housed in institutes and museums throughout Northern Europe. Knowing how or why individuals died will assist in developing appropriate theories.*

Human remains have been discovered in bogs from regions of Canada, Northern Europe, and Florida. The most famous of these bog bodies are from the following countries of Northern Europe: Ireland, Great Britain, the Netherlands, Germany, and

Denmark. They date to periods as early as the Mesolithic period (8000–4500 B.C.E.) and up to as recently as the twentieth century. The word *bog* derives from the Irish *bogach,* meaning soft or marshy ground (McLean 2008). Bog bodies are human corpses that have been preserved naturally within these marshland environments. Hundreds of bog bodies have been unearthed throughout Northern Europe during peat harvesting activities for agricultural purposes, sources of fuel, and iron ore extraction (Giles 2009).

Bog bodies have been discovered within two types of bogs: fen and raised bogs. Their preservation varies depending on the chemical composition of the interment bog. Human remains have been found completely skeletonized, or well-preserved with hair, skin, fingernails, and clothing intact, or as isolated heads and limbs. Fen peat, which has a high calcareous content, will preserve skeletonized remains in fossilized form, but raised bog peat is able to preserve the soft tissue of such individuals in immaculate condition (van der Sanden 1996). If the remains are fully submerged, anaerobic conditions within the bog halt decay with the help of an antimicrobial polysaccharide known as sphagnan. Sphagnan is released from the cell walls of decaying Sphagnum moss found within the bog, gradually converting into humic acid by way of a series of intermediate compounds. Sphagnan, humic acid, and their intermediate compounds bind selectively with calcium and nitrogen contained in the bog environment, initiating a melanoidin or "tanning" reaction that occurs within the skin (Painter 1991). Consequently, calcium is extracted from the immersed human remains, inhibiting the growth of bacteria and any subsequent decay. Decalcification also causes the bones to soften, which can result in distortion due to the overlying weight of accumulated peat, or, under highly acidic conditions, the skeleton may dissolve altogether, leaving only the outer layer of skin (McLean 2008). However, in less acidic conditions, the skin, hair, nails, major organs, and stomach contents of the bog bodies are preserved, along with clothing or objects made of wool, skin, leather, and metal. Though garments made of plant fibers, such as linen, decay within the bog, conserved pollen and macrobotanical remains found in the surrounding peat can provide excellent environmental data in reference to the bog body (Giles 2009).

Discovered bog bodies predominantly date from the Iron Age (ca. 500 B.C.E.–100 C.E.) (Lobell 2010), an era when written history was not commonplace. The absence of such written history about these individuals makes the contextual understanding of their deaths and/or the reason for their interment within the bog a matter of speculation. Bog bodies are enigmas within the fields of wetland archaeology and forensic anthropology. To explain these mysterious remains, many experts in these fields offer generalization, rather than explanation, and fail to analyze each body independently and without assuming that all bog bodies have died for the same reasons.

Reason for Death and Bog Internment Theories

Practicality Theory

To establish a framework accurately to assess the reason for the deaths of bog bodies and their subsequent bog interment, four types of theories can be applied to each bog body on an individual case-by-case basis. The first theory, Practicality Theory, reaffirms the inaccuracy of grouping all bog bodies as victims of sacrifice. Some bodies display no evidence of perimortem (during death) trauma, and in many cases, no definitive cause of death. The possibility of death by natural causes (i.e., disease, sickness, or old age) cannot be overlooked, nor can the use of the bog for interment merely on account of its practicality. Dead bodies are awkward and hard to handle. Carrying a body down-hill and submerging it within a bog would be a rapid and efficient means of disposal. In addition, bog interment eliminates the need for cremation or burial, both of which require a large amount of energy and resource-use to execute.

Social Ritual Theory

The second theory proposed is the Social Ritual Theory. Much more complex than simple practicality, this theory involves the social ritual aspect of early Northern European societies in the form of human sacrifice, whether for religious reasons or judicial punishment. Throughout the ages, Northern European bogs have been reservoirs of abundant resources. These bogs supply such reserves as woodlands, reeds, sedges, and mosses, all of which are used for manufacturing and medicinal purposes. The assortment of food is abundant within the bogs, with profitable means for agriculture, seasonal fishing, fowling, and gaming, as well as their acting as a frequent site to assemble craft, creating metal, glass, and wood (Coles and Minnit 1995). Even today, bogs are one of Northern Europe's primary sources of iron ore and fuel. Such exploitation has greatly reduced both the size and number of bogs that once covered substantial regions of Northern Europe. The majority of discovered bog bodies have been unearthed by peat-harvesting machinery. Therefore, throughout time, bogs have been lucrative locations associated with "production, fertility, and seasonal abundance" (Giles 2006:9). Furthermore, since these marshland sites are replenished annually with additional copious resources, they may have rendered some form of animacy or even identity to those procuring their assets. This may explain why bogs were also often associated with depositional activity, interpreted as areas for providing ritual or votive offerings (Giles 2009). Retrieval of ancient artifacts, including gold and other jewelry, weaponry, battle armor, drinking vessels, and musical instruments from peat bogs supports the use of bogs as a medium for, and a source of, sacramental offerings to religious deities of the past. Written sources provide further corroboration of the Social Ritual Theory, notably those of the Roman historian, Publius Cornelius Tacitus. In his work first published in 98 C.E., Tacitus refers to votive deposits in rivers, lakes, and other bodies of water as commonplace among the Germanic tribes on western frontiers of the Roman Empire (Tacitus 1970). Throughout Greek and Roman history, religious sects, such as the Germanic tribes, have been referred to as providers of both animal and human sacrifices to their deities, their motivation being to appease these deities, to ensure plentiful harvests, or to succeed in battle (Lobell and Patel 2010). For successful transfer of a sacrificial gift to the spirit-world, the bog could have served as a sacrificial medium. As neither land nor water, the bog provided a direct liminal portal for those purposefully deposed of within its midst. Human sacrifices may have been executed and placed in the bog in an effort to appease a single deity, or a ritual combination of actions inflicted on one individual may have been carried out to appease several deities at once.

An example of ritual combination inflicted on one individual is found with the bog body known as Lindow Man. Lindow Man, the mid-twenties-year-old British Iron Age bog body, displays perimortem damage associated with being the victim of triple death sacrifice. This man was subjected to a vicious blow to the back, fracturing a rib; he was also bludgeoned with two strikes to the back of the head, his throat was slit, his neck broken by a garrote, and finally, he was drowned in the bog (Giles 2006). Marcus Annaeus Lucanus (Lucan), a renowned Roman poet of the Middle Ages, referred to triple death as a form of overkill offered by the Celts of Northern Europe to three of their gods: Teutates (represented by drowning), Esus (represented by hanging/garroting), and Taranis (represented by wounding). Plausible reasoning behind this threefold death is the person dies in three ways simultaneously, making the actual cause of death undetermined. An indeterminate death in the eyes of the Celts meant that the person had become immortal and could now live among the gods (Turner 1995). British archaeologist Miranda Green, who specializes in Iron Age and Romano-Celtic sacrificial activities, believes such excessive ritual aggression may have been an important element in the symbolism of sacrifice. The violence inflicted upon a sacrifice may directly link with the "efficacy [of] . . . stimulating regeneration, prosperity or other desired outcomes" (Green 1998). This perspective can also be applied to the many bog bodies that may not have been the victims of triple death, but rather present excessive evidence of perimortem violence. Extreme violence, including strangulation and intentional traumatic injury, such as blunt force trauma and/or throat slitting, may also fall under the Social Ritual Theory as indicators of ritualistic death via human sacrifice.

Two additional examples of bog bodies that may have been victims of ritualistic death are Grauballe Man of Denmark and Yde Girl of the Netherlands. Both individuals demonstrate evidence of perimortem violence. Grauballe Man's throat was so viciously slit that it nearly beheaded him, completely bisecting his larynx. His right temple was also bludgeoned and his leg was broken during death (Asingh 2009). Yde Girl was only 16 or 17 years old when she was murdered, and shows evidence of strangulation using the woolen band with which her body was found, as well as sharp-force trauma from being stabbed near her left clavicle (van der Sanden 1996). The violence inflicted on these two people was methodical and excessive in nature, strongly suggesting that they were the victims of human sacrifice.

The Weerdinge Men of the Netherlands are additional cases of potential sacrifice. One of the men was brutally stabbed in the left side of his abdomen, causing his intestines to extrude from the wound. However, there is no sign of trauma or evident cause of death for the second individual. It is possible this individual was willingly drowned along with his murdered acquaintance because they were related or were lovers. According to the Greek historian Diodorus Siculus, the Gauls or Celts of Western Europe living during the Iron Age and Roman periods disemboweled human sacrifices in an attempt to divine the future by "reading" the victim's entrails and limb convulsions. As Diodorus Siculus states, the Gauls would "kill a man by a knife-stab in the region above the midriff, and after his fall they foretell the future by the convulsions of his limbs and the pouring of his blood" (*Histories* V, 31, 2–5, see Giles 2006:6). Although these historical references strongly reflect the trauma inflicted on numerous discovered bog bodies, one must be cautious that such accounts may deliberately exaggerate or eroticize the "barbaric" traits of the Northern European natives. However, the need for divination and prediction may well have been motivations for ritualistic killings.

Tollund Man, a middle-aged Dane who lived during the Iron Age, is another example of probable human sacrifice by ligature strangulation. As with other bog bodies that fell victim to ligature strangulation, the physical evidence is not only found with the rope or garrote still intact around the neck, but also in deep linear furrows on the sides of the neck that are still present after centuries due to the remarkable preservation of these bodies (Jarcho 1970). However, even though strangulation strongly suggests human sacrifice, if it is the only sign of trauma, strangulation being the result of judicial punishment or murder without ritualistic purpose cannot be overlooked as possible reasons for death. Judicial punishment can be a socially ritualistic activity, but murder may be the intent of a solitary person and may not be ritualistic in nature. Creating a theory based on murder without ritualistic purpose is difficult to construct for the purpose of classification without contextual details to follow, but one cannot discount the possibility that death by another's hand was not a social ritual.

Other common characteristics among discovered bog bodies are unique or unusual physical deformities. Varying in age, it seems that many of these individuals were well treated by society and kept alive to serve a sacrificial purpose. These bodies demonstrate little evidence of heavy manual labor and often present a "well-manicured" appearance. Rather than murdering those born with congenital deformities when their conditions were noticed, these individuals were kept alive, potentially for the purpose of deity-appeasement. The inclusion in bogs of individuals, such as Lindow Man, who did not display unusual physical characteristics, but were well-groomed even in death (i.e., manicured fingernails and a well-groomed beard) suggests that individuals of high social status may have also been sacrificed, possibly to present the archetypal human to the gods to receive the finest rewards in return. Additional examples of such archetypal bog bodies include the Borremose Woman and Haraldskjaer Woman who were both well-nourished and even overweight, while Grauballe Man and Borremose Man demonstrate unblemished hands (Williams 2003). Another interpretation of these individuals who present characteristics of high societal status is that they were elite members of opposing societies captured or taken hostage and deliberately sacrificed after their seizure during a tribal conflict or following a local rebellion against a chief (Giles 2006).

For those presenting physical abnormalities, these individuals may not have necessarily committed any personal crime, but rather were chosen by the community symbolically to represent collective guilt or fear, essentially as a scapegoat (Aldhouse-Green 2001). Roman author Marius Servius Honoratus documented such an incident, which is preserved in a fragment of Petronius (Servius on Virgil *Aeneid* III, 57; Petronius Fragment I). According to this text, whenever an epidemic broke out, a citizen would offer himself as a scapegoat (or in Greek *pharmakos*) in an effort to save his community. At Massalia (modern Marseille, France), for a year prior to the sacrifice, the self-selected victim would be pampered with delicious foods provided by the residents. The *pharmakos* was also crowned with leaves and clad in a sacred robe before being led through the city to be burdened with the community's imprecations and evils. Finally, the victim was cast into the sea, purifying the city and its inhabitants.

There are several bog bodies that could have been chosen to serve as *pharmakos* prior to their death. The Yde Girl and Moora Girl both exhibit scoliosis in their sacra and/or vertebra. These abnormalities would have caused an unusual gait and a curved spine in both of these individuals. The Esterweger Dose Child, a Middle Ages bog body the age of which is estimated between 12 and 14 years old, suffered from what is now known as Legg-Calve-Perthes Disease or LCPD. This involves avascular necrosis of the femoral head. In addition, this unfortunate child also had osteomyelitis or a chronic bone infection in his/her right tibia and fibula. The lesion does show signs of healing, meaning that this child lived with both disorders for an extended period of time. This supports the theory of keeping those with physical deformities alive for sacrifice. However, it cannot be discounted that this child may have succumbed to the leg infection, rather than been sacrificed, since no signs of trauma were found with the remains. The Neu England Man is another example of physical abnormality in bog bodies that also exhibit scoliosis. Scoliosis is a disorder more commonly found in females. This could possibly have made this individual's irregularity stand out even more in his society, facilitating his choice as a sacrifice. Two other interesting cases of physical abnormalities in bog bodies are the third individual found at Lindow Moss, Lindow III, that had a vestigial thumb (Giles 2009), and the Zweeloo Woman, which exhibits skeletal dysplasia that is consistent with achondroplasia. This disorder involves asymmetrical forearms and lower leg lengths. Such noticeable physical irregularities could have made both Lindow III and the Zweeloo Woman prime candidates for human sacrifice.

Demonstrating a visible physical disadvantage, these individuals may have been set apart in some way from the rest of their people, leading to their selection as suitable scapegoats when societal crises arose (Green 1998). Such anomalies may have been viewed in a positive or negative light. From a negative perspective, the practice of pampering individuals with physical anomalies prior to their demise could in part be for compensatory reasons, but was probably more importantly carried out for the perceived symbolic need of raising the victim's status to enhance his/her sacrificial value (Green 1998). However, in a positive light, past societies may have viewed the physically disadvantaged as having distinguishing features that set their "recipient" apart as being "touched" or "favored" by the gods. Having characteristics bestowed by the gods would have made such individuals appropriate intercessors with the gods in times of need (Giles 2009). In other words, offering those with physical abnormalities would procure direct appeal to the deities with the possible reward of reincarnation for the victim (Turner 1999). Whatever the reason for specifically choosing individuals with physical abnormalities, such selection was most likely a communal decision with religious connotations, whether it be for punishment or deity appeasement.

Dehumanization Theory

Dehumanization Theory can be closely linked to the Social Ritual theory, but differs greatly in the reason for the death. According to this theory, the bog bodies may have been criminals, foreign scapegoats, or war captives "dehumanized" during their death. Though ritualistic in nature with partially shaved heads, bound limbs, and fur or leather clothing, these individuals' deaths may represent a form of capital punishment, rather than human sacrifice. Speculation surrounds the application of fur or leather clothing to this theory as an additional means of dehumanization. These individuals may have always worn these types of clothes and other bog bodies that have been found naked may have also been dressed at the time of death, but in plant-based clothing that disintegrated during interment.

An additional aspect surrounding certain bog body deaths that could support the Dehumanization Theory is in cases where stomach contents were available for analysis; the final meals of some bog bodies may also suggest a lack of care, which is another means of degrading the individual prior to death. Individuals such as Grauballe Man and Tollund Man, the last meals of which consisted of gruel, roughly made from a combination of cereals and weeds, could reflect this purposeful neglect and brutalization. However, these meals may have included the plant life growing at the time of their deaths. If the person was murdered during the winter months, grains and weeds may have been the only viable source of food for not only the victim but those committing the act as well. Though this is a feasible explanation for the contents of the last meal, in total, the presumed nakedness or near nakedness of the bodies, the shaving of their hair, as well as the privations of their diet, all suggest that these persons may have been treated roughly and with a lack of respect. In addition, the extreme manner in which these individuals were brutalized during death could have served as a lasting deterrent to others in their communities (Williams 2003). As Tacitus stated in reference to judicial punishment among the Germanic tribes, "The coward, the shirker and the disreputable body are drowned in miry swamps under a cover of wattled hurdles" (*Germania* XII; for a discussion see Aldhouse-Green 2001:117). The bog served as a tomb for those degraded in death for reprehensible crimes committed in life. Such "crimes against honor" that would fall under the Dehumanization Theory were punished by ritual killing, banishing the perpetrator to a liminal world, a place where "the body would not rot, nor would the soul be released into the ancestral realm, but instead was deliberately trapped in a liminal zone" (Giles 2009:86). Differing greatly from the interpretation of the bog as a liminal area of immortality among the gods, as proposed by the Social Ritual Theory, the Dehumanization Theory views this "in-between space" as a trap in which criminals could be held for an eternal sentence.

Kayhausen Boy is a prominent case in bog body discoveries that is strongly suggestive of dehumanization. Only about seven years old when he was savagely murdered, this small child was stabbed several times in the throat and left arm, during which time he was hogtied as if he were an irrepressible beast that needed to be euthanized. The boy also shows evidence of avascular necrosis of the femoral head, similar to that of the Esterweger Dose Child. With such a disability, this young boy could have been another example of human sacrifice. Combining both the Dehumanization Theory and the Social Ritual Theory to explain the death of Kayhausen Boy seems to be an accurate way to analyze this case. Other bog bodies that were tied up or bound prior to deposition in the bog include the Elling Woman, who had her feet bound, and the Huldremose Woman, who had her arms bound (Williams 2003). The use of binding has only one viable explanation: dehumanization. Rendering a victim unable to move as he/she was drowned and/or stabbed could achieve ultimate control over the victim, leaving him/her helpless and stripped of any humanistic characteristics.

Two other bog bodies could be examples of the Dehumanization Theory, but there is much skepticism when trying to label these individuals as such. The Windeby Child, who was 12 to 14 years old at death, was found with a partially "shaved" head and a woolen band covering the eyes. Following the Dehumanization Theory, this individual may have had his/her eyes covered and head shaved to control him/her and degrade him/her in front of the gods and his/her people. However, it is possible that the head was partially exposed to oxygen at some point during its interment in the bog and that the hair in this region decomposed. It is also possible that excavators were careless with their trowels and damaged the hair or even that the hair was damaged by the peat cutting machine that revealed the body in the first place. The woolen band covering may also have been for hair maintenance and fell down while the body settled into the bog. Such ambiguity makes it difficult concretely to explain this individual's death as a result of efforts at dehumanization.

The Yde Girl, previously mentioned with reference to the Social Ritual Theory, may also be explained in terms of the Dehumanization Theory. She was found with half of her long hair cut off. This may be a purposeful act by her murderers to dehumanize her with the removal of her hair. For both the Windeby Child and Yde Girl, direct reference to writings by Tacitus may shed light on the possible act of adultery they both committed in life that resulted in their shaven heads. When commenting on adultery, Tacitus states: "A guilty wife is summarily punished by her husband. He cuts off her hair, strips her naked, and in the presence of her kinsmen turns her out of his house and flogs her through the village" (*Germania* XII; for a discussion see Aldhouse-Green 2001:118). Though there is no mention of deposition within the bog in Tacitus's writings, flogging involves a severe beating, which could have ended in death and subsequent submersion of the dead body; that being said, drowning may have been the final punishment specifically inflicted on these individuals. However, just like with the Windeby Child, the blade of the peat-cutting machine that originally discovered the body could have caused this damage. It is unlikely that a trowel could have removed such a large amount of hair, making the machine blade a much more reasonable culprit. Without definitive evidence for purposeful or accidental hair removal for either of these individuals, their deaths could have been the result of dehumanizing acts of judicial punishment.

Accidental Death or Suicide Theory

The fourth and final theory involves cases of accidental death or suicide. Similar to the Practicality Theory, the individuals involved demonstrate no perimortem trauma indicative of cause of death. However, the reason for death differs from the first theory in that the death was not a natural one that resulted in purposeful body deposition in the bog, but rather was the result of an accident or suicide. The bogs of Northern Europe, particularly during the lifetimes of many of the discovered bog bodies, were known to be dangerous places to travel alone, particularly during foggy weather or at night. Erratically changing from land to water, the terrain of Northern European bogs "was insubstantial and often treacherous [for travelers]" (Giles 2009:87); it was "a desolate landscape with neither roads, nor paths, nor fixed points, just a bottomless deep waiting to engulf the trespasser" (McLean 2008:305). The precariousness of the bogs is evident in the recovered hands of a bog body from the Velne bog in Germany. His hands were grasping tufts of heather, which he most likely grabbed in a futile attempt to escape from the bog. There have also been cases of other bog bodies found clutching sticks (Meredith 2002).

During my own experience taking elemental levels directly in the bog, I too had a very hard time traveling through the bog itself. The underwater dead vegetation can act like quicksand, immobilizing your feet and making it very difficult to extricate yourself. The possibility of death by accidental drowning or even drowning by purposeful suicide is a plausible explanation in these cases of questionable death. Three examples of bog bodies that could be explained using the Accidental Death or Suicide Theory are Juhrdenerfeld Man, Neu England Man, and Husbake Man. All three of these bog bodies demonstrate neither signs of trauma nor a cause of death. One cannot rule out that each of these men may have died accidentally, by suicide, or naturally from sickness or stressful life situations, such as malnutrition. If death were natural for these men, the Practicality Theory may be more applicable for their reason for death.

Conclusion

In conclusion, to explain the reason for death and bog interment of studied bog bodies accurately, it may be necessary to apply more than one of the posited theories. For example, in the cases of the Yde Girl and the Kayhausen Boy, aspects of their deaths may be explained by applying both the Social Ritual Theory and the Dehumanization Theory. Numerous examples strongly suggest human sacrifice, but such an explanation must result from an unbiased analysis of the evidence presented and on a case-by-case basis. Further, one cannot rule out accidental drowning, suicidal drowning, or natural death if there is an absence of perimortem trauma to the bog body. Much of the trauma found on bog bodies was inflicted postmortem by peat-cutting machines, which resulted in their initial discovery, or from mishandling by investigators excavating the remains. Such fragility is common with the bone of bog bodies due to the decalcification process that occurs to the bones within the bog. This again emphasizes the necessity to abstain from grouping all bog bodies as sacrificial victims, but rather each body needs independent examination, so that conclusions about reason and manner of death come from actual evidence and not mere speculation.

ACKNOWLEDGMENTS

The author would like to thank Professor P. Biehl and the Institute for European and Mediterranean Archaeology for making this publication possible.

REFERENCES CITED

Aldhouse-Green, M. 2001 *Dying for the Gods. Human Sacrifice in Iron Age and Roman Europe.* Tempus, Stroud.

Asingh, P. 2009 *Grauballe Man: Portrait of a Bog Body.* Korotan, Slovenia, Moesgård Museum, Århus.

Coles, J., and S. Minnit 1995 *Industrious and Fairly Civilised: The Glastonbury Lake Village.* Exeter, Somerset Levels Project and Somerset County Council Museum Services, Somerset.

Giles, M. 2006 *Bog Bodies: Representing the Dead.* Paper presented at the Respect for Ancient British Human Remains: Philosophy and Practice Conference at the Manchester Museum. Electronic Document, http://www.museum.manchester.ac.uk/medialibrary/documents/respect/bog_bodies_representing_the_dead.pdf.

Giles, M. 2009 Iron Age Bog Bodies of North-Western Europe Representing the Dead. *Archaeological Dialogues* 16(1):75–101.

Green, M. 1998 Humans as Ritual Victims in the Later Prehistory of Western Europe. *Oxford Journal of Archaeology* 17(2):169–189.

Jarcho, S. 1970 Tollund Man and Other Bog Burials. *Bulletin of the New York Academy of Medicine* 46(7):554–558.

Lobell, J. A., and S. S. Patel 2010 Bog Bodies Rediscovered. *Archaeology* 63(3):22–29.

McLean, S. 2008 Bodies from the Bog: Metamorphosis, Non-Human Agency, and the Making of "Collective" Memory. *Trames* 12(62/57), 3:299–308.

Meredith, D. 2002 Hazards in the Bog: Real and Imagined. *Geographical Review* 92(3):319–332.

Painter, T. 1991 Preservation in Peat. *Chemistry & Industry* (12): 421–424.

Turner, R. C. 1995 The Lindow Man Phenomenon: Ancient and Modern. In *Bog Bodies: New Discoveries and New Perspectives,* edited by R. C. Turner and R. G. Scaife, pp. 168–204. British Museum Press, London.

Turner, R. C. 1999 Dating the Lindow Moss and Other British Bog Bodies and the Problems of Assigning their Cultural Context. In *Bog Bodies, Sacred Sites, and Wetland Archaeology,* edited by B. Coles, J. Coles, and M. Schou Jørgensen, pp. 227–233. Wetland Archaeology Research Project, Exeter.

van der Sanden, W. 1996 *Through Nature to Eternity.* Drents Museum, Assen.

Williams, M. 2003 Tales from the Dead: Remembering the Bog Bodies in the Iron Age of North-Western Europe. In *Archaeologies of Remembrance: Death and Memory in Past Societies,* edited by H. Williams, pp. 89–112, Kluwer Academic/Plenum, New York.

PART IV

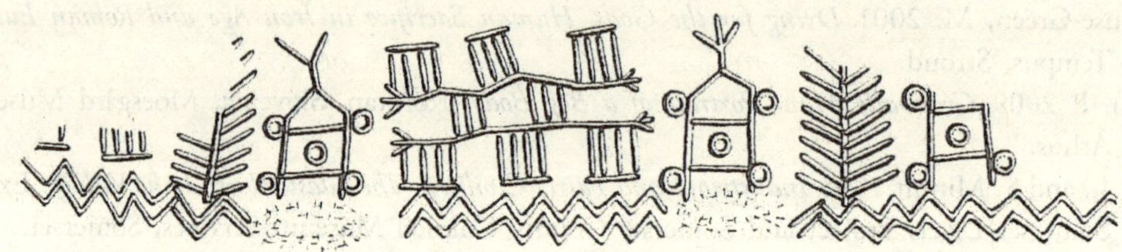

Formularizing and Regularizing Sacrifice

Chapter Twelve

Sacrificing the Sign

The Alphabet as an Offering in Ancient Israel, or, a Classicist's Read on the Ritual Law of the Sotah

Roger D. Woodard

For Sam Paley

שפתי חכמים יזרו דעת

χείλη σοφῶν δέδεται αἰσθήσει

—Proverbs 15.7

Abstract   *The ritual of the Sotah is a curious procedure described in the fifth chapter of the Biblical book of Numbers that can be employed when a man suspects his wife of infidelity. This study examines the record of that rite as it is preserved in the Masoretic Text (MT) of the Hebrew Bible, the Septuagint (LXX), Philo of Alexandria's* De specialibus legibus, *and yet other ancient sources. Egyptian and Mesopotamian procedures showing certain similarities are considered as well. I argue that in order to gain insight into the proper integration of the ritual within Israelite cult, it is necessary to uncouple its synchronic expression from its diachronic developmental pathway. Doing so suggests that through the performance of the rite the body of the suspected wife is rendered, in effect, a symbolic system giving expression to the word of Yahweh.*

An Examination of the Ritual

Asingularly remarkable rite among those prescribed in the Hebrew Bible is that one recorded in Numbers 5.11–31, an instruction of Yahweh, spoken through Moses (v. 11). The ritual-legal procedure there set out is to be followed when a man, seized by

a fit of jealousy (MT v. 14 וְעָבַר עָלָיו רוּחַ קִנְאָה; LXX: ἐπέλθῃ αὐτῷ πνεῦμα ζηλώσεως),
suspects his wife of infidelity. In addition to the Biblical narrative itself, there is a Rabbinic
interpretative tradition of this so-called ordeal of the wayward wife, the *Soṭah* (from שטה
"to turn aside," as in MT v. 12); and the bibliography of modern scholarly treatments is
not slight. In the paper that follows I propose to examine the problem from a perspective
somewhat different, at least partially so, from those of my predecessors in this undertaking, to whom I am of course indebted. I leave aside issues of documentary accretion in the
formation of the text, assiduously examined by earlier critical interpreters,[1] whose views
appear no longer acceptable,[2] and matters of ritual iteration (how many times the priest
performs a particular gesture, and so forth). The ritual procedure can be summarized as
follows. The jealous husband is to bring his wife, together with a grain offering, before
a priest; the grain must not be mixed with oil or incense, "because," we read, "it is an
offering for jealousy" (v. 15). The priest brings the woman into the presence of Yahweh
(v. 16). He then takes a clay vessel containing sacred (MT), or pure (LXX), water and
adds to the water dust from the floor of the tabernacle[3] (v. 17). The priest uncovers the
woman's head[4] and places the grain offering in her hands (v. 18).

In his own hands, the priest holds the vessel of water in which has been dissolved
dust from the tabernacle floor. The Hebrew text refers to this solution as *mê hammārîm,*
traditionally translated in English Bibles as "waters of bitterness" (as if from the root
מרר "to be bitter"); correspondingly, one finds in the Vulgate, the fourth-century Latin
translation associated with St. Jerome, *aquae amārissimae* (superlative of *amārus* "bitter").
Other ancient authorities, however, point to a different sense, and the proper translation
of the Hebrew phrase has been a matter of contention among scholars.[5] The Alexandrian
translators of the Greek Bible, the Septuagint (third century B.C.E. and later), render
the phrase as τὸ ὕδωρ τοῦ ἐλεγμοῦ "the water of refuting" (where ὁ ἐλεγμός equates to
ἡ ἔλεγξις, also a Biblical term, and known from Philostratus; compare ὁ ἔλεγχος "argument
of disproof; testing,"[6] on which see immediately following). In a 1956 study of the passage,
Driver (1956:73) draws attention to a Septuagintal variant attesting not ὁ ἐλεγμός but
ὁ ἐμφανισμός "manifestation; information."[7] As Driver points out, the Samaritan Targum
is in fundamental agreement with the readings of the Septuagint.[8] Philo of Alexandria
has something to contribute to the discussion; the Septuagintal reading reverberates in
his treatment of the cult proceeding: Philo refers to the ritual solution as ποτὸς ἐλέγχου
"the drink of testing" (*De specialibus legibus* 3.61), foreshadowing, as it were, its usage
in the ritual that is unfolding before us.

Questioning Curses

The contentious Hebrew phrase *mê hammārîm* is itself a single constituent within a larger
phrase: *mê hammārîm hamᵉʾārᵉrîm.*[9] While the meaning of *mᵉʾārᵉrîm* is more straightforward, the full construction has likewise drawn scholarly attention. Hebrew *mᵉʾārᵉrîm,* a
participial formation from *ʾārar,* is typically translated as something like "curse-bringing."
For the comparable phrasing the Septuagint provides a participle of ἐπικαταράομαι, a
complex form of the common and archaic verb ἀράομαι meaning "to invoke," "to pray

to/for": the envisioned outcome of the prayer can be for good; more often for bad, the lexicographers tell us. Without a direct object, the sense of ἀράομαι can be "to place a curse" on someone. The complex verb ἐπικαταράομαι occurs frequently in the Septuagint, especially in the Pentateuch, and also in early Christian documents, and is conventionally translated as "to call down curses upon" or simply "to curse."

The Hebrew verb 'ārar (as in the participial *m^e'ār^rîm*) is a part of the Semitic lexicon of religious action, cognate with Akkadian *arāru*. In a study of these terms, Speiser writes, "In all instances the all but invariable translation is 'curse'. This is barely adequate at best. Occasionally, moreover, it is not only misleading but demonstrably wrong. . . . [T]he basic sense of the term is clearly more specific than 'curse' " (1960:198).

Speiser argues that the fundamental meaning of the Akkadian nominal *arratum* is "spell" and that the same sense can be seen to hold for Hebrew 'ārar "in several unambiguous passages," as in Numbers 22, in which a Moabite king recruits the seer Balaam to cast "a spell" (*'ārar*) on the Israelites (22.6). Included among these passages in which Speiser sees 'ārar to convey clearly a verbal notion of "spell" is that of the legal rite of Numbers 5 here under consideration.[10] In this study, Speiser clearly situates such usages within a context of magic, but then somewhat distances himself, or the Hebrew concepts, from that in his conclusion, where he writes, "In course of time, and in view of Israel's progressive aversion to magic practices, 'ārar lost its earlier occult connotation and became a mere synonym for 'curse' in the conventional sense of the term" (1960:200).

Brichto, in part following Speiser, comes to similar conclusions regarding the meaning of 'ārar in a 1968 study (109–112), offering "that which brings on the spell" as the sense of *m^e'ār^rîm* (1968:50).[11] By the use of this phrase, however, Brichto emphasizes not a magical property of the ritual solution of Numbers 5 (*mê hammārîm ham^e'ār^rîm*)—for Brichto, notions of magic are misplaced in interpretations of this rite (a point to which we shall return below)—but its use by God as an agent, a conduit, for accomplishing divine purpose (Brichto 1975:65). The envisioned semantic distinction between "spell" and "curse" appears to be a delicate one in a setting in which magic is not permitted.

In Philo's account of this ritual, his phrase ποτὸς ἐλέγχου "the drink of testing" is not qualified by a form comparable to Hebrew *m^e'ār^rîm,* "curse-bringing," "spell-inducing"; though Philo's phrase does receive additional modification, as we shall see. But in his sentence that immediately precedes, Philo has the priest say to the woman μὴ ἀγνόει πάσαις ἀραῖς ἔνοχος γεγενημένη, "Do not be ignorant of the fact that you have left yourself open to all ἀράς," if she is in fact an adulteress. The Greek nominal ἀρά (source of the verb ἀράομαι) often denotes "prayer" in Homer, but also "imprecation"; it occurs frequently in tragedy, and elsewhere too, with the meaning "curse, imprecation." The noun is found only once in the New Testament (Romans 3:14, in a citation of the Septuagint Psalm 9:28), but the derived complex verb καταράομαι is the common verb, alongside ἀναθεματίζω, meaning "to curse."[12] A lemma search of Philo's works turns up 37 occurrences of the noun ἀρά, the fundamental sense of which looks to be "curse, imprecation, execration," as in the title of his work, as formulated upon the basis of comments by Eusebius (*Historia ecclesiastica* 2.18.5), Περὶ ἀγαθῶν καὶ ἐπιτιμίων καὶ ἀρῶν. (*De praemiis et poenis et De exsecrationibus*) "On Rewards and Punishments and

Curses." It seems likely that at least in the first century, Philo understands the potential outcome of the rite as one that entails the bringing of a curse upon a wayward wife, and in this he looks to be in agreement with the translators of the Septuagint.

TESTING THE WATERS

What sense is then to be made of the Hebrew phrase of Numbers 5.18, *mê hammārîm hamᵉʾārᵉrîm*? As the preceding observations would suggest, commonly encountered translations such as "the bitter water that causeth the curse" (KJV), "the bitter water that brings a curse" (NIV), "the water of bitterness that brings the curse" (NRSV), and so on, are of questionable standing. In the study mentioned above, Sir Godfrey Driver (1956:73–74) contends, regarding the traditional "the water of bitterness," that "the sense so obtained is unsatisfactory; for the addition of a handful of dust to 'clean water' . . . does not make it bitter." Guided by the Greek translation of the Septuagint and the reading of the Samaritan Targum, Driver argues that Hebrew *hammārîm* is to be properly associated with a Semitic root, *mry* (Brockelmann 1913:2, 59–61), that lies behind Hebrew *mārāh* "was rebellious" (compare BDB:598 [מרה]); Syriac *mar(r)î* "rebelled" and *ʾetmar(r)î* "contended"; and Arabic *mirya(tun)* "doubt, ambiguity" and *marīya(tun)* "doubtful matter." Driver thus proposes *mārîm* to be an abstract plural meaning "contention, dispute, doubt" and translates *mê hammārîm* as " 'water(s) of contention, dispute,' by which the truth is elicited and made manifest"—a translation that found its way into the *New English Bible*'s slightly commentarial rendering "the water of contention which brings out the truth" (for the production of which work, Driver served as Joint Director [with C. H. Dodd and W. D. McHardy]): the accompanying participle, *hamᵉʾārᵉrîm*, finds no explicit expression in the NEB. Driver's seems a sensible interpretation of *mê hammārîm*, not only in light of the Septuagint reading, τὸ ὕδωρ τοῦ ἐλεγμοῦ "the water of refuting" (or alternatively ἐμφανισμοῦ "of manifestation"), which Driver invokes, but also in the face of Philo's reformulated ποτὸς ἐλέγχου "the drink of testing" (*Spec.* 3.61).

Nearly two decades subsequent to Driver's study, Brichto (1975) revisited the phrase *mê hammārîm hamᵉʾārᵉrîm*, arguing for a different etymon for *mārîm*: neither the traditional one—"Nothing in the context justifies derivation of *mārîm* from *mrr* 'to be bitter' " (1975:59nl)—nor Driver's. Brichto proposes instead the verbal root *yrh*, meaning (Hiphil) "to point out, show"; "to teach" (see BDB:435), though in his translation of the phrase *mê hammārîm hamᵉʾārᵉrîm*, Brichto opts to leave *mārîm* untranslated, thus rendering it as "the spell-inducing *mārîm* water," but once doing so in conjunction with a note of its "oracular function" (1975:66). Given Brichto's identification of the root, Frymer-Kensky takes the natural step of filling out his translation in her 1984 study of the ritual, rendering *mê hammārîm* as "waters of instruction, waters of revelation" and the full phrase *mê hammārîm hamᵉʾārᵉrîm* as "spell-effecting revelation-waters" (1984:26). Derivation of *mārîm* from *yrh* is, however, cumbersome.[13]

Yet, within a juridical context, the fundamental sense of the Brichto/Frymer-Kensky translation of *mê hammārîm*, "waters of revelation," is not far removed from the Septuagint's τὸ ὕδωρ τοῦ ἐλεγμοῦ "the water of refuting," and hence Driver's "water(s) of dispute," and Philo's ποτὸς ἐλέγχου "the drink of testing"—and is effectively equivalent to the Septuagintal variant τὸ ὕδωρ τοῦ ἐμφανισμοῦ "the water of manifestation." In such a setting, the differences between the two interpretations of the verb root (Driver's *mry* or Brichto's *yrh*) are appreciably negligible. But more than this, as noted above, Philo *does* further modify the phrase ποτὸς ἐλέγχου. The ποτὸς ἐλέγχου, "the drink of *testing*," is the drink ὃ τὰ κεκρυμμένα νῦν καὶ ἀδηλούμενα ἀπαμφιάσει καὶ ἀπογυμνώσει "which will *reveal* and *make visible* those things now hidden and not perceived." Philo weds the two interpretations: "revelation" and "refuting."

AN ORAL AND WRITTEN TEST

But we have yet to see how this potable solution, this "water of contending," is utilized, or even its full list of ingredients. For that we must return to the progression of the ritual. Next, while the priest holds in his hand the vessel of water, he utters an enunciation, declaring how the procedure that is about to be utilized will reveal the guilt or innocence of the woman. These are his words as recorded in Numbers 5:19–22; the translation is that of the New Revised Standard Version with name of the elixir modified per the above discussion:

> "If no man has lain with you, if you have not turned aside to uncleanness while under your husband's authority, be immune to this <u>water of contending that brings a curse</u>. [20]But if you have gone astray while under your husband's authority, if you have defiled yourself and some man other than your husband has had intercourse with you"—[21]let the priest make the woman take the oath of the curse and say to the woman—"<u>may Yahweh</u> make you an execration and an oath among your people, when <u>Yahweh</u> makes your uterus drop, your womb discharge; [22]now may this water that brings the curse enter your bowels and make your womb discharge, your uterus drop!" And the woman shall say "Amen, Amen." (Numbers 5:19–22; modifications are underlined)

The reproductive morbidity that is specified in verses 21 and 22 of this NRSV translation, and which is again the subject of verse 27, is itself an interpretation—there being considerable uncertainty and variance of opinion regarding the intended sense of the Hebrew lexemes.[14] The pathological specifics need not concern us presently; suffice it to say that it is clear that there is an envisaged biological consequence of the actions of the Sotah who has been subjected to this rite.

What is perhaps the most remarkable aspect of this ancient Israelite juridical cult procedure manifests itself in the next sequential element of the procedural syntax. Having uttered these words, the priest then writes this same enunciation—denoted "the curse" (*hā'ālā*) in the Hebrew text—on some appropriate medium (ספר "document, book," etc., verse 23). Most translators of the Numbers passage infer the medium to be a scroll, and the Sotah (2.4) tractate of the Mishnah is explicit in naming the required material to be a scroll of parchment.[15] The Septuagint states that γράψει ὁ ἱερεὺς τὰς ἀρὰς ταύτας εἰς βιβλίον "the priest will write these curses into a book"; and Philo (*Spec.* 3.62) specifies ταῦτα γράψας ἐν χαρτιδίῳ "these things having been written in a little scroll." An interesting variation is recorded by Josephus (*Antiquitates Judaicae* 3.270–271), who states simply, and in seeming contradiction to the Mishnaic material specification, that the priest ἐπιγράφει μὲν τοῦ θεοῦ τὴν προσηγορίαν διφθέρᾳ "writes the name of God upon a piece of hide."

The preparation of the potable substance will now be completed. The priest takes the alphabetic expression of his utterance, his written product, and in some way washes off (MT מחה; "wipe (off); blot out"; cf. LXX ἐξαλείφω "to wash out") the letters into the vessel containing the water and tabernacle-dust solution, completing the preparation of *mê hammārîm hamᵉʾārᵉrîm* "waters of contending that bring a curse." The woman must then ingest this solution of dust and eviscerated letters (verses 24 and 26), the priest having taken from her the grain offering, which he waves before Yahweh, and a portion of which he burns on the altar.[16] If the woman has been unfaithful, her body will display the consequent pathologic expressions of her actions (verse 27); if, however, she is innocent, she will not experience the signaled reproductive morbidity and will be capable of bearing children (verse 28).

What exactly is the *modus operandi* in this most unusual ritual procedure? Briggs is certainly on target when in his recent study (2009:298) he draws attention to "the specific feature of the potion which characterizes the logic of Numbers 5," namely, "the fact that the priest writes the projected curses into a document (ספר, v. 23) and then blots or erases the writing into the potion." Briggs references Schniedewind (2004) on the observation: "As Schniedewind notes, writing is the key ingredient: 'The writing in the water gives the water a magical property. . . . The ritual testifies to the power and magic of written words' (Schniedewind 2004:28–29)."

Schniedewind's remarks are set in the context of a discussion of Egyptian execration texts, offered as an example of what he calls the "numinous power of writing"—among the earliest examples of such, he says (2004:27). The procedure that Schniedewind is referencing is the writing of curses on ceramic vessels or on figurines fabricated to resemble to a degree the person being cursed. The medium on which the curse was inscribed was then shattered in order to effect the curse: "The magical effect is not in the writing itself, but in the ritual breaking," he offers; "The Egyptian was destroyed in a ritual as the curses were recited over it." Schniedewind sees the Biblical rite of the Sotah as providing a parallel to the Egyptian procedure—and envisions that the Hebrew priest had probably written his curse on a sherd, from which it was washed into the water: "The magic water can discern whether the jealous husband is right in his accusation"; he continues: "The similarities between this ritual and the Egyptian rituals suggest that the ancient Israelites had notions of writing that they shared with their neighbors" (2004:29). This last-cited observation is likely accurate: Semitic-speaking peoples of southwest Asia did after all learn to write from the Egyptians (which is not necessarily to suggest that the Israelite rite had its diachronic origin in that distant moment in Canaanite orthographic history). It is less clear to me, however, that the ritual of Numbers 5 is operating on a par with Egyptian execration texts, or with comparable texts from elsewhere in the ancient Mediterranean world. Such maledictory texts are composed for the express end of bringing malevolence. The ritual of the Sotah is designed to reveal if the jealous husband is justified in his suspicions; reproductive morbidity is the signal of confirmation.

QUESTIONING MAGIC

Various swallowing spells are attested from ancient Egypt (see Ritner 1997:102–110 for an overview) and these provide closer analogues to the Israelite cult practice, though the anticipated outcome of the Egyptian practice appears to be an overwhelmingly beneficial one. Pyramid Text offering rituals entail the swallowing of various foods, solid and liquid, whereby there is a " 'consuming' of Horus" (Ritner 1997:103 with n.103). References to ritual swallowing are common in the Coffin Texts of the Middle Bronze Age, a period in which the presence in Egypt of Semitic-speaking peoples from southwest Asia is well evidenced:[17] for example, spell 341 is enunciated over seven drawn images of the Eyes of Horus, which are then "dissolved in beer and natron and drunk by a man" (Ritner 1997:104). Stelae portraying Horus subduing crocodiles and other beasts are known from the time of the Eighteenth Dynasty on into the Roman period (with Byzantine Christian vestiges). Such stelae can themselves be depicted as being held by statuary figures—statues inscribed with beneficent spells. These inscribed spells were not, it seems, meant primarily to be read, but to be swallowed; Ritner (1997:107) reports that "water poured over the stela or statue absorbed the efficacy of the spells and images and was subsequently drunk by the sufferer."

Treatments of magic in the Hebrew Bible have been quite popular in recent years. The interpretation of the juridical procedure of the Sotah as a rite of magic, of "Yahwistic magic" in fact, is pursued in detail in Miller (2010), a study in which the author holds that "the vast majority of scholars [have asserted] that the ritual has, at least in part, a magical character," (2010:4) providing what he calls "a sampling (!)" (2010:5, n. 15) of thirteen works, extending back to 1927, including the articles by Speiser and Frymer-Kensky mentioned above. The characterization, I would say, seems to be accurate in the case of the former, at least to the extent that Speiser contends for *mê hammārîm hamᵉāᵣᵣîm* being waters that are "spell-inducing" rather than "curse-inducing"; but one must remember Speiser's "equivocation" in his conclusion. The characterization is perhaps less appropriate in the case of Frymer-Kensky, who in her own closing remarks includes the statement, with "magical" in quotations (1984:25): "Purgatory oaths may consist of words alone; the words may also be accompanied by ritual, symbolic, or 'magical' actions which effectuate the oath." Drawing in typological evidence, Frymer-Kensky is here responding to the typifying of the Numbers 5 procedure as an example of "trial by ordeal," a concept widely invoked in commentaries on the passage—and also widely denounced. She writes:

> The ritual of the Sotah most closely resembles the classic purgatory oath, in which the individual swearing the oath puts himself under divine jurisdiction, expecting to be punished by God if the oath-taker is guilty. Num. v 11–31 describes a legal "curse" which functions as an oath once the woman has accepted the conditions of the curse by answering "Amen, amen." Conflation with trials by ordeal has resulted in unnecessary confusion about the mechanism and result of the Sotah procedure. The only feature of this procedure that is similar to ordeal trials is the drinking of a potion, which in form looks like the potion-ordeal known from Africa. . . . The drinking of a mystical potion actuates the words of the oath, for the potion is expected to punish the guilty party. The use of such an oath as a means of resolving the societal problem posed by suspicion of adultery is a uniquely Israelite institution. (Frymer-Kensky 1984:24–25)

That this particular author, Frymer-Kensky, is asserting a magical interpretation of this Israelite juridical rite is, I think, not at all clear. But equally unclear is how the drinking of the potion is envisioned to "actuate" the enunciation of the priest, the "legal 'curse' "— how it is that the potion of dust and letters innervates the punishment.

For Miller (2010:8–9), the enunciation of the priest, who invokes the name of Yahweh twice (2010:13), is "intended to harness cosmic energy" (or "Yahwistic energy" [2010:9 n. 36]) and direct that against the one for whom the words are destined. Miller (2010:9–10) takes explicit exception to the treatments of Blank (1950–51), Ashley (1993), and Milgrom (1990 and 1981) as typical of those who view a volitional God, Yahweh, as the sole agent of judgment; though one might note that Milgrom himself (1981:75) writes of the procedure as "an ordeal with its inherent magical and pagan elements," and Blank (1950–51:88) refers to its "primitive spell-like character."[18] Presumably Frymer-Kensky could be added to the company of Blank, Ashley, and Milgrom, in light of the remarks cited immediately above (among others, such as [1984:24]: "In the trial of the Sotah . . . the society has relinquished its control over the woman to God, who will indicate his judgment by punishing her if she is guilty"). Miller sees the written transcription of the enunciation as an incarnation of this "cosmic energy," which is transferred by washing the writing into the elixir, so that "the mixture is now magically charged" (2010:13). When the woman drinks the solution, she takes within herself the "cosmic energy"; the solution so energized is "introduced into her body in an attempt to counteract" another material previously introduced, if she has been unfaithful, namely the semen of her extramarital partner (2010:14). In Miller's view, in general contrast to that of other commentators, the ingested potion with its dust and ink would in any case make the ritual participant ill (2010:14–15); he interprets the cosmic energy-laden concoction as an abortive that lasers in on any issue of the suspected tryst, viewing a miscarriage as the consequent pathologic event. "The power of 'the bitter, curse-inducing water' is potential; it will be activated to cause miscarriage only if the woman is pregnant. The potion is to terminate its program if no wrongdoing (presumably, in the form of a zygote, an embryo, or a fetus) is discovered" (Miller 2010:16). Presumably as well, the captured "cosmic energy" is able to segregate potential targets—an unborn offspring engendered by the woman's husband from one contributed by a paramour. Visions of *Raiders of the Lost Ark* pyrotechnics spring to mind.

An addendum to Miller's list of scholars who view God as the effecting agent in the procedure of Numbers 5 would certainly be Rabbi Brichto, who characterizes the ritual as "untainted by magic" (1975:56), in spite of his endorsement of Speiser's rendering of *meʾārᵉrîm* as "spell-inducing' (by which, as noted above, he indicates agency; see p. 59, note k), and God as "judge and jury" (1975:64). Brichto further advocates that "the essential core of the procedure differs in no way from any oath or adjuration—it is an invocation of Deity to grant a sign of His verdict. In such cases sign and verdict coincide with punishment or its absence" (1975:64); and "The ultimate actor is God, the potion merely an instrument" (1975:65). He continues, bringing into focus what, I believe, moves us toward the heart of the matter:

> Magic is present when the ritual is automatic and impersonal in its effectiveness; when impersonal powers are compelled or deity coerced. Although the very notion of spell and fearsome potion have their roots in magical thinking, so too does sacrifice. And if the biblical understanding of an offering to God is not taken to be magical, then neither is such stricture to be applied to the potion, anymore—for that matter—than to the unbinding of the woman's hair. (1975:65)

I believe that it is clear at this point that what we are here dealing with is an anomalous feature of an ancient Israelite cult—one that scholars have struggled to make sense of. The anomaly perhaps arises from a disjunction between the diachronic and synchronic dimensions of the rite. And perhaps in the addressing of that disjunction a bit more light may be shed on the ritual event and its conceptualization.

THE PHYSICAL RESULT

As we have seen, one interpretation of the phrase *mê hammārîm* is "waters of revelation." In the *juridical context* of the ritual this equates to the Septuagint's τὸ ὕδωρ τοῦ ἐλεγμοῦ "the water of refuting." Philo seconds the sense with his relative clause modifying the denotation of the ritual drink—the ποτὸς ἐλέγχου "the drink of testing" ὃ τὰ κεκρυμμένα νῦν καὶ ἀδηλούμενα ἀπαμφιάσει καὶ ἀπογυμνώσει "which will *reveal* and *make visible* those things hidden and not perceived." The signaling potable solution is concocted of water (pure or sacred), tabernacle dust, and the dissolved visible, alphabetic signs of the priestly enunciation—utterance setting out what will be the inevitable expression of a wife's unsuspected fidelity or suspected, secret infidelity. The inscription of the priest is the visible expression of the priest's utterance—formulaic utterance of which Yahweh is the final author and which Moses transmits to the Israelites—utterance that, again, specifies the visible expression of the wife's status as hidden adulteress or not. With the completion of the ritual it is the wife's *body* that will become the visible *signal* of that status: an expression of no reproductive morbidity reveals her innocence; an expression of reproductive morbidity reveals her guilt.

What transpires between the priest's linguistic enunciation—coupled with its graphic, alphabetic recording—and the wife's parallel bodily enunciation of her fidelity, or lack thereof, is her ingesting of the alphabetic symbolization of the priestly enunciation, her internalization of a signaling event. Briggs and Schniedewind give overt acknowledgment to that which must have for millennia impressed readers of this ritual report—the conspicuousness and seeming novelty of the graphemic ingredient of the potable solution (as described above). What one sees in this ritual is a sequence of signaling events transferred from one domain to another. The primary event is a linguistic event, the priestly enunciation of a curse (*ʾālā*) in the arbitrary signaling system that we call the Hebrew language. The secondary event is a paralinguistic—even pseudolinguistic—event—a second-order signaling event—which, given the dictates of human conceptualizations of writing and language, is interpreted as equivalent to a linguistic event: the priest writes, that is, encodes, the curse in graphic form, utilizing conventionally designated (synchronically) arbitrary graphemic symbols—letters—to represent arbitrary phonemes of Hebrew.

The tertiary event is, I would suggest, a phenomenon of pseudo-writing—a third-order signaling event: the woman's body itself becomes a symbolic system, re-encoding the graphically recorded curse, which encodes the priest's enunciation. That enunciation will be rewritten in the flesh and blood of the suspected wife. But one must remember that there is of course still an additional signaling event—a super primary event—at work here: the entirety of the ritual description is an enunciation of Yahweh—Yahweh's words to Israel expressed via the agency of Moses. There is thus a sense in which the body of the woman is divine word made incarnate.

We must, I submit, allow for the possibility that the much-diagnosed ritual description of the reproductive morbidity that will come upon the wife who has been secretly unfaithful is intentionally, shall we say, fuzzy; in his commentary on Numbers, written more than a century ago, Gray (1903:53) already proposed that "it is doubtful whether any, and, if so, what particular disease is thought of." In the NRSV translation of verses 21–22 rehearsed above, that pathological pronouncement is interpreted as "make your womb discharge, your uterus drop" (as in v. 22; the two symptoms are presented in alternating [chiasmic] order in the two verses). Brichto (1975:60) translates as "to swell belly and shrivel pubis." Slightly less interpretative (that is, more componentially lexically equivalent to the Hebrew) is the translation of the KJV and the NIV: respectively, "thy abdomen to swell and thy thigh to rot"; and "your abdomen swells and your thigh wastes away." Somewhat similarly, the Jewish Study Bible has "the belly to distend and the thigh to sag." The body parts *beṭen* (בטן) "abdomen; uterus" (LXX κοιλία "abdominal cavity; belly" γαστήρ "belly; uterus") and *yārēk* (ירך) "thigh, loin" (LXX μηρός "thigh") may denote in the present context "uterus" and "pubis" respectively (anatomically relevant elements), as scholars have imagined. The verbal notions associated with the body parts *beṭen* and *yārēk* are those of *ṣābāh* (צבה) and *nāpal* (נפל) respectively. The former, *ṣābāh*, is typically identified with the post-Biblical Hebrew verb meaning "to swell"—hence, the "abdomen (etc.) swells"; the Septuagint uses πρήθω "to blow/swell out; to spout." The latter verb, *nāpal*, commonly conveys the sense "to fall, to fall down(ward)," and so "to go to ruin"; the translators of the Septuagint render the concept with διαπίπτω "to fall away/apart, to crumble; to burst (used, for example, of the bursting of bubbles in Aristotle's description of boiling water [*Problemata* 936b 5]); to perish," among yet other senses. The nuances of Hebrew *nāpal* are manifold and not uncommonly used figuratively, as of a word that Yahweh sends against Jacob, a word that *falls* upon Israel in Isaiah 9:8. The term finds expression in the enunciated oracle of the seer Balaam, as he speaks of one who hears the word of God, and one who consequently *falls down* to the ground (Numbers 24:4 and 16). In the enunciation of the priest in the ritual of the Sotah, an enunciation that will be given written form, and a written form that will be dissolved in the potable solution of the rite, the Sotah's *yārēk* "thigh," in whatever sense, is thus "to fall (apart)," "to go to ruin."

The verbal notions expressing the morbidity that will be displayed by the body of the secretly unfaithful wife, a signal of her infidelity to husband and community—notions of swelling and of breaking down—would just as aptly, perhaps more aptly in fact, describe the physical dissolution of the alphabetic expression of the priest's enunciation. When water is applied to the surface on which the utterance has been graphically transfixed, the alphabetic symbols swell, distending as the solvent is absorbed. This graphic bloating would be particularly pronounced if the symbols have been marked on an absorbent medium. As dissolution continues, the symbols break down and, perhaps literally, depending upon the ritual gestures, move *downward,* streaking from the medium into the ritual elixir. The use of *nāpal* to denote the downward movement of liquid is otherwise attested, as in blood dropping to the ground in 1 Samuel 26:20.

The body of the suspected wife becomes a symbolic system, a third-order signaling event, a derivative expression of language—the language of the priest, the language of Moses, preserving the words of Yahweh. In this ritual procedure, that language had previously received graphemic expression, a second-order signaling phenomenon. The trauma to which the alphabetic elements are subjected (*ṣābāh* and *nāpal*) will be replicated in the vitally involved biologic elements of the woman's body if she is an adulteress.

Transformations of Symbols

Is this sympathetic magic? In diachronic perspective, perhaps it is. The Israelite cult procedure as captured in the description of Numbers 5:11–31 is most likely descended from some earlier ritual practice, though one that presumably cannot antedate the use of graphic symbolic systems. In his study of *mê hammārîm* referenced above, Driver (1956:74) draws attention to an Akkadian text found in the royal archives of the Hittite capital of *Hattuša,* the modern Turkish village of Boğazköy. The Akkadian document preserves a rite which Driver characterizes as an "exorcism"—a procedure for driving away fever that entails administering to the patient a potable solution of donkey urine in which has been dissolved "clay from the library." Driver compares this clay to the dust from the tabernacle that is used to prepare the elixir of Numbers 5; he writes: "This will be fine clay, just as the dust 'from the floor of the tabernacle' will be clean, not having been trampled and fouled like that in the surrounding camp" (1956:74).

This is the extent of the comparison that Driver makes; but surely there is something of potentially greater significance here. The Akkadian phrase that he translates as "library" is *bīt ṭuppi,* literally "the house of the tablet," a documentary storehouse and a place for scribal education. Such a "library," of course, houses clay tablets: clay was the principal medium on which Akkadian cuneiform writing was executed. Given the ritual specification of the source of the clay that is to be mixed into donkey urine—clay from the *bīt ṭuppi*—one might well suspect that this is clay scraped or otherwise removed from a tablet, hence clay bearing the graphic symbols of the Akkadian cuneiform script. The two soluble materials of the Israelite potion, dust and alphabetic symbols, would thus jointly comprise an equivalent to the Akkadian ingredient, clay impressed with cuneiform graphemes.

But there is more here: Hebrew *'āpār* (the word we have been translating as "dust") is descended from an ancestral Semitic *'pr* meaning "loose earth, dirt."[19] This sense persists in Hebrew, but at times the term is used to denote "'soil with high clay content,' or maybe just 'clay.'" It is the material, for example, out of which Yahweh-'Elohim creates man—and so, indirectly, woman—in Genesis 2.[20]

The Akkadian procedure may have also left its imprint on the Israelite ritual in the latter's cultic lexical selection. The use of Hebrew *nāpal* to denote the trauma experienced by the *yārēk* "thigh" of the Sotah is perhaps not the most natural of word choices, though if I am right in seeing the vocabulary as reflecting the action of water on inscribed alphabetic symbols, the awkwardness is ameliorated somewhat. Perhaps, however, *nāpal* would likewise not be the most natural of terms for describing the undoing of the graphemes. Hebrew *nāpal* "to fall, to fall down(ward)" has a cognate in Akkadian *napālu* (Greenfield 2001:2:665–667; von Soden 1965–1981:2, 733), meaning "to tear down, demolish" but also "to dig out," as of a dog digging out dust and of digging clay out of a clay pit (CAD 11.1:272–274), and the verb can itself mean (D-stem *nuppulu*) "to kick up dust" (and also "to gouge out, to maim"). Would *napālu* be an appropriate verb to describe the act of digging out the dried clay of a tablet, making a dust to be added to a ritual solution? Seemingly so. And if so, then the Hebrew lexical choice of *nāpal* in Numbers 5 may continue a Semitic magical rite having its origin in a setting in which clay, rather than parchment, was the principal medium for writing.[21] In this regard, the use of Greek διαπίπτω for Hebrew *nāpal* in the Septuagint is remarkably uncanny: among the nuances of the Greek verb is the sense "to crumble" as, for example, in Aristotle's use of διαπίπτω to describe how parched earth falls apart with heavy rain (*Meterologica* 365 b 11).

Such is the diachronic view. If Ferdinand de Saussure taught us anything (and he taught us many things), he showed us that while the diachronic axis and the synchronic axis of structural systems intersect, diachrony and synchrony are discrete and separate phenomena.[22] What is the synchronic Israelite *conceptualization* of the act of transferring the priestly enunciation via alphabetic symbols into the interior of the suspected adulteress? Also one of sympathetic magic? I think not. In my judgment magic—from a synchronic perspective—is what is conceptualized as operating outside of the confines of cult in the Hebrew Bible,[23] as, *mutatis mutandis,* in the New Testament, where apostolic authority substitutes largely for cult.[24] This is in effect the point made by Brichto (1975:65), though worded differently, when he writes, as noted above: "The ultimate actor is God, the potion merely an instrument. Magic is present when the ritual is automatic and impersonal in its effectiveness; when impersonal powers are compelled or deity coerced." What then is the synchronic conceptualization of the bloating and tearing down of these alphabetic symbols? I submit that it must be conceptualized as sacrifice. In one sense—what else could it be within the parameters of Israelite cult?

A Sacrifice of Alphabetic Symbols

The sacrifice of alphabetic symbols admittedly does not fit neatly into the typology of Israelite sacrifice: but regardless of what interpretation one assigns to the cult act, it is an anomalous act; and the typology of sacrifice in ancient Israel is itself not very neat. As Walter Eichrodt noted, now fifty years ago, regarding acts of sacrificial worship (1961:1, 141): the Hebrew Bible "nowhere gives us a direct exposition of the meaning of this worship; it is possible to arrive at various conclusions *a posteriori,* but never with more than a certain degree of probability." Brichto himself, perhaps unwittingly, links the potable solution of Numbers 5 with sacrifice when he observes, as, again, previously noted: "Although the very notion of spell and fearsome potion have their roots in magical thinking, so too does sacrifice. And if the biblical understanding of an offering to God is not taken to be magical, then neither is such stricture to be applied to the potion." In Josephus's description of the ritual, it is worth noting, he treats it together with other Mosaic procedures and identifies the set as matters περὶ μὲν τῶν θυσιῶν καὶ τῆς ἀγνείας τῆς ἐπ᾽αὐταῖς "that concern the sacrifices and the religious observance related to them" (*Antiquitates Judaicae* 3. 273).

The conceptualization of letters bled of life as sacrifice is consistent with fundamental notions of sacrifice among ancient Israelites. Worshipers offer those consumable biological commodities to God, animal and plant, that they receive from God, reminding themselves of that dependency; thus, Eichrodt observes (1961:1, 144), "it is for this reason that their gifts to him take the form of the necessities of life." More generally along these lines, he writes (1961:154): "Sacrifice . . . represents not only the gifts of man to God, but also the gifts of God to man. It is the concept of sacral communion which makes the sacrifice into a true sacrament." The letters that are sacrificed for the juridical procedure of the Sotah are undoubtedly not perceived to be the second-order signaling system that they are, but are perceived to be the first-order signaling system that they graphically encode—language—words. They are the received words of Yahweh, transmitted to Israel through the agency of Moses, enunciated by a priest. And it is abundantly clear in Biblical tradition that the words of Yahweh are deemed to be a necessity of life for the community of Israel. Yahweh made the desert-wandering Israelites hungry and then fed then with manna from heaven, as Moses is presented as reporting in his farewell address to the people (Deuteronomy 8. 3–4): "in order to make you understand that one does not live by bread alone, but by every word that comes from the mouth of the Lord" (NRSV). The priestly words of Numbers 5, words come from Yahweh, are in turn sacrificed, offered back to Yahweh as it were, in a procedure of divine and civic communion through which the community comes to grips with uncertainty surrounding secret unsanctioned behaviors within its midst; revelation is provided by the body of the woman, speaking that which her own words cannot speak with conviction—her innocence, or her guilt. It is she who becomes the mouthpiece of Yahweh, as he speaks again, as his words come once more, through her body, to the community.

Conclusions

The offering of alphabetic characters to a supreme deity is not otherwise unattested in the ancient Mediterranean world. From Mount Hymettos in Attica come sherds dedicated to Zeus, dated from ca. 700 to the early fifth century B.C.E. These sherds are inscribed with abecedaria or with declarations of the act of producing alphabetic symbols; the recipient of the Hymettos votive materials is characterized as *Zeus Semios*, Zeus "of the sign."[25] Some of those inscriptions that encode the act of inscribing bear the lone word εγραφσε "he wrote" or εγραφσα "I wrote." Others give voice to more complex offertory phrases, such as [το Δι]ος ειμι. [————]ας δε μ᾽ εγραφ[σε]ν I belong to Zeus. X wrote me."[26] The sense of the epithet *Zeus Semios* is fundamentally grounded in the sign that Zeus provides as wielder of the thunderbolt. Signs are deemed an appropriate offering—sacrifice—to be given to Zeus, the god who himself gives the sign to humankind. It is a sacrificial act of reciprocal "communing."

The invoking of the Attic phenomenon is not intended to suggest any historical connection between these Greek and Israelite cult practices. But the typological correspondence of making offerings of graphic signs—undoubtedly conceptualized to be linguistic signs by those producing the symbols—to a sovereign deity who is himself the giver of signs, set within fairly narrowly delimited contexts of geography, time, and orthography demands our attention. Signs are offered to Zeus Semios; signs are offered to Yahweh. Alphabetic signs are victims fit for the deity.

Notes

1. See, for example, Gray 1903:48–49 and Brewer 1913, with references to earlier work.

2. See Brichto 1975:55–56, 63–68; compare Fishbane 1974:28–39; Milgrom 1981; Frymer-Kensky 1984:12–18.

3. Again, the procedure is presented as Mosaic instruction (Numbers 5.11). Regarding its dating, Sasson (1972:249) writes: "The narrative has usually been assigned to P [the Priestly stratum of tradition], but in view of comparative Near Eastern data dealing with ordeals, it certainly reflects a tradition deeply embedded in the past." He here footnotes (249n2) Mesopotamian river ordeals. On the notion of the rite as "ordeal," see below.

4. Or "loosens her hair," as in Sasson 1972:250; Brichto 1975:58. See Sasson's note 9 on the act.

5. See, inter alia, Sasson 1972; Driver 1956; Brichto 1975. See especially the summary remarks of Frymer-Kensky 1984:25–26.

6. Greek glosses that appear herein are those of Liddell, Scott, Jones, and McKenzie 1996, though with occasional modification. Unless specified otherwise, Hebrew glosses are drawn from Brown, Driver, and Briggs 1907.

7. On which, see Field 1964:1, 331.

8. See ibid., 1, 231.

9. For a rather different interpretation of *mê hammārîm hamᵉārᵉrîm* from that one espoused herein, see Sasson 1972. Sasson identifies a West Semitic root *mrr* meaning "to bless" and proposes that (p. 250) "the phrase . . . should be considered as a *merismus,* consisting of 'waters that bless' and 'waters that curse,' hence 'waters of judgment'" (250). See the comments of Frymer-Kensky 1984:25–26, reflecting Sasson's own observations (251) regarding a difficulty posed by the approach. In any event, Sasson's final semantic analysis is not far removed from others presented below.

10. Regarding the solution that is characterized as *mᵉārᵉrîm,* Speiser writes (199): "The potion is utilized as an agent 'that implements the spell/ordeal,' which is exactly how it is described."

11. And see Brichto 1975:58–59.

12. See Büchsel 1976:448.

13. John Huehnergard (personal communication 2011) observes: "The derivation of *mārîm* from the root *yrh* is quite problematic; nouns with preformative *m-* from roots with first radical *y* (usually **w* originally, as is true of the root *yrh,* originally *wrw*) rarely, if ever,

have *mā-* in the first syllable; normally in such derived nouns the first syllable has *mô-*, as in *môšab* 'dwelling' (originally **mawšab*; root *w/yšb*), *môrā²* 'fear' (originally **mawra²*; root *w/yr²*), less often *mû-*, as in *mûsar* 'instruction' (**muwsar*; root *w/ysr*), or *mê-* or *mî-*, as in *mêšar* 'uprightness,' *mîšôr* 'plain' (< **mayšar*, **miyšār*, resp.; root *yšr*), but, not *mā-.* So it is highly unlikely that *mārîm* is derived from *yrh.*"

14. See, inter alia, Frymer-Kensky 1984:18–21 (especially 19n15, with a summary of various earlier interpretations); Brichto 1975:62, 66; Sasson 1972:250–251; Driver 1956:74–76; Miller 2010:14, 16.

15. See, for example, the summarizing comments of Destro 1989:6: "The drawing up of the text follows extremely rigid rules: it cannot be written on wood, skin or papyrus, but on a scroll of parchment. Rubber cannot be used nor copper vitriol; only ink is permitted because it must be 'blotted out' (Sot. 2:4)."

16. On the grain offering, see, inter alia, Frymer-Kensky 1984:14–16; Sasson 1972:249n4. On grain offerings generally in Israelite cult, see, inter alia, Preuss 1996:242; von Rad 1962: 1:256–257.

17. The author is indebted to Mary-Ann Pouls Wegner for kindly bringing these materials to his attention and for her guidance with Egyptian matters.

18. Adopting Milgrom's phrasing, Miller contends that (p. 9, n. 36) "to make a distinction between the 'inherent magical powers of the water' and 'the sovereign will of God' is to miss the point; it is Yahwistic energy that gives the water its magical power."

19. For discussion, see Wächter 2001:257–265.

20. P. Kyle McCarter (source of the citation); personal communication. The author expresses his appreciation to Prof. McCarter for reminding him of the semantic range of Hebrew *ʿāpār.*

21. In his discussion of the rite, Fishbane (1974) adduces Akkadian materials, quite different from that referenced herein. Contra Fishbane, see Frymer-Kensky 1984: 17n11.

22. See Saussure 1995, especially 141–260; 2006 *passim.*

23. The practice of magic is strictly prohibited by the injunctions of Deuteronomy 18:9–12. See also, inter alia, Leviticus 19:31; 1 Samuel 15:23; 28; Isaiah 47:9.

24. See Acts 8:9–25.

25. See Langdon 1976:17–21.

26. H 223, H 215, H 181. See Langdon 1976:20.

References Cited

Ashley, T. 1993 *The Book of Numbers.* Eerdmans, Grand Rapids.

Blank, S. H. 1950–51 The Curse, Blasphemy, the Spell, and the Oath. *Hebrew Union College Annual* 23:73–95.

Botterweck, G. J., H. Ringgren, and H.-J. Fabry (editors) 2001 *Theological Dictionary of the Old Testament.* Translated by D. E. Green. Volume 11. Eerdmans, Grand Rapids.

Brewer, J. A. 1913 The Ordeal in Num., Chap. 5. *The American Journal of Semitic Languages and Literatures* 30: 36–47.

Brichto, H. C. 1968 *The Problem of Curse in the Hebrew Bible.* Society of Biblical Literature, Philadelphia.

Brichto, H. C. 1975 The Case of the *Sōṭā* and a Reconsideration of Biblical "Law." *Hebrew Union College Annual* 46:55–70.

Briggs, R. S. 2009 Reading the Sotah Text (Numbers 5:11–31): Holiness and a Hermeneutic Fit for Suspicion. *Biblical Interpretation* 17:288–319.

Brockelmann, C. 1908–1913 *Grundriss der vergleichenden Grammatik der semitischen Sprachen.* Two volumes. Reuther and Reichard, Berlin.

Brown, F., S. R. Driver, and C. A. Briggs 1907 *A Hebrew and English Lexicon of the Old Testament.* Oxford University Press, Oxford.

Büchsel, F. 1976 "ἀρά." In *Theological Dictionary of the New Testament,* edited by G. Kittel, translated by G. W. Bromiley. Volume 1, pp. 448–451. Seventh printing. Eerdmans, Grand Rapids.

Destro, A. 1989 *The Law of Jealousy: Anthropology of Sotah.* Scholars Press, Atlanta.

Driver, G. R. 1956 Two Problems in the Old Testament Examined in the Light of Assyriology. *Syria* 33:70–78.

Eichrodt, W. 1961. *Theology of the Old Testament.* Two volumes. Translated by J. A. Baker. Westminster Press, Philadelphia.

Field, F. 1964 *Origenis Hexaplorum Quae Supersunt, Sive Veterum Interpretum Graecorum in Totum Vetus Testamentum Fragmenta.* Two Volumes. Georg Olms Verlag, Hildesheim.

Fishbane, M. 1974 Accusations of Adultery: A Study of Law and Scribal Practice in Numbers 5:11–31. *Hebrew Union College Annual* 45:25–45.

Friedman, R. E. (editor) 1981 *The Creation of Sacred Literature: Composition and Redaction of the Biblical Text.* University of California Press, Berkeley and Los Angeles.

Frymer-Kensky, T. 1984 The Strange Case of the Suspected Sotah (Numbers V 11–31). *Vetus Testamentum* 34:11–26.

Gray, G. B. 1903 *A Critical and Exegetical Commentary on Numbers.* The International Critical Commentary. Scribner, New York.

Greenfield, J. C. 2001 *Al Kanfei Yonah: Collected Studies of Jonas C. Greenfield on Semitic Philology.* Two Volumes. Edited by P. Shalom, M. E. Stone, and A. Pinnick. Brill, Leiden.

Kittel, G. (editor) 1976 *Theological Dictionary of the New Testament.* Translated by G. W. Bromiley. Volume 1. Seventh printing. Eerdmans, Grand Rapids.

Langdon, M. K. 1976 *A Sanctuary of Zeus on Mt. Hymettos.* Hesperia Supplement 16. Athens.

Liddell, H. G., R. Scott, H. S. Jones, and R. McKenzie 1996 *A Greek-English Lexicon.* Oxford University Press, Oxford.

Milgrom, J. 1981 The Case of the Suspected Adulteress, Numbers 5:11–31: Redaction and Meaning. In *The Creation of Sacred Literature: Composition and Redaction of the Biblical Text,* edited by R. E. Friedman, pp. 69–75. University of California Press, Berkeley and Los Angeles.

Milgrom, J. 1990 *The JPS Torah Commentary: Numbers.* Jewish Publication Society, Philadelphia.

Miller, D. 2010 Another Look at the Magical Ritual for a Suspected Adulteress in Numbers 5:11–31. *Magic, Ritual, and Witchcraft* 5:1–16.

Preuss, H. D. 1996 *Old Testament Theology.* Volume 2. Translated by L. G. Perdue. Westminster John Knox, Louisville.

Ritner, R. 1997 *The Mechanics of Ancient Egyptian Magical Practice.* Studies in Ancient Oriental Civilizations. Third printing. Oriental Institute of the University of Chicago, Chicago.

Sasson, J. 1972 Numbers 5 and the "Waters of Judgment." *Biblische Zeitschrift* 16: 249–251.

Saussure, F. de 1995 *Cours de linguistique général.* Payot, Paris.

Saussure, F. de 2006 *Writings in General Linguistics.* Translated by Carol Sanders and Matthew Pires, with the assistance of Peter Figueroa. Oxford University Press, Oxford.

Schniedewind, W. M. 2004 *How the Bible Became a Book: The Textualization of Ancient Israel.* Cambridge University Press, Cambridge.

Speiser, E. A. 1960 An Angelic "Curse": Exodus 14:20. *Journal of the American Oriental Society* 80:198–200.

von Rad, G. 1962 *Old Testament Theology. Old Testament Library*. Two volumes. Translated by D. M. G. Stalker. Westminster John Knox, Louisville.

von Soden, W. 1965–1985 *Akkadisches Handwörterbuch*. Otto Harrassowitz, Wiesbaden.

Wächter, L. 2001 *ʿāpār*. In *Theological Dictionary of the Old Testament*, edited by G.J. Botterweck, H. Ringgren, and H.-J. Fabry, translated by D. E. Green. Volume 11. pp. 257–265. Eerdmans, Grand Rapids.

CHAPTER THIRTEEN

Ancient Greek Laws on Sacrifice

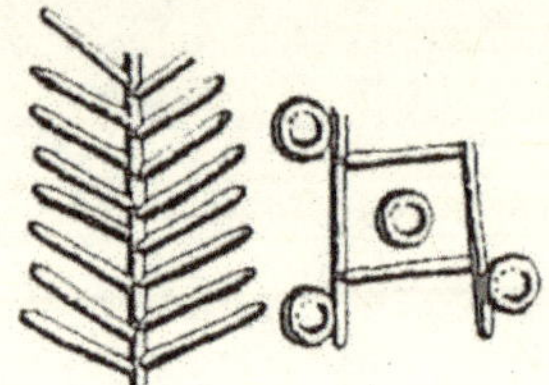

Michael Gagarin

Abstract   *This paper presents a sample of ancient Greek laws on sacrifice. With one exception, they all concern public sacrifice; private sacrifice was rarely regulated by law. Many of these laws are sacrificial calendars—lists of sacrifices to be conducted by a city or other public body. These usually state the date, the animal victim that is to be sacrificed, and the god or hero to whom it is sacrificed. Some also list the cost of victims or other details. The reasons for enacting this legislation were both religious—to ensure that traditional sacrifices were conducted when they were supposed to be—and financial—to authorize the expenditure of public funds and by publishing this authorization help ensure that sufficient funds would be available to conduct all the necessary sacrifices.*

Greek laws that mention sacrifice are far too numerous to treat in detail in a single paper, so I have selected just a few documents that are typical or otherwise informative. These take the form of texts inscribed on stone and displayed in public spaces in Greek cities from the seventh to the fourth centuries B.C.E. I am not aware of any significant literary evidence pertaining to the legal regulation of sacrifice.

PRIVATE SACRIFICE

Sacrifice in Greece could be private or public. Private sacrifices were generally carried out by individuals or small groups of relatives (Rosivach 1994:9–10), who offered something to a god or semi-divine hero or ancestor—a lock of hair, a small cake, a libation of wine, a small animal, almost anything would suffice. The purpose of private sacrifice was commonly to give thanks (after recovery from disease, after childbirth, etc.) or to ask for help and support (for example, before going off to war). Socrates's last words in the *Phaedo* (118a) as he is succumbing to the effects of the hemlock are: "Crito, we owe a cock to Asclepius; please pay it." Socrates intends the cock as a token of thanks to the god of healing for curing him of the sickness of life, and freeing his soul from the weight of his body.

Literature offers other examples of private sacrifices, but only rarely do laws say anything about them. Regulations pertaining to a particular altar or sanctuary may specify who can carry out a private sacrifice, or when or what they may sacrifice, or may prescribe a certain payment to the priest, as in *SEG* 35.923.1–12 (Chios, ca. 400 B.C.E.; see Lupu 2005:303–315). Such regulations are usually enacted or sanctioned by some public authority and can thus be considered to have the force of law. We may perhaps also include decrees set up by the founder of a new altar or sanctuary, who sets conditions for someone who wishes to sacrifice there, and decrees establishing private foundations or associations, which may mention an occasion, usually annual, when the foundation would perform a sacrifice. These may be examples of laws regulating private sacrifices, but in almost all cases sacrifice is a very minor part of the activity regulated by the decree. The 44 lines of *SEG* 31.122, for example, giving regulations for an Athenian *eranos* ("friends") association in the second century C.E. devote just over one line to providing for the annual sacrifice of a boar (Lupu 2005:177–190). Private sacrifice is left up to private individuals.

There is one extraordinary legal document, however, that contains a number of references to private sacrifice: an inscription from the city of Cyrene, probably from the late fourth century B.C.E. (*SEG* 9.72, Appendix 1). The inscription is a decree containing rules for purification that allegedly came from Apollo. Parts of it are quite fragmentary and it presents many problems of text and interpretation which I do not intend to discuss. But several sections mention a type of private sacrifice, sacrifice as part of purification.[1]

A

3. Coming from a woman a man, if he has slept with her by night, will sacrifice [wherever? whatever?] he wishes.

6. If he sacrifices upon the altar a victim which it is not customary to sacrifice, let him remove the remaining fat (?) from the altar and wash it off and remove the other filth from the shrine and take away the ashes (?) from the altar and the fire to a pure spot, and then let him wash himself, purify the shrine, sacrifice a full grown animal as penalty, and then let him sacrifice as is customary.

8. If a grown man is subject to a tithe, having purified himself with blood, he shall purify the shrine; after being sold in the market-place for the most that he is worth, he shall first sacrifice as a penalty before the tithe a fully grown victim, not from the tithe, and then he shall sacrifice the tithe and carry it away to a pure spot; otherwise, the same measures will be necessary. Everyone who sacrifices shall bring a vessel. If a boy is polluted unwillingly, it is sufficient for him to purify himself and a penalty is not necessary. If he is polluted willingly, he shall purify the shrine and sacrifice first as a penalty a fully grown victim.

9. If property is subject to a tithe, he (the owner) shall assess the value of the property, purify the shrine and the property separately, and then sacrifice first as a penalty a fully grown victim,

not from the tithe, and then sacrifice the tithe and carry it away to a pure spot. Otherwise, the same measures will be necessary. From the property, as long as it is subject to a tithe, no one shall make funerary offerings nor shall he bring libations until he pays the tithe to the god. If he brings libations or makes funerary offerings, after cleansing the temple of Apollo he shall first sacrifice as a penalty, according to his offense, a fully grown victim.

10. If a man subject to a tithe dies, after they bury the man he (the heir?) shall place whatever he likes on the tomb on the first day, but nothing subsequent to that, until he pays the tithe to the god, and he shall not sacrifice nor go to the tomb. They shall assess him (the dead man) for the most that he was worth, being a partner to the god. After purifying the temple of Apollo and the property separately, he (the heir) having first sacrificed as a penalty a fully grown victim not from the tithe, in front of the altar, shall sacrifice the tithe in front of the altar and carry it away to a pure spot. Otherwise, the same measures will be necessary.

11. If a man subject to a tithe dies and of the children who are left some live and some die, having assessed the [dead children?] for the most that they are worth he (the heir) shall purify the temple of Apollo and the property separately, shall sacrifice the penalty of the grown man before the altar, and then sacrifice the tithe before the altar. As for the living descendant, having purified himself he shall purify the shrine separately; after being sold in the market place, shall sacrifice the penalty of the grown man, a fully grown animal, and then he shall sacrifice the tithe and carry it away to a pure spot. Otherwise, the same measures will be necessary.

B

1. Any woman who, without doing this, voluntarily incurs pollution, after purifying the temple of Artemis shall sacrifice in addition as a penalty a fully grown animal, and then shall go to the sleeping chamber.

2. A bride must go down to the bride-room to Artemis, whenever she wishes at the Artemisia, but the sooner the better. Any woman who does not go down [shall sacrifice in addition?] to Artemis [what is customary at the Artemesia]; not having gone down, [she shall purify the shrine] and sacrifice in addition [a full grown animal as penalty].

3. But if she incurs pollution, she shall purify herself, purify the shrine, and sacrifice in addition as penalty a full grown animal.

6. Second suppliant, initiated or not initiated, having taken his seat at a public shrine. If an injunction is made, let him be initiated at whatever price is enjoined. If an injunction is not made, let him sacrifice fruits of the earth and a libation annually forever. But if he omits it (?), twice as much next year. If a child forgets and omits it, and an injunction is made to him, he shall pay to the god whatever is told him when he consults the oracle, and sacrifice, if he knows (where it is) on the ancestral tomb, and if not, consult the oracle. (translation by Parker [1983:333–349])

Despite many obscurities, it is clear that the decree prescribes sacrifices as part of purification. The text mentions several polluting acts for which sacrifice is part of the purification: A3 sexual intercourse but only at night, A6 sacrificing an inappropriate victim, A8–11 death (apparently), A8 masturbation (apparently), B1–2 before and after marriage (apparently), B3 childbirth, and B6 something connected with supplication. Some of these events, such as childbirth, are well known to require ritual purification throughout most of the Greek world, but others, such as not visiting the bride-room at the temple of Artemis, are only found here. In either case the law is anomalous, both because sacrifice is seldom required as part of purification, and because private purification is generally dictated by custom, not law, which generally concerns itself with public sacrifices.

PUBLIC SACRIFICE

Public sacrifices were conducted by the city or other public or quasi-public body on many occasions, sometimes in connection with a specific event such as a battle or the harvest, when (like private sacrifice) they could precede the event, seeking the god's favor, or follow it as an act of thanksgiving. But sacrifices directed at specific events are rarely mentioned in laws, which deal almost exclusively with recurring sacrifices often in connection with a civic festival. Animal sacrifices during festivals were very common in Greece, nowhere more so than in Athens, which according to the Old Oligarch ([Xenophon], *Ath. Pol.* 3.8) had more than twice as many as any other city. And most, if not all, of these were in some way regulated by laws, which are found throughout the Greek world beginning with the earliest public inscriptions in the late seventh century.

Perhaps the earliest sacred calendar is from Dreros, from the second half of the seventh century (Van Effenterre 1946:603–604, Appendix 2): ". . . in the Pythion five? . . . in the Agoraion thighs . . ." (translation by author). No dates are given for these sacrifices, although dates may well have been given in parts of the text now lost, but the law is unusual in two ways: instead of the kind of victim, it lists a part of the victim (the thigh), and instead of the name of the god it lists a place, the god's temple or sanctuary. One hesitates to speculate on the basis of such scanty evidence, but it appears that when laws first began to be written down, no standard format had yet developed for listing sacrifices. But the text does show the importance cities attached from the beginning to regulating sacrifices.

In two slightly later fragments, from the first half of the sixth century B.C.E., a more standard pattern begins to emerge. In a fragment from Corinth (*IG* 4.1597, Lupu 2005:65–66, Appendix 3) all that remains is a month and the victims ("In the month Phoinikaios . . . four piglets . . ." [translation by author]). No god is named, though the original text would either have contained the god's name or would have left it to readers to infer that because the inscription was located near or next to the temple of Apollo, he was the recipient of the sacrifice. Another fragment, from Gortyn in Crete (*ICret* 4.3, Appendix 4), contains the three essential elements of most sacrificial calendars—date, victim, and divine recipient:

1 (These) sacred rites have been performed . . . in the month Welkanios . . . on the fifth day

2 . . . a grown (bull?) and a goat on (the? day?), a ewe to Apollo . . . a bull

3 . . . to Hera a ewe, to Demeter a pregnant ewe

4 . . . the two females but the two males and a goat (?) (translation by author)

The text lists the victims and divine recipients of the sacrifices according to the month and the day within that month (line 1 and probably other lines too). This is the standard date format and scholars assume that the sacrifice is to be performed annually on that date.

In addition to annual sacrifices, others were conducted biennially and even quadrennially, and in fact the best-preserved fragment of what is perhaps the most famous Greek sacrificial calendar lists biennial sacrifices. This is the calendar that the Athenian board of Inscribers (*Anagrapheis*) compiled at the end of the fifth century, when the Athenians charged them with reinscribing all the city's laws that were still valid (Andocides 1.82–85). Most of the surviving fragments of this reinscription come from the large calendar of sacrifices compiled and inscribed in 403–399. It is the subject of Lysias's speech *Against Nicomachus* (30), in which the unknown speaker accuses one member of this board, Nicomachus, of taking too long to complete his task and of including too many sacrifices, at too great a cost, in the published calendar. To judge from the surviving fragments, the calendar appears to have been very extensive. Two columns of the longest fragment are fairly well preserved (Oliver and Dow 1935:21, Appendix 5):

The following sacrifices are made every other year [by the Athenians?]

		In Hekatombaion	60	12dr.	to Themis a sheep
		on the fifteenth		15dr.	to Zeus of the forecourt a sheep
		from the Tribe-		12dr.	to Demeter a sheep
		kings' (laws)			to Pherrephatta
35		for the tribe of the Leontes,		17dr.	a ram
		for the Leukotanians'	65	15dr.	to Eumolpos a sheep
		trittys, a sheep		15dr.	to Delichos the hero [a sheep]
	4dr.	without a mark.		15dr.	to Archegetes [a sheep]
	4dr.2ob.	the priestly perquisite		15dr.	to Polyxen[os a sheep]
40		for the Tribe kings			to Thereptos [a ram]
	1dr.	the back.	70	17dr.	of select quality
		for the herald the shoulder,		15dr.	to Dioklo[s a sheep]
	4ob.	feet, head.		15dr.	to Keleos [a sheep].
		On the sixteenth			The Eumolpidae
45		from the Tribe-			[make] these [sacrifices]
		kings' (laws)	75		for the priestess [of Demeter].
		for the tribe of the Leontes,		100dr.	Fees for priests.
		for Zeus of the brotherhood and			From the [stelai?]
		Athena of the		3dr.	a young pig [-]
50		brotherhood, two oxen		12dr.	to Hesti[a a sheep]
	50dr.	without a mark.	80	12dr.	to Athen[a a sheep]
	16dr.	the priestly perquisite		10dr.	to the Gr[aces —]
		for the Tribe kings			[a sheep] to Her[mes]
		the leg.		15dr.	[a sheep]
55		for the herald the chest,		10dr.	———
	2dr.3ob.	feet, head.	85	15dr.	to He[phaistos a sheep]
		for the rearer (of the animals),		15dr.	to D[ionysos a sheep]
		bushels? of barley.			———
		———			

(translation by author)

The heading indicates that these columns contain only the biennial sacrifices; the annual sacrifices, which were certainly more numerous, probably came at the beginning of the calendar, and there was probably also a list of the quadrennial sacrifices and perhaps others at the end. At the top of the first column is Hekatombaion, the first month of the Athenian year. Then we have the day, the fifteenth, and twelve lines later another day, the sixteenth. At the bottom, the column would have continued for an unknown distance, so the next column may represent another day or even another month.

The calendar is clear and well organized. The date is followed by "from (ek) the Tribe-kings,'" an odd expression that is paralleled by "from the [stelai?]" in the next column (line 77). It used to be thought that these "ek-rubrics" indicated the source of funds, but Dow (1953–57:15–21) argued convincingly that they refer to the sources from which Nicomachus drew these laws. His task was to examine all the laws of the city, discard those that were no longer valid, and reinscribe together all those that were still valid. Dow plausibly argues that Nicomachus was protecting himself against critics like Lysias's client who claimed Nicomachus was including too many sacrifices. By citing his sources, Nicomachus was documenting the authenticity of each sacrifice.

After the ek-rubric come the names of the tribe and trittys (a unit of three demes or precincts) who will perform the sacrifice and receive the meat, and finally the victim, a sheep followed by the portion of the animal that will be given to the Tribe kings and the herald after the sacrifice. The rules for the sixteenth day are similar, at least up to the point where the stone breaks off. Column 2 is mostly a long list of sacrifices, presumably all from the same day since there is no mention of a new day; the month (and day) may or may not be the same as in column 1.

In both columns costs are listed to the left, and there is evidence elsewhere in the fragment that at the end of each month came the total expenditure for that month. It is impossible to do more than guess at the total cost of all the sacrifices for Athens, but we should note that most of the sacrifices are of single victims. This was characteristic of Athenian traditional sacrifices such as those on Nicomachus's calendar. Another group of "additional sacrifices" involved many more animals, cost many thousands of drachmas each, and would have provided meat for much of the population on perhaps 40–45 occasions each year (Rosivach 1994:46–67).

On two occasions in column 1, Nicomachus's calendar provides for the distribution of parts of the victim to the tribe kings and the herald. This is a common type of regulation: for example an early fifth-century law in Axos on Crete (*ICret* II.v.9.3–9, Appendix 6) states, "As for the priests, whatever they carry off contrary to what is written, unless someone himself should give (it to them) willingly, let him pay a fine of one stater for each sacrifice and twice (the value) of meat" (translation by author). The law makes clear the public interest in regulating not only the sacrifice but also the distribution of meat from it.

Finally, an example of a calendar of annual sacrifices is the decree of the Salaminioi, a large, well-preserved decree set up in the Athenian agora in 363/2 B.C.E. that records an arbitration settlement between two factions within the *genos* or clan of the Salaminioi— those from Heptaphylai and those from Sounion (*SEG* 21.527, Appendix 7).[2] We know very little about this group, but membership was apparently based to a large extent on ancestry, though tribal affiliation also played a role. The group's functions were mainly social and religious: it administered cults and performed sacrifices. The decree opens in typical fashion with the name of the Athenian archon, followed by the names of the five arbitrators and then the terms of the settlement, most of which concern sacrifices. These are divided into two kinds (lines 20–27):

> Such victims as the polis furnishes from the treasury or as the Salaminioi happen to receive from the *oschophoroi* or the *deipnophoroi*, these both parties shall sacrifice in common and each shall receive half of the flesh raw. Such victims, on the other hand, as the Salaminioi were wont to sacrifice from rentals, they shall sacrifice from their own funds according to their ancient custom, each party contributing half for all the sacrifices. (translation by Ferguson [1938:6])

In other words, the Salaminioi conducted sacrifices with victims provided by the city or by certain groups of individuals, and they also owned property from which they derived income, which paid for a number of sacrifices conducted according to tradition (see Rosivach 1994:40–45). This dual role, performing sacrifices from city funds as well as from their own funds, was unusual and perhaps unique in the Greek world. Not surprisingly, the first group of sacrifices occasioned no dispute: neither party had to pay for them and each received half of the meat. The second group required funding, however, and this was clearly the source of the dispute. This is clear from the preamble to the decree, which was agreed to by both parties, which states its purpose at the end (84–85): "that the archons . . . may know the amount of money each party must contribute for all the sacrifices from the rental of the land at the Herakleion." And because the dispute concerned the cost of these sacrifices, the settlement lists these in detail.

After the preamble, the decree proper presents a list of sacrifices that both sides agree to provide (85–97); it takes the form of a calendar, and is one of the most detailed and best preserved that survives.

> *Mounychion.* At Porthmos: to Kourotrophos a goat, 10 drachmas; to Ioleos a sheep burnt whole, 15 drachmas; to Alkmene a sheep, 12 drachmas; to Maia a sheep, 12 drachmas; to Herakles an ox, 70 drachmas; to the hero at the Hale a sheep, 15 drachmas; to the hero at Antisara a suckling pig, 3 drachmas, 3 obols; to the hero at Pyrgilion a suckling pig, 3 drachmas, 3 obols; to Ion to sacrifice a sheep alternately every other year. Wood for the sacrifices and for those sacrifices which the state gives in accordance with the laws, 10 drachmas. On the eighteenth of the month: to Eurysakes a pig, 40 drachmas. Wood for the sacrifices and incidentals, 3 drachmas.

> *Hecatombaion.* At the Panathenaia: to Athena a pig, 40 drachmas. Wood for the sacrifices and incidentals, 3 drachmas.

> *Metageitnion.* On the seventh: to Apollo Patroos a pig, 40 drachmas; to Leto a suckling pig, 3 drachmas, 3 obols; to Artemis a suckling pig, 3 drachmas, 3 obols; to Athena *agelaa* a suckling pig, 3 drachmas, 3 obols. Wood for the sacrifices and incidentals, 3 drachmas, 3 obols.

> *Boedromnion.* To Poseidon *hippodromios* a pig, 40 drachmas; to the hero Phaiax a suckling pig, 3 drachmas, 3 obols; to the hero Teukros a suckling pig, 3 drachmas, 3 obols; to the

hero Nauseiros a suckling pig, 3 drachmas, 3 obols. Wood for the sacrifices and incidentals, 3 drachmas.

Pyanopsion. On the sixth: to Theseus a pig, 40 drachmas. Incidentals, 3 drachmas. At the Apatouria: to Zeus Phratrios a pig, 40 drachmas. Wood for the sacrifices and incidentals, 3 drachmas.

Maimakterion. To Athena Skiras a pregnant ewe, 12 drachmas; to Skiros a sheep, 15 drachmas. Wood for the altar, 3 drachmas.

Total of the money which both parties have to spend on all the sacrifices, 530 drachmas, 3 obols.

These sacrifices they are to make in common from the rental of the land at the Herakleion at Sounion, each party contributing money for all the sacrifices. If any one moves, or any archon puts a motion, to abrogate any of these provisions or to divert the money to any other purpose, he shall be accountable to the whole genos and likewise to the priests and liable to an action which may be instituted privately by anyone of the Salaminioi who wishes. (translation by Ferguson [1938:7–8])

The calendar is organized chronologically by month. Within each month dates may be given either by the number of the day ("on the sixth") or by the name of an occasion such as the Panathenaia, but some sacrifices have no date; this may mean they could be performed any time within that month. Whether or not a specific date is given, for each sacrifice the calendar states the recipient (a god or a hero), the sacrificial victim, and the cost. Then—and this is highly unusual—at the end of each month it adds an amount for "wood for the sacrifices and incidentals"; the cost is always three drachmas except in Metageitnion, when (for unknown reasons) it is three drachmas, three obols (3 1/2 drachmas). Finally, at the end we are given a total sum for all the sacrifices listed.

All the sacrifices listed are annual with one exception: the last sacrifice listed in the month Mounychion is "to Ion to sacrifice a sheep alternately every other year." The reason for this exception is unknown, but we may note that it is the only sacrifice for which no cost is listed; presumably it would confuse the accounts to list a sum that was only paid every other year together with sums paid annually. It appears, however, that the annualized cost of this sacrifice, which is half the cost of a sheep, needs to be included among the costs in order to reach the total of 530 1/2 drachmas listed at the end of the inscription (Ferguson 1938:64–65).

In many ways this calendar is typical: it gives the three most essential elements of sacrificial calendars: the date, the recipient, and the victim. Only a few of the victims are further described—"a sheep burnt whole," a suckling pig as opposed to a pig, and a pregnant ewe—though in other calendars we often find gender, age, and other details. This calendar probably has little specificity about the victims because it is trying to keep costs to a minimum. As Dow (1953–57) and others have noted, sacred calendars often give a fixed price for victims, although the price must have fluctuated from year to year. This must mean that buyers had the flexibility to buy the best victim they could afford: in a good year with a large supply and low prices, one could afford a good victim; in a bad year, one bought the best one could get for the price. Obviously, the more detail a calendar gives about the victim, the less flexibility a buyer would have regarding cost; thus, the lack of specificity in the calendar of the Salaminioi suggests that the Salaminioi were concerned about cost. And the fact that every single expense including the price of wood is given down to the last obol confirms that cost is a major concern here. Although it is hard to judge, the total cost of a little over 500 drachmas per year, or about the price of a good slave, seems quite modest for this clan, which must have had a good many members. Another indication that the clan is keeping costs down is that in each case there is only a single victim, and these victims are almost all sheep, goats, or pigs, and some of the latter are suckling. These would feed relatively few clan members (Rosivach 1994:47–48), but they would allow the clan to continue to conduct traditional sacrifices from their own funds "according to their ancient custom."

Why Sacrificial Laws?

The laws I have presented thus far give an idea of the main kinds of regulation found throughout the Greek world from the archaic period through the Hellenistic age and beyond. Many are long and detailed, and they raise the question, Why did Greek cities devote so many resources to enacting, inscribing, and publicly displaying these regulations? Lupu (2005:67–68) notes that some texts list the cost of sacrifices in detail, and considers whether these could perhaps be seen as financial rather than religious documents. He argues to the contrary, however, that they are religious documents, intended "to ensure the proper performance of cult." In support, he cites the stated purpose of the decree of the Salaminioi (line 80), "that the Salaminioi may ever sacrifice to the gods and heroes according to ancestral custom." I suggest this is a false dichotomy deriving ultimately from a false sense of the separation of the religious and civic spheres in Greece. Greek religion, or at least that part of Greek religion that involved public sacrifices, was fully part of Greek civic life. Sacrifice was certainly a religious ritual, but it was also a civic ritual, which made a significant contribution to public welfare.

The state certainly had an interest in the proper observation of religious rituals, but it is interesting to note that these public inscriptions do not generally regulate any aspects of the performance other than specifying the date, the victim, the recipient, and sometimes the distribution of meat. If the main purpose of these laws was the proper observation of religious ritual, we might expect something to be said about the personnel involved and details of the act of sacrifice itself. That such details are very rarely included supports the conclusion that in its laws, at least, the state's primary interest was in the cost of such sacrifices. Similarly, the emphasis on cost in the decree of the Salaminioi strongly suggests that the original dispute between the two factions of the clan concerned the cost, not the proper performance of these religious rituals. The Salaminioi wanted to continue sacrificing according to ancestral custom, and they had to make certain that the clan would be able to pay for these sacrifices.

I would thus conclude that most Greek laws on sacrifice are both religious and financial documents, and that the state's primary reason for producing the most common type, the sacrificial calendar, was to specify in detail its obligation to provide victims for

these sacrifices. This concern is evident from the beginning of Greek legislation and was
probably present even earlier. Sacrifices cost money, and in most cases, the city had to
pay for them.

Appendix

1. The Cyrene Cathartic Law (SEG 9.72). Text from Solmsen-Fraenkel, no. 39

SIDE A

3. [ἀπ]ὸ γυναικὸς ἀνὴρ τὰν νύκτα κοιμαθὲς θυσεῖ, ὅ[κα κα] δήληται.

6. αἴ κα ἐπὶ βωμῶι θύσηι ἰαρήιον ὅ τι μὴ νόμος θύεν, τ[ὸ] ποτιπίαμμα ἀνελὲν ἀπὸ
τῶ βωμῶ καὶ ἀποπλῦναι καὶ τὸ ἄλλο λῦμα ἀνελὲν ἐκ τῶ ἰαρῶ καὶ τὰν ἴκνυν ἀπὸ τῶ
βωμῶ καὶ τὸ πῦρ ἀφελὲν ἐς καθαρόν, καὶ τόκα δὴ ἀπονιψάμενος καθάρας τὸ ἰαρὸν
καὶ ζαμίαν θύσας βοτὸν τέλευν, τόκα δὴ θυέτω ὡς νόμος.

8. αἴ κα δεκατὸς ἦι ἄνθρωπος ἠβατάς, καθάρας αὐτὸς αὐτὸν αἵματι καθαρεῖ τὸ ἰαρὸν
καὶ πωλη[θ]ὲς ἐν τᾶι ἀγορᾶι ὁπόσσω κα πλείστω ἄξιος ἦ[ι] προθυσεῖ πρὸ τᾶς δεκάτας
ζαμίαν βοτὸν τέλ[ε]υν, οὐκ ἀπὸ τᾶς δεκάτας, καὶ τόκα δὴ θυσεῖ τάν [δε]κάταν καὶ
ἀποισεῖ ἐς καθαρόν. αἰ δὲ μή, τῶν αὐ[τῶ]ν δησῆτα[ι]. σκοίκιον δὲ οἰσεῖ πᾶς ὁ θύων.
[ἄ]νηβος αἴ μή τί κα ἐκὼμ μιᾶι, ἀποχρεῖ καθάρασ[θ]αι αὐτὸν καὶ ζαμίας οὐ δεῖ, αἰ
δέ κα ἐκὼμ μιᾶι, κα[θ]αρεῖ τὸ ἰαρὸν καὶ ζαμίαν προθυσεῖ βοτὸν τέλευν.

9. [αἴ] κα χρήματα δεκατὰ ἦι, ἐκτιμάσας τὰ χρήματ[α κ]αθαρεῖ τὸ ἰαρὸν καὶ τὰ
χρήματα δίχα καὶ τόκα [δὴ] προθυσεῖ ζαμίαν βοτὸν τέλευν, οὐ τᾶς δεκάτ[ας] καὶ
τό[κα] δὴ θυσεῖ τὰν δεκάταν καὶ ἀποισεῖ ἐς [κα]θαρόν. αἰ δὲ μή, τῶν αὐτῶν δησεῖ.
των δὲ χρημά[τω]ν ἇς κα δεκατὰ ἦι ἐντόφιον οὐκ ἐνθησεῖ οὐδὲ ἓν οὐδὲ χύτλα οἰσεῖ,
πρίν κα τῶι θεῶι ἀπο[δεκατε]ύσει. αἰ δέ κα χύτλα ἐνίκει ἢ ἐντόφια ἐνθῆι, κα[θάρ]ας
τὸ Ἀπολλώνιον ζαμίαν προθυσεῖ κατὰ τὰν [ἁμα]ρτίαν βοτὸν τέλευν.

10. [αἴ κ]α δεκατὸς ἐὼν ἄνθρωπος ἀποθάνηι, κατακομ[ίξαν]τες τὸν ἄνθρωπον τᾶι
μὲν πρατίσται ἀμέρα[ι ἐπιθ]ησεῖ ὅ τι κα δήληται ἐπὶ τὸ σᾶμα, δεύτερον [δὲ οὐ]δὲ ἕν,
πρίγ κα ἀποδεκατεύσει τῶι θεῶι, καὶ ο[ὐδὲ θυ]σεῖ οὐδ' ἐπὶ τὸ σᾶμα εἴτι. ἐκτιμασέντι
δὲ ὀπ[όσσω πλ]είστω ἄξιος ἧς κοινὸς ἐὼν τῶι θεῶι. καθάρα[ς δὲ τὸ] Ἀπολλώνιον
καὶ τὰ χρήματα δίχα προθυ[σάμενο]ς ζαμίαν βοτὸν τέλευν, οὐκ ἀπὸ τᾶς δεκά[τας
προ]βώμιον θυσεῖ τὰν δεκάταν προβώμιον [καὶ ἀποι]σεῖ ἐς καθαρόν. αἰ δὲ μή, τῶν
αὐτῶν δησεῖτ[αι].

11. [αἴ κα ἀπ]οθάνηι δεκατὸς ἐών, καὶ τὰ τέκνα καταλι[πόμενα τὰ μὲν ζῶι, τὰ δὲ
ἀποθάνηι, ἐκτιμάσας τὰ [ἀπογενό]μενα, ὁπόσσω κα πλείστω ἄξια ἦι, καθάρα[ς τὸ
Ἀπολλώ]νιον καὶ τὰ χρήματα δίχα προθυσεῖ ζα[μίαν τὰν τῶ ἠβ]ατᾶ προβώμιον καὶ
τόκα δὴ θυσεῖ τὰν δε[κάταν προ]βώμιον. τὸν δὲ ζόον, καθάρας αὐτὸς αὐτὸ[ν αἵματι

κ]αὶ τὸ ἱαρὸν δίχα πωληθὲς ἐν τᾶι ἀγορᾶι [προθυσεῖ τ]ῶ ἡβατᾶ ζαμίαν βοτὸν τέλευν καὶ τόκ[α δὴ θυσεῖ τὰ]ν δεκάταν καὶ ἀποισεῖ ἐς καθαρόν. αἰ [δὲ μή, τῶν αὐτ]ῶν δησεῖ.

SIDE B

1. ἃ [δ]έ κα ταῦτα μὴ ποιήσ[αισ]α μιᾶι ἔκασσα, καθάραισα τὸ Ἀρταμίτιον ἐ[πιθυ]σεῖ ζαμίαν βοτὸν τέλευν καὶ τόκα δὴ ε[ἴτι ἐς] τὸ κοιτατήριον.

2. [νύ]μφαν δὲ τὸ νυμφήιον ἐς Ἄρταμιν κατ[ενθ]ὲν δεῖ ὁπόκα κα δήληται Ἀρταμιτίοις, [ὡς τά]χιστα δὲ λῶιον. ἃ δέ κα μὴ κατένθηι, [ἐπιθυ]σεῖ τᾶι Ἀρτάμιτι ἃ ν[ομίζετ]αι τοῖς [Ἀρταμιτίοι]ς. μὴ κατεληλε[υθυῖα δὲ καθαρεῖ τὸ ἱαρὸν] καὶ ἐπιθυσεῖ ζ[αμίαν βοτὸν τέλευν].

3. αἰ δέ κα μιᾶι καθ[α]ραμένα αὐτὰ καθαρεῖ τὸ ἱαρὸν καὶ ἐπιθυσ[εῖ] ζαμίαν βοτὸν τέλευν.

6. ἱκέσιος ἅτερος, τετελεσμένος ἢ ἀτελής, ἱσσάμενος ἐπὶ τῶι δαμοσίωι ἱαρῶι. αἰ μέγ κα προ[φέ]ρηται, ὁπόσσω κα προφέρηται, οὕτως τελίσκ[ε]σθαι. αἰ δέ κα μὴ προφέρηται, γᾶς καρπὸν θ[ύ]εν καὶ σπονδὰν καθ᾿ ἔτος ἀεί. αἰ δέ κα παρῆι, ἐ[ς] νέω δὶς τόσσα. αἰ δέ κα διαλίπηι τέκνον ἐγλ[α]θόμενον καὶ οἱ προφέρηται, ὅ τι κα οἱ μαντε[υ]ομένωι ἀναιρεθῆι, τοῦτο ἀποτεισεῖ τῶι θεῶι [καὶ] θυσεῖ, αἰ μεγ κα ἴσαι, ἐπὶ τὸμ πατρῶιον, αἰ δέ μή, [χρή]σασθαι.

2. Dreros (*BCH* 70 [1946]:603–604, no. 6)

1. [---] ἐν τε Πυτίοι | πεν[τ---]
2. [---] ἐν Ἀγ[ο]ραίοι | μῆρος Ρ[---]

3. Corinth (*IG* 4.1597)

A 1.   Φοινικ[αίο - -
   2.   - - τέτο]ρες χο
   3.   ῖροι - -

4. Gortyn (*ICRET* 4.3)

1 *a-c.*   - - ἱα]ρὰ | τετελημέ[να-c. 6 -] · υι | τõι [Ϝ]ελκανί[õι - -
   d.   - -]αι | ἐν τᾶι πένπτα[ι - -
2 *a-c.*   - -]ν | τέληον | καὶ αἶγα | ἐν [τᾶι ἔκται] ὄιν θήλε[ι]αν | τõι Ἀπ[έλλονι - -
   d.   - -]ερ[· ·]ς | ταῦρος | ἐσ · [- -
3 *a-c.*   - - τᾶι Ἥραι | ὄις | θή[λ]ε[ια | τᾶι Δάμ]ατρι | ὄις | ἐπίτεκ[ς - -
4 *a-c.*   - - αἰ μὲν δύο | θήλει[αι, οἱ δὲ δύ]ο ἔρσενες | καὶ τρ[άγος - -

5. ATHENIAN SACRED CALENDAR (OLIVER AND DOW 1935:21)

τάδε τὸ ἔτερον ἔτος θυέται Ἀ[θήνησιν]

		Ἑκατομβαιῶνος	60	Δ⊢⊢	Θέμιδι οἶς
		πέμπτηι ἐπὶ δέκα		ΔΓ	Διὶ Ἑρκείωι ο[ἶς]
		ἐκ τῶν φυλο-		Δ⊢⊢	Δήμητρι οἶς
		βασιλικῶν			Φερρεφάττη[ι]
35		Γλεόντων φυλῆι		Δ⊢⊢	κριός
		Λευκοταινίων	65	ΔΓ	Εὐμόλπωι ο[ἶς]
		τριττύϊ οἶν		ΔΓ	Δελίχωι ἥ[ρωϊ οἶς]
	⊢⊢⊢	λειπογνώμονα		ΔΓ⊢	Ἀρχηγέτη[ι οἶς]
	⊢⊢⊢‖	ἱερεώ[σ]υνα		ΔΓ	Πολυξέν[ωι οἶς]
40		Φυλοβ[α]σιλεῦσι			Θρεπτῶι [- - -]
	⊢	νώτο	70	ΔΓ⊢⊢	κριτός
		κήρυκι ὤμο		ΔΓ	Διόκλ[ωι οἶς]
	‖‖	ποδῶν κεφαλῆς		ΔΓ	Κελεῶι [οἶς]
		ἕκτηι ἐπὶ δέκα			Εὐμολπ[ίδαι]
45		ἐκ τῶν φυλο-			ταῦτα [θύοσιν]
		βασιλικῶν	75		ἱερέα[ι Δήμητρος]
		Γλεόντων φυλῆι		Η	ἀπόμ[ετρα]
		Διὶ Φρατρίωι καὶ			ἐκ τῶν σ[- - -]
		Ἀθηναίαι Φρα-		(⊢)⊢⊢	χοῖρ[ος — — —]
50		τρίαι βόε δύο		Δ⊢⊢	Ἑστί[αι οἶς]
	⅂	[λ]ειπογνώμονε	80	Δ⊢⊢	Ἀθην[αίαι οἶς]
	:ΔΓ⊢	ἱερεώσυνα		Δ	Χάρ[ισιν — — —]
		φυλοβασιλεῖ			Ἑρ[μῆι - - -]
		σκέλος		ΔΓ	Ἐν[- - - οἶς]
55		κήρυ[κ]ι χέλυος		Δ	[— — — — — —]
	⊢⊢‖‖	ποδ[ῶν] κεφαλῆς	85	ΔΓ	Ἡ[φαίστωι? οἶς]
		τ[ροφ]εῖ κριθῶν		ΔΓ	Δ[ιονύσωι? οἶς]
		μ[έδιμ]νοι			- - - -
		- - - -			

6. AXOS (*ICRET* II.v.9)

τοῖς δ᾽ ἰαροῦσ-
ι, ὅτι κα πέρονται πὰρ τὰ ἠγ-
ραμένα, αἰ μή τις αὐτὸς δοίη μ-
ἠ ὑπ᾽ ἀνάνκας, τιτουϝέσθο σ-
τατῆρα κατὰν θυσίαν ϝεκάστ-
αν καὶ τὸ κρίος τὰν διπλεία-
ν· πορτιπονὲν δ᾽ αἴπερ τὸν ἄλ-
ον.

     5

7. The Decree of the Salaminioi (SEG 21.527). Text from Ferguson 1938:3–5

Lines 20–27: ὅσα μὲν ἡ πόλις παρέχει ἐκ τὸ δημοσίο ἢ παρὰ τῶν ὠσκοφόρων ἢ παρὰ τῶν δειπνοφόρων γίγνεται λαμβάνειν Σαλαμινίοις, ταῦτα μὲν κοινῆι ἀμφοτέρος θύοντας νέμεσθαι τὰ κρέα ὠμὰ τὰ ἡμίσεα ἑκατέρος· ὅσα δὲ ἀπὸ τῆς μισθώσεως ἔθυον Σαλαμίνιοι παρὰ σφῶν αὐτῶν θύειν κατὰ τὰ πάτρια, τὸ ἥμυσυ ἑκατέρος συμβαλλομένος εἰς ἅπαντα τὰ ἱερά·

Lines 85–97: Μουνιχιῶνος. ἐπὶ Πορθμῶι· Κουροτρόφωι αἶγα Δ, Ἰολέωι οἶν ὁλόκαυτον ΔΓ: Ἀλκμήνει οἶν Δ⊢Μα, Μαίαι οἶν Δ⊢Ἡρ, Ἡρακλεῖ βοῦν ϜΔΔ ἥρωι ἐπι τεῖ ἀλεῖ οἶν ΔΓ, ἥρωι ἐπ’ Ἀντισάραι χοῖρον ⊢⊢⊢|||, ἥρωι ἐπὶ Πυργιλίωι χοῖρον ⊢⊢|,|||, Ἴων(ι) οἶν θύειν ἐναλλὰξ παρ’ ἔτος· ξύλα ἐφ’ ἱεροῖς καὶ οἷς ἡ πόλις δίδωσιν ἐκ κύρβεων Δ· ὀγδόει ἐπὶ δέκα Εὐρυσάκει : ὗν : ΔΔΔΔ· ξύλα ἐφ’ ἱεροῖ(ς) καὶ εἰς τἄλλα ⊢⊢⊢|||. Ἑκατονβαιῶνος. Παναθηναίοις Ἀθηνᾶι ὗν : ΔΔΔΔ· ξύλα ἔφ’ ἱεροῖς καὶ εἰς τἄλλα ⊢⊢⊢|||. Μεταγειτνιῶνος. ἑβδόμει Ἀπόλλωνι Πατρώιωι ὗν : ΔΔΔΔ, Λητοῖ χοῖρον (90) ⊢⊢⊢|||. Ἀρτέμιδι χοῖρον ⊢⊢⊢|||, Ἀθηνᾶι Ἀγελάαι χοῖρον ⊢⊢⊢|||· ξύλα ἐφ’ ἱεροῖς καὶ εἰς τἄλλα ⊢⊢⊢|||. Βοηδρομιῶνος. Ποσειδῶνι Ἱπποδρομίωι ὗν : ΔΔΔΔ, ἥρωι Φαίακι χοῖρον ⊢⊢⊢|||, ἥρωι Τεύκρωι χοῖρον ⊢⊢⊢|||, ἥρωι Ναυσείρωι χοῖρον ⊢⊢⊢|||· ξύλα ἐφ’ ἱεροῖς καὶ τἄλλα ⊢⊢⊢. Πυανοψιῶνος. ἔκτει Θησεῖ ὗν ΔΔΔΔ· εἰς τἄλλα ⊢⊢⊢. Ἀπατουρίοις Διὶ Φρατρίωι ὗν ΔΔΔΔ· ξῦλα ἐφ’ ἱεροῖς καὶ τἄλλα ⊢⊢⊢. Μαιμακτηριῶνος. Ἀθηνᾶι Σκιράδι οἶν ἐνκύμονα Δ⊢⊢⊢, Σκίρωι οἶν ΔΓ· ξύλα ἐπὶ τὸν βωμὸν ⊢⊢⊢. κεφάλαιον οὗ δεῖ ἀναλίσκειν ἀμφοτέρος ἐς ἅπαντα τὰ ἱερὰ ϜΔΔΔ|||. ταῦτα θύειν κοινεῖ ἀπὸ τῆς μισθώσεως τῆς γῆς τῆς ἐφ’ Ἡρακλείωι (95) ἐπὶ Σονίο, ἀργύριον συμβαλλομένους ἑκατέρους ἐς ἅπαντα τὰ ἱερά· ἐὰν δέ τις εἴπει ἢ ἄρχων ἐπιψηφίσει τούτων τι καταλῦσαι ἢ τρέψει ποι ἄλλοσε τὸ ἀργύριον, ὑπεύθυνον εἶναι τῶι γένει ἅπαντι καὶ τοῖς ἱερεῦσι κατὰ ταὐτὰ καὶ ἰδίαι ὑπόδικον καὶ τῶι βουλομένωι Σαλαμινίων.

Notes

1. The very useful study of this text by Robertson (2010:259–374) came to my attention only after this paper was completed. The text, with a translation and brief commentary, can also be found in Rhodes and Osborne 2003:495–505.

2. This text, with a translation and brief commentary, can also be found in Rhodes and Osborne 2003:182–193.

References Cited

Dow, S. 1953–57 The Law Codes of Athens. *Proceedings of the Massachusetts Historical Society* 71:2–36.

Ferguson, W. S. 1938 The Salaminioi of Heptaphylai and Sounion. *Hesperia* 7:1–74.

Lupu, E. 2005 *Greek Sacred Law: A Collection of New Documents (NGSL)*. Brill, Leiden.

Oliver, J. H., and S. Dow 1935 The American Excavations in the Athenian Agora: Sixth Report: Greek Inscriptions. *Hesperia* 4:5–90.

Parker, R. 1983 *Miasma: Pollution and Purification in Early Greek Religion.* Oxford University Press, Oxford.

Rhodes, P. J., and R. Osborne 2003 *Greek Historical Inscriptions 404–323 BC.* Oxford University Press, Oxford.

Robertson, N. 2010 *Religion and Reconciliation in Greek Cities. The Sacred Laws of Selinus and Cyrene.* Oxford University Press, New York.

Rosivach, V. J. 1994 *The System of Public Sacrifice in Fourth-Century Athens.* Scholars Press, Atlanta.

Solmsen, F., and E. Fraenkel 1930 *Inscriptiones graecae ad illustrandas dialectos selectae.* Fourth edition. Teubner, Stuttgart.

Todd, S. C. 1996 Lysias *Against Nikomachos*: The Fate of the Expert in Athenian Law. In *Greek Law in Its Political Setting: Justifications Not Justice,* edited by L. Foxhall and A. D. E. Lewis, pp. 33–56. Oxford University Press, Oxford.

CHAPTER FOURTEEN

In What Way Is Christ's Death a Sacrifice?

Theories of Sacrifice and Theologies of the Cross

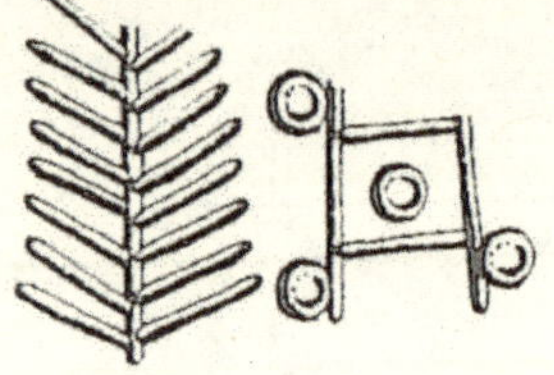

S. Mark Heim

Abstract   *There is irony in the fact that Christian ideas stood behind much early modern anthropological theorizing about sacrifice, given that those ideas relate to an event—crucifixion—with so little similarity to the usual ritual activities under that heading. This paper notes a certain gap between the event of Jesus's death as described in early Christian texts and the typical anthropological categories for sacrifice, illustrates this by contrasting early Christian texts and early Christian visual artifacts, and then suggests some of the implications of this gap for relations between theories of sacrifice and theologies of the cross. At the very least, this gap is of interest in considering the influence that the model of the cross as a sacrifice has exercised on anthropological study. In using categories from the practice of temple offerings to describe Jesus's death, early Christian usage clearly links it to wider ritual activity in the history of religion. In interpreting the cross through the types of Isaac, Job, Jonah, Daniel, and Susanna these Christians also linked it to social dynamics whose relation with ritual is less obvious. This tension is reflected in the gospel narratives of the passion, in which differing rationales for the crucifixion compete. The paper considers René Girard's theory of sacrifice and his suggestion that the biblical literature contains an anti-sacrificial reading of the phenomenon of scapegoating violence. Girard's hypothesis has been sharply criticized by many anthropologists, but is notable for directly addressing the gap this essay describes and for encouraging the consideration of sacrifice in a wider evolutionary perspective.*

The Shadow of Biblical Ideas in
Anthropological Study of Sacrifice

If one were to weigh contemporary human discourse about sacrifice by brute volume, religious discourse would likely be the weightiest portion (alongside a not insubstantial military sector: "He made the ultimate sacrifice"). Such reference is manifest daily in liturgies, rituals, scripture study, and theological conversations. Anthropological study of sacrifice cannot be fully separated from these ongoing streams of thought and practice, whether found in churches, mosques, and synagogues or among indigenous peoples. The complex question of what kinds of thing sacrifice was can never be entirely unaffected by our concerns about what sacrifice is. This is plainly evident in the history of such study.

Christian ideas, rooted in biblical texts and historical theology, stood in the background of much early modern anthropological theorizing about sacrifice as a feature in human history.[1] Where the models of Jewish and Christian religion were firmly in mind, there was a tendency to look at other cultures and practices in those terms, to presume that they defined a feature of religion as such. Other traditions were viewed through the lens of the Bible, with an assumption that the superiority of biblical revelation implied the primitive and subordinate character of other forms. In a sense, little changed with the later generation of anthropologists who "having benefited from the historical-critical method and its critique of dogmatic theology, in effect promptly reasserted the supercessionism and progressivism of their theological predecessors within their newly secularized context" (Astell, Goodhart 2011:9). The normativity of biblical tradition could survive within the critical inclination to relativize it, for instance in a stress on the cultural ubiquity of elements, such as the narrative of a dying and rising god, that were once thought uniquely characteristic of Christian gospels. To make the point that biblical tradition was much like others, it was common to emphasize the way the others were like the biblical tradition. Alternatively, repugnance for the biblical models could lead to an overemphasis on those features in other settings that were deemed totally distinct. Such readings were, in their own way, as determined by the biblical starting point as prior ones had been (see McClymond 2008). Some participants in this conference remark upon the fact that sacrifice has become much less prominent as a topic in anthropology and/or that it has become much less obvious what is to be comprehended in the term (see, for instance, the contributions of Stevens and Berggren in this volume). This would indicate that in a more pluralistic setting the shadow of biblical ideas has significantly lifted, making it possible to revisit both the data of sacrifice and the biblical traditions in a fresher light.

The Oddity of the "Sacrifice of Christ"

The emphasis on sacrifice that derives from the influence of Christian culture stems from the centrality in that tradition of the "sacrificial" death of Jesus. This is odd on its face in that there is nothing sacrificial about Jesus's death in an anthropological respect (see Ullucci 2012:6–7). If we did not have any textual sources interpreting that death, if, for instance, we were to have only archaeological evidence—whether physical remains related to Jesus's individual death or remains and records related to people who died in the same manner—there would be nothing to suggest classifying that event as a sacrifice. No libations or formal invocation of deities, no ritual implements, no altar, no sacred sites, no specialized treatment or disposition of the body would be indicated by such evidence, as indeed they are not indicated in the written descriptions. The death of Jesus is an execution. Simple parallels are more readily found in the political than the ritual realm. If the cross is the central paradigm of sacrifice in Western culture, a primary driver of interest in that category, it is strange that this model should be so lacking in the elements that otherwise characterize the practice. The meaning of this event as a sacrifice must be in some measure imported or constructed.

There is a gap, if you will, between the description of Jesus's death and the descriptors of "sacrifice." There is not much overlap between the two save for the bare fact of death, which is a feature of at least some sacrifices. Thus, the bridge between the two tends to be a focus on sacrificial death and killing, which perhaps helps to explain the bias toward this dimension of ritual sacrifice in earlier anthropological study. It is precisely the identification of sacrifice with blood that many contemporary historians contest, pointing to the many ritual cases where there is no killing and no direct reference to it.

There is no doubt that early Christians connected the crucifixion and sacrifice. In texts (from Paul and Ignatius in the first century through Clement, Origen, Tertullian, and later) and in the eucharistic liturgies of the churches there is abundant emphasis on the saving significance of Jesus's death and frequent reference to its sacrificial character. Both the Epistle to the Hebrews and the Epistle of Barnabas compare Jesus's death to the Jewish liturgy of sacrifice. Melito of Sardis wrote an entire sermon in the second century comparing Jesus to the Passover lamb.[2] The celebration of the eucharist as a memorial of the cross provided all the liturgical elements absent in the death itself: an altar, a ritual, a meal, apportioning of the "body," and "blood." In many and varied ways the texts and worship of the church explicitly emphasize Jesus's death as a sacrifice. In addition, it appears that early Jewish Christians continued to take part in the animal sacrifices of that tradition, while gentile Christians did not, and both (like Jews generally) shunned the traditional sacrifices of their Roman and Greek neighbors. This divergence came to an end with the destruction of the second temple. Early Christians reinterpreted sacrifice in light of Jesus's death, but only over time did this distill into the view that all ritual sacrifice had been abolished in principle. The process was more complicated for those eventually predominant Jesus followers who retained Hebrew scriptures and their sacrificial content, in contrast with those who simply rejected these texts, their deity, and their practices (Ullucci 2012).

The Absence of an Image

Interestingly, this contrast between the event itself and the terms used to describe it in early Christian scriptures is paralleled in the next few centuries by another anomaly: a contrast between the textual tradition and the visual one. Up through the fifth century C.E., while the textual sources continue their extensive treatment of the crucifixion in the language of sacrifice, the physical, iconographic artifacts of Christian life are entirely devoid of explicit representations of Jesus's death on the cross. Some have argued that this absence of images of the crucifixion proves that death and sacrifice played no central role in early Christian faith, which was instead focused on divine empowerment (see Nakashima Brock and Parker 2008). As one writer concluded, there are no early symbols that "signify suffering, death, or self-immolation. . . . There is no place in the third century for a crucified Christ, or a symbol of divine death" (Graydon Snyder, quoted in Jensen 2000:145).

Because the death of Jesus carries no self-evident character as a sacrifice, its significance must often be gathered from the other images or types used to interpret it. That is, a picture of a dying criminal by itself suggests nothing religious or ritual in nature and could have any number of connotations.[3] This is illustrated by an apparent exception to the lack of crucifixion images with Christian reference in the first four centuries, which is a scrap of supposed graffiti found in Rome, depicting a crucified human figure with the head of an ass, with another person standing beside/below and a caption "Alexamenos: worship God" (Lanciani 1888:122). Most likely the graffito is anti-Christian mockery. But in the absence of the ass's head, it would be virtually impossible to know whether this image was pro-Christian, anti-Christian, or without any religious reference at all.

It is thus perhaps not surprising that the religious meaning of the cross might be represented under another image, since the naked picture of the thing itself did not encode that meaning. But that possibility magnifies the visual ambiguity. To this we can add the reality of martyrdom and the cult of the martyrs among early Christians. It may be that in these actual executions and the stories and relics attached to them believers saw commentaries on Jesus's death more powerful and self-explanatory than art. If the crucifixion itself is absent in art, this is not so for the cross, which could be taken as a summary representation of the event. It is widely found, in the form of an anchor, a ship's mast, or a military standard, not to mention explicit images of a bare cross, or the emerging practice of Christians making the sign of the cross on their own bodies. Christian scribes adopted conventions such as the contracted combination of the letters *tau* and *rho,* yielding a crude icon of a cross with a human head inclined to one side (Hurtado 2006).

The ambiguity of such images in isolation was balanced with images drawn from other scriptural stories. For instance, a relatively common scene in early Christian art is Abraham's offering of Isaac. Some scholars see this as a typological reference to Jesus's death, a representation by analogy of the crucifixion and its meaning. Others maintain that at least in the early centuries that image conveys a simple, non-cross-related message of hope and deliverance for Christians facing persecution (Jensen 2000:145). Only in the mid-fourth century in some versions of this image does the figure of Isaac appear for the first time bound on the altar (rather than standing nearby), suggesting to some the development at that point of a more explicit sacrifice-crucifixion analogy. We will see below that other images were similarly used to interpret Jesus's death by association.

There seems no way to blink this fact: explicit reference to Jesus's death and explicit sacrificial interpretation of it are prominent in the textual tradition from the beginning, but absent (or ambiguously referenced) in the visual grammar for the first four hundred years.[4] Whatever else this may indicate, it seems to suggest the constructed nature of reference to Jesus's death as a sacrifice. Such a reference had to be narrated and could only be ambiguously represented in direct signs. The image of Isaac and Abraham may be a clear sacrificial reference (an interrupted sacrifice, but presumably one completed with a ram instead of Isaac as the offering). No image of Christ's death alone is. Only after many centuries, in the early middle ages, would it become so, when "sacrifice" itself had received a different connotation by assimilation with the crucifix figure.

Scriptural Types for the Meaning of Sacrifice-crucifixion

There is another twist to consider. We have noted the ambiguity of the bare image of Christ's death, which prompted Christians to use other visual representations. There are types from Hebrew scripture that are consistently used to expound the significance of Jesus's death and the cross. While the "sacrifice" of Isaac from Genesis is one of these favored images, the list also includes Jonah, Job, Daniel (in the lions' den), and Susanna. Archaeological and iconographic materials from early Christianity offer all of these images, with Jonah being the most common (Jensen 2000:10). Here, the textual traditions and the visual traditions converge, emphasizing these same biblical types in interpreting the cross.

But of course these Hebrew types all come with their own attendant narratives. And there is something all these cases have in common. We have just noted that the fact of death was the one element clearly tying the passion to sacrificial practices. Yet all of the scriptural types on our list are cases of people who precisely do not die. They are not killed, despite accusations and attempts to do so, often in God's name. Each of these stories is the story of someone's deliverance from death, a deliverance engineered or directly effected by God. In Isaac's case it is the non-killing that is highlighted in the term used for this event in Jewish tradition, the *akedah* or the "binding" of Isaac. Christian references to this as the "sacrifice" of Isaac often reflect a sense of superiority, in that Jesus's offering was actually realized and complete. Isaac's case is a prefiguration of what was carried through in Jesus. But early Christian deployment of the story stresses commonality more than difference. The moral of God's action in averting Isaac's death and in reversing Jesus's death is taken to be the same.

We have an apt illustration of these themes woven together in a fourth-century artifact, the Brescia casket, where Christ's passion is paralleled with the Jonah, Susanna, and Daniel stories (Tkacz 2002). No representation of the crucifixion is present, but the lid and front of the casket prominently display the elements of the passion story: Christ in the garden of Gethsemane, Christ's arrest, the betrayal of Peter, Jesus before Pilate, and Jesus before Herod. These images are paralleled with those of Susanna taken by the elders in a garden, Susanna on trial, Susanna vindicated, as well as those of Jonah thrown to the whale, saved on the beach, and sitting under a vine, and of Daniel in the lion's den and then redeemed.

The choice of interpretive types such as these seems to turn around and cut the sole thread of connection that links Jesus's death to the terminology of sacrifice: the death itself. To put it somewhat baldly, early Christians stretched to use sacrificial language to describe a crucifixion that on its face had no sacrificial qualities, stressing the death as one element that connected it with those sacrifices that immolated a victim. They then used narrative types to represent the meaning of that event, types in which the protagonists by deliverance avoided death altogether, whether that death was explicitly a ritual one (as with Isaac) or more "political" or judicial, as with Susanna or Daniel.

This alerts us that the very explicit sacrificial language used of Jesus has taken on a different and doubled character. Sacrificial language is not just used to lay meaning on Jesus's death. The language itself is skewed in the process. Jesus's passion is described in these terms not to categorize it as another instance of this class, but to signify a disturbance in the pattern of its normal operation. This is made very explicit in the Letter to the Hebrews, where Jesus's death is clearly spoken of as "once for all," a sacrifice to end sacrifice.[5] The same is true in early Christian writers who rework the language to describe what they themselves practice in the wake of the cross as "a bloodless sacrifice," "a sacrifice of praise," "a living sacrifice."[6]

Two Sides of the Texts

In fact, the various elements we have described can be seen to have roots in the passion narratives of the gospel texts. The narratives are all very clear that the crucifixion is a political/social event, an execution in a setting of repression. The scriptural accounts go to some length to detail this picture: the problematic accusations, the bribed betrayal, the collusive interests of Herod and Pilate, the catalytic role of the crowd, the frightened passivity of the disciples. As we observed at the outset, Jesus's death is not a ritual or religious event in any obvious way in the gospel telling, any more than it is in iconographic representation.

Superimposed on this account there are at least two interpretations with "sacrificial" character that do not cancel the political account but stand alongside. The first of these is embedded within the narrative in the viewpoint of players with whom the reader is clearly not intended to sympathize. An example would be found in the Gospel of John when fear is expressed that Jesus's popularity may alarm the Roman occupiers and lead them to take reprisals against the people of Israel and its holy places. Caiaphas, the high priest, says, "You do not understand that it is better for you to have one man die for the people than to have the whole nation destroyed" (John 11:45–53). There is a clear rationale for Jesus's death here, one that is sacrificial not according to any ritual prescription but to a political one. The same rationale shows up in the curious verse in the Gospel of Luke that comments that after Jesus has been passed back and forth between Herod and Pilate, "That same day Herod and Pilate became friends with each other; before this they had been enemies" (Luke 23:12). Jesus's death is reconciling and prevents conflict: this is both the intent and the actual result for his killers, the verse suggests. A similar point may be made about Pilate's offered substitution of Jesus for Barabbas, the prisoner that the crowd prefers to have freed. Jesus is selected as the one whose death will bring the least conflict in its wake. This treatment of Jesus as a convenient offering to discharge conflict and foster social peace (a "sacrifice" only according to a much later usage) is more or less continuous with the straightforward description of the mechanisms of his indictment and execution. That is to say, it also explains that death without recourse to the religious and ritual qualities of sacrifice.

Superimposed on all this is yet another perspective, the one that communicates to the reader most directly the projected viewpoint of Jesus and/or that of the writer. And this is the perspective in which the death of Jesus is, finally, presented in explicitly sacrificial terms that reference ritual and religious behavior. This is seen in the words attributed to Jesus at the last supper, "This is my blood, poured out for you," the words said of Jesus in John's gospel "Behold the lamb of God who takes away the sins of the world," or the interpretive scheme of the writer of the letter to the Hebrews, "For if the blood of goats and bulls . . . sanctifies those who have been defiled . . . how much more will the blood of Christ, who through the eternal spirit offered himself without blemish to God, purify our conscience from dead works to worship the living God" (Matthew 26:26–28 and parallels; John 1:29; Hebrews 9:12–14).

Here we now have unequivocal identification of Jesus's death, and particularly his shed blood, with the similar death and blood of an animal offered in Israel's religious practices—temple sacrifice, Passover rituals. The use of such language expresses a positive value in the death of Jesus. But this, the most explicit terminology, is at the same time highly contrastive. The writer of Hebrews sharply distinguishes the effect as well as the setting of Jesus's bloodshed from that in the temple. In the report of the last supper, Jesus's ritual plays upon familiar language and actions but transposes them with contrasts that would have struck his listeners (Chilton 1992:150ff). In light of the community's experience of Jesus's resurrection, these bread and wine rituals referring to Jesus's death are to be done in memory of him. They are to take pride of place among and to become the reference point for assessing other forms of sacrifice.

Theologies of the Cross and Theories of Sacrifice

Enough has been said, I believe, to illustrate the problematic character of the crucifixion as a paradigm of sacrifice. We might say that the most prominent historical theologies of the cross grow up in the gap we have described, the gap between descriptions of ordinary ritual sacrifice in the Greco-Roman world and the description of a social-political event. They either attribute some saving significance to Jesus's death without invoking sacrifice in any but a derivative metaphorical sense (thus the so-called moral influence theory) or reconstruct a literal sacrificial dynamic to fit the case (substitutionary atonement), or treat its significance in other terms entirely, such as battle with demonic powers or a ransom paid to the devil (for further discussion of these theologies see Heim 2006).

As consumers of theories of sacrifice, theologians have an obvious bias toward those that see in sacrifice some widespread pattern (as opposed to a collection of varied practices with varying purposes). Early Christian views of the cross all involved a profound sense of human solidarity as the premise for its effects. The influence of French ethnology—notably the work of Emile Durkheim, Marcel Mauss and Claude Lévi-Strauss—is significant in this respect, as these writers explored the social and communal bonds involved in sacrifice, elements that they saw as structurally characteristic of societies in general.[7] For similar reasons, theology has been interested in mythic and psychological theories, such as those of Joseph Campbell, Sigmund Freud, or Carl Jung, which hypothesize shared psychic dynamics underlying ritual and religious practices. Structuralist and psychological theories may be problematic for religious perspectives because of reductionist tendencies, and problematic for anthropologists because of their totalizing reach. But a common strength is that both offer perspectives in which sacrifice remains relevant to our condition, even if the overt assumptions of those who practiced it in the past do not.

Ritual sacrifice is ubiquitous in the history of human civilization. It would seem that the purpose and function of anything so widespread in our developmental past ought to be clear to us. Two centuries of study in anthropology and the history of religions have made this a highly detailed puzzle, but no less a mystery. We do not lack for theories, theories that link sacrifice to the hunt and human dependence upon animals as prey, theories that link it to the maintenance of fertility in humans, animals, and crops, theories that see it as a bargaining exchange with divine powers, theories that see it as an artificial patriarchal construction of kinship to supplant the pattern in which women are preeminent as the birth givers.[8] Some contend that the mystery is misconceived, that there is no single explanation because there is no single thing designated by the word *sacrifice*. There are only various acts with various purposes and meanings, grouped semantically under this term.[9]

Few besides specialized scholars show any interest in the contest among theories of sacrifice just referenced, because we are confident its resolution has no immediate importance. Our ancestors made mistakes. It doesn't much matter which ones. We may not know what one thing or many things sacrifice meant in the past, but we are sure it means nothing now. Our modern script on early human religion expresses certainty that sacrifice was deluded technology, and must recede where knowledge of real scientific causes advances, or was mistakenly projected psychology, which ought to be relocated to the realm of literature or imagination.

An Anti-sacrificial Reading of the Cross

More than any other contemporary, René Girard has challenged the assumptions we have just described. For him, sacrifice is neither a catchall category for varied phenomena or epiphenomena in traditional religions, nor an antiquarian topic whose relevance died with its prescientific assumptions. It is a key element in human social evolution. Its origins date from a crucial transitional moment, when life in the earliest social groups was just in the process, literally, of making us human. Sacrifice is a discovery that stands at the structural origin of both human society and human religion, helping explain why the two emerge hand in hand. Girard maintains there is a genre of sacrifice based on an actual cause and effect relation, one as real today as it ever was. Humans develop awe for a mysterious power of the "sacred" and society overcomes its first political problems because sacrifice works.[10]

His theory of sacrifice bridges the anthropological and the theological, combining elements from both the structuralist and psychological approaches. The structuralist element is represented by Girard's revised reading of sacrifice's role in social dynamics. The psychological element is represented in his mimetic theory, which illuminates the genesis of the problems that sacrifice addresses as well as the means by which it operates (Girard and Williams 1996). Embedded in both, Girard sees a theological dimension. He finds in Jewish and Christian scriptural texts both manifestations of these elements and a commentary on them that is tributary not only to the biasing influence in early anthropology already noted, but also to a much wider social and moral anxiety regarding hidden victims. He explicitly recognizes the gap we have been discussing and addresses it by arguing that though Jesus's death is far from being a sacrifice in the obvious sense, the process the passion narratives describe illustrates an underlying dynamic that is generative of more ritualized, mythologized, and typical forms of sacrifice: the dynamic of scapegoating violence. In starting from the violent fact of a criminal death to reconstruct its own appropriation of sacrificial terms, Christian tradition was retracing the path already followed in the ritualization of that violence and the path of awareness of this dynamic already given in Hebrew texts and types.

Contemplating the anomalies or gap that we have earlier described, Girard sees one clear connecting link in the various Christian interpretations of Jesus's death. It can be summed up in the word *victim,* most particularly a victim of the collective, for the benefit of the collective (see especially Girard 1982). It is a word that applies to each of the cases and yet adds a distinctive and unifying perspective to each. To say that a political execution has a victim is to say something about the justice of that act. To say that someone is a victim of sacrifice is to raise a question about the religious rationale underlying that act. To use both inflections in describing the same act is to suggest an underlying unity between the sociopolitical practice and the ritual, religious one. It is precisely this connection that Girard articulates in his thought, and which he sees comprehended in portions of Hebrew scripture and portions of the New Testament.

We can quickly sketch the original situation as Girard imagines it. What distinguished emergent humans from other primates was an increased mental plasticity coupled with susceptibility to cultural formation, a combination that spurred an explosion beyond simple genetic selection.[11] In practical terms, this meant that humans developed a radical mimetic capacity, a capacity not only to imitate others' behavior, but to form inner life and consciousness on models we infer through the empathetic reading of other minds. The result is a dramatic new level of novelty and creative advance, even though the process operates largely beyond conscious human control.[12]

This dynamic draws humans together into intense communities where culture becomes as important as biology. This breakthrough comes with a dramatic drawback. As quickly as people are drawn together by these emergent sensibilities, they are driven apart by a parallel new class of interpersonal conflicts.[13] Mutual responsiveness communicates destructive dynamics as quickly as constructive ones, with none of the innate limitations of purely biological inheritance. Anger, suspicion, and fear ricochet quickly from one mind to another like light bouncing from mirror to mirror, and their power multiplies. Social life is a fragile shoot, fatally subject to plagues of rivalry and vendetta. Girard proposes that in a situation with no legal power and no mediating institutions, the contagious escalation of retributive violence is the archetypal social disease. Without a cure, human community cannot get off the ground.

The ability to break this vicious cycle appears spontaneously as a kind of miracle. At some point, when feuding threatens to dissolve a community, spontaneous and irrational mob violence erupts against some distinctive person or minority in the group. They are accused of the worst crimes the group can imagine, crimes that by their very enormity might have caused the terrible plight the community now experiences. They are lynched.

The sadly effective reality is that this scapegoating works to "clear the air." In its wake, communities find that this sudden war of all against one has delivered them from the war of each against all. The sacrifice of one person as a scapegoat discharges the pending acts of retribution. This benefit seems a startling, even magical result from a simple execution. The sudden peace confirms the desperate charges that the victim had been behind the crisis to begin with. If the scapegoat's death is the solution, the scapegoat must have been the cause. The death has such reconciling effect that it seems the victim must possess supernatural power. So the victim becomes a god, memorialized in myth, and the practice of sacrifice is institutionalized as both preventive medicine and remedy in crisis. Myth is the story the community tells itself about this event, and it provides the pattern for its repetition and ritualization.

At least some major forms of sacrifice originated and are maintained because of this dynamic, says Girard. They were tools to fend off social crisis. There is nothing primitive about their character, for in varied forms both the problem they address and the solution they represent are with us still. The prescription is that divisions in the community must be reduced to but one division, the division of all against one common victim or one minority group. Prime candidates are the marginal and the weak, or those isolated by their very prominence. Humans are the original sacrificial offerings in this sense. The moral ambiguity of the practice combines the arbitrary fate of its victims with the implicit aim to forestall yet worse human violence. The substitution of animals or other sacrificial objects is an advance, but one that relies for its effectiveness on maintaining association with the prototype. This, in a nutshell, is Girard's account of the origin of sacrifice, which is central to the origin of religion.[14] No one thought out this process, and its effectiveness depends on a certain blindness to its workings. Myth reflects the scapegoat event but does not accurately describe it.

The passion narratives are notably nonmythical in this sense, because they describe the sociopolitical mechanisms from the point of view of the victim and subsequent identification with the victim. The ambiguous position of God with regard to such sacrifice through the biblical tradition (sometimes represented as initiator and guarantor of the sacrificial process, sometimes as defender of the victim) is tipped in favor of an anti-sacrificial position by reference to the many types in Hebrew scripture that exemplify deliverance of the collective victim and by reference to God's identification with the crucified one. Thus, Christians readily made common cause with critiques of sacrifice already present in philosophical circles, while at the same time emphasizing the language of sacrifice with their particular connotations.[15]

Girard highlights an anti-sacrificial dimension of the tradition of the cross which helps to explain why Jesus's death is such an atypical model, with little outward similarity to other cases. It helps to explain why Christians use the same word for what they most strongly reject (such as sacrifice to the emperor) and what they most strongly affirm (the sacrifice of Christ and their own "sacrifice of praise" or "living sacrifice"). His analysis also clarifies some of the tensions in Christian theologies as well, which have had to balance a positive account of sacrifice as part of Christ's work with adequate attention to the sociopolitical dimensions of the passion and the anti-sacrificial themes we have identified.

Sacrifice and the Cross: Odd Partners or Not?

There has been widespread criticism of Girard.[16] These objections usually acknowledge that scapegoating violence is a reality, one present in some cases under religious forms. But critics argue that most actual sacrificial practices fall outside Girard's scheme, having no ostensible connection to issues of violence.[17] They object that his view is infected with a Christian exceptionalism, whereby the cross—at best an outlier case of "sacrifice"—reappears as an interpretive key.[18] At the same time, Girard is often critiqued by theologians for his repudiation of traditional Christian doctrine on the cross and for reducing the meaning of the gospels to an anthropological insight on social reconciliation. To his unfashionable interest in biblical texts as a source as well as an object of interpretation, he adds an interest in viewing questions of sacrifice in a wider, evolutionary perspective.[19] Here too, his emphasis falls less on the specific meaning practitioners attach to sacrificial rituals and more on their place in the large story of hominization.[20] Thus, there is no doubt that Girard fails to privilege what many anthropologists arduously seek: the self-understanding of those participating in such rituals. In his view, performers of sacrifice need not understand themselves as addressing social violence for this to be true, any more than those engaged in scapegoating need regard themselves as persecutors to be so. From his critics' view, this separation between function and meaning allows Girard an interpretive license that is almost unlimited.

The interest of Girard's theory in the context of our discussion is that it directly focuses on the anomalies that we have discussed. Indeed, for most of his career, Girard saw the described divergence as unbridgeable. Contrary to Christian tradition, he refused to use the word *sacrifice* to apply to the death of Jesus precisely because of its differences from "ordinary" sacrifice. But he changed his mind, because he came to believe that the meaning of the cross was intrinsically dependent on that background.[21] Whatever special value Christians attributed to the crucifixion as a saving death had to be grounded in the ways in which it was not a unique event, but a typical one, a scapegoating like others. Its anti-sacrificial character could only be expressed in sacrificial terms. Whether or not Girard's reading is accepted, it highlights the relevance of the gap we have described, and the fact that even within the Christian tradition there is no simple answer to the question that heads this essay.

We began by noting that the death of Jesus served as a kind of model for early anthropology in understanding sacrifice, even though the model was almost entirely dissimilar to the class of events it supposedly exemplified. The one point of linkage was killing, a feature of the passion as of some sacrificial rituals. In early Christianity this divergence was reflected in the absence of any images of the death itself, since the picture of a crucified criminal conveyed no obvious religious meaning. The meaning of Jesus's death as a sacrifice was thus a novel construction, achieved by idiosyncratically applying the language of second temple Jewish ritual to it, instigating a ritual Eucharistic remembrance of it and gathering other biblical narratives around it, narratives whose protagonists were delivered from threatened (sometimes ritual) death. Christian theologies developed various versions of this tension, unable to dispense with the category of sacrifice but required to revise its prior definitions. Girard and his critics represent the continuing disagreement over the marriage between the crucifixion and the category of sacrifice, between those who believe they belong together for mutual illumination and those who hold that a sharper separation would clarify the nature of each one.

Acknowledgments

I want to express my appreciation for the conference underlying this volume. The interdisciplinary nature of the discussions provided an unusual opportunity to address the issues in this essay from new perspectives. I want to express my appreciation to the organizers and especially to Carrie Murray for the privilege of participating in such a stimulating event and for their careful facilitation.

Notes

1. A classic statement of this argument can be found in Smith, 1990. See also McClymond 2008.
2. For a discussion of this literature see Daly 2009:75–94.
3. This contrasts with many images from antiquity presented at the IEMA 2011 conference, scenes of libations or animals being offered on altars, which would immediately have registered with ancient viewers as they do with us as representations of cultic sacrifice.
4. This statement refers specifically to images of the crucifixion or the suffering Jesus. As we have already indicated, there is no shortage of images that refer to the passion events as an ensemble—representations of the cross without the body of Jesus on it, or the *chi-rho* symbol. See Jensen 2000, 2005 and Hurtado 2006 for very nuanced treatments of the evidence.
5. Hebrews 7:27 "Unlike the other high priests, he has no need to offer sacrifice day after day, first for his own sins, and then for those of the people: this he did once for all when he offered himself." Scriptural quotations are from the New Revised Standard Version.
6. See Daly 2009, particularly chapter 9.
7. For responses to such approaches, see Burket et al. 1987.
8. A representative sampling is given in Carter 2003. For an interpretive summary of many of these theories see Milbank 1995.

9.   As, for instance, argued in McClymond 2008.

10.   There are more or less maximal readings of Girard's theory. Much criticism is directed at his perceived insistence on subsuming all sacrifice and ritual under one dynamic. He does use words such as *founding* and *original* to refer to the scapegoating dynamic in religion, but I think this need not be interpreted to mean sole and exclusive. For the purposes of fruitful discussion, it is only necessary to entertain the possibility that some crucial portion of what goes under the anthropological heading of sacrifice is in fact rooted in the dynamic he describes, a dynamic that is particularly relevant to the case of Jesus.

11.   This seems to cohere well with much current scientific work on cognitive development. See Heim 2004.

12.   This is a shorthand statement of Girard's "mimetic theory," which is the subject of books in its own right. Girard has most notably traced this dynamic in literature. See, for instance, Girard 1961.

13.   This view assumes that violence was a common problem in early human groups and that normal life was marked by the reality and the anticipation of this threat. If violent conflict among humans arose only much later, then Girard's theory of origins has the wrong time line, though it could still be quite accurate as an empirical description of a later "fall" into mimetic conflict. Despite a tendency among many anthropologists during a certain period to assume the peacefulness of early societies, there is evidence that points strongly in the opposite direction. See for instance Keeley 1996; and LeBlanc and Register, 2003.

14.   See especially Girard 1972, 1982. Though Girard draws his illustrations from many cultural settings, the familiarity of Greek history allows us to point to Athens in the fifth century B.C.E., a city that continued an ancient practice of maintaining a stable of captives and criminals as sacrificial victims for times of special crisis. The word for such persons was *pharmakos,* derived from *pharmakon,* a word that can mean both poison and remedy. Likewise, Girard would point to the myth of Oedipus, whose many interpretations presume the guilt of Oedipus but which Girard regards as bearing the marks of a classic scapegoat accusation. It is interesting to note that the Parthenon frieze itself is thought by many to depict a procession, which includes sacrificial animals and vessels, long thought to be a procession for a celebration of a festival of Athena, the patron goddess of Athens. It has recently been proposed that instead the central scene of the procession depicts a mythical founding event for the city, when to save it from defeat, the king offered his three daughters as sacrifices. See Connelly 2014.

15.   In the manuscript for a German encyclopedia article on *"Opfer,"* Robert J. Daly addresses this topic in greater depth, and I thank him for the use of that manuscript in preparing this article. Brief discussion may be found in Daly 2009.

16.   See, for instance, Strenski 1993 and Boustan 2011.

17.   See critics already cited and also Heyman 2007.

18.   Many critics do not seem to have followed Girard's more recent tracing of similar anti-sacrificial themes in other religious traditions. See, for instance, his treatment of Hindu tradition in Girard 2011.

19.   See Girard, Antonello, and Rocha 2004.

20.   A good example of the background Girard has in mind is sketched in Bellah 2011. Bellah does not address sacrifice extensively, but his presentation of the crucial role of ritual in human development is very harmonious with Girard's vision. See Heim 2014 for a summary of Bellah's perspective.

21.   In Girard's terms, sacrifice is the appropriate description when the act of scapegoating violence (or a derivative form) is associated with mythic mis-description and validation of it, while in the passion narratives the act is present but in association with a non-mythic description. His change of mind is described in Girard 2001.

References Cited

Astell, A., and S. Goodhart 2011 Introduction. In *Sacrifice, Scripture, and Substitution: Readings in Ancient Judaism and Christianity*, edited by Ann Astell and Sandor Goodhart, pp. 1–38. University of Notre Dame Press, South Bend.

Bellah, R. N. 2011 *Religion in Human Evolution: From the Paleolithic to the Axial Age*. Belknap Press of Harvard University, Cambridge.

Boustan, R. S. 2011 Confrounding Blood: Jewish Narratives of Sacrifice and Violence in Late Antiquity. In *Ancient Mediterranean Sacrifice*, edited by Jennifer Wright Knust and Zsuzsanna Varhelyi, pp. 265–286.Oxford University Press, Oxford.

Brock, R. N., and A. P. Rebecca 2008 *Saving Paradise: How Christianity Traded Love of This World for Crucifixion and Empire*. Beacon Press, Boston.

Burkert, W., R. Girard, J. Z. Smith, and R. Hamerton-Kelly 1987 *Violent Origins: Walter Burkert, René Girard, and Jonathan Z. Smith on Ritual Killing and Cultural Formation*. Stanford University Press, Stanford.

Carter, J. (editor) 2003 *Understanding Religious Sacrifice: A Reader, Controversies in the Study of Religion*. Continuum, London.

Chilton, B. 1992 *The Temple of Jesus: His Sacrificial Program within a Cultural History of Sacrifice*. Pennsylvania State University Press, University Park.

Connelly, J. B. 1996 *The Parthenon Enigma*. Knopf, New York.

Daly, R. J. 2009 *Sacrifice Unveiled: The True Meaning of Christian Sacrifice*. T and T Clark, London.

Girard, R. 1961 *Mensonge Romantique Et Vérité Romanesque*. B. Grasset, Paris.

Girard, R. 1972 *La Violence Et Le Sacré*. B. Grasset, Paris.

Girard, R. 1982 *Le Bouc Émissaire*. B. Grasset, Paris.

Girard, R. 2001 Théorie Mimétique Et Thélogie. In *Celui Par Qui Le Scandale Arrive*, pp, 63–84. Hachette, Paris.

Girard, R. 2011 *Sacrifice*. Michigan State University Press, East Lansing.

Girard, R., P. Antonello, and J. C. de Castro Rocha 2004 *Les Origines De La Culture*. Desclée de Brouwer, Paris.

Girard, R., and J. G. Williams. 1996 *The Girard Reader*. Crossroad, New York.

Heim, S. M. 2006 *Saved from Sacrifice: A Theology of the Cross*. Eerdmans, Grand Rapids.

Heim, S. M. 2004 A Cross-Section of Sin: The Mimetic Character of Human Nature in Biological and Theological Perspective. In *Evolution and Ethics: Human Morality in Biological and Religious Perspective*, edited by Philip Clayton and Jeffrey Schloss, pp. 255–272. Eerdmans, Grand Rapids.

Heyman, G. 2007 *The Power of Sacrifice: Roman and Christian Discourses in Conflict*. Catholic University of America Press, Washington, District of Columbia.

Hurtado, L. W. 2006 *The Earliest Christian Artifacts: Manuscripts and Christian Origins*. Eerdmans, Grand Rapids.

Jensen, R. M. 2000 *Understanding Early Christian Art*. Routledge, London.

Jensen, R. M. 2005 *Face to Face: Portraits of the Divine in Early Christianity*. Fortress Press, Minneapolis.

Keeley, L. H. 1996 *War before Civilization*. Oxford University Press, Oxford.

Lanciani, R. A. 1888 *Ancient Rome in the Light of Recent Discoveries*. Houghton, Mifflin, Boston.

LeBlanc, S. A., and K. E. Register 2003 *Constant Battles: The Myth of the Peaceful, Noble Savage*. First edition. St. Martin's Press, New York.

McClymond, K. 2008 *Beyond Sacred Violence: A Comparative Study of Sacrifice*. Johns Hopkins University Press, Baltimore.

Milbank, J. 1995 Stories of Sacrifice. *Contagion* 2:75–103.

Smith, J. S. 1990 *Drudgery Divine: On the Comparison of Early Christianities and the Religions of Late Antiquity*. University of Chicago Press, Chicago.

Strenski, I. 1993 At Home with René Girard: Eucharistic Sacrifice, the "French School," and Joseph Demaistre. In *Religion in Relation: Method, Application and Moral Location*, edited by Ivan Strenski pp. 202–216. University of South Carolina Press, Columbia.

Tkacz, C. B. 2002 *The Key to the Brescia Casket: Typology and the Early Christian Imagination*. Christianity and Judaism in Antiquity Series. University of Notre Dame Press, Notre Dame, Indiana, and Institut d'Etudes Augustiennes, Paris.

Ullucci, D. C. 2012 *The Christian Rejection of Animal Sacrifice*. Oxford University Press, Oxford.

Contributors

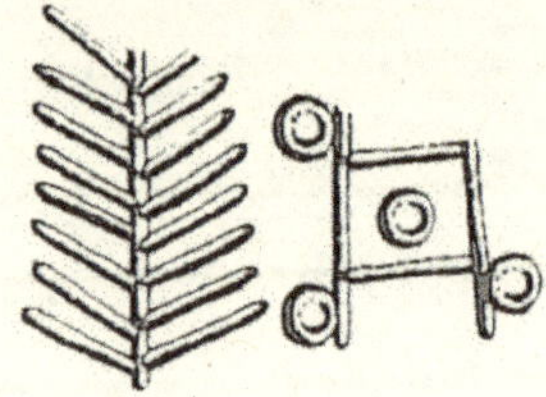

Rose-Marie Arbogast, MISHA, UMR 7044, 5, allée du Général Rouvillois, F-67083 Strasbourg

Silja Bauer, Ludwigstraße 14, D-67346 Speyer

Åsa Berggren, Sydsvensk Arkeologi, Lund University, Sweden

Bruno Boulestin, CNRS, UMR 5199—PACEA, Université Bordeaux 1, Avenue des Facultés—B8, F-33405 Talence, France

Lídia Colominas, Laboratory of Zooarchaeology. Universitat Autònoma de Barcelona, Spain

Anne-Sophie Coupey, CNRS, UMR 6566, CReAAH, Université Rennes 1, Campus de Beaulieu, F-35042 Rennes, France

Anthony Denaire, Antea-Archéologie, 11, rue de Zurich, F-68 440 Habsheim, France

Michael Gagarin, James R. Dougherty Jr. Centennial Professor Emeritus, Department of Classics, University of Texas at Austin

Guinevere Granite, Research Lead Specialist Clinical, Adjunct Professor, University of Maryland, Baltimore, School of Medicine & School of Dentistry

Nancy T. de Grummond, M. Lynette Thompson Professor of Classics, Distinguished Research Professor at Florida State University

Fabian Haack, MA, Ludwigstraße 14, D-67346 Speyer, Germany

S. Mark Heim, Samuel Abbot Professor of Christian Theology, Andover Newton Theological School

Samantha Hurn, University Lecturer, Department of Anthropology, University of Exeter, United Kingdom

Christoph Huth, Professor of European Archaeology, Institute of Archaeology, Department of Prehistoric Archaeology, University of Freiburg, Germany

Christian Jeunesse, Université Marc Bloch—Strasbourg II, Institut des Antiquités nationales, 9, place de l'Université, F-67084 Strasbourg Cedex, France

Carrie Ann Murray, Assistant Professor of Roman Archaeology, Department of Classics, Brock University, Canada

Enriqueta Pons, Museum of Archaeology of Catalonia-Girona, Spain

Mary-Ann Pouls Wegner, Associate Professor of Egyptian Archaeology, Department of Near & Middle Eastern Civilizations, University of Toronto, Director, Toronto Abydos Votive Zone Project, Penn-Yale-IFA Expedition to Abydos

Maria Saña, Laboratory of Zooarchaeology, Universitat Autònoma de Barcelona, Spain

Dirk Schimmelpfennig, Burgunderstrasse 44, CH-3018 Bern, Switzerland, dirk@schimmelpfennig.name

Jeffrey H. Schwartz, Professor, Departments of Anthropology and History and Philosophy of Science, University of Pittsburgh

Tyler Jo Smith, Associate Professor, McIntire Department of Art, University of Virginia

Phillips Stevens Jr., Associate Professor, Department of Anthropology, University at Buffalo, The State University of New York

Rouven Turck, MA, Abteilung Ur- und Frühgeschichte des Historischen Seminars, Universität Zürich, Karl-Schmid-Str. 4, CH-8006 Zürich, Switzerland, rouven.turck@uzh.ch

Roger D. Woodard, Andrew V. V. Raymond Professor of the Classics, Department of Classics, University at Buffalo, The State University of New York

Andrea Zeeb-Lanz, Generaldirektion Kulturelles Erbe Rheinland-Pfalz, Direktion Landesarchäologie, Speyer, Germany

Index

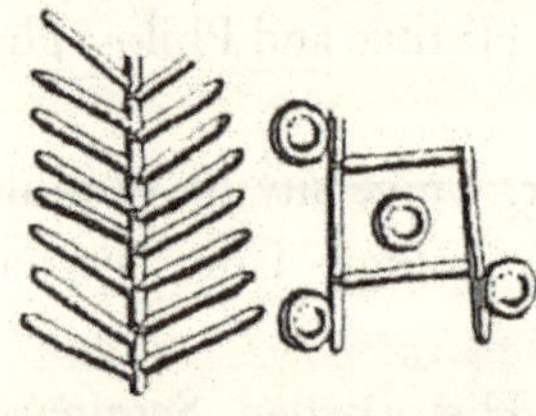